AMOS

BHLXX

Baylor Handbook on the Septuagint
Sean A. Adams and Seth M. Ehorn
General Editors

OTHER BOOKS IN THIS SERIES

2 Maccabees 1–7
Seth M. Ehorn

Amos
A Handbook on the Greek Text

W. Edward Glenny

BAYLOR UNIVERSITY PRESS

© 2022 by Baylor University Press
Waco, Texas 76798

All Rights Reserved. No part of this publication may be reproduced, stored in a retrieval system, or transmitted, in any form or by any means, electronic, mechanical, photocopying, recording, or otherwise, without the prior permission in writing of Baylor University Press.

Cover design by Kasey McBeath
Cover image: Shiloh Byzantine basilica mosaic, © Todd Bolen/BiblePlaces.com
Book design by Baylor University Press; typeset by Scribe Inc.

The Library of Congress has cataloged this book under
ISBN 978-1-4813-1670-5.

Printed in the United States of America on acid-free paper with a minimum of thirty percent recycled content.

CONTENTS

Series Introduction	vii
Preface	xv
Abbreviations	xvii
Introduction	xxi
Amos 1:1–2	1
Amos 1:3–5	7
Amos 1:6–8	16
Amos 1:9–10	20
Amos 1:11–12	21
Amos 1:13–15	24
Amos 2:1–3	28
Amos 2:4–5	31
Amos 2:6–16	35
Amos 3:1–8	55
Amos 3:9–15	69
Amos 4:1–3	83
Amos 4:4–13	91
Amos 5:1–17	109
Amos 5:18–27	140

Amos 6:1–14	157
Amos 7:1–3	188
Amos 7:4–6	195
Amos 7:7–9	198
Amos 7:10–17	205
Amos 8:1–3	218
Amos 8:4–14	222
Amos 9:1–7	240
Amos 9:8–15	255
Glossary	273
Works Cited	281
Grammar Index	291
Author Index	296

SERIES INTRODUCTION

There has been something of a renaissance in Septuagint studies among biblical scholars in the twentieth and twenty-first centuries, evidenced by the production of critical editions of the Septuagint, new translation projects, commentaries on individual books, new reading tools and introductions, and the induction of various centers for study of the Septuagint. Yet despite this growing international interest in the Septuagint, there is a dearth of language resources that are aimed at helping facilitate rapid reading and translation of the Septuagint. The Baylor Handbook on the Septuagint (BHLXX) is designed to fill this lacuna and meet the needs of students, teachers, and scholars who are interested in reading the Septuagint.

Each volume of the BHLXX treats a septuagintal book (or portion of a book) verse-by-verse, guiding the reader through the Greek text of the Septuagint. Contributors cannot comment on every aspect of the text, but every significant grammatical or syntactical issue will receive attention. In this respect, the BHLXX differs from the Brill Commentary on the Septuagint and *La Bible d'Alexandrie*, which provide historical, theological, and literary comments rather than detailed comments on the Greek text itself.

There is need to clarify what is meant by "Septuagint." It is widely acknowledged that *septuaginta*, from which the English transliteration "Septuagint" derives, was originally a designation used to refer to the Greek Pentateuch. However, the name "Septuagint" has been extended and applied more broadly than these first five books, encompassing the entire Greek versions of the Hebrew Bible as well as a selection of so-called Apocryphal books. In accordance with this standard usage, the BHLXX includes books from this widest grouping and often employs the term "Septuagint" or "LXX" in this general sense. For additional discussion on terminology, interested readers should consult Jobes and Silva (14–17).

Greek-Based Approach

Septuagint studies has been dominated by investigations that have used the Greek text primarily as a way to understand better the Hebrew *Vorlage* (or source text) or ancient approaches to translation (e.g., Boyd-Taylor). Although these are valid approaches to the Septuagint, they are by no means the only ways to engage critically with the text. Recently, there has been a move to understand the Septuagint as a Greek text on its own terms and not only as a derivative text. Tessa Rajak (143–44) provides two strong reasons for understanding the text in this way:

1. Greek translations in due course *did* stand alone, in fact sooner rather than later, and they therefore rapidly proved usable and fully intelligible in their ancient context.
2. The degree of interference from the source language is sometimes overstated. While sometimes Septuagint Greek can be awkward, it is very rarely unintelligible.

This approach fits with a growing movement within Septuagint scholarship that seeks to prioritize the Greek text and to understand how the Septuagint would have been understood in its wider Greek context (see, e.g., Aitken; Lee 2004; 2018). This perspective requires a rethinking of the linguistic and grammatical approaches to the text as well as a new set of tools that understands the Greek of the Septuagint as a *text* and not just as a *translation*.

The BHLXX operates on the assumption that the Septuagint represents one aspect of post-classical Greek. This claim needs qualification, but represents a growing trend in Septuagint studies to prioritize the Greek text that expresses natural idioms. In a significant study on *The Greek of the Pentateuch*, John Lee (2018, 22) claimed,

> It is too easy to assume that anything in the LXX that is not immediately recognizable as normal Greek is due to Semitic interference. Our procedure ought rather to be to assume that it *might* be normal Greek, that is, to begin with the presumption of innocence, and not decide on a verdict until the evidence on both sides has been fully investigated.

Lee's point is not that the Septuagint is free from Hebrew interference. Rather, he rightly points out that foreign or unusual constructions have, all too often, been explained away as examples of Semitic interference without much evidence. But as our knowledge of post-classical Greek has grown, many alleged instances of Semitic interference have turned out to be idiomatic Greek. In agreement with Lee's arguments, the BHLXX is a resource that attempts to take the Greek of the Septuagint seriously before assuming that it represents translation Greek.

As a result of this adopted perspective, BHLXX series authors will make limited recourse to the Hebrew, mainly doing so when it is necessary to understand the Greek grammar or syntax. The difference in approaches can be illustrated by an example from Exod 1:1-5a:

> ¹Ταῦτα τὰ ὀνόματα τῶν υἱῶν Ισραηλ τῶν εἰσπεπορευμένων εἰς Αἴγυπτον ἅμα Ιακωβ τῷ πατρὶ αὐτῶν — ἕκαστος πανοικίᾳ αὐτῶν εἰσήλθοσαν — · ²Ρουβην, Συμεων, Λευι, Ιουδας, ³Ισσαχαρ, Ζαβουλων καὶ Βενιαμιν, ⁴Δαν καὶ Νεφθαλι, Γαδ καὶ Ασηρ. ⁵Ιωσηφ **δὲ** ἦν ἐν Αἰγύπτῳ.

> ¹These are the names of the sons of Israel who had entered into Egypt with Jacob their father. Each with their whole household went in: ²Reuben, Simeon, Levi, Judah, ³Issachar, Zebulun and Benjamin, ⁴Dan and Nephtali, Gad and Asher. ⁵**But** Joseph was in Egypt.

In this passage the translator(s) of LXX Exodus rendered the Hebrew connective *vav* (ו) in several different ways. As Muraoka (§72j) observes more generally, recourse to Hebrew in *this* passage shows that *vav* (ו) is left untranslated (3 times), translated as καί (3 times), and translated as δέ (1 time). But one could also approach the text by reading it as a Greek document, observing that the connective δέ (rather than καί) is a common way to signal a change of subject (cf. Smyth §2836). Whereas 1:1-4 concerns the sons of Israel, 1:5 introduces a new subject, Joseph, and this development in the narrative is marked by δέ. The grammar is understandable to a Greek reader and we should seek to read it as such.

In addition to grammar and syntax, we must also ask a similar question about Septuagint lexicography. Should vocabulary be studied in relationship to underlying Hebrew terms or studied discretely as Greek terms? Because the aim of the BHLXX is to facilitate reading of the Greek text of the Septuagint, we have opted for the latter approach, generally preferring definitions that are derived from Muraoka's *A Greek-English Lexicon of the*

Septuagint (*GELS*) or the *Brill Dictionary of Ancient Greek* (*GE*). Muraoka's lexicon is a welcome new resource that focuses on the meaning of Greek terms, distinct from Hebrew terms, building upon his prior methodological work on the relationship between Greek and Hebrew in Septuagint studies. In a programmatic essay, Muraoka (1990, 44–45) stated,

> Notwithstanding one's recognition of the basic character of the LXX for most of its parts as a work of translation, it is equally important to recognise that the LXX *is* a Greek document, and one must attempt to read it as such, and it has been so read down the ages.... Before one concludes, out of despair perhaps, that a particular rendition is merely an attempt mechanically to reproduce the Hebrew, every attempt ought to be made to comprehend the translation as a Greek document.

By treating the Septuagint as Greek literature itself and not as a translation document, the BHLXX focuses on the unique aspects of the Greek language. As such, Muraoka's lexicon as well as other Greek lexicons covering Hellenistic literature provide the most logical choice for reference tools that focus on reading the Septuagint itself. Readers may also want to consult the lexicon produced by Johan Lust, Erik Eynikel, and Katrin Hauspie, *A Greek-English Lexicon of the Septuagint* (LEH), which adopts a different theoretical approach and is also full of rich data. The differences between these two lexica are informative of how methodological approaches influence decisions at even a lexical level. For important critiques of the methodological weaknesses of each lexicon, see Aitken (9–15).

Another major difference between *GELS* and LEH is that the former attempts to place lexical items in their literary context, not only identifying the part of speech the item typically holds, but also highlights collocations and words that are grammatically, contextually, and semantically linked. This additional information provides a more robust understanding of how Greek words work in context as well as a wider perspective of how the language functions as a whole.

Septuagint lexicography is one of the big scholarly topics at the moment and new works are expected to be available soon. Arguably the most important in this field will be E. Bons and J. Joosten, *Historical and Theological Lexicon of the Septuagint*. This multivolume work will be published by Mohr Siebeck with the first volume expected in 2020. Readers with very little knowledge of the Septuagint will find the introduction by Karen Jobes and Moisés Silva, *Invitation to the Septuagint*, to be the best point of entry into the field. Now in its second edition, the book introduces readers to key questions and provides up-to-date bibliographic entries on many important topics in Septuagint studies.

Greek Text and Translations of the Septuagint

Volumes in the BHLXX use the Rahlfs-Hanhart (R-H) 2006 edition of the Septuagint as a base text. The rationales for this decision are that this text is complete, it is the most widely accessible edition of the Septuagint, and it is traditionally the one most used by those initially interested in the LXX. However, contributors to the BHLXX will also consult the Göttingen edition on text-critical matters and, where beneficial, variation units from volumes in that edition are considered in the handbook. This critical edition focuses on individual books of the LXX and represents the best attempts at reconstructions based on extant Greek manuscripts. Unfortunately, not all of the LXX books have been completed and published. As a result, some BHLXX volumes will not be able to engage with this significant resource.

A further difficulty occurs when determining which text to produce. As is well known in septuagintal studies, certain LXX books have multiple, distinct Greek texts (e.g., Judges, 1–4 Kingdoms, Daniel, Tobit, etc.). In these books the amount of textual overlap between the different versions is often significant, although the number of pluses and minuses create distinctive characteristics in each recension. It is not possible for each handbook to treat every version, and so the decision has been made to follow one version in its entirety—to be determined by the handbook author and discussed in their introduction—and to include the additional material found in the other version where appropriate. This additional material will be marked in the text of the handbook for ease of identification. The goal of this decision is to allow for maximum coverage with minimal redundancy.

The BHLXX also serves an important scholarly function in providing a fresh translation of the R-H Septuagint from a Greek-language perspective. Previous translations, such as *A New English Translation of the Septuagint* (NETS), adopt a different approach to the Greek text. Specifically, NETS adopts an "interlinear" approach, which aims "to bring the Greek reader to the Hebrew original" (Pietersma and Wright, xiv). Lancelot Brenton's translation, now quite dated, is a diplomatic text based on Codex Vaticanus. Most recently, *The Lexham English Septuagint*, edited by Ken Penner (2019), provides a fresh translation of the LXX without recourse to the Hebrew text. For ease of reading, the BHLXX standardizes the spelling of proper names in translation following the NRSV.

Getting Started

Each volume of the BHLXX offers a verse-by-verse discussion of the Septuagint text, guiding the reader through the intricacies of the Greek text. This work is not designed to be an exhaustive resource for discussions of grammar, syntax, or lexicography, but each author will seek to provide commentary on any significant questions arising from the Greek text. The goal of this series is to support students of Greek as they navigate their way through unfamiliar and sometimes difficult texts. The handbooks are thus designed to serve as companions to the Septuagint and complement standard commentaries, where they exist, which may or may not discuss the intricacies of the primary language.

A reasonable level of knowledge of Greek grammar is presupposed by this tool. Students should be aware of a few Greek grammars that focus on the Septuagint. The first is that of F. C. Conybeare and St. George Stock, *Grammar of the Septuagint*. Second, Henry St. J. Thackeray, *A Grammar of the Old Testament in Greek According to the Septuagint*. These grammars may prove useful in helping to solve difficult issues of syntax or morphology; however, as they are over a century old, they are not informed by modern linguistic study or the deeper understanding of the Septuagint that has emerged in recent decades. More recently, Muraoka has completed his *A Syntax of Septuagint Greek*, a comprehensive work on the morphosyntax and syntax of Septuagint Greek that compares the LXX text with contemporary Greek literature. Although not without its flaws, this is a significant contribution to Septuagint scholarship and will no doubt be a foundational resource for future scholarship. Beyond these grammars that explicitly focus on the Septuagint, we recommend the following grammars of classical Greek: Herbert Smyth's *Greek Grammar*; Evert van Emde Boas, Albert Rijksbaron, Luuk Huitink, and Mathieu de Bakker, *The Cambridge Grammar of Classical Greek*; Heinrich von Siebenthal, *Ancient Greek Grammar*. Additionally, the following grammars on Greek papyri are useful: Mayser, *Grammatik der griechischen Papyri aus der Ptolemäerzeit*; Palmer, *A Grammar of the Post-Ptolemaic Papyri*; Gignac, *A Grammar of the Greek Papyri of the Roman and Byzantine Periods*.

Contributors to the BHLXX typically employ standard grammatical labels such as those found in intermediate and advanced Greek grammars. These labels (e.g., a participle of *manner* or *subjective* genitive) represent not only a morphological determination, but also a contextual judgment about the function of the word. These categories are contested with different scholars categorizing the Greek text differently. Although one system will be adopted in each volume, we would recommend examining a range of resources to understand alternate viewpoints.

Each handbook consists of the following features. The Introduction draws the readers' attention to some of the distinctive features of the Greek text in question and treats some of the broader issues relating to the text as a whole in a more thorough fashion. The handbook proper consists of two parts. The text is divided into sections based on the overall structure of the book and each section is introduced with a translation that illustrates how the insights gleaned from the analysis that follows may be expressed in natural English. Following the translation is the heart of the handbook, which offers a detailed analysis of the Greek text. The Greek text of each verse is followed by comments on syntactic, lexical, text-critical, and other significant issues.

Each page of the handbook includes a header to help readers quickly locate comments on a particular passage. Terminology used in the comments that is potentially unfamiliar to many users is included in a glossary at the end of each handbook. Each volume also includes an index that provides an exhaustive list of grammatical or syntactical phenomena occurring in the text. This feature provides a valuable resource for Greek teachers wanting to illustrate a particular phenomenon or develop exams or exercises. Finally, each handbook concludes with a bibliography of works cited, providing helpful guidance in identifying resources for further research on the Greek text.

It is our hope that through engagement with the BHLXX volumes students will be better suited to engage with and understand the unique context(s) of the Septuagint as a text in its own right. Along the way, students will encounter readings that differ from what they know to be derived from the Hebrew Bible. Such discoveries will be well worth the effort.

Sean A. Adams
University of Glasgow, Scotland

Seth M. Ehorn
Wheaton College, USA

PREFACE

My interest in LXX Amos began about fifteen years ago when I decided to write a dissertation on the translation technique in this Septuagint book. Robert Gordon encouraged me to work on this portion of the LXX, and in the beginning stages of the dissertation my advisor, Melissa Harl Sellew, met with me regularly for over a year to review my exegetical work and to help me work through the translation of Septuagint Amos. Through sabbatical times at Tyndale House, Cambridge, I received invaluable direction and needed confirmation from Robert Gordon, James Palmer, and Jennifer Dines. The finished dissertation was published as *Finding Meaning in the Text: Translation Technique and Theology in the Septuagint of Amos* (Brill 2009), and it was followed by a commentary on the Greek text of Amos in the Brill Septuagint Commentary series (Brill 2013b). After writing those two works on LXX Amos, I was interested in doing a work on this LXX book that would be something like the works in the BHGNT and BHHB series, and I talked with Carey Newman about it before the BHLXX ever existed. When the series was established and Sean Adams and Seth Ehorn became the editors, I was pleased to receive an official invitation to be a part of the series. That was a few years ago, and the handbook on LXX Amos has taken longer than I had expected, but hopefully it is better for the process. I have gone back over the text of LXX Amos and gained new insights and entertained new questions in doing so. Sean and Seth have been a great help to me. Seth's volume on 2 Maccabees, which initiated the series, has established a high standard, and their feedback on my work has helped me grow and has helped conform this volume to the style that they envision and desire for the series. I am very thankful for their help. Thanks also to the students in my 2020–2021 Intermediate Greek class at the University of Northwestern–St. Paul for their helpful feedback and questions as we worked through some of the material in this handbook in our class. Special thanks to Tori Hinsverk for her help in proofreading, compiling the Grammar and Author Indexes, and rechecking the differences between R-H and Ziegler's editions of LXX Amos. Her work and that of the editors has saved me from many errors and helped me clarify and more consistently present the material in the Handbook. Of course, I alone am responsible for any errors or deficiencies that remain.

Volumes in the BHGNT series have been helpful to me, especially those of Brookins and Longenecker (1 Corinthians), my dissertation advisee Rodney Decker (Mark), Olmstead (Matthew), and Dubis (1 Peter). Particularly helpful was Ehorn's volume on 2 Maccabees 1–7, the first in the BHLXX series. These all provided direction and set a high standard for me to attempt to follow.

I also want to thank the good people at Baylor University Press for their help in bringing the volume to completion. Among others, Cade Jarrell, David Aycock, Jenny Hunt, Kasey McBeath, Michelle McCaig, and Carrie Watterson have had an important part in the completion of this project.

I would be remiss if I did not thank the University of Northwestern–St. Paul for supporting my work and providing opportunities for me to complete this project, especially a sabbatical during the school year 2019–2020. Lastly, I thank my wife, Jackie, for her continued support and encouragement in my writing projects. Without her partnership in life, this would not be possible.

ABBREVIATIONS

Abbreviations of primary sources follow the *Society of Biblical Literature Handbook of Style*. Works cited in the Handbook also utilize the author-date format or, when only one work by an author is cited, the name of the author alone.

=	corresponding to; this symbol is used, for example, when a reading corresponds to a reading in the Masoretic Text (MT)
A	Codex Alexandrinus
*	An asterisk denotes an original reading
a, b	A superscript letter denotes a corrector of a manuscript (1st, 2nd, etc.)
1st	first person
2nd	second person
3rd	third person
ABD	Freedman, *Anchor Bible Dictionary*, 1992
acc	accusative
act	active
aor	aorist
B	Codex Vaticanus
Bd'A	*La Bible d'Alexandrie*
BDAG	Danker, *A Greek-English Lexicon of the New Testament*, 2000
BDF	Blass, Debrunner, and Funk, *A Greek Grammar of the New Testament*
BHGNT	Baylor Handbook on the Greek New Testament
BHLXX	Baylor Handbook on the Septuagint

Brenton	Brenton's translation of the LXX, found in *The Septuagint Version, with Apocrypha, Greek, and English*, 1976
c	corrector, correction
C	The Recension of Catena Magna in Prophetas Inventa
CD	Damascus Document
CGCG	Van Emde Boas, *Cambridge Grammar of Classical Greek*
dat	dative
EDB	Freedman, *Eerdmans Dictionary of the Bible*, 2000
esp.	especially
ESV	English Standard Version
fem	feminine
fut	future
gen	genitive
GE	Montanari, *The Brill Dictionary of Ancient Greek*
GELS	Muraoka, *A Greek English Lexicon of the Septuagint* (2009)
HALOT	Koehler and Baumgartner, *The Hebrew and Aramaic Lexicon of the Old Testament*, 2 vols., 2001
H-R	Hatch and Redpath, *A Concordance to the Septuagint*, 1983
impf	imperfect
impv	imperative
ind	indicative
inf	infinitive
L	Lucianic recension; this is taken from R-H.
LEH	Lust, Eynikel, and Hauspie, *A Greek–English Lexicon of the Septuagint*, 2015
LES	*The Lexham English Septuagint*
LSJ	Liddell, Scott, and Jones, *A Greek-English Lexicon*, 1996
LXX	Septuagint
LXX.D	Kraus and Karrer, *Septuaginta Deutsch: Das griechische Alte Testament in deutscher Übersetzung*, 2009
LXX.E	Karrer and Kraus, *Septuaginta Deutsch: Erläuterungen und Kommentare zum griechischen Alten Testament*, 2 vols., 2011
masc	masculine
MBG	Mounce, *The Morphology of Biblical Greek*
MHT	Moulton, Howard, and Turner, *A Grammar of New Testament Greek*, 4 vols., 1908–1963

mid	middle
MM	Moulton and Milligan, *The Vocabulary of the Greek New Testament*
MS(S)	manuscript(s)
MT	Masoretic Text
Muraoka	Muraoka, *A Syntax of Septuagint Greek*, 2016
NETS	*New English Translation of the Septuagint*
neut	neuter
NIDNTTE	Silva, *New International Dictionary of New Testament Theology and Exegesis*, 2014
nom	nominative
NRSV	New Revised Standard Version
opt	optative
pass	passive
pl	plural
PP	prepositional phrase
pres	present
prf	perfect
ptc	participle
Q	Codex Marchalianus
R-H	Rahlfs-Hanhart, *Septuaginta*, 2006
S	Codex Sinaiticus
sg	singular
subj	subjunctive
s.v.	*sub verbo* (under the word)
Swete	Swete, *The Old Testament in Greek According to the Septuagint*, 1925–1930
TDNT	Kittel and Friedrich, *Theological Dictionary of the New Testament*, 1964–1976
Th	Theodotian text of Daniel
V	Codex Venetus
v.l.	*varia lectio* (variant reading)
W	Washington Papyrus (mss V in the Freer collection)
Ziegler	Ziegler, *Duodecim prophetae. Septuaginta*, 1984

INTRODUCTION

In keeping with the purposes of the Baylor Handbook on the Septuagint (BHLXX) series, this handbook on LXX Amos attempts to address every significant grammatical and syntactical issue in the Greek text. This handbook is not a full-scale commentary (although at times it is necessary to comment on issues in the text to accomplish the purposes of the handbook), and many historical, cultural, theological, and contextual issues that one would discuss in a commentary would not be appropriate for this handbook. The handbook is a word-by-word and phrase-by-phrase guide through the Greek text of LXX Amos, trying to answer questions a reader of Greek might have. However, it is also a handbook on a translation, and this opens up other issues behind the Greek text that are relevant to its discussion and are occasionally worthy of comment. For example, in places I refer to the reading of the Hebrew where it might be helpful or especially interesting to a student of the LXX. In this regard the discussion will include some things not found in a handbook on a LXX book originally written in Greek (e.g., 2 Maccabees).

Resources for studying the text of LXX Amos are limited. The much-anticipated commentary in the volumes of *La Bible d'Alexandrie*, by Jennifer Dines and Eberhard Bons, has not appeared yet, and no commentaries in the SBL Septuagint Commentary Series have been published. The main resources that I have consulted, and which are referenced often in this handbook, are Jennifer Dines' 1991 dissertation, my own commentary on the text of Amos in Codex Vaticanus for the Brill Septuagint Commentary Series (2013b), and my earlier published dissertation, *Translation Technique and Theology in the Septuagint of Amos* (2009). Although this handbook builds upon those works, it is different and, in many ways, independent of them. For example, the text that is employed in this handbook is the Rahlfs-Hanhart text of the Septuagint, whereas in my commentary I worked with the text in Codex Vaticanus. The primary lexicon cited in this handbook is Muraoka's *Greek-English Lexicon of the Septuagint* (*GELS*), although several others were also employed and are also cited in the handbook (BDAG, *GE*, LEH, and LSJ). For a history of interpretation of LXX Amos, see Glenny 2013b, 1–5.

Where there are important questions concerning the text, meaning, or grammar in a passage, I present exegetical options. My editors have pushed me to make decisions on them. Sometimes those decisions are tentative, and where that is the case, I have communicated what I think are the most likely options, giving evidence for the most important options. I have not addressed every occurrence of καί or of the Greek definite article, thinking that this would become repetitious and unnecessary; however, I have tried to address most occurrences, including those that have special significance for understanding the text.

In the remainder of this introduction, we will consider the Greek edition and translation of LXX Amos in this handbook, the structure of LXX Amos, the place of LXX Amos in LXX Twelve, the unity and date of the translation of the Twelve, Greek verbs in LXX Amos, and the character of the translation of LXX Amos and its language, style, and syntax. These topics will help orient readers of the handbook to LXX Amos and provide a holistic perspective to the localized discussions.

Greek Edition and English Translation of LXX Amos

Greek Edition. The BHLXX uses the Rahlfs-Hanhart (R-H) 2006 edition of the Septuagint because it is complete, it is the most widely accessible edition, and it is traditionally the one used by those beginning work in the LXX (see the Series Introduction); this edition is a "moderate revision" of Rahlfs' first edition, published in 1935 (R-H, xi). The Göttingen edition on the Twelve Prophets, which is edited by Joseph Ziegler (1984), is referred to often in the handbook, and it is essential for scholarly work on the text of the LXX Twelve (see Bons, 439, for differences between Rahlfs' and Ziegler's approaches to textual decisions). In the Handbook, I tried to give the evidence from the major uncials for different readings in the text of Amos. (The uncials Vaticanus [B] and Alexandrinus [A] contain Amos, and the Washington papyrus [W] from the third century is the earliest manuscript witness.) I did not comment on minor textual differences (spellings, word order, etc.) that did not impact the meaning of the text. I also did not normally mention textual issues where R-H agreed with the Göttingen Septuagint text of

Amos. Although I commented on textual variants, I employed the text in R-H, without variation, as the basis of the study. It is possible to compare the text in R-H with the text in Vaticanus (B), which is the basis of Swete's text (*The Old Testament in Greek according to the Septuagint*, 1925–1930) and translation, by comparing the text and translation in this volume with the text and translation in my commentary on LXX Amos (Brill 2013b). For an introduction to the text of the Twelve in the Septuagint, see Glenny (2021).

Park (2001, 139–42) has a chart of the differences in the text of Amos between the LXX editions of Swete (1925–1930), Rahlfs (1935), and Ziegler (1984). To aid in the use of this handbook, I have also compiled the following list of differences between the 2006 R-H text and Ziegler's 1984 Göttingen edition (see also Ziegler 1984, 134–35). The differences between the two editions are relatively few. Differences in breathing marks, accents, and final *nu* (always present in R-H and absent in Ziegler where it differs) are not included in the list.

1. Punctuation difference (1:2; 2:9; 3:6, 11; 4:1^2, 2; 5:8, 21, 26; 6:9; 8:4, 5, 7, 14).
2. Inflection difference (1:5; 3:7; 5:8; 8:11; 9:1).
3. Versification difference (7:17/8:1 and 8:1/8:2).
4. Simple vs. compound verb form (7:9).
5. Omission or addition of word(s) (3:2, 7, 9^2, 11, 15; 4:3, 8; 5:3, 19, 22^2, 25; 6:2, 12, 14; 7:7, 12; 8:9; 9:5, 12).
6. Spelling variation (4:8; 5:11; 7:10; 9:10).
7. Different word choice(s) (4:10; 5:19; 6:1).
8. Variation in word order (8:3).

English Translation. As with other volumes in the BHLXX, this handbook seeks to help readers understand the grammar and syntax of the Greek text of the Septuagint. Accordingly, the translation of LXX Amos in the handbook attempts to follow the general phrase and clause order of the Greek text. Words in the translation that are understood but not explicitly stated in the *Vorlage* are placed in brackets. The vocabulary in LXX Amos is not especially difficult, but I have tried to gloss most rare and unusual words in the entries in the handbook. Where words are not glossed in the entries, the translation will hopefully clarify the meaning of the Greek words.

I have not attempted to interpret or analyze the Greek of LXX Amos primarily as a translation of the Hebrew, but I have tried to read and understand the LXX text as an independent Greek document and interpret it as a text in its own right. That is not to say that there is no place for reading the LXX as a translation, and where there are major differences between the LXX and the MT I try to mention them, but the focus of this handbook is on the Greek text as it stands. Where I do list differences between the Hebrew and Greek texts, I often try to explain briefly the logic behind the discrepancy.

The translation was influenced by my previous translation in my commentary on Amos in Codex Vaticanus (2013b), but this translation is updated and changed to reflect the R-H text. I regularly consulted the *New English Translation of the Septuagint* (NETS), and I often checked the translation in Dines (1991). In the last stage of my work, I was also able to use *The Lexham English Septuagint* (2019). The influence of my commentary, NETS, and Dines can be seen throughout the handbook.

The sections in the handbook are based on the divisions of the text in Ziegler and R-H, which agree in every instance. Occasionally one section contains more than one oracle or it has other natural divisions that could be divided into subsections, and when that occurs it will be mentioned, often before the first entry for the verse that begins the subsection.

The Structure of LXX Amos and Its Place in the Twelve

Amos in LXX Twelve. The collection of the Twelve Prophets, which are also referred to as the Minor Prophets, is mentioned first in Sirach 49:10 ("May the bones of the twelve prophets send forth new life from where they lie," NRSV), first written in Hebrew about 180 BCE. The evidence from the Judean Desert manuscripts, dating back to the second century BCE, confirms the evidence for such a collection (Fuller 1996). From as far back as our evidence goes these twelve books have been read together as a collection in both Hebrew and Greek, and they comprise one book in the Jewish canon. Furthermore, in addition to the historical evidence for this collection, scholars have found literary coherence in the content and order of the books. This evidence supports reading the Twelve not only as individual books but also as a "coherent literary whole" (Sweeney 2000, 49).

The LXX Minor Prophets are distinct from the Hebrew version not only in their language but also in their order. The dominant order of the first six books of the Twelve in the LXX is Hosea-Amos-Micah-Joel-Obadiah-Jonah, and the order of the last six books agrees with the Hebrew, probably deriving from it. The order of the first six book in the LXX may result from an attempt to arrange the books more chronologically (Swete 1989, 227). It could also be influenced by the length of the books, although the last book, Jonah, is longer than Obadiah, which precedes it. In this regard, Jonah may have been placed last because of its narrative content, which differs from the oracles in the other books.

Especially important for LXX Amos is its relationship to Hosea and Micah, which precede and follow it in the LXX. Hosea and Amos are both addressed to the Northern Kingdom. The prophet Hosea is from the Northern Kingdom and prophesies to it, the prophet Amos is from the Southern Kingdom and is called to minister to the North, and Micah is from the Southern Kingdom and ministers there. Thus, in the first three books of the Twelve there is a sequence in the home countries of the first three prophets, related to their ministries to the Northern and Southern Kingdoms. Also, all the kings named in the superscription in Hos 1:1 are the same kings named in the combined superscriptions in Amos and Micah. So, the superscription in Hosea provides the framework for the first three prophets in LXX Twelve. Jones (192) writes, "The information contained within the superscriptions unites and organizes the three books under the rubric of chronology and also explains the position of Hosea at the head of the collection." It is also possible that the epilogue of Hosea (14:10) provides the motto for the collection, functioning like Psalm 1 does in the Psalter (Seitz, 215). That verse reads: "Who is wise and will understand these things, or prudent and will comprehend them? For the ways of the Lord are upright, and the just will walk in them, but the impious (ἀσεβής) will be weak in them" (NETS).

Themes and catchwords may also have influenced the order of these three books. The word "impious" (ἀσεβής) in the epilogue of Hosea also connects Hosea with the Oracles to the Nations in Amos 1–2, each of which contains the adjective ἀσέβεια in the repeated clause: "On account of three ungodly acts (ἀσέβεια) of . . . and on account of four I will not let them go unpunished." Then the Oracles against the Nations in Amos 1–2 give examples of the kinds of "ungodly" people referred to in the last verse in Hosea. It is also noteworthy that, in the Hebrew Bible, Joel 4:16 describes the Lord "roaring from Zion" connecting with the same verb in Amos 1:2 (שאג) and forming a link between the two books. However, in the LXX where Joel does not precede and connect with Amos, two different words are used to translate the Hebrew verb (see Glenny 2013a, 8).

Just as with the book's opening, the ending of LXX Amos forges a different link with the following book(s) than the Hebrew version of Amos does. In Amos 9:12, the Hebrew phrase "that they may possess the remnant of Edom" connects the text with Obadiah, which follows it in the Hebrew version, whereas the corresponding words in the Greek, referring to "nations" coming to the Lord—"that the remnant of people and all the nations (ἔθνος) may seek [me]"—do not form a link with

Obadiah in the LXX where such a link is not necessary since Micah follows Amos in that version (see Glenny 2013a, 8). However, the LXX version of Amos 9:12a does form a link with Micah, the book following it in the LXX, by means of the programmatic verses in Mic 4:1–3 which describe the "nations" (ἔθνος) coming to Jerusalem to seek the Lord. This important distinction between the Hebrew and Greek of Amos 9:12a connects Amos with the two different books following it in the Hebrew and Greek traditions; the Greek rendering making a thematic and verbal connection with the nations coming to Jerusalem to seek the Lord in the Greek of Micah and the Hebrew version forming a verbal link with Edom in the Hebrew of Obadiah (see Glenny 2013b, 6–16, for more on the order of the Twelve in the LXX).

Structure of LXX Amos. The divisions of LXX Amos in this handbook follow the two main critical editions, R-H and Ziegler, which agree with each other exactly on their paragraph divisions. The only place I have differed from the divisions in these two editions is in combining 1:1 and 1:2, which R-H and Ziegler divide into separate paragraphs.

The main features of the structure are as follows. The first verse is the superscription, containing the name of the author and a description of his words, and 1:2 summarizes the message of the book. The first two chapters are a series of eight oracles addressed to nations around Israel, concluding with a longer oracle addressed to Israel that leads into the content of the oracles against Israel's sin and prophecies of Israel's judgment in chapters 3–6. Five visions comprise the main structure of 7:1–9:7, with further development following the last three visions. And the book concludes with a final prophesy of judgment (9:8a) and promises of future deliverance and blessing (9:8b-15).

1:1–2	Superscription and Motto
1:3–5	Oracle against Damascus
1:6–8	Oracle against Philistia
1:9–10	Oracle against Tyre
1:11–12	Oracle against Idumea
1:13–15	Oracle against Ammon
2:1–3	Oracle against Moab
2:4–5	Oracle against Judah
2:6–16	Oracle against Israel
3:1–8	The Lord Must Judge Israel's Sin
3:9–15	The Lord Calls Witnesses against Israel and Prophesies Judgment
4:1–3	The Judgment of the Self-Indulgent Rich
4:4–13	Israel's Empty Worship and Judgment

5:1–17   Lament and Call to Seek the Lord
5:18–27   The Day of the Lord
6:1–14   Condemnation of Israel's Enemies and Israel
7:1–3   First Vision: Grasshoppers
7:4–6   Second Vision: Fire
7:7–9   Third Vision: Hard Metal
7:10–17   Amos and Amaziah
8:1–3   Fourth Vision: A Fowler's Cage
8:4–14   Empty Religion and Resulting Judgment
9:1–7   Fifth Vision: The Lord Standing on the Altar
9:8–15   Judgment and Eschatological Blessing

A different, but noteworthy, structure of LXX Amos is found in Codex Vaticanus, where the copyists employed two means of indicating divisions in the text. The original scribe made thirty-four paragraph divisions by beginning each paragraph on a new line and using *ekthesis* (i.e., extending the text of those lines slightly into the left margin). These paragraph divisions vary greatly in length, and after chapters 1–2 it is often difficult to understand the point of the divisions. A later method of indicating divisions in LXX Twelve in Vaticanus is the use of numeral capital letters at the beginning of major sections of the book. There are six such major divisions in LXX Amos in Vaticanus, beginning at 1:1 (also at 2:4; 3:1; 5:16; 7:10; and 9:11). All of these six major divisions correspond with one of the thirty-four original paragraph divisions in Vaticanus, mentioned above (see Glenny 2013b, 5–7).

The Translation of LXX Amos

The Unity of the Greek Translation of LXX Twelve. Although several scholars have challenged the unity of the Greek translation of the Twelve, those challenges have been answered to the satisfaction of most scholars, and the general consensus is that the translation of all twelve books should be attributed to one translator.

In 1920 in his Schweich Lectures H. St. John Thackeray proposed that the Twelve were translated by a single translator (Thackeray 1921). Shortly thereafter Johannes Hermann and Friedrich Baumgärtel (1923) disagreed with Thackeray, arguing that there were two translators of the Minor Prophets. They proposed the first six books in the LXX ordering, Hosea–Jonah, were the work of one translator, and the last five books, Habakkuk–Malachi, were the product of a second; Nahum, between these two groups, belonged to both. Joseph Ziegler (1934) disputed this thesis, emphasizing the similarities between the Greek in the two main groups of the Twelve Hermann and Baumgärtel had proposed and arguing that a difference in style does not necessarily point to a different translator. Ziegler explained the difference in style "on the basis of a versatile translator who felt no urgency to use the same correspondent consistently for a given Hebrew word or phrase" (NETS, 780).

The number of translators of LXX Amos has been a special focus of attention. Johnson (1936) maintained that one translator was responsible for chapters 1–4 and 7–9, and chapters 5–6 were the work of a different translator, or they were reworked following the translation of the whole book. He considered the translation of chapters 5–6 to be distinguished from the rest of the book by "strikingly idiomatic Greek," "double rendering[s]," "syntactical blunders," several renderings of words differing from the way the words were rendered elsewhere in the book, and "peculiarities in the translation of Hebrew moods and verses" (Johnson 1936, 25, 36–37, 67). George Howard (1970) also proposed there were two translators for LXX Amos, but he divided their work differently than Johnson. He contended that one translated 1:1–8:11 and 9:11–15, and the other translated 8:12–9:10. He pointed to things like the different renderings of the place-name "Beersheba" (באר שבע), which in 5:5 is rendered "the well of the oath" (τὸ φρέαρ τοῦ ὅρκου) and in 8:14 is translated Βηρσαβεε (on these differences, see the handbook proper). T. Muraoka (1970) answered Howard and argued that the differences in style in Amos could be explained by differences in context and the flexibility of a single translator. Muraoka judged Ziegler's previous work on this issue to be important and valuable and took a position similar to him. In his introduction to the translation of the Twelve Prophets in NETS (781), Howard revised his earlier judgment and concluded that "although the differences in style within the Greek Minor Prophets are sometimes striking, they do not necessarily suggest that more than one translator was at work." His one exception to that conclusion is Habakkuk 3, which exists in two versions, the majority text found in most manuscripts and the textual tradition represented in Codex Barberinus and a small number of other manuscripts (often called the Barberini text). Besides this text, he suggests "stylistic differences" in LXX Twelve can be explained by an early corrector who worked through the original translation, making some revisions; his work was hasty and haphazard, and he left the text as it exists "with some stylistic inconsistencies" (NETS, 781).

Tov (1976, esp. pp. 17, 135–55) proposed the same translator made the original translation of the Twelve, Jeremiah, and Ezekiel. Since the latter parts of Jeremiah and Ezekiel reflect the work of a reviser or editor, the original translation of those two books is only preserved in Jeremiah 1–28 and Ezekiel 1–27.

Thus, the consensus is that the evidence suggests one translator, or possibly one group of translators, for the Twelve (Dines 2004, 22). It is also possible this same translator was responsible for parts of Jeremiah and Ezekiel, but this is less certain.

The Time and Place of the Translation of LXX Twelve. Since it is generally held that one translator was responsible for the translation of LXX Twelve, we will consider the time and place of the translation of the Twelve rather than focusing only on LXX Amos. The translation of the Twelve must have been completed by the last third of the second century BCE, on the basis of the reference to the Greek "twelve prophets" in Sirach 49:10 (Bons, 441; Wright, 413). This is the time Ben Sirach's grandson translated Sirach into Greek, referring in his prologue to the parts of the Hebrew Bible as translated into Greek and including the "twelve prophets" along with other biblical authors and characters in chapters 44–50. However, it is impossible to establish a precise *terminus post quem* for the translation. Dines (2004, 45–51) suggests the interest to translate books like the Psalms and the Prophets into Greek may have been spurred by the Jewish struggles with the Ptolemies and Seleucids and the Maccabean Revolt in the second century BCE, which created a need in Greek-speaking Judaism for a further prophetic message from the Lord to speak to their times. Thus, it is best to place the translation of the Twelve about the middle of the second century (Dines 2004, 46, 50; Glenny 2009, 262–63). (On the date of the translation and its relationship to the dates of the translation of other books, see further Bons 2019, 440–41; Dines 2015, 441; Dogniez 2019, 425–26; Glenny 2017, 617.) Linguistic evidence regarding the date of the translation of the Twelve is inconclusive (Dines 2004, 46, 50).

Although the translation of LXX Twelve could have taken place in Palestine, the limited evidence available suggests an Egyptian provenance is more likely. In LXX Amos 7:14 the prophet describes himself as "a scratcher of sycamore tree fruit" (κνίζων συκάμινα), referring to a practice that was necessary for the fruit to ripen so it was edible, and which was especially attested in Egypt. Furthermore, Bons (441) notes that in Egypt the noun τὸ συκάμινον designated sycamore figs, as it does in LXX Amos 7:14, and the noun ἡ συκάμινος designated the sycamore tree itself (see further Muraoka 2009, 644; LSJ, 955; Glenny 2009, 264; Dines 1991, 242). Another translation in LXX Amos that is consistent with an Egyptian provenance is the rendering in 6:14:

οὖ μὴ εἰσελθεῖν εἰς Εμαθ καὶ ἕως τοῦ χειμάρρου τῶν δυσμῶν

so that you will not enter into Hamath and as far as the wadi of the west

ולחצו אתכם מלבוא חמת עד נחל הערבה

and they shall oppress you from Lebo-hamath to the Wadi Arabah (NRSV)

While the Hebrew refers to oppression of people *within* the borders of the Northern Kingdom (Wolff, 289), the LXX gives the perspective of someone *outside* the land, who cannot enter any part of it, from the northern border to the border with Egypt. Such a perspective would be fitting for a person considering the land from outside of it, perhaps in Egypt.

Bons also mentions the clause "the reaping shall last until the vintage" (καταλήμψεται ὁ ἀλοητὸς τὸν τρύγητον) in LXX Amos 9:13, which is an almost verbatim equivalent to LXX Lev 26:5 (although the corresponding Hebrew texts differ from each other). This suggests the translator of the Twelve was familiar with the translation in Leviticus, and, since it is a pronouncement of salvation, he was relying on it. Bons (441) summarizes, "Such a course of action is only plausible when the translator addresses a Greek-speaking audience living in Egypt that had access to the LXX Pentateuch." In addition, Dines (2015, 441) gives evidence of "Egyptian terminology" in LXX Twelve and the translator's "wide technological knowledge," suggesting a wide-ranging education and making Alexandria a likely location, although she acknowledges "there were Greek-speaking Jewish communities elsewhere in Egypt and beyond (e.g., Leontopolis in Egypt or Cyrene)."

The Character of the Translation

When considering the character of a LXX translation, it is helpful to remember that the Greek translation can differ from the Hebrew text we use today (MT) for several different reasons: (1) a different Hebrew *Vorlage*; (2) changes made by a copyist to the Hebrew or Greek text during its transmission; or (3) changes made by the translator (Glenny 2021, 319–23). This discussion usually focuses on different *Vorlagen* or changes made in translation, and Tov thinks that most differences are caused by the latter, which he describes as "inner-translational factors, especially in the area of exegesis" (2012, 117); my own studies in Amos concur with Tov's analysis (Glenny 2007 and 2009).

The translation of LXX Amos is similar to the rendering of the rest of the Twelve (see Glenny 2009; 2017, 618–21). The translator was a scholar-scribe who was adequate in Hebrew but struggled with some of the more difficult sections in his source text (Glenny 2009, 71–108). Specifically, it is in the sections containing difficult Hebrew or visually ambiguous phenomena, like words with homonyms or homographs, that his translation most often varies from the sense of the source text. I have argued that difficult and ambiguous contexts in the source text are often used by the translator to communicate his unique ideology and theology on an ad hoc basis (Glenny 2009), but others believe the differences between the source text and translation are more likely the result of obscurities, like indistinct writing, in the source text used by the translator of Amos (Gelston 2002) or differences between the source text used by the translator and the proto-MT (see Dines [2015, 442] for some examples of textual variants that may have influenced the translator of the Twelve).

The translator worked from a *Vorlage* that was close to the consonantal text of the MT, and for the most part he showed respect for it, trying to reflect it in his translation, preserving its word order and seldom adding or deleting elements. I have found only seven differences in word order, and six of them are minor (Glenny 2009, 44–46; see pp. 47–51 on omissions and additions in LXX Amos). The sporadic divergences in representation of the Hebrew in LXX Amos indicate "that the translator did not feel tied to the text, but instead he was free to add or subtract elements where necessary to meet requirements of Greek style or grammar or to attempt to clarify his desired meaning" (Glenny 2009, 51). The resulting translation is "competent" (Dines 2004, 22) and generally represents the Hebrew well.

Dines (2015, 440) writes concerning the translator of the Twelve that his "Koine Greek is usually good, sometimes elegant, although marked by Semitic interference and stereotyping common in LXX." Some evidence for interference includes (1) employing a Greek verb and participle to render a Hebrew verb and infinitive absolute (5:5), (2) προστίθημι plus an infinitive to communicate "to continue doing" (for *hiphil* of יסף plus an infinitive; 5:2; 7:8, 13; 8:2), (3) redundant use of genitive personal pronouns immediately following a noun (3:7; 4:9), (4) pleonastic use of a personal pronoun in relative clauses (2:9; 4:7; Bons 2019, 439–40, where he also lists other examples; see also Howard 2007, 777).

There are several indications of rhetorical consciousness and good Greek style in LXX Amos. One of the main evidences of the translator's interest in style is *variatio*, or literary variation. Whereas Hebrew authors tend to repeat the same word over and over again, Greek style prefers the use of synonyms. And there seems to be evidence that "*Variatio*, in the rhetorical sense of the term, was an effect consciously pursued" by some of the LXX translators (Joosten 2011, 16; see also Glenny 2009, 58–63). Although faithfulness to the original is their overriding concern, "[i]n small details, however, one observes sensitivity to the genius of the Greek language. Literary taste prevails over strict literalism: a lexical equivalent is altered for variety; words are chosen for the way their sound interacts with other elements in the clause; and grammatical forms are varied for the sake of elegance" (Joosten 2011, 22). In Amos 4:7–11 the phrase "you did not return to me, says the Lord" (ולא שבתם עדי נאם יהוה) is repeated five times. The first two times, in 4:6 and 4:8, the translator employed the simple negative οὐκ, and then in the last three occurrences of this clause in 4:9, 10, and 11 he uses the stronger negative οὐδ' ὥς. In 4:7 he also varies between καί and δέ in rendering the Hebrew *waw*, and this is one of only five times δέ occurs in LXX Amos (see also 2:9; 7:11, 13, 17). There are also many examples of literary variation in the rendering of the Oracles against the Nations in 1:3–2:6, and several examples are given in the notes on 1:3. (See also Dines 2004, 55–56; 2019, 40–42, for examples of *variatio* in the Oracles against the Nations in LXX Amos 1:3–2:6.)

Bons (2019, 440) illustrates the Greek style and rhetoric in LXX Amos by "plays on words" (2:14; 9:9) and "alliteration and homoioteleuton" (5:6; 6:11; 8:3, 5; 9:14). Dines (2019) points out the "fourfold alliteration in *kappa*" in 2:13; the "threefold alliteration in *lambda*" in 9:9; the avoidance of a Hebrew chiastic structure (7:12), which would have been offensive to Greek speakers' ears; and a host of other literary effects that occur throughout the LXX Amos and will be enumerated in the introduction to the forthcoming volume on Amos in *La Bible d'Alexandrie*. She also suggests (2019, 35) that clusters of literary effects in 1:3–2:6, chapter 6, and chapter 9 may "mark a change in tempo or a rise in moral temperature, so to speak, or a sense of a set piece meriting special attention (as in Amos 1:3–2:6)."

Greek Verbs in LXX Amos

In the R-H text there are 577 verbals in LXX Amos (indicative, subjunctive, imperative, participles, and infinitives). Of these, 370 are in the indicative mood, 52 are subjunctive, and 40 are imperative.

Interestingly the translator used no optative verbs, and, of the 370 indicative mood verbs, almost half (177) are future tense, as seems consistent in prophetic literature. There are also 92 participles and 23 infinitives (for a survey of the translation of Hebrew verbals in LXX Amos, see Glenny 2009, 51–57). The following chart gives an overview of the distribution of verbs in LXX Amos and in LXX Twelve, the larger translation unit of which Amos is a part. The percentages are rounded off and thus not exact, but they are deemed sufficiently exact for a summary evaluation.

Verbs in LXX Amos (577)	Verbs in LXX Twelve (4,083)
Indicative verbs 370 (64%)	*Indicative verbs 2,786 (68%)*
Present tense 73 (13%)	Present tense 388 (10%)
Future tense 177 (31%)	Future tense 1250 (31%)
Imperfect tense 16 (3%)	Imperfect tense 123 (3%)
Aorist tense 98 (17%)	Aorist tense 925 (23%)
Perfect tense 6 (1%)	Perfect tense 94 (2%)
Subjunctive verbs 52 (9%)	*Subjunctive verbs 231 (5%)*
Present tense 3 (0.5%)	Present tense 19 (0.4%)
Aorist tense 49 (8%)	Aorist tense 211 (5%)
	Future tense 1 (0.02%)
Imperative verbs 40 (7%)	*Imperative verbs 309 (8%)*
Present tense 10 (2%)	Present tense 97 (2%)
Aorist tense 30 (5%)	Aorist tense 211 (5%)
	Perfect tense 1 (0.02%)
Optative verbs 0	*Optative verbs 3 (0.01%)*
Participles 92 (16%)	*Participles 571 (14%)*
Present tense 76 (13%)	Present tense 474 (12%)
Future tense 2 (0.3%)	Future tense 3 (0.07%)
Aorist tense 0	Aorist tense 17 (0.4%)
Perfect tense 14 (2%)	Perfect tense 77 (2%)
Infinitives 23 (4%)	*Infinitives 183 (4%)*
Present tense 2 (0.3%)	Present tense 59 (1%)
Aorist tense 21 (4%)	Aorist tense 124 (3%)

Although the text under consideration is a translation, and we are not comparing it with the verb forms in its source text, we can still make several interesting observations. First, the proportionate use of different verb forms charted in LXX Amos is in overall general agreement with the proportionate use of the same forms in LXX Twelve, which is consistent with the theory that there was one translator of the Twelve. Striking is the proportion of future-tense verbs used in both Amos and the Twelve. This is probably due to the fact this is prophetic literature and is filled with references to the future. The translator preferred the aorist tense over the present in the subjunctive and imperative moods and in the use of infinitives, and he seldom employed the optative mood, never in Amos. With participles the tendency is to favor the present tense, and peculiarly there is not one aorist participle in LXX Amos. Nor are there any pluperfect-tense verbs.

More specific observations may be helpful. The frequent use of the aorist subjunctive is partly due to its frequent use with οὐ μή in strong negation and with ἐάν in third-class (vivid future) conditional sentences. The main reason the present-tense indicative is used seventy-three times in LXX Amos is the forty-two occurrences of the form λέγω, often introducing the words of the Lord. The infrequent occurrence of perfect (6) and imperfect (16) indicative verbs in Amos and LXX Twelve makes their presence all the more marked. Interestingly, they tend to occur in clusters, perfects in 5:15 (2x); 5:21 (2x); 6:8; and 9:12, and imperfect-tense verbs appear in 1:3, 13; 2:12 (2x); 2:7–9 (6x); 5:3 (2x); 5:11; 6:6; and 7:14 (2x). Especially striking is the use of the imperfect tense, six of the sixteen times it occurs in LXX Amos, in 2:7–9; the imperfect tense is very appropriate in this context, describing the sins of Israel, because it puts special stress on the continuous or repetitive nature of their sin. The imperfect also emphasizes the sin of the last and climactic oracle against Israel, the main addressee in the book. Because there are other places where it could have also been appropriate to use the imperfect tense and because of the pattern of clustering occurrences of imperfect and perfect tenses, one gets the impression that the use of indicative forms of these tenses in LXX Amos tends to recur when for some reason the use of these verb forms came to the translator's mind, and once he used a perfect or imperfect verb it was on his mind and he was prone to use it again.

Levels of prominence and the different uses of the Greek verb tenses in various contexts (e.g., ingressive, constative, consummative, etc.) are not part of the inherent meanings of the different verbal aspects communicated by the tense forms but are determined by the broader context. However, references to prominence and uses of verb tenses will be included in the discussion of verbs in this handbook where it is deemed appropriate to describe how verbs are functioning in their contexts. The same is true of different categories of the use of noun cases and other grammatical features in the text; categories have been employed in the handbook to describe how different grammatical forms function in their contexts, but such categories of usage are not an inherent part of the forms of those words. They are simply functions possible for those forms that are judged to be useful for explaining their meanings in said contexts.

Verb Tense. Some contend that "tense forms in Greek are not primarily time based (i.e., tense is not grammaticalized in Greek)" (Porter 1993, 107–8), and others contend that verbs in the indicative mood grammaticalize both tense and aspect (Fanning, 8–29, esp. 28–29, 420–22; *CGCG* §33). The position assumed and followed in this handbook is that Greek verb-tense labels describe how the action of the verb is located in time in relation to some other moment; in main clauses the time is relative to the time of speaking or writing, and in subordinate clauses it is usually in relation to another temporal reference in the context (*CGCG* §33.1–3; Ehorn, xxix). Although there are anomalies, normally the temporal significance of Greek verbs (i.e., past, present, and future) is grammaticalized in indicative mood verbs (e.g., augments) and signified by the surrounding co-text.

Verbal Aspect. The primary semantic feature that is grammaticalized in the various verb stems is verbal aspect, and verbal aspect refers to the way the author elected to describe the action of the verb. That is, from the author's subjective viewpoint, the different verb stems present or look at the action of the verb from different perspectives. The aorist (perfective aspect) views the action of the verb externally and as a whole. The present (imperfective aspect) affords an internal view of the action of the verb and sees the action as continuing and ongoing. The imperfect stem, which is built on the present-tense stem, expresses the same aspect as the present stem, only in past time. With the perfect stem the action of the verb is stative in its aspect. The future stem does not express aspect, only time.

A few other notes concerning the treatment of verbs in this handbook will be helpful for the reader. Instead of employing the term "deponent" to refer to verbs whose morphology is middle, passive, or middle/passive and are considered to be "active" in meaning, I have used the traditional morphological categories middle and passive. The term "deponent" is "borrowed from Latin grammar" (*CGCG* §35.6), and there are better explanations than deponent for the use of such middle and passive forms (see *CGCG* §35.1–36; and Aubrey, 563–625). I have labeled all middle-morphology verbs as such and used the categories suggested by Suzanne Kemmer (1993) for middle verbs to classify them. I have also parsed all -θη/η- aorist verbs as passive voice, although during the Koine period middle morphology was being replaced by passive morphology (esp. the -θη- morpheme; Decker 2014b, xii; see also the discussion in Mathewson and Emig, 152; and *CGCG* §35.27), and many verbs that have a passive form are not passive in meaning. *CGCG* (§14.1) notes that not only are there verbs whose passive aorist does not have (or only rarely has) passive meaning, but also only a minority of passive aorists formed with -η- regularly has passive meaning. For an up-to-date discussion of Greek verbs, see the 2016 volume edited by Runge and Fresch and the discussion of verbs in *CGCG*.

Syntax and Style

As noted above, the Koine Greek in LXX Amos is generally good, but it is not of a high register. It has characteristics consistent with translation Greek, and it is generally isomorphic, following closely the order in its *Vorlage*. There is an absence of Greek features like genitive absolute constructions, μέν ... δέ constructions (only twice in LXX Twelve [Hag 1:4; Zech 1:15]), optative mood verbs, periphrastic constructions, first-class condition constructions, and pluperfect verb forms. The conjunction ἵνα occurs only once in LXX Amos, in the construction ἵνα τί with the sense "why?" (5:18).

A few other points could be added concerning the syntax. By far the dominant conjunction employed in LXX Amos is καί, which occurs 312 times, illustrating the predominantly paratactic style of the translation Greek. By contrast δέ occurs merely 5 times (see above), ἀλλά is found only twice (7:14; 8:11), and τέ does not occur at all in LXX Amos. The translator also used asyndeton (e.g., 3:8; 4:9, 13; 5:8, 11; 6:1, 5; 8:6; 9:2, 3, 10), often in contexts where the relationship between clauses is clear or there is development or transition to a new topic or thought (see Runge, 20–23).

Some examples of hypotaxis in the translation are found in the use of ἐάν to introduce vivid future (third-class) conditions, the employment of ὅπως with purpose or result clauses, several occurrences of ὅτι introducing causal clauses, and the use of διὰ τοῦτο and διότι in causal and inferential clauses (see the grammatical index for examples).

The Greek is straightforward, and the *Vorlage* often controls the style, and yet on occasion LXX Amos evidences a more elegant style. Several elements of the Greek style in LXX Amos are discussed above in the section addressing the translation, but a few more could be added here. Bons (440) notes a certain "ornamentation" in the Greek that cannot be completely explained by the underlying Hebrew in wordplay in 2:14 (ὁ κραταιὸς οὐ μὴ κρατήσῃ; see also Dines 2013, 404) and 9:9 (λικμιῶ ... λικμᾶται ... λικμῷ) and in "alliteration and homoioteleuton" in 5:6 (ἐκζητήσατε ... ζήσατε), 6:11 (θλάσμασιν ... ῥάγμασιν), 8:3 (πολὺς ὁ πεπτωκὼς ἐν παντὶ τόπῳ), 8:5 (μικρὸν μέτρον), and 9:14 (κατοικήσουσιν ... καταφυτεύσουσιν ... φυτεύσουσιν κήπους ... φάγονται ... καρπὸν). I have also found various literary features in LXX Amos. Some reflect the source text, and some are the work of the translator. Either way, they are part of the text and worthy of mention. In the handbook there are several references to literary variation in the translation (see 1:3; 2:15; and the section above on the translation). Other literary features include assonance (9:11), rhetorical questions (introduced by εἰ in 3:3–6), inclusion (5:1 and 16), merism (1:2), hyperbaton (1:1; 4:7; 6:4), and homoioteleuton (i.e., rhyming in 4:1; 8:8). It is also noteworthy that there are several neologisms in LXX Amos (e.g., 3:9; 9:13); LEH is helpful in identifying these.

A HANDBOOK ON THE GREEK TEXT OF AMOS

Amos 1:1-2

¹The words of Amos, which came [to him] in Nakkarim of Tekoa, which he saw concerning Jerusalem in the days of Uzziah king of Judah and in the days of Jeroboam the son of Joash king of Israel two years before the earthquake. ²And he said, "The Lord has spoken out of Zion, and out of Jerusalem he has given his voice, and the pastures of the shepherds mourned, and the summit of Carmel was dried up."

The first two verses of LXX Amos introduce the book, giving the title (Λόγοι Αμως) in 1:1 and a summary of its message in 1:2. The title or superscription in verse 1 contains the author's name, the location where he received his words, a general description of the content of his visions, and the time of his ministry.

1:1 Λόγοι Αμως, οἳ ἐγένοντο ἐν νακκαριμ ἐκ Θεκουε, οὓς εἶδεν ὑπὲρ Ιερουσαλημ ἐν ἡμέραις Οζιου βασιλέως Ιουδα καὶ ἐν ἡμέραις Ιεροβοαμ τοῦ Ιωας βασιλέως Ισραηλ πρὸ δύο ἐτῶν τοῦ σεισμοῦ.

Λόγοι. Nominative absolute, a type of nominative that occurs only in introductory material, such as the opening formula of a book, which is not to be construed as a sentence (Wallace, 49–51). Smyth (§940) notes, "The nominative may be used independently in the citing of names of persons and things."

Αμως. Possessive genitive. This proper noun is indeclinable. Amos 7:11–17 gives some background on Amos. Normally in the introduction to the prophetic books "the word of the Lord" comes to the prophet (see ἐγένοντο); in Amos it is "the words of Amos," which came [to him] (see also MT Jer 1:1).

οἳ ἐγένοντο ἐν νακκαριμ ἐκ Θεκουε. The first of two relative clauses modifying λόγοι ("the words [of Amos]"). In the MT the corresponding relative clause modifies Amos (עמוס) and explains his location and occupation ("among the shepherds of Tekoa").

οἳ. Nominative relative pronoun, subject of ἐγένοντο.

ἐγένοντο. Aor mid ind 3rd pl γίνομαι. This verb is employed regularly in the first verse of the LXX Prophets to describe the word of the Lord coming to the prophet (Jer, Hos, Joel, Jonah, Mic, and Zech; see also Jonah 3:1; *GELS*, 130–31.2.f) or coming "by the hand" of the prophet (Hag 1:1). The corresponding verb in the Hebrew (היה) is third-person singular, describing Amos. This Greek verb form is sometimes called deponent, but it is better to call it middle. It is clear that the subject is affected by the state or copulative relationship described. See the discussion of so-called deponent verbs in the Introduction.

ἐν νακκαριμ. Locative (*GELS*, 231.1), modifying ἐγένοντο. The rendering "in Nakkarim" (ἐν νακκαριμ) is apparently a result of a misunderstanding of the Hebrew בנקדים ("among the herdsmen"), which was taken to be a place-name, based on its proximity in the text to the place-name Tekoa. It is likely that the translator did not know the Hebrew word נקד since it occurs only one other time in the Hebrew Scriptures (2 Kgs 3:4), and thus he attempted to transliterate it. However, in the transliteration he seems to have read the Hebrew *dalet* in נקדים as a *resh*. (See the discussion of this rendering in Glenny 2013b, 12.) The Greek MSS B, A, and Q have Ἀκκαρείμ, and *L* and *C* have καριαθιαρειμ, which is clearly an attempt to identify the word with Kiriath-Jearim. It appears that all the readings in the LXX MSS are place-names, apparently near Tekoa, Amos' hometown. Since all the early Greek MSS have Ἀκκαρείμ, probably an early copyist (or translator) confused the *nu* at the end of ἐν and the one at the beginning of the transliteration of נקדים (i.e., νακκαριμ) and dropped the *nu* at the beginning of νακκαριμ, resulting in the early reading Ἀκκαρείμ. The choice of the reading νακκαριμ in R-H (which is also in Ziegler) is influenced by the Hebrew (נקדים) and the versions. Dines (1991, 42–43) notes that LXX Amos has about twice as many "indeclinable forms of proper nouns [as] declinable ones" (see, for example, Αμως [1:1], Εφραιμ [6:7], Ιερουσαλημ [1:1, 2; 2:5], Σιων [1:2; 6:1], and Ισραηλ [29x in LXX Amos]), and it is likely that "Nakkarim" (νακκαριμ) is another of these.

ἐκ Θεκουε. Partitive, modifying νακκαριμ. The preposition ἐκ should probably be understood to point to "an entity out of which a component or part is singled out" (*GELS*, 201.2). The translator understood the words to come to Amos in Nakkarim, which is a part or portion of Tekoa. MS B and Swete have the preposition ἐν here, which would have a slightly different sense, emphasizing more that Nakkarim was located within the environs of Tekoa than that it was a part of it; Θεκουε, the genitive object of ἐκ, is another indeclinable proper noun that occurs six times in the LXX (see also 1 Kgdms 10:28 [2x]; 2 Kgdms 22:14; Ezra 10:15; Jer 6:1).

οὓς εἶδεν ὑπὲρ Ιερουσαλημ. This relative clause further describes the words of Amos.

οὓς. Accusative direct object of εἶδεν, referring to the antecedent λόγοι.

εἶδεν. Aor act ind 3rd sg ὁράω. Constative aorist, presenting a summary of the action. This verb suggests prophetic visions, like those found in chapters 7–9. Since this relative clause modifies λόγοι, the words of Amos are related to the visions he saw.

ὑπέρ Ιερουσαλημ. Reference, modifying εἶδεν. The preposition ὑπέρ functions as a "marker of general content, whether of a discourse or mental activity" (BDAG, 1031.A.3; see also *GELS*, 696.2; and *GE*, 2194.B, D mentioning that this use of ὑπέρ with the genitive = περί with the genitive); see parallel uses of this preposition in Joel 1:3; Jonah 4:10; Nah 1:14; and esp. Mic 1:1, where ὑπέρ with the genitive is parallel to περί with the genitive. It is noteworthy that in the Greek the things Amos saw are "concerning Jerusalem," while in the Hebrew they are "concerning Israel"; on this rendering, see Dines (1991, 42) and also the discussion in Park (177). It is possible that the translator rendered Israel as Jerusalem because he understood Israel to be the Northern and Southern Kingdoms and Jerusalem as their legitimate capital (LXX.E, 2345–46).

ἐν ἡμέραις Οζιου βασιλέως Ιουδα. Temporal. This is the first of three PPs modifying the preceding verb εἶδεν but also apparently giving the time of the previous parallel relative clause, "which came [to him] in Nakkarim in Tekoa." All three of these PPs have a temporal sense (temporal use of ἐν [2x] and πρό), giving the time when Amos received the content of the book.

Οζιου. Genitive of description, and "the days of Uzziah" are the days when Uzziah lived or ruled (see Wallace, 81 n. 26).

βασιλέως. Genitive in simple apposition to Οζιου, referring to him and further clarifying who he is.

Ιουδα. Genitive of subordination, meaning that Uzziah ruled "over Judah" (Wallace, 103–4, who calls it "a subset of the subjective genitive").

καί. Coordinating conjunction, connecting parallel phrases (*GELS*, 352.1). This links the second PP that modifies εἶδεν. The καί connects the times when Uzziah and Jeroboam II ruled, so both are synchronized with the time when Amos saw his visions.

ἐν ἡμέραις Ιεροβοαμ τοῦ Ιωας βασιλέως Ισραηλ. Temporal. This is the second PP explaining the time when Amos received the content of this book and ministered. See earlier in 1:1 on ἐν ἡμέραις.

Ιεροβοαμ. Genitive of description. See also Οζιου above in 1:1.

τοῦ Ιωας. Genitive of relationship, meaning Joash is the father of Jeroboam II (see Smyth §1301; Wallace, 83–84). This indeclinable noun is genitive, as indicated by the article.

βασιλέως. Genitive in simple apposition to Ιωας. See βασιλέως above in 1:1.

Ισραηλ. Genitive of subordination. See Ιουδα above in 1:1.

πρὸ δύο ἐτῶν τοῦ σεισμοῦ. Temporal. This is the third PP modifying εἶδεν. The preposition πρό means "prior to, before." Here the preposition is "followed by the genitive of a noun denoting a period of time at the end of which an event denoted by another, immediately following, genitive takes place" (GELS, 583.1.b; see also BDAG, 864.2; and the same construction in 4:7). This construction, placing the preposition before the time period rather than before its object, is "a Hellenistic Greek idiom for indicating duration of time" (MHT 3:246, 260; see also Robertson, 423–24, who calls this unusual word order hyperbaton).

δύο ἐτῶν. Interpositional genitive. An adjective modifying ἐτῶν and supplying the amount of time before "the earthquake" takes place. It is placed between the preposition and its object ἐτῶν, which is a genitive of time. BDF (§186, 2) discusses genitive of time within which something takes place and genitive of a point of time; this is probably closer to the latter, i.e., at a point of time two years before the earthquake (see also Muraoka §22.h).

τοῦ σεισμοῦ. Genitive object of πρό. The article is employed because the "earthquake" is well known (Wallace, 225). Although earthquakes have occurred often in Israel, this earthquake must have been "extremely violent and unparalleled" because it was not only used to date this book, but it was also referred to by Zechariah (14:4–5) hundreds of years later (Paul, 35–36).

1:2 Καὶ εἶπεν Κύριος ἐκ Σιων ἐφθέγξατο καὶ ἐξ Ιερουσαλημ ἔδωκεν φωνὴν αὐτοῦ, καὶ ἐπένθησαν αἱ νομαὶ τῶν ποιμένων, καὶ ἐξηράνθη ἡ κορυφὴ τοῦ Καρμήλου.

After a two-word introduction (Καὶ εἶπεν; "and he said"), referring to Amos, this verse involves two pairs of parallel clauses. The first pair of clauses describes the Lord speaking, apparently in an audible voice from

Jerusalem, and the second pair pictures the effects of his voice, apparently in the form of judgments. The first two clauses are a translation of the Hebrew found also in Joel 4:16, and the two passages are translated exactly the same way in the two LXX passages with the exception of one verb in the first clause: Joel has the verb ἀνακράζω, and Amos has φθέγγομαι.

Καὶ. The καί is conjunctive, connecting this clause with the previous verse and introducing the result or consequence of the Lord speaking to Amos, as described in 1:1. See the same use of καί at the beginning of an utterance in Hos 1:2 (*GELS*, 353.1.h).

εἶπεν. Aor act ind 3rd sg λέγω. Amos is the subject (see Λόγοι Αμως in 1:1). This is the first of five aorist verbs in this verse. The next four aorists are renderings of future-tense verbs in the Hebrew; their presence in the LXX gives the impression that the summary of what Amos prophesied (i.e., what "Amos said") was written after he prophesied (see Garrett, 13, for the rendering of the Hebrew imperfects as future).

Κύριος ἐκ Σιων ἐφθέγξατο. The first of two parallel clauses, describing how the words of the Lord came to Amos (1:1). The two parallel clauses have the same word order: subject–PP–predicate. The subject is given in the first sentence and understood in the second.

Κύριος. Nominative subject of ἐφθέγξατο. Fronted and emphatic; it is the main topic of the first two clauses. Although the order of the Greek in LXX Amos follows the Hebrew closely (Glenny 2009, 44–46), as it does here in 1:2, to the Greek reader the position of Κύριος would be emphatic by its position. Κύριος "as a ubiquitous standard translation of the *nomen sacrum*, יהוה, is very often anarthrous except in the dative" (Muraoka §5b; he adds that in 83 percent of LXX renderings of the tetragrammaton Κύριος is anarthrous).

ἐκ Σιων. Origin, modifying ἐφθέγξατο; the preposition ἐκ "indicates origin, point of departure, source" (*GELS*, 201.5.b; see also BDAG, 296.3). The language in this verse locates the Lord in "Sion" and "Jerusalem," apparently in the temple in Jerusalem, which is his proper dwelling place or sanctuary on earth (Jer 32:30; Joel 3:17). The position of the PP before the verb emphasizes the phrase.

ἐφθέγξατο. Aor mid ind 3rd sg φθέγγομαι. Constative aorist, viewing the action as a whole. The middle voice focuses attention on the subject and his or her self-interest (see Kemmer, 133–34, 269, on speech actions with middle markings). The verb φθέγγομαι occurs three times in LXX Twelve (see also Nah 2:8 and Hab 2:11, both referring to animals uttering sounds), and it can be used of human or animal utterance. In this context with no object, it indicates the Lord spoke out loud (see *GE*, 2271–72; *GELS*, 714). Perhaps the translator was trying to tone down the zoomorphic language in the Hebrew (שׁאג, "roar") with this rendering, but the Lord does "roar" (שׁאג) in LXX Hos 11:10. Anthropomorphic language is found often in LXX Twelve (e.g., references to God's eyes in Amos 9:3, 4, 8, and references to God's hand in Amos 1:8; 7:7; 9:2). The suggestion of LXX.E (2346) that the aorist of the Septuagint points to a single past event is not necessary in this context and makes too much of the grammaticalization of the action by the Greek verb.

ἐξ Ἰερουσαλημ. Origin. See above on ἐκ Σιων.

ἔδωκεν. Aor act ind 3rd sg δίδωμι. Constative aorist, viewing the action as a whole. The active voice focuses more on the situation than the previous middle-voice aorist, which focuses more on the subject. The phrase "given his voice" (ἔδωκεν φωνὴν αὐτοῦ; see also 3:4) is often employed in the LXX in contexts describing the Lord's miraculous deeds and manifestations of his power, such as thunder, hail, and earthquakes (2 Kgdms 22:14; Pss 17:14; 45:7; Joel 2:11; 3:16).

φωνὴν. Accusative direct object of ἔδωκεν.

αὐτοῦ. Possessive genitive, referring to the Lord.

ἐπένθησαν. Aor act ind 3rd pl πενθέω. Constative aorist, viewing the action as a whole. This verb is in the first of two parallel clauses that give the result or consequence of the Lord's speech described earlier in the verse and, following the Hebrew, have the same word order: verb–subject–genitive modifier.

αἱ νομαὶ. Nominative subject of ἐπένθησαν. The "pastures" (νομαί) and the "summit of Carmel" (κορυφὴ τοῦ Καρμήλου) in the next clause constitute a merism (north/south, low/high, minimal vegetation / fertile), implying complete devastation.

τῶν ποιμένων. Possessive genitive, presuming the pastures belong to the shepherds. If they do not belong to them, it is a simple genitive of description. The use of articles with both nouns in the "head noun–genitive noun" construction follows Apollonius' canon (Wallace, 239–40, 250–52; MHT 3:180).

ἐξηράνθη. Aor pass ind 3rd sg ξηραίνω. Consummative aorist, stressing the accomplishment or attainment of the state; it is completely dried up. No agent is expressed or required with this passive verb; God is the understood ultimate agent.

ἡ κορυφὴ. Nominative subject of ἐξηράνθη. The article is used with a monadic (one-of-a-kind) noun.

τοῦ Καρμήλου. Partitive (sometimes called wholative) genitive (BDF §164; Wallace, 84–86), denoting the whole mountain of which the "summit" is a part. The use of articles with both nouns in the genitive construction follows Apollonius' canon (MHT 1963, 180; Wallace, 239–40, 250–52).

Amos 1:3-5

³And the Lord said, "On account of three ungodly acts of Damascus and on account of four I will not let him go unpunished, because with iron saws they were sawing the pregnant women from the people of Gilead. ⁴And I will send out fire against the house of Hazael, and it will consume the foundations of the son of Hader. ⁵And I will crush the bars [of the gates] of Damascus, and I will utterly destroy the inhabitants from the plain of On, and I will cut in pieces the tribe of the men of Haran and the alien people of Syria will be led into captivity," says the Lord.

This section (1:3-5) is the first of eight woe Oracles against the Nations in 1:3-2:16. The oracles have a similar structure, but they differ in many details. The differences in structure and the apparent literary variation in the LXX's renderings will be addressed below in the individual verses.

1:3 Καὶ εἶπεν κύριος Ἐπὶ ταῖς τρισὶν ἀσεβείαις Δαμασκοῦ καὶ ἐπὶ ταῖς τέσσαρσιν οὐκ ἀποστραφήσομαι αὐτόν, ἀνθ᾽ ὧν ἔπριζον πρίοσιν σιδηροῖς τὰς ἐν γαστρὶ ἐχούσας τῶν ἐν Γαλααδ·

Καὶ εἶπεν κύριος. This phrase is unique in the Oracles against the Nations in chapters 1-2. All the judgment oracles have the same introduction in the Hebrew, which is rendered Τάδε λέγει κύριος in the other seven oracles. Here the Hebrew כה is rendered with καί rather than the normal τάδε ("thus"), and the Hebrew verb is rendered in the aorist tense (εἶπεν) instead of the present. The coordinating conjunction (καί) often occurs at "the start of an utterance or book" (*GELS*, 353.1.h; see καὶ εἶπεν κύριος in Hos 1:2); here it connects the first oracle with the introductory material. And the aorist tense of the verb (εἶπεν), which matches the verb describing Amos' speech in 1:2, gives the impression that the first oracle is a continuation of what Amos "said" in 1:2 (Park, 169-70).

The words εἶπεν κύριος render the Hebrew אמר יהוה ("Yahweh said"), a formula that occurs nineteen times in the Hebrew of Amos (1:3, 5, 6, 9, 11, 13, 15; 2:1, 3, 4, 6; 3:12; 5:4, 16, 17, 27; 7:3, 17; 9:15). These Hebrew words are normally rendered λέγει κύριος (this formula occurs forty times in LXX Amos), except in 1:3 and 5:17, where they are rendered εἶπεν κύριος; in two other places the Hebrew has וימר יהוה (7:8; 8:2), with a different form of the Hebrew verb, and these two occurrences of the formula are also rendered εἶπεν κύριος. Wolff (143-45) understands this Hebrew formula to differ from the formula

נאם יהוה ("utterance/oracle of Yahweh"), which occurs sixteen times in MT Amos and is always rendered λέγει κύριος (except in 6:8 and 14, where the LXX has nothing corresponding to these Hebrew words). He proposes that אמר יהוה is sometimes employed in the Oracles to the Nations (1:3–2:16) to convey "messenger speech," and נאם יהוה is "the divine oracle formula," used particularly in 2:16 to emphasize the conclusion of the (divine) oracle against Israel. Wolff includes the evidence he deduces from these formulas in his discussion of the literary redaction of the Hebrew version of Amos. What is most important for LXX Amos is that the translator made no distinction between the two formulas, normally translating both with the words λέγει κύριος, unless he uses the aorist form of this verb. It is also noteworthy that he employs λέγει κύριος to render both אמר אדני (in 1:8; 3:11; 5:3; 7:6) and נאם אדני (in 3:13; 4:5; 8:3, 9, 11; in 6:14 there is nothing corresponding to the Hebrew in the LXX); the single variation is in 7:8, where the translator rendered ויאמר אדני with εἶπεν κύριος. On the basis of his translation of these two Hebrew formulas, it appears the translator understood both of them to be divine speech formulas, pointing to an oracle from the Lord. These formulas can appear at the beginning (introduction) of oracles, in the middle of them (medial) or at their conclusion.

εἶπεν. Aor act ind 3rd sg λέγω. Constative aorist, viewing the action as a whole.

κύριος. Nominative subject of εἶπεν.

Ἐπὶ ταῖς τρισὶν ἀσεβείαις ... ἐπὶ ταῖς τέσσαρσιν. Causal. Coordinate PPs modifying ἀποστραφήσομαι. The preposition ἐπί, which is the first word in the formula in all eight oracles ("on account of the three ..."), and which is repeated again in the next parallel phrase ("on account of the four ..."), gives the cause, ground, or reason why the Lord "will not turn away" from the judgment (*GELS*, 265.II.6). The dative object of ἐπί (ἀσεβείαις) is explicit in the first occurrence of the preposition in the formula, and it is implicit in the second. All eight oracles begin with this formula. See Thackeray (§13.3) on the apparent assimilation of syllables that produces the dative form of τέσσαρες (τέσσαρσιν).

The Greek uses the article with the cardinal numbers ("the three" and "the four") in these phrases throughout the Oracles against the Nations (1:3–2:16). The Hebrew does not have the article, so the translator was not following the Hebrew text strictly here. The cardinal numbers "three" and "four" in the oracles are attributive modifying "ungodly acts" (ἀσεβείαις). Almost certainly the Greek uses the article because the "ungodly acts" and the numbers are abstract "without reference to any definite object" (Smyth §1125; see also Wallace, 226–27); this understanding is supported by the absence of the article with the cardinal numbers in the numerical sayings in Proverbs 30, where the numbers refer to specific objects (the exception in Prov 30:15 is a demonstrative construction). It has been suggested the article with the cardinal numbers in these oracles should be understood to indicate that it is bad enough to commit three sins, but four cannot be forgiven (following b. Yoma 86b, which quotes Amos 2:6). It is also possible that three and four represent components of seven, symbolizing completeness, and thus the sins of all the nations, including Israel and Judah, are filled up (see the other lists of seven in Amos 2:14–16; 4:6–12; 9:1–4). It is better to understand the formula as Nogalski (278) suggests. He comments that since none of the oracles lists three or four specific sins, it is more likely that the numbers should be understood abstractly, and the formula refers to "a significant number and then some" (see the helpful discussion of this formula in Nogalski, 278–79; see also Smyth §1125; and Wallace, 226–27). Since the numbers do not refer to definite objects (see the following), the articles are not translated.

The reason for the punishment in each oracle is the "ungodly acts" (ἀσεβείαις) of the city or nation addressed. The word (ἀσέβεια) has the idea of "ungodliness" or "impiety" and is more specific than the corresponding Hebrew word, "transgression" (פשע); see LXX.E (2346). It can refer to sin in the abstract, and that is possible here since the acts are not described or specified (see also the discussion of numbers above). But with the references to "three" or "four" (and the mention of some specific acts of sin later in each oracle), it is best to render ἀσεβείαις as "ungodly acts."

Δαμασκοῦ. Subjective genitive.

οὐκ. Muraoka (§83.a) states that in LXX Greek "the fundamental distinction between [the two negatives οὐ and μή] is that οὐ and its compounds are objective negations, a speaker or writer rejecting the reality of an affirmation, whilst μή and its compounds are subjective, a speaker or writer rejecting a wish or will, a possibility or likelihood, and a hypothesis from his or her perspective." However, he goes on to list several exceptions to this general rule (Muraoka §83.a, b, ba-bh). Thus, the Greek of the LXX seems to be closer to classical Greek's more complicated distinction between these two negatives than the Koine of the NT, where negation can be summarized in one rule: "οὐ negates the indicative, μή the remaining moods, including infinitive and participle. Individual words and phrases are always negated by οὐ" (BDF §426).

ἀποστραφήσομαι. Fut pass ind 1st sg ἀποστρέφω. Predictive future; simple passive without agency expressed. This is a second future passive form with a stem vowel shift from ε to α and the shortened future-passive-tense formative ης (rather than θης found in the first future passive). The phrase says, "I will not be turned away from him" (BDAG, 122–23.1; LSJ, 220.II; Thackeray, 286), which in this context means "I will not let him go unpunished" (*GELS*, 85.I.4). The clause οὐκ ἀποστραφήσομαι αὐτόν occurs in each of the eight Oracles against the Nations.

αὐτόν. Accusative of person (*GELS*, 85.I.4; see also *CGCG* §30.10; 35.13; the accusative functions like Wallace's category of accusative of thing with a passive verb, Wallace, 438–39). While the Hebrew verb corresponding to ἀποστραφήσομαι always has a masculine, singular, third-person suffix, the object of the Greek verb in the LXX differs from the MT in 1:6 and 1:11 (masc pl 3rd) and in 1:9 (fem sg 3rd). The changes in the gender and number of the pronominal objects of the passive verb require that the object refer to the preceding addressees in the formula "for three transgressions of . . . and for four," because the changes in gender and number would not make sense referring to the judgments, and they can be explained as referring to the preceding addressees. In five of the eight oracles in the LXX, the gender and number of the pronoun agrees with the gender and number of its antecedent, the addressee in the formula, as expected (1:9 ["Tyre," fem sg]; 1:13 ["sons of Ammon" referring to "Ammon," masc sg]; 2:1 [masc sg]; 2:4 [masc sg]; and 2:6 [masc sg]). In two instances (1:6, 11) the change from the Hebrew masculine singular suffix to a masculine plural pronoun (αὐτούς) in the Greek could be explained as a change from a reference to the city or country addressed in the oracles (Gaza and Idumea) to the inhabitants of the respective locales. There is support for this in the contexts following each of the two uses of αὐτούς as the object of οὐκ ἀποστραφήσομαι. In 1:6 following αὐτούς, the "inhabitants" (pl) of Gaza as well as other Philistine cities are mentioned in 1:8. And in 1:11 following the use of αὐτούς for the object of ἀποστραφήσομαι, the people of "Idumea" are described again in the third-person plural, repeating the same pronoun (αὐτούς); thus, the contexts may have influenced the translator to employ a plural pronoun, or the translator may have wanted to vary the pronouns. In the other oracle (in 1:3), the accusative pronoun following ἀποστραφήσομαι does not agree with its antecedent in gender. The addressee, "Damascus," is feminine singular and the pronoun referring to "Damascus" is masculine singular (αὐτόν). Here it is possible that the translator rendered the pronoun αὐτόν to agree with the corresponding Hebrew suffix or was possibly looking ahead in the oracle to references to Damascus as the "house (οἶκος) of Hazael" or "Hader" in 1:4 and the "people (λαός) of Syria" in 1:5, since both of the head nouns in these descriptions are masculine singular.

ἀνθ' ὧν. Causal. This construction is the contracted form of the preposition ἀντί that occurs before a rough breathing mark (Decker 2014a, 157) followed by its genitive object. It is equivalent to ἀντὶ τούτων ὅτι (BDF §294.4). The construction functions like a causal conjunction indicating the reason for something (BDAG, 88.4; Robertson, 574).

The translator varied the way that he renders the identical causal phrase in the Hebrew (על with infinitive construct and suffix). In the LXX ἀνθ' ὧν (1:3, 9, 13; 2:1, 6) and ἕνεκεν-α (1:6, 11; 2:4) are used alternatively to show the cause of the Lord's judgment of the nations ("because"). The translator always used an aorist or imperfect verb to describe the crime following ἀνθ' ὧν and a genitive articular infinitive following ἕνεκεν-α, because this preposition requires a genitive object. The pronouns with the infinitives or the verbs in the descriptions of the addressees' crimes are always third-person plural in the LXX, varying twice from the MT (1:11 ["he" to "they"]; and 2:1 ["he" to "they"]). The two different prepositional constructions would have had a slightly different sense to the sophisticated reader; in classical Greek the construction ἀνθ' ὧν often refers to something preceding that is the antecedent of the relative pronoun and cause or reason for what follows (LSJ, 153.A.3; similarly, in the LXX as explained in *GELS*, 57–58), whereas with ἕνεκεν-α, its genitive object, which most often follows it, is the cause. In the LXX there is no difference in the meaning of the two constructions, as indicated by their use in this passage (see BDF §208 for a list of Hebrew causal constructions rendered by ἀνθ' ὧν in the LXX), and in the oracles in Amos 1–2 ἀνθ' ὧν always refers to or describes what follows it, just as ἕνεκεν-α does. See Dines (2004, 54–57) for a discussion of the literary variation in the stock formulas at the beginning of the judgment oracles.

ἔπριζον. Impf act ind 3rd pl πρίζω, a later, mainly Hellenistic variant of πρίω, only here in the LXX (Dines 1991, 46 n. 7; LSJ, 863). Iterative imperfect, pointing to repeated action, "were sawing." The imperfect-tense verb is significant, or prominent, because the translator only used this tense sixteen times, and he chooses it here in the description of the first sin in the oracles in Amos 1–2. It emphasizes this first sin.

πρίοσιν. Dative of means or instrument. Language similar to "saw with a saw" is found in 2 Kgdms 12:31, the parallel in 1 Chr 20:3, and Sus 59. The context in 2 Kgdms indicates the language there is figurative, referring to torture (LEH, 514), but later uses of the language in Sus 59 and Heb 11:37 are best taken literally (see Dines 1991, 48–52). The use of this noun with its cognate verb (πρίζω) creates a new cognate pairing not found in the Hebrew (דושם בחרצות; "they threshed with threshing sledges") giving a "new literary effect" (Dines 2013, 404).

σιδηροῖς. Dative adjective modifying πρίοσιν.

τὰς ἐν γαστρὶ ἐχούσας. The idiom "to have in belly" (ἐν γαστρὶ ἔχειν) means to be pregnant (*GELS*, 126, s.v. γαστήρ). This phrase is not found in this verse in the MT and may have been borrowed from 1:13 (Paul, 47). However, the corresponding Hebrew is found in a fragment from Qumran (5QAm[4]1), dated to the first century CE (DJD 3 [Baillet, Milik, and de Vaux], 173, plate xxxvi, line 4), and so it may have been in the translator's *Vorlage*.

τάς . . . ἐχούσας. Pres act ptc acc fem pl ἔχω (substantival). Direct object of πρίζω. This should probably be understood as a gnomic present tense, describing a timeless truth that has no time limits. It is feminine because it refers to women.

ἐν γαστρὶ. Locative. The PP indicates a place "in which some object is found or placed" (*GELS*, 231.1), and it modifies the participle construction in which it is enclosed.

τῶν. The article functions as a nominalizer, changing the PP (ἐν Γαλααδ) into a genitive of source ("the pregnant women from the people of Gilead") rather than partitive ("the pregnant women who are a part of the people of Gilead").

ἐν Γαλααδ. Locative. The preposition ἐν indicates a place "in which some object is found or placed" (*GELS*, 231.1).

1:4 Καὶ ἐξαποστελῶ πῦρ εἰς τὸν οἶκον Αζαηλ, καὶ καταφάγεται θεμέλια υἱοῦ Αδερ·

ἐξαποστελῶ. Fut act ind 1st sg ἐξαποστέλλω. Predictive future. See Decker (2014a, 353–55) and *MBG* (§44.3) on the morphology of future tense liquid verbs.

With only one exception this judgment by fire is described with the same words in both the Greek and Hebrew in the seven oracles that contain it (1:4, 7, 10, 12, 14; 2:2, 5): "I will send out fire . . . and it will consume the foundations" (ἐξαποστελῶ πῦρ . . . καὶ καταφάγεται θεμέλια). In 1:14 the Greek has "I will kindle a fire" (ἀνάψω πῦρ), corresponding to the Hebrew. The prepositional prefix in the verb "I will send out" (ἐξαποστέλλω) connects the judgment in the oracles with the judgment described in 1:2 that comes ἐκ Σιων and ἐξ Ιερουσαλημ.

πῦρ. Accusative direct object of ἐξαποστέλλω. Seven of the eight oracles refer to judgment by fire; the final oracle, which refers to Israel, is the exception.

εἰς τὸν οἶκον. Direction, modifying ἐξαποστέλλω. The preposition εἰς "indicates a target, aim, or focus of action" (*GELS*, 196.3.a), and in the context of judgment it could be rendered "against." The "house" refers to the dynasty of Hazael. The article is used with a monadic noun.

Although in the Hebrew the preposition modifying the recipients of the fiery judgment is always the same (ב), in the LXX the preposition employed to modify the recipients of the judgment fire varies between εἰς (1:4, 12) and ἐπί (1:7, 10, 14; 2:2, 5). The difference is best attributed to literary variation on the part of the translator, since there is no consistent relationship between the prepositions employed and their objects ("the house" 1:4; "the walls," 1:7, 10, 14; "Thaiman," 1:12; "Moab," 2:2; and "Ioudas," 2:5) that explains the variation of the prepositions. I have translated both prepositions "against" to emphasize the seriousness of the hostile acts of judgment described (BDAG, 290.4.c.α; GELS, 266. III.4.a; see Glenny [2013b, 45–46] for further discussion about the translation of these prepositions). See Glenny (2013b, 43–46) for further introductory material on the oracles of judgment in LXX Amos 1–2.

Αζαηλ. Possessive genitive of this indeclinable proper noun. The dynastic title "house of Hazael" should probably be understood as a reference to Syria (see Paul, 51; Glenny 2013b, 46).

καταφάγεται. Fut mid ind 3rd sg κατεσθίω. Predictive future; the middle voice is marked by the affectedness of the subject of the verb, and the self-interest of the subject is clear with this verb. The sense of the verb ἐσθίω is often intensified in this compound form (NIDNTTE, 2:290).

θεμέλια. Accusative direct object of καταφάγεται. This anarthrous noun is definite since its genitive modifier is definite; they follow Apollonius' corollary ("when both nouns are anarthrous, both will usually have the same semantic force"; Wallace, 250–51). Thus, they are translated, "the foundations of the son of Hader." The word corresponding to θεμέλια in the MT is ארמון ("palace, fortress"), a word that gave the Septuagint translators trouble because it is rare in postbiblical Hebrew. This Hebrew word occurs twelve times in Amos. In the oracles to the nations, the translator always rendered it with θεμέλια ("foundation"); see also 1:7, 10, 12, 14; 2:2, 5, and Glenny (2009, 78–79). In its five occurrences outside of the oracles to the nations (3:9–11 and 6:8), it is always rendered with χώρα ("district"); see 3:9.

υἱοῦ. Possessive genitive. The anarthrous noun is definite since the following genitive specifies its reference. See θεμέλια.

Αδερ. Genitive of relationship. Ben Hadad is normally translated "Ben Hader" or "son of Hader" in the LXX (3 Kgdms 11:14, 17, 18–20; 15:20; 21:1; etc.), with one exception (3 Kgdms 20:17) where it is rendered "king of Syria," and every one of the thirty-nine times that "Ben Hader" or "Hader" occurs in the LXX, it is a translation of Ben Hadad or a translation of a pronoun referring to Ben Hadad. Here "son of Ader" is a synecdoche for Syria. See Glenny (2009, 46, 176–77).

1:5 καὶ συντρίψω μοχλοὺς Δαμασκοῦ καὶ ἐξολεθρεύσω κατοικοῦντας ἐκ πεδίου Ων καὶ κατακόψω φυλὴν ἐξ ἀνδρῶν Χαρραν, καὶ αἰχμαλωτευθήσεται λαὸς Συρίας ἐπίκλητος, λέγει κύριος.

καὶ. Coordinating conjunction, connecting independent clauses (*GELS*, 352.1.b).

συντρίψω. Fut act ind 1st sg συντρίβω. Predictive future, "I will crush."

μοχλοὺς. Accusative direct object of συντρίψω. The noun refers to a "long piece of hard material placed across" a door or gate to secure it and keep out intruders (*GELS*, 469). A phrase like "of the gates" is implied here, modifying μοχλούς. By synecdoche the "bars" of the gates entail the gates; when the "bars" are destroyed, the gates are useless.

Δαμασκοῦ. Genitive of place, i.e., in Damascus.

ἐξολεθρεύσω. Fut act ind 1st sg ἐξολεθρεύω. Predictive future, "I will utterly destroy."

κατοικοῦντας. Pres act ptc acc masc pl κατοικέω (substantival). Direct object of ἐξολεθρεύσω. The substantival use of the participle without an article is common in the LXX (Muraoka §2; §31.ba, bbb). The MT has a singular participle here, parallel to "the one who holds the scepter" in the next line; the LXX refers to a "tribe" rather than a "scepter" (see φυλήν), and it naturally requires a plural participle here.

ἐκ πεδίου Ων. Dissociation, modifying ἐξολεθρεύσω; the inhabitants will be utterly destroyed "out of" or "from" the plain of On (*GELS*, 201.1).

Ων. Genitive of place, i.e., in "On." "On" is explicitly connected with Heliopolis in LXX Gen 41:50, which has "Potiphar the priest of Heliopolis," instead of "On" (און), which is the reading it the MT (see also LXX Jer 50:13 and the LXX plus in Exod 1:11 "and On which is Heliopolis"). Heliopolis was located at the southern tip of the Nile Delta in Egypt and was the main cult center of Re, the sun-god (see LXX Ezek 30:17; and *ABD*, 1:529). In Amos 1:5, Ων probably refers to a cult center in Syria, and Greek readers probably would have understood it to refer to Baalbek, the cult center in Lebanon, dedicated to Baal, since Greek and Roman authors called Baalbek Heliopolis (Paul, 53); in the third or second century BCE, the town and shrine were renamed Heliopolis, "City of the Sun" (*ABD*, 1:556). The corresponding Hebrew word is און ("Aven"), which means "idolatry" or "iniquity," which the Hebrew text uses to make a derisive wordplay. But the translator either missed the wordplay or on purpose rendered it as its homograph "On" (see also the same rendering in Hos 4:15; 5:8; and 10:5); see LXX.E (2346–47) and Glenny (2009, 63–64).

κατακόψω. Fut act ind 1st sg κατακόπτω. Predictive future. There is nothing in the MT corresponding to the idea of this verb; the corresponding Hebrew word is a participle from תמד ("hold, support"). It has the sense "cut in pieces, destroy" (LSJ, 895).

φυλὴν. Accusative direct object of κατακόψω. Definite with the genitive modifiers, referring to a specific tribe. "Tribe" is a "community of people" that is "united by local habitation" (*GELS*, 723–24.c). The LXX translator read the Hebrew שבט as "tribe" rather than "rod, scepter," as in the MT (*HALOT*, 2:1388–89.1 and 2).

ἐξ ἀνδρῶν. Source, modifying φυλήν. The preposition ἐξ indicates origin or source (*GELS*, 201.5). The Hebrew corresponding to ἀνδρῶν is בית; see Χαρραν.

Χαρραν. Genitive of place. This indeclinable proper noun is probably meant to refer to Haran in northern Mesopotamia, where Abraham lived for a time (see BDAG, 1081 for Scripture references). The Hebrew corresponding to this word is עדן ("Eden"); see also ἐξ ἀνδρῶν. The rendering of these last two words is very difficult to explain. Perhaps the translator had a *Vorlage* that was the basis of these renderings, or he was possibly trying to broaden the scope of the prophecy.

αἰχμαλωτευθήσεται. Fut pass ind 3rd sg αἰχμαλωτεύω. Predictive future; no agency is expressed for the passive verb because "the focus of the passage is on the subject" (Wallace, 436).

λαὸς. Nominative subject of αἰχμαλωτευθήσεται. The "people of Syria" in 1:5 are another group of Syrians, in addition to those mentioned earlier in the verse, who will be taken into captivity, and at the time the LXX was translated they may have been "foreigners" or "aliens" who were enemies of "Jerusalem" (1:2).

Συρίας. Genitive of place.

ἐπίκλητος. Nominative adjective, modifying λαός. The basic sense of ἐπίκλητος is "called," "designated," or "appointed," although its use with the sense "called" is first century BCE and later (LSJ, 638–39). Elsewhere in the LXX ἐπίκλητος is rendered "appointed" or "designated" (Josh 20:9), "called" in the sense of "famous, renowned" (Num 1:16; 26:9), or "convocation" (Num 28:18, 26; 29:1, 7, 12). *GELS* (274.1) suggests the meaning "bearer of the name" in Amos 1:5. The word often has a negative connotation, and Herodotus (*Hist*. 5.75; 7.203) and Thucydides (*Hist*. 4.61) used it for people from abroad who were summoned or called upon as mercenaries. Plutarch used the word for secondary guests who were not invited by the host but by one of his honored guests (*Mor.* 2.707a; see Dines 1991, 59–62). In some contexts the word has the connotation of foreign or barbaric (Dionysius of Halicarnassus 6.53.1, see also 2.76; Josephus *A.J.* 15.2.5; and LSJ, 639), and that unusual sense is preferred in this context where it describes the Syrians (Dines 1991, 53, 59–62; NETS renders it "important"). Although H-R finds no Hebrew correspondence for this word, it is possible the translator read קִירָה ("unto Kir") as קָרִיא ("person called" *HALOT*, 2:1141).

λέγει κύριος. This is the first of five oracles that conclude with "says the Lord" (1:5, 8, 15; 2:1, 16). See the discussion of Καὶ εἶπεν κύριος in 1:3.

λέγει. Pres act ind 3rd sg λέγω. The present tense in introductory formulas could be understood as an aoristic present taking place at the moment the words are spoken (BDF §320), but that would be more the sense "the Lord said." It could also be understood to emphasize the continuing relevance of the content of earlier speech, i.e., "the Lord says" (see *CGCG* §33.188). This is the use of the present tense in an introductory formula, emphasizing the continuing results of the Lord speaking in the past (his words still have relevance, like an OT quotation in the NT; see Eph 4:8; 5:14; Wallace, 532–33). This verb form is very common in LXX Amos; there are 73 present-tense indicative verbs, and 41 are this exact verb form, often occurring in divine speech formulas.

κύριος. Nominative subject of λέγει.

Amos 1:6–8

⁶This is what the Lord says, "On account of three ungodly acts of Gaza and on account of four I will not let them go unpunished, because they led captive the captives of Solomon to confine [them] in Idumea. ⁷And I will send out fire against the walls of Gaza, and it will consume the foundations of her. ⁸And I will utterly destroy the inhabitants from Azotus, and a tribe will be removed from Ashkelon, and I will bring my hand against Ekron, and the survivors of the foreigners will perish," says the Lord.

1:6 Τάδε λέγει κύριος Ἐπὶ ταῖς τρισὶν ἀσεβείαις Γάζης καὶ ἐπὶ ταῖς τέσσαρσιν οὐκ ἀποστραφήσομαι αὐτούς, ἕνεκεν τοῦ αἰχμαλωτεῦσαι αὐτοὺς αἰχμαλωσίαν τοῦ Σαλωμων τοῦ συγκλεῖσαι εἰς τὴν Ἰδουμαίαν·

Τάδε λέγει κύριος. This introductory formula is found at the beginning of all of the oracles except the first (1:3) and recurs thirteen times in the book (1:6, 9, 11, 13; 2:1, 4, 6; 3:11, 12; 5:3, 4, 16; 7:17). See the discussion of Καὶ εἶπεν κύριος in 1:3.

Τάδε. Accusative direct object of λέγει. This demonstrative pronoun is cataphoric, referring to what follows in the narrative context (see BDAG, 689–90, s.v. ὅδε; *GELS*, 485.2; see also Thackeray §14.3).

λέγει. Pres act ind 3rd sg λέγω (see λέγει κύριος at the end of 1:5).

κύριος. Nominative subject of λέγει. Monadic noun that is definite with or without the article.

Ἐπὶ ταῖς τρισὶν ἀσεβείαις Γάζης καὶ ἐπὶ ταῖς τέσσαρσιν οὐκ ἀποστραφήσομαι αὐτούς. See the discussion of this formula in 1:3. See Glenny (2013b, 47–48) for a summary of the history of the Philistine cities and the updating of their names in the LXX. Here and in 1:11 the masculine plural pronoun αὐτούς differs from the corresponding third-person singular masculine suffix found in the Hebrew in all of these formulas (אשיבנו); the translator likely varied the number to fit the context or for literary purposes (see the discussion under αὐτόν in 1:3).

ἕνεκεν τοῦ αἰχμαλωτεῦσαι. Causal. Improper preposition used with the genitive to indicate cause or reason (BDAG, 334; *GELS*, 237.1); it is parallel with ἀνθ᾽ ὧν, which is employed in some of the other oracles in chapters 1–2 (see 1:3). The PP modifies the preceding negated verb (οὐκ ἀποστραφήσομαι), and it gives further explanation why the Lord will not let Gaza go unpunished; ἕνεκεν also occurs in 1:11; 2:4; 6:10.

τοῦ αἰχμαλωτεῦσαι. Aor act inf αἰχμαλωτεύω. Constative aorist, looking at the action as a whole, and a causal genitive articular infinitive construction, which is the object of the governing preposition ἕνεκεν (Muraoka §30.aba).

αὐτούς. Accusative subject of the infinitive αἰχμαλωτεῦσαι (Porter 1994, 202–3).

αἰχμαλωσίαν. Accusative cognate object of αἰχμαλωτεῦσαι. Muraoka (*GELS*, 18) suggests that in the unique contexts of 1:6 and 1:9 the singular form of αἰχμαλωσία is best understood as the collective idea "captives," which is a frequent sense of this word elsewhere in the LXX (Hab 1:9; Num 3:12; 2 Chr 28:5; Ezek 39:25; see also BDAG, 31). See Glenny (2013b, 48) on this word and its modifiers.

τοῦ Σαλωμων. Objective genitive. The Hebrew has שלמה ("whole"), and perhaps the translator read that word as the homograph "Solomon" (see LXX.E, 2347; Glenny 2009, 137–38). The article is often used with indeclinable proper nouns in the LXX, esp. in the oblique cases (Muraoka §5.c-cab).

τοῦ συγκλεῖσαι. Aor act inf συγκλείω (purpose genitive articular infinitive construction [Muraoka §30.ab]; cf. Porter 1994, 199–200). Consummative aorist, emphasizing the cessation or completion of the action, "to confine" (Wallace, 559). An object of this infinitive ("them") is implied.

εἰς τὴν Ἰδουμαίαν. Location, modifying συγκλεῖσαι. The preposition εἰς indicates a position within a certain area (BDAG, 289.1.a.δ). On the complexity of the use of articles with place-names in the LXX, see Muraoka (§5.cb). The LXX tends to update the place-name Edom found in the Hebrew, especially in the Prophets and Writings, and in the Twelve "Edom" in the Hebrew (7x) is always "Idumea," except in Amos 9:12.

1:7 καὶ ἐξαποστελῶ πῦρ ἐπὶ τὰ τείχη Γάζης, καὶ καταφάγεται θεμέλια αὐτῆς·

ἐξαποστελῶ πῦρ . . . καταφάγεται θεμέλια. See 1:4 and 1:10.

ἐπὶ τὰ τείχη Γάζης. Direction, modifying ἐξαποστελῶ. The preposition ἐπί indicates that to which the action is directed. I have translated it "against" to emphasize the seriousness of the hostile acts of judgment described (BDAG, 366.12.b; GELS, 266.III.4.a; see the use of ἐπί in Mic 7:6; and Glenny 2013b, 45–46, for further discussion about the translation).

τὰ τείχη. Accusative object of ἐπί. Accusative article specifying the walls from the other parts of Gaza, i.e., its use is "simple identification" (Wallace, 216–17).

Γάζης. Possessive genitive.

αὐτῆς. Possessive genitive. The pronoun refers to Gaza. Muraoka (§20.c.iii) notes, "Names of *countries* and *cities* are treated as fem[inine], most probably on account of γῆ, χώρα, πόλις."

1:8 καὶ ἐξολεθρεύσω κατοικοῦντας ἐξ Ἀζώτου, καὶ ἐξαρθήσεται φυλὴ ἐξ Ἀσκαλῶνος, καὶ ἐπάξω τὴν χεῖρά μου ἐπὶ Ακκαρων, καὶ ἀπολοῦνται οἱ κατάλοιποι τῶν ἀλλοφύλων, λέγει κύριος.

This verse consists of four parallel clauses introduced and connected by καί (4x), describing the Lord's punishment of the Philistine cities. The verse concludes with an attribution of these words to the Lord (λέγει κύριος).

ἐξολεθρεύσω. Fut act ind 1st sg ἐξολεθρεύω. Predictive future. The verb with the suffix has a more intensive sense, "utterly destroy" (see *NIDNTTE*, 3:485; LSJ, 597).

κατοικοῦντας. Pres act ptc acc pl masc κατοικέω (substantival). Customary present, showing an ongoing state. This participle functions as the direct object of ἐξολεθρεύσω ("inhabitants"). See Muraoka (§31.ba) on anarthrous participles functioning as substantives in the LXX.

ἐξ Ἀζώτου. Derivation, modifying κατοικοῦντας, and the preposition ἐκ indicates origin or derivation (BDAG, 296.3.c). The noun is an updated form of "Ashdod" (אשדוד).

ἐξαρθήσεται. Fut pass ind 3rd sg ἐξαίρω. Predictive future; passive without agency expressed because it is a divine passive. The Lord, who is the subject of the other four verbs in the verse, all active voice, is the agent.

φυλὴ. Nominative subject of ἐξαρθήσεται. "Tribe" is a "community of people" that is "united by local habitation" (*GELS*, 723–24.c).

ἐξ Ἀσκάλωνος. Separation, modifying ἐξαρθήσεται. The preposition ἐκ indicates the place from which the separation or removal takes place (BDAG, 295.1.a).

ἐπάξω. Fut act ind 1st sg ἐπάγω. Predictive future. The clause refers to God moving his punitive hand against a nation with hostile intent (see *GELS*, 256.1).

τὴν χεῖρά. Accusative direct object of ἐπάξω.

μου. Possessive genitive.

ἐπὶ Ακκαρων. Direction, indicating that to which the action is directed. I have translated it "against" to emphasize the seriousness of the hostile acts of judgment described (BDAG, 366.12.b; *GELS*, 266.III.4.a; see the use of ἐπί in 1:7). Ekron was one of the five main Philistine cities.

ἀπολοῦνται. Fut mid ind 3rd pl ἀπόλλυμι. Predictive future; the future middle of ἀπόλλυμι is intransitive and has the sense "perish" (*GELS*, 78.I.1 BDAG, 116.1.b.α); the specific feature of the middle voice is "the *affectedness* of the subject of the verb in, or by, the event denoted by the verb," and in this regard middle-voice verbs are "subject-focused" (Bakker, 24; the emphasis is original).

οἱ κατάλοιποι. Nominative subject of ἀπολοῦνται.

τῶν ἀλλοφύλων. Partitive genitive or the genitive of the divided whole (BDF §164); in such constructions the head noun (here κατάλοιποι) is a part of the genitive modifying it (ἀλλοφύλων). According to Muraoka (*GELS*, 29), apparently based on the constituent parts of the word, ἀλλόφυλος means "of another tribe." But in the LXX from Judges on, it is employed almost exclusively to render פלשתי (see also Conybeare and Stock, 225, 231). NETS has consistently rendered the word "allophyles," basically transliterating the Greek. I have rendered the word as "foreigner" the three times it occurs in LXX Amos (1:8; 6:2; 9:7), following Dines (1991) and *LES*, because in Jewish writings it had the sense non-Jew or foreigner, and even though the context here is referring to Philistines, the word would not have had a definite reference to the Philistines for the original readers (see the discussion of the word in LXX Joel 3:4 and Zeph 2:5 in *Bd'A*, 23.4–9, 73, 351; see also 1 Macc 5:15, where it must mean foreigner or gentile). The article with the head noun and the genitive noun follows Apollonius' canon (Wallace, 239–40).

λέγει κύριος. See 1:3 and 5. Here the one divine name renders two Hebrew names אדני יהוה (LXX.E, 2347).

Amos 1:9–10

⁹This is what the Lord says, "On account of three ungodly acts of Tyre and on account of four I will not let her go unpunished, because they confined Solomon's captives in Idumea and did not remember the covenant between brothers. ¹⁰And I will send out fire against the walls of Tyre, and it will consume the foundations of her."

1:9 Τάδε λέγει κύριος Ἐπὶ ταῖς τρισὶν ἀσεβείαις Τύρου καὶ ἐπὶ ταῖς τέσσαρσιν οὐκ ἀποστραφήσομαι αὐτήν, ἀνθ᾽ ὧν συνέκλεισαν αἰχμαλωσίαν τοῦ Σαλωμων εἰς τὴν Ιδουμαίαν καὶ οὐκ ἐμνήσθησαν διαθήκης ἀδελφῶν·

Τάδε λέγει κύριος Ἐπὶ ταῖς τρισὶν ἀσεβείαις Τύρου καὶ ἐπὶ ταῖς τέσσαρσιν οὐκ ἀποστραφήσομαι αὐτήν. See the discussion of this formula in 1:3 and 1:6. This is the only oracle addressed solely to a city-state, Tyre, and there is no reference to Sidon or other Phoenician cities.

ἀνθ᾽ ὧν. Causal, modifying οὐκ ἀποστραφήσομαι. See 1:3.

συνέκλεισαν. Aor act ind 3rd pl συγκλείω. Consummative aorist, focusing on the completion and cessation of the act (Wallace, 559); see also 1:6 where the infinitive is employed. The corresponding word in the MT is an infinitive construct with a third-person masculine plural suffix (הסגירם).

αἰχμαλωσίαν τοῦ Σαλωμων. See 1:6; in both of these verses the Hebrew גלות שלמה is rendered αἰχμαλωσίαν τοῦ Σαλωμων ("Solomon's captives").

αἰχμαλωσίαν. Accusative direct object of συνέκλεισαν.

τοῦ Σαλωμων. Objective genitive.

εἰς τὴν Ἰδουμαίαν. See 1:6. In MSS B and Aᶜ Solomon's captives are confined in Judea (Ιουδαίαν).

ἐμνήσθησαν. Aor pass ind 3rd pl μιμνήσκομαι. Constative aorist, looking at the action as a whole. The θη- morpheme is a dual-voice form, and this verb should be considered to be middle/passive (Aubrey, 563–625; Caragounis, 153; and see the comments in the Introduction). The idea here is not "they are being reminded" (passive). In this context the verb has the idea of being concerned about and paying attention to (something) (BDAG, 652.3).

διαθήκης. Genitive complement of ἐμνήσθησαν. Verbs of remembering usually take a genitive object (Smyth §1356; BDF §175; Muraoka §22.p).

ἀδελφῶν. Subjective genitive. For a genitive to function as a subjective genitive, the head noun that it modifies must be a verbal noun, normally having a cognate verb (Wallace, 112); the cognate verb of διαθήκη is the middle form of διατίθημι (BDAG, 228). A plural subjective genitive provides the subjects that affect or effect the action denoted by the head noun (Muraoka §22.v.xii). The genitive ἀδελφῶν is rendered "between brothers" rather than "of brothers" (NETS), because a covenant is by its nature an agreement or bond between two or more parties.

1:10 καὶ ἐξαποστελῶ πῦρ ἐπὶ τὰ τείχη Τύρου, καὶ καταφάγεται θεμέλια αὐτῆς.

καὶ ἐξαποστελῶ πῦρ ἐπὶ τὰ τείχη Τύρου. See 1:7.
καὶ καταφάγεται θεμέλια αὐτῆς. See 1:4 and 1:7.

Amos 1:11–12

[11]This is what the Lord says, "On account of three ungodly acts of Idumea and on account of four I will not let them go unpunished, because they pursued his brother with the sword, and he ravaged a womb in the land, and he seized his trembling anger for a witness, and he preserved his violent impulse forever. [12]And I will send out fire against Thaiman, and it will consume the foundations of her walls."

1:11 Τάδε λέγει κύριος· Ἐπὶ ταῖς τρισὶν ἀσεβείαις τῆς Ἰδουμαίας καὶ ἐπὶ ταῖς τέσσαρσιν οὐκ ἀποστραφήσομαι αὐτούς, ἕνεκα τοῦ διῶξαι αὐτοὺς ἐν ῥομφαίᾳ τὸν ἀδελφὸν αὐτοῦ καὶ ἐλυμήνατο μήτραν ἐπὶ γῆς καὶ ἥρπασεν εἰς μαρτύριον φρίκην αὐτοῦ καὶ τὸ ὅρμημα αὐτοῦ ἐφύλαξεν εἰς νῖκος·

Τάδε λέγει κύριος· Ἐπὶ ταῖς τρισὶν ἀσεβείαις τῆς Ἰδουμαίας καὶ ἐπὶ ταῖς τέσσαρσιν οὐκ ἀποστραφήσομαι αὐτούς. The introductory formula of this oracle is the same as 1:6 (τάδε λέγει κύριος), and the clause following it is discussed in 1:3 and 1:6. The LXX consistently renders אדום ("Edom") with Ἰδουμαία ("Idumea"), but note the exception in 9:12. After the Nabataeans captured Mount Seir and its capital, Petra, in 300 BCE, the Edomites pressed into the then empty lands west of the Arabah. This land then came to be known by the Greek name Idumea, and the people were called the Idumeans (1 Macc 4:29, 61; 5:65). The variety of pronouns referring to Idumea (αὐτούς; αὐτοῦ;

αὐτῆς) complicates the interpretation of the oracle. Most of the pronouns correspond to the gender and number in the MT, but there is one significant difference. The Hebrew corresponding to ἀποστραφήσομαι αὐτούς in this verse is אשיבנו, with the third-person masculine singular suffix corresponding to the pronoun αὐτούς. See the discussion under αὐτόν in 1:3.

ἕνεκα τοῦ διῶξαι αὐτούς. Causal, modifying οὐκ ἀποστραφήσομαι. The preposition ἕνεκα often indicates "a reason, cause or ground" (*GELS*, 237.1). See the discussion of this grammatical construction in 1:6 and in Muraoka (§30.aba).

διῶξαι. Aor act inf διώκω. Causal infinitive with ἕνεκα (Porter 1994, 200); constative aorist.

αὐτοὺς. Accusative subject of the infinitive διῶξαι. There are two accusatives related to the infinitive διῶξαι, and since they are not in apposition, one is the subject of the infinitive and one is its direct object. Normally, in this kind of construction, the first of the two accusatives is the subject, as here; the general context is also important for determining the function of the accusatives (Muraoka §69A.ai; Porter 1994, 202–3).

ἐν ῥομφαίᾳ. Manner, modifying διῶξαι. The preposition ἐν has the sense "equipped with" (*GELS*, 232.7).

τὸν ἀδελφὸν. Accusative direct object of διῶξαι. Accusative article with the monadic noun ἀδελφόν (see Wallace, 223–24; Young, 61). Jacob (Israel) was Edom's (Esau's) only brother.

αὐτοῦ. Genitive of relationship, referring to Idumea.

ἐλυμήνατο. Aor mid ind 3rd sg λυμαίνω. Consummative aorist, here an accomplishment or climax type of verb, which implies a natural endpoint or termination to the action, and found in a context implying resistance to the action (Fanning, 263–64). The sense of the verb is "to cause or inflict serious harm and damage to" (*GELS*, 435–36), and this use of the middle voice involves the subject's self-interest and is describing a naturally reciprocal event. This verb sometimes has the connotation of sexual violence in the LXX (Ezek 16:25; 4 Macc 18:8), and the reading "womb" (μήτρα) here in R-H (and Ziegler) certainly makes a reference to sexual violence appropriate (see also Jdt 9:2). Dines (1991, 70 n. 71) notes that "the whole verse sounds highly charged."

μήτραν. Accusative direct object of ἐλυμήνατο. The three parallel clauses in the verse, describing other specific sins of Idumaea, all have a third-person singular pronoun modifying the objects of the verbs, but there is no pronoun in this clause modifying μήτραν ("womb"). This reading is found in A, Q, W, and followed by R-H and Ziegler; this etymological or exegetical reading of the Hebrew רחמים

("compassions") takes it concretely. It is rendered μητέρα ("mother") in B and V. See the discussion of this rendering in Glenny (2009, 100) and LXX.E (2347).

ἐπὶ γῆς. Locative, modifying λυμαίνω. The words ἐπὶ γῆς have nothing corresponding to them in the Hebrew; see the similar expression in Gen 38:9 (Paul, 65 n. 219). The anarthrous object of the preposition is apparently definite without the article (see Wallace, 247); it is difficult to determine if it refers to the "ground" (NETS) or the "land" (Dines 1991, 70, mentions this possibility). Understanding it as the land "is consistent with the expansion of Edom into southern Israel after 300 BCE" (Glenny 2013b, 50).

ἥρπασεν. Aor act ind 3rd sg ἁρπάζω. Constative aorist, viewing the action as a whole, "he seized" (*CGCG* §33.28).

εἰς μαρτύριον. PP modifying ἥρπασεν. This phrase occurs thirteen times in the LXX, and it has the idea of "as a witness" or "for a witness"; here the preposition εἰς probably indicates the result (or state that results) from Edom's actions (*GELS*, 197.7, s.v.; BDAG, 290.4.d, s.v.; cf. Mic 7:18 where the Lord does not retain his anger εἰς μαρτύριον). Although the anarthrous object of the preposition could be definite (Wallace, 247), here it is not. The translator rendered the consonants עד, which are understood to mean "forever" in the MT, as the homograph "witness" (see *HALOT*, 2:786–88; Glenny 2009, 132–34).

φρίκην. Accusative direct object of ἥρπασεν. Dines (1991, 70 n. 71) suggests this word is "very odd as a rendering of אף ['anger']"; it has the sense "shivering fear" (*GELS*, 720), and it only occurs twice in the LXX (see also Job 4:14).

αὐτοῦ. Possessive genitive.

τὸ ὅρμημα. Accusative direct object of ἐφύλαξεν. It is normal for an article to be used with a head noun when it is modified by a possessive pronoun (Wallace, 239), but there is also a sense in which this article could be anaphoric, denoting the previous references to Edom's violence and anger. The word refers to an outburst of anger or indignation (*GELS*, 506.1; see also Hos 5:10), and its position at the front of the clause is emphatic.

αὐτοῦ. Possessive genitive.

ἐφύλαξεν. Aor act ind 3rd sg φυλάσσω. Constative aorist.

εἰς νῖκος. Extent of time. An idiomatic PP (see 8:7, which is also difficult). The preposition εἰς indicates "an extent of time" (*GELS*, 196.4). The basic sense of νῖκος, which is a later form for νίκη, is "victory" (*GELS*, 474–75; BDAG, 673; LSJ, 1176), and some suggest the idiom εἰς νῖκος means "until victory is won" (Caird, 136). Muraoka comments that already at 2 Kgdms 2:26 it could mean "to the bitter end, i.e., till one has defeated the other" (*GELS*, 475). In this context the meaning "until victory" or "until victory is won" would be attributing victory to Edom in a judgment oracle on Edom. The phrase has the idea "forever, permanently, resolutely" in 2 Kgdms 2:26 and Jer 3:5, and the Old Latin and Armenian versions understood the phrase to mean "forever" (*GELS*, 475), which is the meaning of the Hebrew base text. Thus, it seems likely the LXX reader would be familiar with this idiom, apparently emphasizing that Edom holds on to its "violent impulse" permanently, resolutely, or "forever" (Kraft, 155–56). For the spelling of νῖκος as νεῖκος in some MSS, see Glenny (2013b, 14).

1:12 καὶ ἐξαποστελῶ πῦρ εἰς Θαιμαν, καὶ καταφάγεται θεμέλια τειχέων αὐτῆς.

This verse gives the Lord's judgment of the Idumaeans for their sins, described in 1:11. This wording is similar to 1:4 and 1:7, and there are only a few things that need comment.

εἰς Θαιμαν. Direction, modifying ἐξαποστέλλω. Thaiman was the southernmost city or region in Edom along the ancient King's Highway that ran from Damascus to the Gulf of Aqaba. "Her walls" corresponds to the Hebrew term Bozrah, which was the northernmost city or region in Edom. See below on τειχέων and Glenny (2009, 51). On the translation "against," see 1:8 on ἐπὶ Ακκαρων.

τειχέων. Partitive genitive, with the head noun θεμέλια ("foundations"); the genitive denotes the whole, the "walls," of which the head noun, "foundations," is a part (*CGCG* §30.29). This Greek word also occurs in 1:7, 10, and 14 in reference to the walls of different cities, and this may have influenced the translator in his rendering. The corresponding Hebrew is בצרה ("Bozrah"), which occurs only eight times in the MT, and only this one time in the Twelve; perhaps the translator did not know this place-name, and he took it as the consonants צר ("rock") with the prepositional prefix ב and the ה as a pronominal suffix ("her"); in the context with all the other references to walls (1:7, 10, and 14), he interpreted it as the rocks in walls, or as walls. See Glenny (2009, 95, 125–26).

αὐτῆς. Possessive genitive. See the discussion of τειχέων above.

Amos 1:13–15

[13]This is what the Lord says, "On account of three ungodly acts of the sons of Ammon and on account of four I will not let him go unpunished, because they were ripping up the pregnant women of the Gileadites so

that they might widen their borders. ¹⁴And I will kindle a fire upon the walls of Rabba, and it will consume her foundations with shouting in the day of war, and she will be shaken in the day of her destruction. ¹⁵And her kings will go forth in captivity, their priests and their rulers together," says the Lord.

1:13 Τάδε λέγει κύριος Ἐπὶ ταῖς τρισὶν ἀσεβείαις υἱῶν Αμμων καὶ ἐπὶ ταῖς τέσσαρσιν οὐκ ἀποστραφήσομαι αὐτόν, ἀνθ᾽ ὧν ἀνέσχιζον τὰς ἐν γαστρὶ ἐχούσας τῶν Γαλααδιτῶν, ὅπως ἐμπλατύνωσιν τὰ ὅρια αὐτῶν·

Τάδε λέγει κύριος Ἐπὶ ταῖς τρισὶν ἀσεβείαις υἱῶν Αμμων καὶ ἐπὶ ταῖς τέσσαρσιν οὐκ ἀποστραφήσομαι αὐτόν. See the discussion of these formulaic clauses above in 1:3 and 1:6.

υἱῶν. Subjective genitive. See also 2:4, where the introductory formula in the oracle refers to the "sons of Judah" (not in MT); in 1:13 υἱῶν corresponds with the MT.

Αμμων. This indeclinable proper noun is functioning as a genitive of relationship. Ammon was Israel's neighbor to the northeast, bordering Gilead and Aram.

ἀνθ᾽ ὧν. Causal, modifying οὐκ ἀποστραφήσομαι. See 1:3, 9.

ἀνέσχιζον. Impf act ind 3rd pl ἀνασχίζω. Iterative imperfect, pointing to repeated action in past time, and here it is distributive, indicating individual acts of multiple agents (Wallace, 546–47). The corresponding word in the MT is an infinitive construct with a third-person masculine plural suffix (בִּקְעָם). The use of the imperfect tense gives prominence to this verb (see the Introduction and ἔπριζον in 1:3).

τὰς ἐν γαστρὶ ἐχούσας. This is an idiom referring to pregnant women. See 1:3.

τάς … ἐχούσας. Pres act ptc acc fem pl ἔχω (substantival). Direct object of ἀνέσχιζον.

ἐν γαστρί. Locative, modifying the participle construction that encloses it. The preposition ἐν indicates a place "in which some object is found or placed" (*GELS*, 231.1.a).

τῶν Γαλααδιτῶν. Partitive genitive, with the head noun "pregnant women" denoting a part of the whole, the "Gileadites." The Ammonites often fought with the Gileadites, attempting to gain parts of fertile Gilead (Judg 3:12–14; 10:7–9, 17; 11:4–33; 1 Kgdms 11:1–11; 14:47; 2 Kgdms 8:12; 10:1–11; 2 Chron 20:1–13; 24:26). Following Apollonius' canon, a genitive noun normally has an article when the head noun has one (Turner, 180).

ὅπως. Conjunction introducing a purpose clause that modifies ἀνέσχιζον. This clause is one of the examples Muraoka employs (*GELS*,

502.4) to demonstrate the use of ὅπως in a "final, purposive" subordinate clause with a present tense subjunctive verb.

ἐμπλατύνωσιν. Pres act subj 3rd pl ἐμπλατύνω. Subjunctive in a purpose clause with ὅπως. The corresponding word in the MT is an infinitive construct (הרחיב). See Glenny (2013b, 14) for the varying spellings of this word in the texts and versions.

τὰ ὅρια. Accusative direct object of ἐμπλατύνωσιν. It is normal for a head noun modified by a possessive pronoun to have an article (Wallace, 239).

αὐτῶν. Possessive genitive. MS B, followed by Swete, has the reflexive pronoun ἑαυτῶν, which is unnecessarily emphatic; furthermore, Muraoka notes that when the reflexive pronoun functions as a possessive in the LXX, in seventeen of its eighteen occurrences it stands between the article and the substantive it modifies (*GELS*, 183.1.b). MS A, followed by R-H and Ziegler, has αὐτῶν, which is more fitting in this context. The pronouns referring to the subject, Ammon, in 1:13–14 vary between singular (1:13 and 14) and plural (1:13) and between masculine (1:13) and feminine (1:14).

1:14 καὶ ἀνάψω πῦρ ἐπὶ τὰ τείχη Ραββα, καὶ καταφάγεται θεμέλια αὐτῆς μετὰ κραυγῆς ἐν ἡμέρᾳ πολέμου, καὶ σεισθήσεται ἐν ἡμέρᾳ συντελείας αὐτῆς·

ἀνάψω. Fut act ind 1st sg ἀνάπτω. Predictive future. In the other six oracles describing judgment by fire (1:4, 7, 10, 12; 2:2, 5) the LXX has ἐξαποστελῶ πῦρ corresponding to ושלחתי אש. Here where the Hebrew varies its language (והצתי אש), the LXX follows the variation with ἀνάψω πῦρ. Garrett (45) notes that the Hebrew author "uses formulas and repetition without rigidly adhering to fixed patterns," and the translator did the same. Therefore, it is no surprise the translator followed closely the variation in the Hebrew here.

πῦρ. Accusative direct object of ἀνάψω.

ἐπὶ τὰ τείχη. Direction, modifying ἀνάψω and indicating that to which the action of the verb is directed, here involving hostile action (*GELS*, 266.III.4). See the discussion of ἐπὶ τὰ τείχη in 1:7 (also in 1:10).

Ραββα. Indeclinable proper noun functioning as a possessive genitive.

καὶ καταφάγεται θεμέλια αὐτῆς. See 1:7.

μετὰ κραυγῆς. Accompaniment, modifying καταφάγεται; the preposition μετά has the sense "accompanied by" (*GELS*, 452.I.2); shouting will accompany the fire that will consume the foundations of Rabba.

ἐν ἡμέρᾳ. Temporal, modifying καταφάγεται and indicating the point in time when the event will take place (*GELS*, 231.I.3).

πολέμου. Attributive genitive. It specifies the innate quality of the day (Wallace, 86–88).

σεισθήσεται. Fut pass ind 3rd sg σείω. Predictive future, "she will be shaken." Ραββα is the understood subject, and in this context the Lord is the understood agent of the action. With the passive voice and no agent given, the focus is on the subject, not on the agent, of the action. The Hebrew has a preposition and a noun corresponding to this verb (בסער, "with a whirlwind").

ἐν ἡμέρᾳ. Temporal, modifying σεισθήσεται and indicating the point in time when the event will take place (*GELS*, 231.I.3).

συντελείας. Attributive genitive, specifying the innate quality of the day (Wallace, 86–88). This is earthquake imagery, probably related to the Day of the Lord. This word, meaning "destruction," is often employed in eschatological contexts referring to divine vengeance (see 8:8 and 9:5; Glenny 2013b, 141). MS A has the reading ἡμέρᾳ συντελείας, which is followed by both R-H and Ziegler; B* has the reading ἡμέραις συντέλει, which could be rendered, "in the days it will destroy her," but has basically the same sense; B^ab, V, and Q have ἡμέραις συντελέιας (see the discussion in Glenny 2013b, 14, 51). The word corresponding to συντελείας in the MT is סופה ("windstorm"), which the translator may have read as סוף ("end") with a feminine singular suffix (see Glenny 2009, 126). Gelston (2010, 79*) notes that the LXX renders this same noun (סופה) by the same Greek noun, only without αὐτῆς, in Nah 1:3.

αὐτῆς. Possessive genitive. The MT does not have this pronoun; see συντελείας above for the likely source of this pronoun.

1:15 καὶ πορεύσονται οἱ βασιλεῖς αὐτῆς ἐν αἰχμαλωσίᾳ, οἱ ἱερεῖς αὐτῶν καὶ οἱ ἄρχοντες αὐτῶν ἐπὶ τὸ αὐτό, λέγει κύριος.

πορεύσονται. Fut mid ind 3rd pl πορεύομαι. Predictive future. The main characteristic of the middle voice is that the subject is affected by the action of the verb, and it is clear that that holds true with this verb; Kemmer (269) categorizes the action in the middle voice of πορεύομαι ("come, go") as "translational motion," describing the subject's movement from one place to another (see also the discussion of deponent/middle verbs in the Introduction to this book).

οἱ βασιλεῖς. Nominative subject of πορεύσονται. Apparently, the translator read the third plural suffix in "their king" (מלכם) as a plural morpheme, resulting in "kings." It is normal for an article to be used with a head noun that is modified by a possessive pronoun.

αὐτῆς. Possessive genitive.

ἐν αἰχμαλωσίᾳ. Direction, modifying πορεύσονται; the preposition ἐν indicates movement or extension toward a state or condition where one might normally expect the use of εἰς (*GELS*, 233.17; BDAG, 327.3; Thackeray §3). Here αἰχμαλωσία has its more normal sense ("captivity"; see also 4:10; 9:4, 14), rather than "captives," as in 1:6 and 1:9.

οἱ ἱερεῖς. Nominative subject of πορεύσονται. "Priests" here (and in 3:12) is not in the MT (cf. Jer 49[LXX 30]:3).

αὐτῶν. Possessive genitive. The antecedent of this possessive pronoun could be the "sons of Ammon," or it could be "the kings." Dines (1991, 78–79) argues that the antecedent is the nearer noun, "the kings," and that the LXX refers to the recent history of Ammon (see also Glenny 2013b, 52–53).

οἱ ἄρχοντες. Pres act ptc nom masc sg ἄρχων (substantival). Subject of πορεύσονται.

αὐτῶν. Possessive genitive. See comments on αὐτῶν above. The corresponding text in the MT has מלכם ("their king"), and the translator may have taken the third-person suffix as a plural ending.

ἐπὶ τὸ αὐτό. Direction. This idiomatic PP can communicate several different but related ideas: "at the same place, at the same time, together" (BDAG, 153–54.3.b, s.v. αὐτός; LEH, 95, s.v. αὐτός; esp. *GELS*, 267. III.12, s.v. ἐπί). Here it means "together."

λέγει κύριος. See 1:3 and 1:5.

Amos 2:1–3

¹This is what the Lord says, "On account of three ungodly acts of Moab and on account of four I will not let him go unpunished, because they burned the bones of the king of Idumea into dust; ²and I will send out fire against Moab, and it will consume the foundations of her cities, and Moab will perish in helplessness with shouting and with the sound of a trumpet. ³And I will utterly destroy a judge out of her, and I will kill all the rulers of her together with him," says the Lord.

2:1 Τάδε λέγει κύριος Ἐπὶ ταῖς τρισὶν ἀσεβείαις Μωαβ καὶ ἐπὶ ταῖς τέσσαρσιν οὐκ ἀποστραφήσομαι αὐτόν, ἀνθ᾽ ὧν κατέκαυσαν τὰ ὀστᾶ βασιλέως τῆς Ιδουμαίας εἰς κονίαν·

Τάδε λέγει κύριος Ἐπὶ ταῖς τρισὶν ἀσεβείαις Μωαβ καὶ ἐπὶ ταῖς τέσσαρσιν οὐκ ἀποστραφήσομαι αὐτόν. See the discussion of these formulaic clauses above in 1:3 and 6.

Μωαβ. The descendants of Moab are the brother nation of Ammon (see 1:13–15). Moab is the area east of the southern half of the Dead Sea, and the sin of Moab is not against Israel or Judah but against Idumea (see 1:11–12 on Idumea), their neighbor and adversary across the Brook Zered to their south.

ἀνθ᾽ ὧν. Causal, modifying οὐκ ἀποστραφήσομαι. See 1:3, 9, 13.

κατέκαυσαν. Aor act ind 3rd pl κατακαίω. Consummative aorist, stressing the accomplishment of the act (Robertson, 834–35, calls this use of the aorist the effective aorist).

τὰ ὀστᾶ. Accusative direct object of κατέκαυσαν. Article of simple identification, pointing out a particular object (Wallace, 216–17).

βασιλέως. Possessive genitive, modifying ὀστᾶ.

τῆς Ἰδουμαίας. Genitive of subordination, meaning that the king ruled "over Idumea" (Wallace, 103–4, calls it "a subset of the subjective genitive"); the proper noun is a "Grecized form . . . of אדום" (BDAG, 468). Muraoka (§5.cb) concludes that with place-names it is "difficult to lay down a generally applicable rule" concerning the presence or absence of the article. "Each place-name appears to behave in its own way."

εἰς κονίαν. Result, modifying κατέκαυσαν. The preposition εἰς indicates transformation and points to "the transitive transform of the preceding" (*GELS*, 197.6.b; see also BDAG, 290.4.e: it points to the result of the action). *The Targum of the Minor Prophets* has the king of Moab doing the burning, and it explains what he did with the "dust," or lime, left from the burned bones: he "used them for plaster in his house" (see Cathcart and Gordon, 78, and Garrett, 48–49).

2:2 καὶ ἐξαποστελῶ πῦρ ἐπὶ Μωαβ, καὶ καταφάγεται θεμέλια τῶν πόλεων αὐτῆς, καὶ ἀποθανεῖται ἐν ἀδυναμίᾳ Μωαβ μετὰ κραυγῆς καὶ μετὰ φωνῆς σάλπιγγος·

καὶ ἐξαποστελῶ πῦρ ἐπὶ Μωαβ. See the discussion of this expression in 1:7 and 1:10, which differ from 2:2 in their rendering "against the walls [of the city]" (ἐπὶ τὰ τείχη), rather than "against [the city]" (ἐπὶ Μωαβ); see also 2:5. In 1:7 and 1:10 the fire devours "the foundations of it" (θεμέλια αὐτῆς), whereas here it devours "the foundations of her cities" (θεμέλια τῶν πόλεων αὐτῆς), a reading only found here in the oracles in 1:3–2:8.

ἐπὶ Μωαβ. Direction, modifying ἐξαποστελῶ. The preposition ἐπί indicates that to which the action is directed. On the translation "against," see 1:8 on ἐπὶ Ακκαρων.

καὶ καταφάγεται θεμέλια. See the discussion at 1:4. This phrase is found without the article in the first seven oracles in Amos 1–2. MS B and Swete have the article (τά) before θεμέλια, but R-H and Ziegler rightly do not include it.

τῶν πόλεων. Partitive genitive, signifying the whole of which the head noun (θεμέλια) is a part. It is normal to have an article with a head noun modified by a possessive pronoun (Wallace, 239; see Muraoka §3.b for exceptions to this pattern). The translator apparently read the Hebrew place-name הקריות ("Kerioth") as קריה ("city"); compare the Targum's הקריה ("the city"; see LXX.E, 2347).

αὐτῆς. Possessive genitive, modifying πόλεων; Μωαβ is its antecedent.

ἀποθανεῖται. Fut mid ind 3rd sg ἀποθνῄσκω. Predictive future; this verb does not have an active form in the future tense, and the future middle form is probably best understood as a dynamic middle, indicating particularly intense involvement of the subject (Muraoka §27.ce). It could also be classified as a spontaneous event middle (Kemmer, 269). This verb has the sense "to come to the end of one's physical existence" (*GELS*, 74). BDAG (111; also, LSJ, 199) notes that this verb is the intensive of θνῄσκω.

ἐν ἀδυναμίᾳ. Manner. This is the first of three PPs modifying ἀποθανεῖται. The preposition ἐν indicates the manner (*GELS*, 231.5; BDF §219.4) or marks the circumstances or condition under which Moab will perish (BDAG, 329.7).

Μωαβ. The indeclinable noun Μωάβ is functioning as the nominative subject of ἀποθανεῖται.

μετὰ κραυγῆς. Accompaniment. The second of three PPs modifying ἀποθανεῖται. The preposition marks "a trait or accompanying action which characterizes an action" (the death of Moab) (*GELS*, 452.I.2 a) or phenomena that accompany the end of Moab's existence (BDAG, 637.A.3.b). It is difficult to determine whether the shouting describes the people of Moab or the army attacking them; the same phrase occurs in 1:14, where it is also difficult to determine who is crying and shouting, and it may be best to understand it to be a general description of the noise of war, as the following μετὰ φωνῆς σάλπιγγος suggests.

μετὰ φωνῆς. Accompaniment. The third of three PPs modifying ἀποθανεῖται. See the preceding treatment of μετὰ κραυγῆς.

σάλπιγγος. Genitive of source.

2:3 καὶ ἐξολεθρεύσω κριτὴν ἐξ αὐτῆς, καὶ πάντας τοὺς ἄρχοντας αὐτῆς ἀποκτενῶ μετ' αὐτοῦ, λέγει κύριος.

ἐξολεθρεύσω. Fut act ind 1st sg ἐξολεθρεύω. Predictive future.

κριτὴν. Accusative direct object of ἐξολεθρεύσω. The noun could be understood to be generic, and sometimes nouns can have the generic idea without an article (Muraoka §1.d; Wallace, 253–54). But here with the third-person pronoun (αὐτοῦ) following, which apparently refers to a single judge, it is best to take the anaphoric noun to be indefinite, referring to one judge rather than the class of judges, even though this is a bit awkward. The corresponding word in the MT (שֹׁפֵט), which is also anarthrous, is usually taken to refer to the "ruler" or "governor" (*HALOT*, 2:1624.E.6.c.β, s.v. שׁפט), and it makes sense to understand it to be definite. The LXX translates the word literally as "judge" (κριτήν), a word that does not fit well with a monadic or par-excellent (Wallace, 222–23) understanding, and thus is not easily understood to be definite in this context. See the related discussion of αὐτοῦ below.

ἐξ αὐτῆς. Source, modifying ἐξολεθρεύσω. The preposition ἐκ indicates the source from which the judge comes or originates (*GELS*, 201.5; BDAG, 296.3.5).

πάντας τοὺς ἄρχοντας. Accusative direct object of ἀποκτενῶ. See Muraoka §38.b.i on this construction with the adjective πᾶς.

τοὺς ἄρχοντας. The accusative article is probably an article of simple identification, distinguishing the rulers from others, but it is normal to have an article with a head noun modified by a possessive pronoun, and the article is also expected in this construction with πᾶς (Muraoka §38.b.i). The words τοὺς ἄρχοντας are not in MS B and Swete but are rightly included in R-H and Ziegler, following the Hebrew.

αὐτῆς. Genitive of subordination, indicating that which is "subordinated to or under the dominion of the head noun," i.e., that which the rulers rule over (Wallace, 103–4).

ἀποκτενῶ. Fut act ind 1st sg ἀποκτείνω. Predictive future.

μετ᾽ αὐτοῦ. Accompaniment, modifying ἀποκτενῶ. The preposition (μετά) places the subject of the verb, the rulers, in association or company with the object of the preposition, αὐτοῦ (BDAG, 636.A.1; *GELS*, 451.I.1). The pronoun (αὐτοῦ) could refer to Moab or to the previously mentioned judge. Since the rulers and judges are both leaders in authority over the people and naturally thought of together, it is best to understand this pronoun as referring to the previously mentioned "judge" (κριτήν) who would be killed with the rulers. The change in gender (feminine "judge" and masculine pronoun referring to the "judge") is in keeping with the pattern seen elsewhere in these oracles (see the discussion under αὐτόν in 1:3) and also may reflect the translator's sensitivity to what he probably thought to be the natural gender of the "judge."

λέγει κύριος. See 1:3 and 1:5.

Amos 2:4–5

⁴This is what the Lord says, "On account of three ungodly acts of the sons of Judah and on account of four I will not let him go unpunished,

because they rejected the Law of the Lord, and his commands they did not keep; and their vain things, which they made, led them astray, which things their fathers followed after. ⁵And I will send out fire against Judah, and it will consume the foundations of Jerusalem."

There are several similarities between this passage and the description in 5:25–27 of Israel's sins that led to their captivity. Both passages (2:4 and 5:25–27) implicate earlier and later generations of the nation in the sins described. The sins of the fathers became paradigmatic to the children, indicating a long history of disloyalty to the covenant (see Glenny 2013b, 54).

2:4 Τάδε λέγει κύριος Ἐπὶ ταῖς τρισὶν ἀσεβείαις υἱῶν Ιουδα καὶ ἐπὶ ταῖς τέσσαρσιν οὐκ ἀποστραφήσομαι αὐτόν, ἕνεκα τοῦ ἀπώσασθαι αὐτοὺς τὸν νόμον κυρίου καὶ τὰ προστάγματα αὐτοῦ οὐκ ἐφυλάξαντο καὶ ἐπλάνησεν αὐτοὺς τὰ μάταια αὐτῶν, ἃ ἐποίησαν, οἷς ἐξηκολούθησαν οἱ πατέρες αὐτῶν ὀπίσω αὐτῶν·

Τάδε λέγει κύριος. See 1:3 and 1:6.

Ἐπὶ ταῖς τρισὶν ἀσεβείαις υἱῶν Ιουδα καὶ ἐπὶ ταῖς τέσσαρσιν οὐκ ἀποστραφήσομαι αὐτόν. See 1:3.

υἱῶν. Subjective genitive. In the Oracles against the Nations (Amos 1:2–2:16) in the LXX the noun υἱῶν ("sons") is found in the designation of the nation only in 1:13 (also in MT) and here (not in MT), where it clarifies that the oracle refers to the people ("members of the community," *GELS*, 694.2) and not to the locale (cf. 1:5). It also emphasizes that the people as a whole are guilty and not only the "fathers" mentioned specifically later in the verse (Glenny 2013b, 53–54).

Ιουδα. Genitive of relationship. Thackeray (§11.6) notes that the indeclinable form of Ιουδας (i.e., Ιουδα) stands only for the nominative and accusative; here Ιουδα is the genitive of the more common declinable form, Ιουδας (see also BDAG, 479).

αὐτόν. Accusative of person (*GELS*, 85.I.4, s.v. ἀποστρέφω; see also *CGCG* §30.10; 35.13). See the discussion of the clause at 1:3.

ἕνεκα τοῦ ἀπώσασθαι. Causal. Improper preposition that "functions as a preposition with a genitive to indicate cause of or reason for something" (BDAG, 334.1; see also LSJ, 563.1; *GELS*, 237.1); see discussion at 1:6 on ἕνεκεν. The following clause gives the first and main reason why the Lord will not let Judah go unpunished.

τοῦ ἀπώσασθαι. Aor mid inf ἀπωθέω. Constative aorist, looking at the action as a whole. It could be a consummative aorist emphasizing the actual accomplishment or end point of their rejection of the

Lord, but the two clauses that follow seem to point to a summary view of their rejection as a whole in this context. This verb is found in the middle voice only in biblical literature, and the verb, meaning "reject, push aside" (BDAG, 126–27.2; also *GELS*, 88.1), involves the subject in a volitional activity that affects the subject. It could be called an indirect middle, in which the subject acts somehow in relation to herself (Wallace, 419–20). This causal genitive articular infinitive construction is the object of the governing preposition ἕνεκα. The two parallel clauses that follow will use indicative verbs; this awkward verbal pattern follows the Hebrew.

αὐτοὺς. Accusative subject of the infinitive ἀπώσασθαι (Muraoka §69.A.ab; Porter 1994, 202–3).

τὸν νόμον. Accusative direct object of ἀπώσασθαι. Article with a well-known or monadic noun (Smyth §1120.a; Wallace, 223–24). The only other occurrence of νόμος in LXX Amos is the free translation in 4:5, where it refers to the "written and authoritative divine Law, especially the Pentateuch," as it does in this verse (Glenny 2013b, 54); this is a common meaning of this word in the LXX (*TDNT* 4:1046–47).

κυρίου. Possessive genitive.

τὰ προστάγματα. Accusative direct object of ἐφυλάξαντο. Article with a well-known noun (Smyth §1120.a; Wallace, 223–24). The "commandments" are contained in the Law (see τὸν νόμον above), which the people of Judah rejected.

αὐτοῦ. Possessive genitive, referring back to κυρίου.

οὐκ ἐφυλάξαντο. Aor mid ind 3rd pl φυλάσσω. Constative aorist; indirect middle with the subjects acting in relation to themselves (Robertson, 804) and the actions affecting the subjects. The negative particle οὐ is what is expected with the indicative-mood verb.

ἐπλάνησεν. Aor act ind 3rd sg πλανάω. Constative aorist, "led astray."

αὐτοὺς. Accusative direct object of ἐπλάνησεν.

τὰ μάταια. Nominative subject of ἐπλάνησεν. The neuter form of this adjective suggests it refers to "things," and the following context confirms that. The article could simply identify the "vain things" and distinguish them from others, but it is more likely cataphoric, pointing to the references to them that immediately follow (ἃ ἐποίησαν and οἷς ἐξηκολούθησαν οἱ πατέρες αὐτῶν; see Wallace 220–21).

αὐτῶν. Possessive genitive, referring to the people of Judah who have been the subject of the last three clauses.

ἅ. Accusative direct object of ἐποίησαν. This is the first of two relative clauses further describing τὰ μάταια αὐτῶν. This phrase has nothing corresponding to it in the Hebrew, and its presence in this context in the LXX leaves no doubt that τὰ μάταια are idols (see Lev 17:7; 4 Kgdms

17:15; Hos 5:11; Jer 2:5 for other places that this language is used for idols; see also Glenny 2009, 178–79; Stuart, 307; Theocharous, 99).

ἐποίησαν. Aor act ind 3rd pl ποιέω. Constative aorist. There are several similarities between the description of Judah's sins here and the description of Israel's sins in the wilderness in 5:25–27 (Glenny 2013b, 54); one of the main similarities is that both passages describe their idols as things they made.

οἷς ἐξηκολούθησαν οἱ πατέρες αὐτῶν ὀπίσω αὐτῶν. This is the second relative clause further describing τὰ μάταια αὐτῶν. The relative clause is "a pleonastic resumptive element," and the relative pronoun as well as the object of the preposition (αὐτῶν) both refer back to τὰ μάταια αὐτῶν (Muraoka §86.caa–cabb, esp. cabb).

οἷς. Dative complement of ἐξηκολούθησαν, referring back to and describing τὰ μάταια.

ἐξηκολούθησαν. Aor act ind 3rd pl ἐξακολουθέω. Constative aorist. The verb takes its object in the dative case.

οἱ πατέρες. Nominative subject of ἐξηκολούθησαν. The article refers to a well-known object, here their forefathers or ancestors.

αὐτῶν. Genitive of relationship.

ὀπίσω. This adverb functions here as a preposition with a genitive (i.e., a "marker of position behind an entity that precedes," BDAG, 716.2.a).

αὐτῶν. Genitive object of ὀπίσω. This pronoun, which corresponds with the Hebrew, seems redundant, and to avoid confusion it is left untranslated. It is clear from the context that it refers to the idols they had made. But if it is translated it can be confused with the referent of the same pronoun that occurs two words ahead in the verse (αὐτῶν), i.e., the people of Judah, resulting in the nonsensical meaning that the fathers of Judah followed the later generations (i.e., people of Judah) in their idol worship. Muraoka (§86.cabb) discusses this construction among several other pleonastic constructions in the LXX; see a parallel construction in Lev 17:7.

2:5 καὶ ἐξαποστελῶ πῦρ ἐπὶ Ιουδαν, καὶ καταφάγεται θεμέλια Ιερουσαλημ.

καὶ ἐξαποστελῶ πῦρ ἐπὶ Ιουδαν. See 1:4 and 1:7; also 1:10, 12 and 2:2. The preposition εἰς occurs in this formula in 1:4 and 12.

ἐπὶ Ιουδαν. Direction, modifying ἐξαποστελῶ. On the translation of ἐπί as "against," see 1:8 on ἐπὶ Ακκαρων (and also the same use of ἐπί in 1:7, 10, 14; 2:2).

καὶ καταφάγεται θεμέλια Ιερουσαλημ. This clause is found in the first seven oracles; see esp. 1:4. See 4 Kgdms 25:9–10 on the image of Jerusalem burning to its foundations.

Ιερουσαλημ. Genitive of place. This indeclinable form of Jerusalem should probably be understood to be genitive feminine singular. This proper noun occurs most often without the article (BDAG, 471–72; BDF §261.3).

Amos 2:6–16

[6]This is what the Lord says, "On account of three ungodly acts of Israel and on account of four I will not let him go unpunished, because they sell a righteous man for money and a poor man for sandals, [7]things which tread upon the dust of the earth; and they were striking at the heads of the needy; and they pervert the way of the lowly; and a son and his father were going in to the same slave girl so that they profane the name of their god; [8]and binding together their garments with cords, they were making curtains adjacent to the altar; and they were drinking wine [obtained] from extortion in the house of their god. [9]But I destroyed the Amorites from before them, whose height was as the height of the cedar, and he was strong as the oak, and I destroyed his fruit above and his roots below. [10]And I brought you up out of the land of Egypt, and I led you around the wilderness forty years to inherit the land of the Amorites. [11]And I chose from among your sons for prophets and from among your young men for consecration; are not these things so, sons of Israel," says the Lord? [12]"But you were giving the consecrated ones wine to drink, and you were giving orders to the prophets, saying, 'Do not ever prophesy!' [13]Therefore, behold, I am rolling under you in the manner that the wagon that is full of straw is rolled along. [14]And flight will perish from the runner, and the strong man will not retain possession of his strength at all, and the warrior will not save his life. [15]And the archer will not be able to stand his ground, and the one who is swift on his feet will in no way be delivered, nor will the horseman save his life. [16]And he will find his confidence in a powerful army; the naked man will flee on that day," says the Lord.

This eighth and last oracle was especially important for Amos' prophecy, since Amos was sent specifically to Israel (7:15). Whereas the previous seven oracles addressed various neighbors and enemies of Israel, this eighth and last oracle is presented *to Israel*. In its original presentation this oracle would apparently have had an unexpected rhetorical effect, following the complete number (seven) of oracles against Israel's neighbors and enemies. Readers of the LXX would not have had such a close connection with Israel, and many probably would have known what was coming, so it is unlikely the position of this oracle had as much rhetorical effect on them. This is by far the longest of the eight oracles in chapters 1–2, and in keeping with that fact it contains the most detailed list of charges of any of the oracles. Furthermore, the accusations in this oracle differ from those in the first seven oracles. In the first six they deal with military violence, and in the seventh (Judah) they deal with idolatry. But after the standard introduction (2:6a), this oracle contains a list of seven immoral and unethical actions that show Israel's infidelity to the covenant (2:6b-8). The oracle then continues with reminders of the Lord's past goodness to the nation (2:9–11), further examples of Israel's rebellion and lack of response to the Lord (2:12), and the unavoidable punishment resulting from their sins (2:13–16). The placement of this oracle at the end of the series, the length of it, and the number of specific sins mentioned all show that it was the ultimate rhetorical target of the sequence of oracles (Nogalski, 284).

2:6 Τάδε λέγει κύριος Ἐπὶ ταῖς τρισὶν ἀσεβείαις Ισραηλ καὶ ἐπὶ ταῖς τέσσαρσιν οὐκ ἀποστραφήσομαι αὐτόν, ἀνθ᾽ ὧν ἀπέδοντο ἀργυρίου δίκαιον καὶ πένητα ἕνεκεν ὑποδημάτων,

Τάδε λέγει κύριος. See 1:3 and 1:6.

Ἐπὶ ταῖς τρισὶν ἀσεβείαις Ισραηλ καὶ ἐπὶ ταῖς τέσσαρσιν οὐκ ἀποστραφήσομαι αὐτόν. See 1:3.

Ισραηλ. Subjective genitive. Here this indeclinable noun refers to the ten tribes of the Northern Kingdom, which separated from the tribes of Judah and Benjamin, the Southern Kingdom.

ἀνθ᾽ ὧν. See 1:3.

ἀπέδοντο. Aor mid ind 3rd pl ἀποδίδωμι. Gnomic aorist, expressing a general fact, not referring to a particular event, and translated as present tense (*CGCG* §33.31; Robertson, 836–37; Wallace, 562). The generic sense of the direct object supports this understanding of the verb. See *GELS* (73.II.1) and LSJ (197.III) for this meaning ("sell") of the verb in the middle voice. The affectedness of the subject is clear with this use of the middle voice, and the verb is an indirect middle, with the subject acting in her own interest (Wallace, 419–23).

ἀργυρίου. Genitive of price or value (Smyth §1372; Muraoka §22.l); this is an adverbial genitive, related to ἀπέδοντο and parallel with the following PP, ἕνεκεν ὑποδημάτων (see the discussion of adverbial genitives in Wallace, esp. 121–22; *CGCG* §33.31).

δίκαιον. Accusative direct object of ἀπέδοντο. This is a substantival use of the adjective, and the substantive is generic, representing the class of the righteous (Wallace, 253). It is common for generic nouns to be anarthrous (Muraoka §1.d).

καί. Coordinating conjunction, connecting parallel direct objects and their modifiers (*GELS*, 352.1.a). It is possible to understand the verb ἀπέδοντο to be repeated with the second object, but that does not seem necessary.

πένητα. Accusative direct object of ἀπέδοντο; an anarthrous generic noun, representing the class of the poor (Wallace, 253). On the anarthrous use of a generic noun, see δίκαιον above.

ἕνεκεν ὑποδημάτων. Exchange, modifying ἀπέδοντο. Improper preposition with the sense "in return for, in exchange for," which usage is not attested prior to the LXX (*GELS*, 237.4; see also Isa 5:23). The genitive object of the preposition, "sandals" (ὑποδημάτων), is used in a similar context in 8:6; in both contexts it emphasizes the "paltry sum" for which the oppressors seek to buy the lowly (see Glenny 2013b, 55, and 1 Kgdms 12:3).

2:7 τὰ πατοῦντα ἐπὶ τὸν χοῦν τῆς γῆς καὶ ἐκονδύλιζον εἰς κεφαλὰς πτωχῶν καὶ ὁδὸν ταπεινῶν ἐξέκλιναν, καὶ υἱὸς καὶ πατὴρ αὐτοῦ εἰσεπορεύοντο πρὸς τὴν αὐτὴν παιδίσκην, ὅπως βεβηλώσωσιν τὸ ὄνομα τοῦ θεοῦ αὐτῶν,

τὰ πατοῦντα ἐπὶ τὸν χοῦν τῆς γῆς. This participial phrase is "grammatically loose" (Dines 1991, 85), but it must modify the noun ὑποδημάτων at the end of 2:6. Muraoka (§77.da) notes that sometimes a phrase in the nominative is in apposition to a preceding phrase in an oblique case, as here. Thus, the phrase continues the description of the last sin in 2:6. The Lucianic version (*L*) apparently tried to improve this grammatical connection by rendering the participle in the genitive case ("of the one who is walking"), producing a more logical connection with the ὑποδημάτων (Dines 1991, 85). In the Hebrew the participial phrase begins the description of the third sin of the Israelites in verse 7 ("those who trample the head of the poor into the dust of the earth," ESV).

τὰ πατοῦντα. Pres act ptc nom neut pl πατέω (substantival). The participle refers back to the sandals. Gnomic present, describing a timeless fact. The article functions as a substantiver with the participle.

ἐπὶ τὸν χοῦν τῆς γῆς. Locative, modifying πατοῦντα. The preposition ἐπί has the sense "on the surface of" (*GELS*, 265–66.III.1).

τὸν χοῦν. Accusative object of ἐπί. The article with the head noun and modifying genitive is consistent with Apollonius' canon (Porter 1994, 111–12).

τῆς γῆς. Genitive of place, i.e., on the earth.

ἐκονδύλιζον. Impf act ind 3rd pl κονδυλίζω. Customary imperfect, describing a regularly occurring event ("they were striking"; Muraoka §28.c.ii; Wallace, 548). This verb has nothing corresponding to it in the Hebrew and was probably added because the first part of the description of this sin in the Hebrew ("the head of the poor") is connected with the previous sin in the LXX (see above and Glenny 2013b, 57); this is the only place in LXX Amos where a verb could be understood to be an addition to the Hebrew text, other than some possible double translations (see Glenny 2009, 49 n. 66). This is the first of six imperfect-tense verbs in 2:7-9 (see the Introduction); this rare verb form in LXX Amos (16x) emphasizes the sins of Israel in 2:7-8, and the imperfect points to the ongoing or repetitive nature of these sins; the two imperfects of εἰμί in 2:9 are not as marked, because the imperfect is the normal past tense for that verb.

εἰς κεφαλὰς. Direction, modifying ἐκονδύλιζον. The translator apparently included εἰς because he was following his Hebrew *Vorlage* closely; it corresponds to the ב preposition in the Hebrew. It probably "indicates a target aim or focus of action" (*GELS*, 196.3.a). I have rendered it "at"; i.e., "they were striking at the heads of the needy" (*GELS*, 406, s.v. κονδυλίζω, suggests the translation "they boxed the poor on the head," but this rendering of the preposition ["on"] is not consistent with the sense of εἰς; it has more the sense "against," referring to hostile action; *GELS*, 196.3.a). The accusative object of εἰς (κεφαλὰς), indicates the target of the blows and can be understood to be definite without the article. There is no article with the head noun or with its genitive modifier (Apollonius' canon applies; Porter 1994, 111-12).

πτωχῶν. Possessive genitive. The adjective is used substantivally and is generic, referring to a class of people. It is common for generic nouns to be anarthrous (Muraoka §1.d; Wallace, 253-54). "The πτωχός is often a beggar or someone so poor they literally have nothing" (Glenny 2013b, 56; see 55-57 for a discussion of the meaning of this noun and other words in the same semantic field).

ὁδὸν. Accusative direct object of ἐξέκλιναν. No article with head noun nor with its genitive modifier (Apollonius' canon applies; Porter 1994, 111-12; Wallace, 250-51).

ταπεινῶν. Subjective genitive. The adjective is used substantivally and is generic, referring to a class of people (see Muraoka §1.d; and Wallace, 253-54, on generic nouns without an article). See Glenny (2013b, 55-58) on this semantic field in the LXX.

ἐξέκλιναν. Aor act ind 3rd pl ἐκκλίνω. Gnomic aorist, expressing a general fact, not referring to a particular event, and translated as the present tense (Robertson, 836–37; Wallace, 562). Dines (1991, 86–87) suggests that this verb could have at least three different translations here: (1) "to deny justice to," (2) "to ignore or reject," and (3) "to cause to turn aside" (for a fuller discussion of this issue, see *GELS*, 209–10.I.1; Glenny 2013b, 58–59). The first meaning would have to be read into this context, and the second understanding does not seem serious enough for this context. Therefore, the third, the causative sense, perhaps with the idea "pervert," is the simplest and most likely in this verse.

υἱός. Nominative subject of εἰσεπορεύοντο. The noun is generic, referring to a class of people (see Muraoka §1.d; and Wallace, 253–54, on generic nouns without an article). This is also the sense of the MT, which has "man" (אִישׁ); the LXX clarifies that the "man" is the "son" of the "father" mentioned next. They comprise the compound subject in this clause.

πατὴρ. Nominative subject of εἰσεπορεύοντο. This is another generic noun; see above.

αὐτοῦ. Genitive of relationship. This pronoun does not refer to a specific son, but the point of this generic language is that fathers and their sons are doing this together.

εἰσεπορεύοντο. Impf mid ind 3rd pl εἰσπορεύομαι. Customary imperfect, pointing to something that regularly occurred or was a pattern. The middle voice could be classified as a "translational motion" middle (Kemmer, 269); the subject is clearly affected by the action of the verb. Here the word is a euphemism for sexual relations (see Gen 6:4; Esth 2:13–14; Tob 7:11; Ezek 23:44; and the discussion in Glenny 2013b, 59).

πρὸς τὴν αὐτὴν παιδίσκην. Direction, modifying εἰσεπορεύοντο. The preposition πρός with the accusative indicates the direction or that toward which they were entering in (*GELS*, 589.III.1; this preposition is often used in this sense "with verbs of physical movement . . . and mostly with accusative of person"). Combined with the force of the prepositional prefix on the verb (εἰσ-), the sense is one of moving toward and entering into.

The accusative article with the third-person personal pronoun (τὴν αὐτὴν) is the adjectival-identifying use of the pronoun and expresses "the notion of total identity, that of 'one and the same'" (Muraoka §14.a; see also Decker 2014a, 101–3). The accusative object of πρός (παιδίσκην) is always used in the LXX and related literature to refer to a "slave girl" (BDAG, 750; LEH, 456), and the sin described here may not only be the breaking of the prohibition of close relatives having sexual relationships with the same person (Lev 18:17) but also the sexual exploitation of the weak and vulnerable (see Glenny 2013b, 59).

ὅπως. Conjunction introducing a subordinate (dependent) clause giving the result (or consequence) of the sin described in the previous clause. Muraoka (*GELS*, 501.2) describes this use of ὅπως as indicating "a result which was not necessarily intended by the subject marked by the verb in the main clause but was bound to ensue."

βεβηλώσωσιν. Aor act subj 3rd pl βεβηλόω. Used with ὅπως to indicate a direct result (or consequence). Gnomic aorist, expressing a general fact, not referring to a particular event, and translated as a present tense (Robertson, 836–37; *CGCG* §33.31; Wallace, 562). The verb communicates the idea of causing "something highly revered to become identified with the commonplace, profane, desecrate" (BDAG, 60; see also Spicq 1:284; *GELS*, 116; and Glenny 2013b, 60). MSS B, V, and Swete have the present subjunctive form (βεβηλῶσιν), which is perhaps a mistake (homoioteleuton).

τὸ ὄνομα. Accusative direct object of βεβηλώσωσιν. Article with head noun and article with genitive modifier (Apollonius' canon applies).

τοῦ θεοῦ. Possessive genitive.

αὐτῶν. Possessive genitive. This could also be a genitive of subordination, if the emphasis is on God's dominion over them; however, in this context the emphasis seems to be on their covenant relationship with God, and in that sense he belongs to them. The Hebrew has "so that my holy name is profaned" (למען חלל את שם קדשי), apparently referring to the Lord's name, but the LXX refers to "the name of their god," an ambiguous phrase that suggests they are not worshipping the God of Israel (see also "their god" [τοῦ θεοῦ αὐτῶν] in 2:8).

2:8 καὶ τὰ ἱμάτια αὐτῶν δεσμεύοντες σχοινίοις παραπετάσματα ἐποίουν ἐχόμενα τοῦ θυσιαστηρίου καὶ οἶνον ἐκ συκοφαντιῶν ἔπινον ἐν τῷ οἴκῳ τοῦ θεοῦ αὐτῶν.

τὰ ἱμάτια. Accusative direct object of δεσμεύοντες. The article is commonly used with a head noun modified by a possessive pronoun (Wallace, 239–40).

αὐτῶν. Possessive genitive.

δεσμεύοντες. Pres act ptc nom masc pl δεσμεύω (means). Customary present describing something that regularly or repeatedly occurs, "binding together."

σχοινίοις. Dative of material. Wallace (169–70) distinguishes this use from the dative of means in that with the dative of means the item used is a tool and with the dative of material the item is not a tool but material, "with cords."

παραπετάσματα. Accusative direct object of ἐποίουν. This word is a *hapax* in biblical Greek, and it has the sense of "that which is spread before something" (*GELS*, 530). Here it apparently refers to some sort of "curtains" that are composed of "garments" bound together "with cords." The precise nature of the sin described here is unclear. It may have involved committing fornication on these curtain-garments, or perhaps the curtains were used to conceal sinful activity, or perhaps the curtains have idolatrous connections (see Ezek 16:16; and Glenny 2013b, 60–61). The mention of "the altar" in 2:8 suggests the sin involved putting something profane in close contact with it.

ἐποίουν. Impf act ind 3rd pl ποιέω. Customary imperfect, pointing to something that regularly occurred or was a pattern.

ἐχόμενα. Pres mid ptc neut acc pl ἔχω (circumstantial). The present middle participle of ἔχω has the meaning "neighboring, adjacent to" as here (*GELS*, 311.II.2.a; Smyth §1734; *GE*, 888.2.D), and it is describing the noun παραπετάσματα, but its relationship to it is complex. Muraoka (§31.df) describes this participle as circumstantial; he explains that in such cases the participle introduces a circumstantial clause in an oblique case with a noun phrase in an oblique case, to which the participle is subordinate, and the participle concords with its grammatical subject. Elsewhere Muraoka (§59; 61.c) differentiates this participle construction (ἐχόμενα τοῦ θυσιαστηρίου) from a typical object complement construction, which would here be in apposition to παραπετάσματα; in this verse the participle is not necessary to complete the clause, and an equative sentence like "they were near the altar" seems to be implied.

τοῦ θυσιαστηρίου. Genitive object of ἐχόμενα, indicating what is being designated as nearby the present middle participle of ἔχω (*GELS*, 311.II.2.a, s.v. ἔχω). Since it is not certain what altar is referred to here, I have classified this use of the article as "well-known" (see the discussion in Wallace, 225); if we could be certain the altar referred to is the altar in the Temple in Jerusalem, it would be the use of the article with a monadic noun. This sin is described as worship of "their god" (2:7 and 2:8), and if it was taking place in Jerusalem, it points to a Hellenized Jerusalem priesthood. See the discussion in Glenny (2013b, 60–61; see also the use of this noun in 3:14 and 9:1). The Hebrew has "beside every altar," but the Greek refers to a specific altar. In this regard, it is noteworthy that according to the title in 1:1, the contents of LXX Amos contain the things Amos saw "concerning Jerusalem" (see ὑπέρ Ιερουσαλημ in 1:1), whereas the Hebrew title reads "concerning Israel."

οἶνον. Accusative direct object of ἔπινον.

ἐκ συκοφαντιῶν. Source, modifying οἶνον (*GELS*, 201.5.a). The noun means "extortion" (*GELS*, 645), and Muraoka suggests the translation "wine obtained through extortion."

ἔπινον. Impf act ind 3rd pl πίνω. Customary imperfect, pointing to something that regularly occurred or was a pattern.

ἐν τῷ οἴκῳ. Locative, modifying ἔπινον. The preposition ἐν indicates the place where the drinking takes place (*GELS*, 231.1.b). The dative τῷ οἴκῳ is the object of ἐν. This dative article is difficult to classify; it could be an article of simple identification, and it could also be a "well-known" use of the article, pointing to a well-known "house" (see the discussion in Wallace, 225); but οἴκῳ could also be a monadic noun, if this god has only one "house."

τοῦ θεοῦ. Possessive genitive. The two articles in the head noun-genitive modifier construction at the end of this verse (τῷ οἴκῳ τοῦ θεοῦ) follow the pattern for Apollonius' canon. The noun τοῦ θεοῦ with the genitive modifier (αὐτῶν) is monadic.

αὐτῶν. Possessive genitive. The phrase "in the house of their god" leaves open the possibility of various and false gods (see also "their god" in 2:7).

2:9 ἐγὼ δὲ ἐξῆρα τὸν Αμορραῖον ἐκ προσώπου αὐτῶν, οὗ ἦν καθὼς ὕψος κέδρου τὸ ὕψος αὐτοῦ καὶ ἰσχυρὸς ἦν ὡς δρῦς, καὶ ἐξῆρα τὸν καρπὸν αὐτοῦ ἐπάνωθεν καὶ τὰς ῥίζας αὐτοῦ ὑποκάτωθεν·

ἐγὼ δὲ. These words mark a "new development" in the oracle against Israel (see Runge, 31–36, on the function of δέ). The particle δέ is only found five times in LXX Amos (see also 4:7; 7:11, 13, 17), and it occurs much less often than καί in LXX Twelve. In 2:9 δέ seems to be doing more than marking a transition; it is also marking a contrast between the sins of the Israelites and the Lord's goodness and faithfulness to them, which is described in the Lord's direct speech in 2:9–11. The emphatic nominative pronoun at the beginning of the verse introduces a new and contrasting subject (moving from Israel to the Lord).

ἐξῆρα. Aor act ind 1st sg ἐξαίρω. Consummative aorist, stressing attainment or accomplishment (Fanning, 263–65). In this context the verb has the sense "remove, get rid of, efface, obliterate" (*GELS*, 244–45.4), and I have rendered it "destroyed."

τὸν Αμορραῖον. Accusative object of ἐξῆρα. Apparently, this is a name for the combined inhabitants of Canaan during the time of the conquest, which is in view in this verse. The singular proper noun, representing the people, is generic, referring to a class. I have translated it as a plural because it refers to a class and not an individual. The names of ethnic groups are usually articular in the LXX (Muraoka §5.cae; see 2:10); Muraoka (§1.d) discusses the use of an article with a generic noun.

ἐκ προσώπου. Dissociation, modifying the verb ἐξῆρα. The preposition ἐκ indicates dissociation "with verbs of expelling, annihilating, removing" (*GELS*, 201.1.a). This phrase has the idea of "from before [them]" and with the verb ἐξαίρω indicates removal (see *GELS*, 601.6.d, s.v. πρόσωπον). On the rendering and meaning of the phrase ἐκ προσώπου, see Sollamo (33–34, 85–86, 328–29). The anarthrous genitive object of ἐκ (i.e., προσώπου) is definite, as is often the case with objects of prepositions (see BDF §255).

αὐτῶν. Possessive genitive, referring to the Israelites on their way to the promised land. This classification of the genitive is based on a literal understanding of the phrase "away from their face [presence]."

οὗ. Possessive genitive, indicating the one whose ὕψος ("height") is being described. The relative pronoun refers back to τὸν Αμορραιον.

ἦν. Impf act ind 3rd sg εἰμί. Customary imperfect, describing the ongoing state of "the Amorite." It is employed here to give background information (*CGCG* §33.22).

καθώς. This conjunction shows similarity and comparison (*GELS*, 352.1.a); it functions adverbially here, modifying ἦν and comparing the height of "the Amorite" to the height of a "cedar."

ὕψος. Nominative in comparative phrase with καθώς. Both the head noun and the genitive modifier are anarthrous (Apollonius' canon applies); ὕψος is definite, with the following genitive modifier giving it specificity.

κέδρου. Subjective genitive. The noun is generic, referring to a class of trees, the "cedar." Since both the head noun and the genitive modifier are anarthrous (Apollonius' canon applies), we would expect both to "have the same semantic force," or definiteness (Apollonius' corollary; see Wallace 250–51). Furthermore, it is good to note that "the use of . . . a generic article is optional" (Muraoka §1.d).

τὸ ὕψος. Nominative subject ("the height") of the first half of the compound relative clause. See *GELS* (352.1.a, s.v. καθώς) on the repetition of the same term (ὕψος) in both members of the comparison. The article marks this occurrence of ὕψος as the subject of the relative clause.

αὐτοῦ. Subjective genitive, referring back to τὸν Αμορραιον; this pronoun is not explicitly translated, since it overlaps in function with the preceding relative pronoun (οὗ).

καί. Coordinating conjunction, connecting parallel clauses (*GELS*, 352.1.b). The relative clause introduced by οὗ is compound, and this conjunction connects the two parts of that clause.

ἰσχυρὸς. Predicate nominative. This adjective ("strong, powerful, mighty"; LEH, 291) would be awkward as a subject. It is simpler to understand the subject of this clause to be included in the following verb (ἦν) and to understand ἰσχυρός to be a predicate nominative ("he was strong"). GELS (748.I.5, s.v. ὡς) comments that in the LXX "only rarely is the *tertium comparationis* [quality two things compared have in common] expressed" in a ὡς phrase, as it is here.

ἦν. Impf act ind 3rd sg εἰμί. Customary imperfect, describing the state of the Amorite.

ὡς. Introduces a comparative clause where "the predicate [is] in an equational sentence" (GELS, 748.I.7.a).

δρῦς. Nominative in a comparative phrase with ὡς. GELS (748.6, s.v. ὡς) comments that in the LXX "in similes the noun following ὡς is usually anarthrous." This anarthrous noun is generic, referring to a class of trees, and it could be definite ("strong as the oak"). See the discussion above concerning ὕψος κέδρου; if "cedar" (κέδρος) is definite, probably "oak" (δρῦς) in the parallel clause is also.

ἐξῆρα. Aor act ind 1st sg ἐξαίρω. Consummative aorist, stressing attainment or accomplishment (Fanning, 263–65). See the occurrence of the same verb form in the first main clause in 2:9, translating the same Hebrew verb (שמד but a different form). This verb form (from ἐξαίρω) is the reading in *L* and the modern editions by R-H and Ziegler; MSS B, A, Q, W, and Swete have the verb ἐξήρανα (from ξηραίνω meaning "to dry"). The latter reading was apparently not favored by modern editions since it is an imprecise rendering of the Hebrew verb שמד ("destroy"), and it differs from the rendering of the same Hebrew verb earlier in the verse; thus, it appears to be a transcriptional error. However, there are several factors that support ἐξήρανα as the original LXX rendering: it is found in earlier MSS, it makes sense in the context, and it is consistent with the pattern of literary variation found elsewhere in the translation of Amos (see 1:3 for several examples of such literary variation in the Oracles against the Nations). Either verb makes sense here, and it is a difficult decision. I have chosen to work with the reading in the main modern versions. This clause has a compound direct object.

τὸν καρπόν. Accusative direct object of ἐξῆρα. This is an article of simple identification, "the fruit" (Wallace, 216–17).

αὐτοῦ. Possessive genitive.

ἐπάνωθεν. Adverb of place ("above"; GELS, 260; Muraoka §26.e). BDF (§104) notes that "adverbs in -θεν answer the question 'whence?'" but goes on to comment that the ending "is stereotyped and meaningless for the most part" in some situations; the usage in this verse does not seem to add any special sense that needs to be rendered "from" or in some such manner emphasizing "whence." There is a correspondence between this word and the following ὑποκάτωθεν, matching the corresponding terms ממעל and מתחת in Hebrew; in Greek the corresponding terms rhyme (see Dines 2013, 400).

τὰς ῥίζας. Accusative direct object of ἐξῆρα; article of simple identification (Wallace, 216–17).

αὐτοῦ. Possessive genitive.

ὑποκάτωθεν. Adverb of place ("below"; GELS, 702; Muraoka §26.e; see ἐπάνωθεν above in this verse).

2:10 καὶ ἐγὼ ἀνήγαγον ὑμᾶς ἐκ γῆς Αἰγύπτου καὶ περιήγαγον ὑμᾶς ἐν τῇ ἐρήμῳ τεσσαράκοντα ἔτη τοῦ κατακληρονομῆσαι τὴν γῆν τῶν Αμορραίων·

ἐγώ. Nominative subject of ἀνήγαγον. Mirroring the Hebrew (אנכי), the pronoun is emphatic, repeating the pronoun at the beginning of 2:9 and continuing the description of the Lord's work.

ἀνήγαγον. Aor act ind 1st sg ἀνάγω. Consummative aorist, emphasizing the completion of the action, "I brought you up," viewing the action as a whole. See the similar phrase in Mic 6:4.

ὑμᾶς. Accusative direct object of ἀνήγαγον. Whereas the work of the Lord in 2:9 was directed toward "the Amorite," Israel is the direct recipient of his work in this verse (ὑμᾶς, 2x).

ἐκ γῆς. Separation, modifying ἀνήγαγον. The preposition ἐκ indicates dissociation from (GELS, 201.1) or separation from (BDAG, 295–96.1) the object of the preposition (γῆς); this differs from the simple idea of origin or source. γῆς refers to a "land or ground," that is, "belonging to or inhabited by a particular ethnic group or nation" (GELS, 129.4.d). The genitive object of ἐκ (γῆς) is definite because the following genitive (Αἰγύπτου) specifies what land it is and because an object of a preposition is commonly definite when anarthrous (BDF §255; 259).

Αἰγύπτου. Genitive of apposition, giving an example of the category in the head noun (Wallace, 95).

περιήγαγον. Aor act ind 1st sg περιάγω. Constative aorist, viewing the action as a whole. The emphatic ἐγώ at the beginning of the verse is the subject of this verb, which is coordinated (by καί) with ἀνήγαγον.

ὑμᾶς. Accusative direct object of περιήγαγον.

ἐν τῇ ἐρήμῳ. Locative, modifying περιήγαγον. The preposition ἐν indicates a place in which an action takes place (GELS, 231.1.b); the article (τῇ ἐρήμῳ) points out a well-known object, "the wilderness" (Wallace, 225).

τεσσαράκοντα ἔτη. Adverbial accusative, indicating duration or extent of time and modifying περιήγαγον (BDAG, 401; Wallace, 201-3). MS B and Swete have the numerical sign (μ´) rather than the full spelling of the adjective τεσσαράκοντα, and it is difficult to know which form should receive priority. For Greek abbreviations of numbers, see Smyth (§347). "Forty years" here clearly refers to Israel's desert experience when they came out of Egypt (see 5:25).

τοῦ κατακληρονομῆσαι. Aor act inf κατακληρονομέω (purpose or goal; BDF §400 on the genitive articular infinitive; Wallace, 591). This verb could have the sense "to inherit" here, referring to Israel's inheritance of the land, or it could have the sense "to give as a possession," referring to the Lord's giving of the inheritance (*GELS*, 372-73.1 and 4). The former meaning is found in 2:10, and where it has the latter meaning there is usually a dative indicating the recipient; thus, the former sense is more likely here. The aorist is consummative, stressing attainment or accomplishment (Fanning, 263-65). Ehorn (224) explains that "purpose (which emphasizes the *end* of an action) and cause (which emphasizes the *beginning* of an action) are conceptually similar" (emphasis in original). Thus, the explanation of the τοῦ + infinitive construction denoting purpose may be the ablative sense of the genitive case (see Burk, 63-67)

τήν γῆν. Accusative direct object of κατακληρονομῆσαι; the article points out a monadic noun, "the land of the Amorites."

τῶν Ἀμορραίων. Possessive genitive. In genitive phrases both the head noun and genitive noun normally have or lack the article (Apollonius' canon applies; Wallace 239-40) The Hebrew הָאֱמֹרִי is rendered as a generic singular in 2:9 ("the Amorite") and as a plural here ("the Amorites"); either is a possible rendering (*HALOT*, 1:67-68), but the difference points to the translator's penchant for literary variation.

2:11 καὶ ἔλαβον ἐκ τῶν υἱῶν ὑμῶν εἰς προφήτας καὶ ἐκ τῶν νεανίσκων ὑμῶν εἰς ἁγιασμόν· μὴ οὐκ ἔστιν ταῦτα, υἱοὶ Ισραηλ; λέγει κύριος.

ἔλαβον. Aor act ind 1st sg λαμβάνω. Constative aorist, viewing the action as a whole; here the action was iterative. The verb has two main prepositional phrases modifying it, both with the preposition ἐκ, and therefore it could be understood as two different works of the Lord (choosing "from among your sons for prophets and from among your young men for consecration").

ἐκ τῶν υἱῶν. Partitive, modifying ἔλαβον. The preposition ἐκ is employed to indicate "an entity out of which a component or part is singled out ('partitive')" (*GELS*, 201.2). The article points out a well-known object (Wallace, 225). Here υἱῶν refers to male descendants (*GELS*, 694.1).

ὑμῶν. Genitive of relationship, since this pronoun refers to the progenitors of the noun it is modifying.

εἰς προφήτας. Purpose, modifying ἔλαβον. The preposition marks the goal of the Lord choosing sons from Israel; the preposition indicates the vocation, use, or end and is rendered "for, as" (BDAG, 289–90.4.d).

ἐκ τῶν νεανίσκων. Partitive, modifying ἔλαβον. See the parallel entry above on the function of ἐκ and the article in this PP.

ὑμῶν. Possessive genitive; this differs from the use of this pronoun earlier in the verse, because here there is no necessary family relationship involved (Wallace, 83).

εἰς ἁγιασμόν. Purpose, modifying ἔλαβον. On εἰς, see above in this verse. The noun ἁγιασμόν has the sense "consecration, sanctification" (LSJ, 9; LEH, 4), and that is how NETS renders it. The corresponding Hebrew word (נזיר) can function as an adjective or a substantive (*HALOT*, 1:683), and the translator rendered it with two different senses in 2:11 and 12. In 2:11 it apparently refers to "consecration for a cultic or sacral office" like the priesthood (2 Macc 2:17) or a Nazarite vow (*GELS*, 5.1). But in 2:12a it refers to consecrated ones, who are Nazirites, or perhaps priests, who were being defiled (parallel with "prophets" in both verses). As is often his practice, the translator varied his rendering of a word in a context (נזיר in 2:11 and 2:12), apparently referring to consecration to an office in 2:11 and the ones so consecrated in 2:12; see ἡγιασμένους in 2:12 and Dines (2013, 405).

μὴ οὐκ. Muraoka (§83.ce) thinks μή should be understood to be rhetorical, and the οὐκ negates the following proposition, resulting in something like "Are not these things so [true]?" He classifies it as a "negatived question introduced with a rhetorical negator." The construction of the rhetorical question is unusual. Smyth (§2752) discusses the use of μὴ οὐ "with the indicative in doubtful assertions" (see also §1772) and notes that in such constructions the οὐ after μή "belongs to a single word, not to the sentence" (§2651.d); this makes good sense here where οὐκ ἔστιν corresponds to אִין. This order of the two negatives occurs only about ten times in the LXX, and in five other passages it is found in a rhetorical question expecting a positive answer, as here (Judg 14:3; 3 Kgdms 6:3; Eccl 6:6; Isa 50:2; 59:1). Rather than strictly following the Hebrew (הַאַף אֵין זֹאת), the translator gave the sense of the construction (μὴ οὐκ ἔστιν ταῦτα).

ἔστιν. Pres act ind 3rd sg εἰμί. Gnomic present. The singular verb "preponderates with words having non-personal meaning" (BDF §133) and is the norm with neuter plural subjects.

ταῦτα. Nominative subject of ἔστιν.

υἱοί. Vocative of address, indicating to whom the rhetorical question is spoken. Here the word υἱοί refers to the members of the community of Israel, and the emphasis is not on progenitors and their descendants. "Sons of Israel" means "Israelites" (*GELS*, 694.2).

Ισραηλ. Genitive of relationship.

λέγει κύριος. See 1:3 and 1:5.

2:12 καὶ ἐποτίζετε τοὺς ἡγιασμένους οἶνον καὶ τοῖς προφήταις ἐνετέλλεσθε λέγοντες Οὐ μὴ προφητεύσητε.

After the Lord's speech about himself in 2:9–11, Israel is once again the subject in this verse, and the Lord gives two more examples of the nation's rebellion and lack of response to him.

καί. Coordinating conjunction, connecting clauses; what follows is a contrast or logical contradiction with the Lord's goodness to his people, as described in 2:9–11, and it should be rendered "but," as is often the case with καί in the LXX (so NETS here; see *GELS*, 353.4).

ἐποτίζετε. Impf act ind 2nd pl ποτίζω. Customary imperfect, describing regularly occurring or habitual activity ("were giving to drink"). The imperfect tense is marked and stands out, after the more default aorists, describing the Lord's actions in 2:9–11.

τοὺς ἡγιασμένους. Prf mid ptc acc masc pl ἁγιάζω (substantival). Direct object (person) of ἐποτίζετε in a person-thing double accusative construction. Intensive use of the perfect tense, focusing on the results or present state produced by the sanctification. The middle voice is indirect middle, affecting the subject; Kemmer (268) describes the indirect middle as being found with "verbs of coming into possession, desiring to come into possession" (see also Wallace, 419–23, who calls it the "benefactive" middle). "The consecrated ones" are in this context Nazarites or priests; see the discussion in 2:11 on εἰς ἁγιασμόν. The accusative article functions as a substantiver with the participle.

οἶνον. Direct object (thing) of ἐποτίζετε in a person-thing double accusative.

τοῖς προφήταις. Dative indirect object of ἐνετέλλεσθε. The article is employed to point out a well-known object (Wallace, 225).

ἐνετέλλεσθε. Impf mid ind 2nd pl ἐντέλλω. Customary imperfect, describing regularly occurring or habitual activity ("command, give orders to"). This verb is exclusively middle in biblical literature (BDAG, 339). The category of the middle voice is probably "speech action," involving emotion (Kemmer, 269).

Amos 2:11–13

λέγοντες. Pres act ptc nom masc pl λέγω (means, redundant adverbial participle with a verb of commanding used to introduce direct discourse; Wallace, 649–50). The time of the present participle is contemporaneous with the time of the main verb.

Οὐ μή. Double negative with an aorist subjunctive verb. This is the first of 22 instances of the double negative οὐ μή in Amos, almost always with aorist subjunctive verbs (the only exception is its use with a present subjunctive in 7:10). This is the strongest negation in Greek, and when used with the subjunctive mood (or future indicative), it rules out the possibility or future potential of the affirmation (Wallace, 468; see also Muraoka [§83.ca], who mentions the "ring of authority" with this double negator).

προφητεύσητε. Aor act subj 2nd pl προφητεύω. Muraoka (§29.ba.ii-a) remarks that in the LXX a subjunctive with a double negative "may be used for stringent prohibition" (see Gen 3:1; Amos 8:14; 9:10, 15; and Smyth §1800, 2756), as it is here. Muraoka (ibid.) also notes that the subjunctive with the double negative is "almost always aorist" (see Muraoka §83.c-cf).

2:13 διὰ τοῦτο ἰδοὺ ἐγὼ κυλίω ὑποκάτω ὑμῶν, ὃν τρόπον κυλίεται ἡ ἅμαξα ἡ γέμουσα καλάμης·

διὰ τοῦτο. Inferential. This phrase could be classified as causal or inferential. Many lexicons do not include the inferential sense in their discussion of διά with the accusative case but instead just refer to the causal sense (*GE*, 478–80.III.C; *GELS*, 148.II.1.a). A causal sense is expressed in English with phrases like "because of" or "on account of," while an inferential sense is expressed with phrases like "therefore" or "as a consequence." Although the two ideas are closely related, the difference is that cause emphasizes and focuses on the preceding reason, but inference emphasizes and focuses on the resulting consequence. (For a discussion of the developing uses of διά see Zerwick §82.) BDAG (225–26.B.2.b) mentions that "in real and supposed answers and inferences" διὰ τοῦτο often has the sense "therefore," especially in the Septuagint. The development of the inferential sense of διά is apparently because of the close relationship of causes that give rise to something and the resulting consequences, which can often be closely related to or part of the cause (see Zerwick §82 on final causes). The neuter demonstrative pronoun τοῦτο refers to "a general situation, circumstances, or an argument made" (Muraoka §12.g).

This phrase occurs eight other times in LXX Amos (3:2, 11; 4:12; 5:11, 13, 16; 6:7; 7:17), and each time it occurs the context must determine if the focus of διὰ τοῦτο is on the cause or on what is being inferred. Also, the translations "because of" and "therefore" are flexible enough that either could be used for all occurrences of διὰ τοῦτο in LXX Amos; *LES* employs "on account of this" for eight of them (using the unusual phrase "thanks to this" in 3:11 where the other rendering is not fitting), and *NETS* always employs "therefore." There is nothing corresponding to these two Greek words in the MT of 2:13, and their inclusion in the LXX suggests the translator was reading the text closely and wanted to clarify the flow of the argument for his readers. Six times where this phrase is found in LXX Amos, the corresponding Hebrew is לכן; in 3:2 it is על כן, and in 5:11 it is לכן יען (see the discussion there). The basic sense of לכן and על כן is "therefore" (*HALOT* 1:530.1; 1:833–34). Here the phrase clarifies the relationship between Israel's sins and rejection of the Lord's goodness and ministry to them (2:6–12) and the Lord's judgment of them (2:13–16), which is the consequence of their sins.

ἰδού. Although this is technically a verbal form (aor mid impv 2nd sg εἶδον, i.e., ἰδοῦ), it is best to understand ἰδού to be "a presentative particle used to draw the hearer's or reader's attention to what follows," and "it is accented with the acute when used as a particle" (BDAG, 468). Here it is "not clausal initial" (*GELS*, 337–38.h); it is a "marker of strong emphasis" (BDAG, 468.2).

ἐγώ. Nominative subject of κυλίω. This pronoun is not necessary, because the subject is embedded in the following verb. Thus, it is emphatic, and its position after ἰδού further corroborates its emphasis (see ἰδού above). The pronoun identifies the speaker and subject as the same ἐγώ who spoke in 2:9–11 (the Lord), in contrast to the Israelites, who were the subjects in 2:12.

κυλίω. Pres act ind 1st sg κυλίω. Futuristic present, describing the coming day of the Lord (2:14–16) and stressing the certainty of the event; it has the meaning "roll" (*GELS*, 418.1).

ὑποκάτω ὑμῶν. Locative, modifying κυλίω; ὑποκάτω functions here as a preposition (it can also function as an adverb), meaning "under, underneath" and indicating "where some object is moved or moves to" (*GELS*, 702.I.c).

ὃν τρόπον. This is an idiomatic adverbial accusative phrase (BDF §160; Smyth §1608), which indicates the manner in which something happens, and introduces a clause, "emphasizing comparability and analogy"; it has the sense "just as, exactly as" (*GELS*, 688.2.b, d; BDAG, 1016–17). The phrase also occurs in 3:12; 5:14, 19; and 9:9. Here it introduces a subordinate clause that compares and further explains the action in the main clause; the comparison is between things that are similar, not between things that are antithetical to each other (as in Zech 8:13 and 14).

κυλίεται. Pres pass ind 3rd sg κυλίω. Gnomic present, describing a general, timeless event. The present middle/passive form is best understood to be passive here (so NETS, "is rolled"). See also the passive sense in Sir 27:27 ("it will be rolled," NETS); in Zech 9:16 and Amos 5:24 the passive idea is not as clear.

ἡ ἅμαξα. Nominative subject of κυλίεται. Generic noun, describing a class of things; it is common to have an article with a generic noun, but it is not required (Muraoka §1.d).

ἡ γέμουσα. Pres act ptc fem nom sg γέμω (attributive). The nominative article marks the function of the participle as adjectival, modifying ἅμαξα, i.e., "the wagon that is full" (second attributive position, Wallace, 306–7).

καλάμης. Genitive of content (Wallace, 92–94), modifying γέμουσα. This substantive is always singular in the LXX (18x), even though it refers to an object that consists of many units (Muraoka §21.d, suggesting the rendering "the wagon laden with stubble"). The description of God rolling under the Israelites like a wagon is difficult to understand, and LXX readers probably would have understood it to mean something like "I will press you down, like a wagon full of sheaves presses down" (similar to MT; see Glenny 2013b, 62).

2:14 καὶ ἀπολεῖται φυγὴ ἐκ δρομέως, καὶ ὁ κραταιὸς οὐ μὴ κρατήσῃ τῆς ἰσχύος αὐτοῦ, καὶ ὁ μαχητὴς οὐ μὴ σώσῃ τὴν ψυχὴν αὐτοῦ,

The description of the Lord's judgment in 2:14–15 begins with a future-tense verb, and then that verb is followed by five aorist subjunctives with οὐ μή, emphasizing the inescapable nature of the judgment. The vocabulary in 2:14–16 suggests that the judgment will come by means of a foreign army (φυγή, μαχητής, τοξότης, ἱππεύς). The following descriptions of judgment are more literal and concrete than the figurative and more general description of judgment in 2:13.

ἀπολεῖται. Fut mid ind 3rd sg ἀπόλλυμι. Predictive future. There is a pronounced difference between the transitive active ("I destroy") and intransitive middle ("I perish") meanings of ἀπόλλυμι. It does not appear that the passive form of this verb occurs in the LXX, although the verb occurs 366 times (see *GELS*, 78–79; BDAG, 115–16; LEH, 70–71; LSJ, 207).

φυγὴ. Nominative subject of ἀπολεῖται. This word is related to φεύγω, and it means "flight" (BDAG, 1067).

ἐκ δρομέως. Separation, modifying ἀπολεῖται; ἐκ indicates dissociation "with verbs of expelling, annihilating, removing, taking" (*GELS*, 201.1). Its sense here could also be described as "separation" (BDAG, 295–96.1). The noun δρομεύς means "runner" (*GE*, 555).

ὁ κραταιὸς. Nominative subject of κρατήσῃ. This generic subject, meaning "strong" (*GELS*, 410), describes a class. The LXX has rendered the Hebrew with the stylish cognate expression κραταιὸς οὐ μὴ κρατήσῃ connecting the subject and verb; the Hebrew does not contain such a cognate expression (Dines 2013, 404). The article with a generic noun is common, but it is not required (Muraoka §1.d); here the article substantivizes the adjective.

οὐ μὴ κρατήσῃ. Aor act subj 3rd sg κρατέω. Aorist subjunctive of emphatic negation with οὐ μή; see the entry on οὐ μή in 2:12. This verb can have the sense "to lay hold of, grasp" or "to gain control over," but here it probably has the idea "to have at one's disposal," i.e., to have use of one's own strength (*GELS*, 411). Verbs meaning "to touch, take hold of" often take their objects in the genitive, and the genitive often is a "genitive of part," referring to part of the thing, as fits here (BDF §170).

τῆς ἰσχύος. Genitive complement of κρατήσῃ. An article is almost invariably used with a noun that has a possessive pronoun attached to it (Wallace, 239). The article is also often employed with abstract nouns, as here, to define them more closely; here with the possessive pronoun αὐτοῦ, the ἰσχύος is distinguished (Wallace, 226–27; see also BDF §258).

αὐτοῦ. Possessive genitive.

ὁ μαχητής. Nominative subject of σώσῃ. The generic noun describes a class, "the warrior"; generic nouns often have an article (Muraoka §1.d).

οὐ μὴ σώσῃ. Aor act subj 3rd sg σῴζω. Aorist subjunctive of emphatic negation with οὐ μή (see above in 2:12). This verb and its negative modifier (οὐ μὴ σώσῃ) correspond to the first of three occurrences of the Hebrew verb and negative לֹא יְמַלֵּט ("he will not save") in Amos 2:14–15; the Hebrew phrase is rendered in two different ways in 2:15: οὐ μὴ διασωθῇ and οὐ μὴ σώσῃ (see Dines 2013, 408). R-H and Ziegler have the reading σώσῃ, but MSS B, V, Q, and Swete have the future tense (σώσει). The string of aorist subjunctive verbs in this context with the double negation supports the subjunctive reading here also.

τὴν ψυχήν. Accusative direct object of σώσῃ; the article is almost invariably used with a noun that has a possessive pronoun modifying it (Wallace, 239). Here the noun refers to "physical life" (*GELS*, 743.1).

αὐτοῦ. Possessive genitive.

2:15 καὶ ὁ τοξότης οὐ μὴ ὑποστῇ, καὶ ὁ ὀξὺς τοῖς ποσὶν αὐτοῦ οὐ μὴ διασωθῇ, οὐδὲ ὁ ἱππεὺς οὐ μὴ σώσῃ τὴν ψυχὴν αὐτοῦ,

ὁ τοξότης. Nominative subject of ὑποστῇ. The generic noun ("the archer") describes a class (on the article with a generic noun, see Muraoka §1.d).

οὐ μὴ ὑποστῇ. Aor act subj 3rd sg ὑφίστημι. Aorist subjunctive of emphatic negation with οὐ μή (see 2:12). *GELS* (708.1.c) suggests the idea of ὑφίστημι is "to bear up, endure [suffering]," but in this context the absolute use of the verb has more the sense "stand one's ground, face the enemy" (LSJ, 1909.IV).

ὁ ὀξὺς. Nominative subject of διασωθῇ. The adjective functions as a substantive and is a generic noun describing a class (on the article with a generic noun, see Muraoka§1.d). The article also substantivizes the adjective. The basic idea of this word is "sharp, keen," but when it refers to motion or movement it has the idea "quick, swift" (see esp. LSJ, 1236.IV).

τοῖς ποσὶν. Dative of respect (Muraoka §22.wc). The meaning of the phrase ὀξὺς τοῖς ποσίν is "quick-footed" (*GELS*, 500.1, s.v. ὀξύς). It is normal to have an article with a noun modified by a possessive pronoun.

αὐτοῦ. Possessive genitive.

οὐ μὴ διασωθῇ. Aor pass subj 3rd sg διασῴζω. Aorist subjunctive of emphatic negation with οὐ μή (see 2:12). There is no agency expressed with the passive verb, further emphasizing that it is certain the subject will not be delivered. This verb and its negative modifier (οὐ μὴ διασωθῇ) correspond to the second of three occurrences of the Hebrew verb and negative לא ימלט in Amos 2:14–15; the Hebrew phrase is rendered οὐ μὴ σώσῃ in the other two occurrences, giving the passage a degree of literary variation in comparison with the Hebrew (see Dines 2013, 408).

οὐδὲ. Negative conjunction, which is a combination of οὐ and δέ (7x in Amos; see also 4:9, 10, 11; 7:14; 8:11; 9:10). Here it is "preceded and followed by another negative" and best rendered "neither, nor" (see BDAG, 734–35; *GELS*, 512.d).

ὁ ἱππεὺς. Nominative subject of σώσῃ. The generic noun describes a class, "the horseman" (on the article with a generic noun, see Muraoka §1.d).

οὐ μὴ σώσῃ. Aor act subj 3rd sg σῴζω. Aorist subjunctive of emphatic negation with οὐ μη, "will not save" (see 2:12). Note the triple negation in this clause (Muraoka §83.cf). R-H and Ziegler have the aorist subjunctive, but MSS B, V, W, and Swete have the future tense (σώσει). There is no difference in meaning between the two readings, and the string of aorist subjunctives in 2:14–15 suggests that was also the original reading here, which was changed for literary variation.

τὴν ψυχήν. Accusative direct object of σώσῃ. See 2:14.

αὐτοῦ. Possessive genitive.

2:16 καὶ εὑρήσει τὴν καρδίαν αὐτοῦ ἐν δυναστείαις, ὁ γυμνὸς διώξεται ἐν ἐκείνῃ τῇ ἡμέρᾳ, λέγει κύριος.

This verse is very difficult in the LXX. The first clause in R-H and Ziegler, καὶ εὑρήσει τὴν καρδίαν αὐτοῦ ("and he will find his confidence"), does not seem to fit in this context, and it does not correspond closely to the Hebrew; one of the main problems with the clause in the LXX is that the antecedent of the subject is not clear.

εὑρήσει. Fut act ind 3rd sg εὑρίσκω. Predictive future. Vaticanus has a double negative in this clause and a subject (ὁ κραταιός), resulting in a meaning that fits well in the context: "*the strong man* will never find his confidence in a powerful army" (see the discussion of LXX variants in Glenny 2013b, 18). The first two correctors of Vaticanus have removed the negative particles, and ὁ κραταιός in the original Vaticanus reading seems to be an addition, not corresponding to the Hebrew, to try to make sense of the difficult LXX text. *L* has the subjunctive of εὑρίσκω, which is consistent with the variation of the future tense and subjunctive mode throughout this section.

τὴν καρδίαν. Accusative direct object of εὑρήσει. I have rendered καρδία as "confidence" (see *GELS*, 363.5; NETS renders it "heart"). An article is almost invariably used with a noun that has a possessive pronoun attached to it (Wallace, 239).

αὐτοῦ. Possessive genitive.

ἐν δυναστείαις. Source, modifying εὑρήσει and indicating "an object to which some emotion or thought is directed" (*GELS*, 232.9). The dative object of the preposition (δυναστείαις) could be a reference to "power, mighty deeds" (LEH, 122), "a powerful army" (*GELS*, 179.2), "acts of dominance" (NETS), or perhaps "oppressive regimes," following the prevalent political use of the term in non-biblical Greek (Dines 1991, 103 n. 28). I have taken the plural noun to be a reference to "a powerful army" here because of all the war and military language in 2:14–16 (so *GELS*, 179.2); see the discussion in Glenny (2013b, 63). The subject is directing his heart to his army to find his confidence there.

ὁ γυμνός. Nominative subject of διώξεται. The adjective functions as a generic substantive (with the article), describing a class (on the article with a generic noun, see Muraoka §1.d). The asyndeton at the beginning of this clause follows the Hebrew, and so one should not make too much of it. This is an instance where the relationship between the clauses can be gleaned from the context (see Runge, 20–23). The LXX has changed the MT's בגבורים ערום ינוס ("the strong man will flee away naked") to ὁ γυμνὸς διώξεται ("the naked man will flee"), bringing to mind Jews like those described in 1 Macc 1:14–15 and 2 Macc 4:9–15, who enrolled in the gymnasium and adopted the Greek way of life (see Glenny 2013b, 63).

διώξεται. Fut mid ind 3rd sg διώκω. Predictive future. The middle voice is often used for translational motion when something moves itself from one place to another, and the middle future form of διώκω is often used in this way in the LXX Twelve (Hos 6:12; Amos 6:12; Nah 1:8); in this intransitive construction it probably should be understood to mean "run" (see also Amos 6:12; Hab 2:2; Hag 1:9), apparently in the sense "move away with speed," hence "flee" (*GELS*, 173.II.1).

ἐν ἐκείνῃ τῇ ἡμέρᾳ. Temporal, modifying διώξεται and giving the "point in time when something takes place" (*GELS*, 231.3). The far, or remote, demonstrative (ἐκείνῃ) is employed to contrast the coming day of judgment with the present time of the writer or audience (Wallace, 325). The LXX transposes the order of the demonstrative and noun found in the MT; on the fronted position of the demonstrative here, see Muraoka (§34.c). The article is normal with a noun modified by a demonstrative pronoun.

λέγει κύριος. See 1:3 and 1:5.

Amos 3:1–8

¹Hear this word which the Lord has spoken against you, O house of Israel, and against the whole tribe which I brought up out of the land of Egypt, saying, ²"Only you have I known out of all tribes of the earth; for this reason, I will bring punishment upon you for all your sins. ³Will two ever start out on a journey together if they do not know each other? ⁴Will a lion roar out of its thicket without having a prey? Will a young lion ever give its roar from its den unless it has taken something? ⁵Will a bird fall on the ground without a fowler? Will a trap on the ground spring up without catching something? ⁶Will a trumpet sound in a city and the people not be terrified? Will there be distressing circumstances in a city, which the Lord has not made? ⁷Therefore, the Lord God will never do anything unless he reveals his instruction to his servants, the prophets. ⁸A lion will roar, and who will not be afraid? The Lord God has spoken, and who will not prophesy?"

Chapters 3–6 make up the second major section of Amos, and asyndeton marks the new thought or topic at the beginning of each of these four chapters. Chapters 3–5 all begin with almost identical introductory formulas (3:1; 4:1; and 5:1 differs slightly), and chapter 6 begins with a woe oracle. These chapters are also characterized by the fact that they are all made up of relatively brief units (see Nogalski, 291). Chapter 3 has two main units (following R-H and Ziegler), which could be further subdivided into five relatively independent units (3:1–2, 3–8, 9–11, 12, and 13–15; following NETS).

3:1 Ἀκούσατε τὸν λόγον τοῦτον, ὃν ἐλάλησεν κύριος ἐφ᾽ ὑμᾶς, οἶκος Ισραηλ, καὶ κατὰ πάσης φυλῆς, ἧς ἀνήγαγον ἐκ γῆς Αἰγύπτου, λέγων

Ἀκούσατε. Aor act impv 2nd pl ἀκούω. Summary command in the aorist (constative), focusing on the action as a whole (Wallace, 485; CGCG §33.28), and emphasizing the urgency of the specific action (Fanning, 369). When the verb ἀκούω has as its object what one hears, it usually stands in the accusative case, as here (Smyth §1361–66; BDF §173, 416); and when its object is the person being heard it is usually in the genitive case. In LXX Amos its object is always in the accusative case.

τὸν λόγον τοῦτον. Accusative direct object of ἀκούσατε. The article is invariably present with a head noun modified by a demonstrative (Muraoka §34.a); the near or proximate demonstrative is employed here to refer to what follows immediately in the context (cataphoric; see Muraoka §12.c).

ὅν. Accusative direct object of ἐλάλησεν. The relative pronoun modifies or refers back to λόγον.

ἐλάλησεν. Aor act ind 3rd sg λαλέω. Constative aorist, viewing the action as a whole.

κύριος. Nominative subject of ἐλάλησεν.

ἐφ᾽ ὑμᾶς. Opposition, modifying ἐλάλησεν; the preposition (ἐπί) indicates the ones to whom the speech is directed, here in a hostile sense ("against," GELS, 266.III.4.d). The parallel PP with κατά (below) has this same sense. The accusative plural pronoun ὑμᾶς, which is the object of ἐπί, refers to the people addressed, the "house of Israel" and "the whole tribe," both of which refer to the same people.

οἶκος. Nominative for a vocative. It functions like a vocative of address in apposition to ὑμᾶς, clarifying to whom the utterance is addressed (Muraoka §22.ya–yb). Here the οἶκος refers to the clan of people descended from a common ancestor, thus the idea here is "descendants," or better "nation" (BDAG, 699.3).

Ισραηλ. Genitive of apposition or, possibly, source. If functioning as a genitive of apposition, this indeclinable proper noun further identifies the "house" or "nation" as Israel (see Wallace, 95–100); it is possible to call it a genitive of source if the emphasis is on the fact that the nation is made up of the descendants of the patriarch Jacob, or Israel.

καί. Coordinating conjunction, connecting parallel PPs (*GELS*, 352.1.a). Park (144) calls it a syntactic link, and it clarifies that there are two different descriptions of the recipients of the judgment in this verse.

κατὰ πάσης φυλῆς. Opposition, modifying ἐλάλησεν. The preposition has the sense "against" in a context designating "hostile speech" (BDAG, 511.A.2.b.β). This genitive adjective (πάσης) could be distributive ("*every* tribe"; Dines 1991, 104) or collective ("*all* the tribe, the whole tribe"; Brenton, NETS, MT); on this construction (πᾶς + singular noun) see especially Muraoka (§38.b.i) and MHT (3:199–200). With the distributive use there is usually no article with the related noun, as here, and with the collective use the related noun is usually articular (Conybeare and Stock §63; MHT, 3:199–200; see also Smyth §1174). However, this pattern has many exceptions, and πᾶς with an anarthrous noun can be collective (see Wallace, 253; Muraoka §38.a–b.ib; and esp. Moule, 94–95). Furthermore, the object of a preposition is often definite without an article (Smyth §1128; BDF §255). Consequently, the decision must be made on the basis of the context, and the remainder of the verse clearly refers to all of Israel, including Judah, which the Lord led out of Egypt (see also 9:7). Thus, πᾶς is most naturally understood to be collective, referring to the "whole tribe," and further defining the "house of Israel" (so also NETS and *LES*).

The noun φυλή has the sense of a community of people (*GELS*, 723.a), and it can refer to a "subgroup of a nation characterized by a distinctive blood line" or a larger group like a "race" or "nation" (BDAG, 1069.1 and 2). The word occurs four times elsewhere in Amos. It seems to refer to a subgroup in 1:5, 8; and 3:12 (see discussion there), but in 3:2 the plural of φυλή seems to refer to all the other nations in contrast to the nation of Israel, which is the object of the Lord's special love; thus, in 3:2 it is a collective plural. In this verse where it is parallel to οἶκος Ισραηλ it makes sense to understand it as a collective singular ("the whole tribe") referring to the whole nation, "the house of Israel."

ἧς. Genitive relative pronoun, attracted to the case of its antecedent φυλῆς (see the helpful discussion in Wallace, 338–39) and functioning here as the direct object of ἀνήγαγον.

ἀνήγαγον. Aor act ind 1st sg ἀνάγω. Consummative aorist, stressing the completion of the act.

ἐκ γῆς. Separation, modifying ἀνήγαγον. The preposition ἐκ indicates dissociation from (*GELS*, 201.1) or separation from (BDAG, 295–96.1); this differs from the simple idea of origin or source. The genitive object of the preposition (γῆς) refers to a "land or ground" that is "belonging to or inhabited by a particular ethnic group or nation" (*GELS*, 129.4.d).

Αἰγύπτου. Genitive of apposition, giving a specific example of the category in the head noun (Wallace, 95). See the use of this phrase in 2:10 and 9:7.

λέγων. Pres act ptc nom masc sg λέγω (means; redundant adverbial participle used to introduce direct discourse; Wallace, 649–50). The present tense communicates action that is contemporaneous with the action of the main verb (ἐλάλησεν), which this adverbial participle modifies. The participle is modal and probably best classified as a participle of means. However, λέγων is employed so often in the LXX to "signal the onset of direct speech" (Muraoka §31.daa; 90.e) that this could be considered a separate category of the use of the participle in the LXX.

3:2 Πλὴν ὑμᾶς ἔγνων ἐκ πασῶν φυλῶν τῆς γῆς· διὰ τοῦτο ἐκδικήσω ἐφ' ὑμᾶς πάσας τὰς ἁμαρτίας ὑμῶν.

Πλὴν. Adverb used as a conjunction at the beginning of a sentence or clause and marking something contrastingly added for consideration (BDAG, 826.1; *GELS*, 564.3), here with the sense "only, solely." Interestingly, Symmachus revises it to μόνους. This verse begins the Lord's words to Israel that were announced in 3:1.

ὑμᾶς. Accusative direct object of ἔγνων. The second-person plural pronoun is fronted for emphasis and then repeated two more times in this short verse. See the discussion of it in 3:1.

ἔγνων. Aor act ind 1st sg γινώσκω. Constative aorist, viewing the action (relationship) as a whole. The Targum (Cathcart and Gordon, 80) renders the phrase "In you alone have I taken pleasure," apparently not wanting to limit God's knowledge; perhaps the LXX translator understood that the Lord's knowledge in 3:2 refers to his love and election of his people. The verb is used "in contexts relating to familiarity acquired through experience or association" (BDAG, 199).

ἐκ πασῶν φυλῶν. Partitive, modifying ὑμᾶς. The preposition is "indicating an entity out of which a component or part is singled out" (*GELS*, 201.2; BDAG, 295–96.1). This is the collective use of πᾶς ("all") with an anarthrous noun. See the discussion of this adjective in 3:1 and esp. Muraoka (§38.b.i) on this particular construction with πᾶς.

τῆς γῆς. Possible possessive genitive, showing that to which the tribes "belong"; but more likely this is an attributive genitive, giving an innate quality of the tribes: they are "of the earth," i.e., mortal and human in contrast to the Lord, who is sovereign over creation (4:13). It is common to have an article with a monadic noun (Wallace, 223–24).

διὰ τοῦτο. Causal. See 2:13. The flow of the argument is difficult to trace, and the sense of the phrase could also be inferential; either construal would make sense.

ἐκδικήσω. Fut act ind 1st sg ἐκδικέω. Predictive future. Although this verb can have the sense of "avenge," in this context it is better understood to mean to "bring punishment upon" (*GELS*, 206; see also 3:14).

ἐφ᾽ ὑμᾶς. Opposition, modifying ἐκδικήσω. The preposition ἐπί indicates those toward whom hostile action is directed (*GELS*, 266. III.4.a), as it often does in Amos (see ἐφ᾽ ὑμᾶς in 3:1). This preposition seems redundant in Greek, but it is the result of the translator following closely the Hebrew *Vorlage*, and ἐπί is often employed with ἐκδικήσω in the LXX (see *GELS*, 206.1). The accusative object of ἐπί (ὑμᾶς) picks up the earlier references to Israel (ὑμᾶς) in this verse and in 3:1 (also ἐφ᾽ ὑμᾶς).

πάσας τάς ἁμαρτίας. Accusative direct object of ἐκδικήσω; see *GELS* (206.1, s.v. ἐκδικέω) for a list of various attested constructions with ἐκδικήσω. The construction found here after ἐκδικήσω follows the pattern τι ἐπί τινα ("your sins upon you"). The article is expected with the noun in a collective πᾶς + noun construction (see the discussion of the collective us of πᾶς in 3:1).

ὑμῶν. Subjective genitive.

Each of the seven rhetorical questions in 3:3–6 is introduced by the conditional particle εἰ, and all seven expect a negative answer. The first six lead up to the climactic seventh question. On the basis of the inevitable connection between sin and punishment, the prophet argues in 3:7 that there is also a necessary connection between the words of the prophets and the acts of the Lord. The two questions in 3:8 are the conclusion and main point of this LXX context (3:1–8).

3:3 εἰ πορεύσονται δύο ἐπὶ τὸ αὐτὸ καθόλου ἐὰν μὴ γνωρίσωσιν ἑαυτούς;

εἰ. The conditional participle is often used to introduce direct yes/no questions in biblical Greek (see Muraoka §88; Conybeare and Stock §100; BDAG, 278.5.a; BDF §440.3; *GELS*, 190.3; cf. *CGCG* §42.3), and this is its function seven times in 3:3–6. In each of the seven sentences in which it occurs the two clauses of the sentences function much like a conditional sentence; in six of the implied conditions, if the action or state described by the verb in the second clause occurs, then the action or state in the first (εἰ) clause is expected to follow (like the protasis and apodosis of conditional sentences). The logic of the first sentence in 3:6 is opposite, and the εἰ clause contains the implied protasis (see 3:6). It is unlikely that this use of εἰ is a semitism, because, as Muraoka mentions (§88), it occurs several times in the LXX where there is no corresponding Hebrew particle (אם). In the five occurrences of εἰ in 3:3–5, it corresponds to an interrogative ה in Hebrew, and in its two occurrences in 3:6 it corresponds to the Hebrew conditional אם (see Muraoka §88 and Ehorn, 279, on the use of εἰ to introduce questions in the LXX).

πορεύσονται. Fut mid ind 3rd pl πορεύομαι. The future here is used instead of a subjunctive in a deliberative real question. The question is one of possibility (see Wallace, 465–67). Muraoka (*GELS* 577.I.1.c) suggests the meaning "to set off on a journey" in this context, but the verb could also mean "to journey, to travel." Verbs of translational motion are typically employed using the middle voice; it is clear that the subject is affected by the action of such verbs.

δύο. Nominative subject of πορεύσονται.

ἐπὶ τὸ αὐτὸ. Direction. This PP modifies πορεύσονται and is an idiom meaning "together" in this context (*GELS*, 267.III.12; BDF §233.1; see also 1:15). The construction τὸ αὐτό (article with the third-person personal pronoun, *GELS*, 104.2) is an adjectival identifying use of αὐτός, usually rendered "the same" (see Decker 2014a, 101–2).

καθόλου. Adverb, modifying πορεύσονται. Its meaning is flexible: "in any way, if ever" (*GELS*, 351), "on the whole, in general, at all" (LSJ, 856), or "entirely, completely" (BDAG, 493). In this context it emphasizes the certainty of the statement, and it underscores the proverbial or general nature of the truth communicated by the rhetorical question. Muraoka (§6.ea) comments that this adverb has the same sense whether articular or anarthrous.

ἐὰν μὴ. The conditional particle ἐάν plus a subjunctive verb constitute the protasis of a third-class conditional clause (Smyth §2323). With these "prospective conditions" the writer or speaker "presents fulfillment of the condition as very well possible/likely" in the future (*CGCG* §49.6). The conditional particle ἐάν and the negative particle (μή) are sometimes combined, mostly with the aorist subjunctive, as here, resulting in the meaning "if not, unless" (BDAG, 267–68.1.c.β).

γνωρίσωσιν. Aor act subj 3rd pl γνωρίζω. Constative aorist; the subjunctive is normally used with ἐὰν μή, and the sense is similar to the protasis of a conditional sentence ("If two do not know each other, how can they . . .").

ἑαυτούς. Accusative direct object of γνωρίσωσιν. The reflexive pronoun is functioning here like a reciprocal pronoun ("one another") and underscores "*the participation of the subject* in the verbal action" (Wallace, 350–51; emphasis in original).

3:4 εἰ ἐρεύξεται λέων ἐκ τοῦ δρυμοῦ αὐτοῦ θήραν οὐκ ἔχων; εἰ δώσει σκύμνος φωνὴν αὐτοῦ ἐκ τῆς μάνδρας αὐτοῦ καθόλου ἐὰν μὴ ἁρπάσῃ τι;

εἰ. See 3:3.
ἐρεύξεται. Fut mid ind 3rd sg ἐρεύγομαι. The future here is used instead of a subjunctive in a deliberative real question. The question is one of possibility (see Wallace, 465–67). "Roaring" is communicated in Greek in the middle voice, apparently because the subject is acting in its own interests (what Wallace, 418–19, classifies as the indirect middle), perhaps by calling attention to itself; Kemmer (267–70) notes that many speech and body action verbs are middle verbs in Greek. See also the synonym ὠρύομαι, which is always middle voice (*GELS*, 748; LSJ, 2038). This verb (ἐρεύγομαι) is used four times in the LXX to describe the roaring of a lion, or the Lord roaring like a lion; see also 1 Macc 3:4; Hos 11:10; and Amos 3:8. The word is used metaphorically of volcanoes discharging themselves, and it often has the sense "belch out" or "utter" when used of speech (LSJ, 686; see also BDAG, 391).

λέων. Nominative subject of ἐρεύξεται. The noun is indefinite, referring to "one member of a class, without specifying which member" (Wallace, 244).

ἐκ τοῦ δρυμοῦ. Origin, modifying ἐρεύξεται. The preposition ἐκ indicates the direction from which something comes (BDAG, 296.2), or the point of departure from (*GELS*, 201.5), i.e., "out of its thicket"; it does not indicate source, since the lion is the source. "Almost invariably the article is used when a possessive pronoun is attached to the noun" (Wallace, 239).

αὐτοῦ. Possessive genitive.
Θήραν. Accusative direct object of ἔχων. The noun is indefinite, referring to "one member of a class [a 'prey'], without specifying which member" (Wallace, 244).

οὐκ. Negative particle with the participle ἔχων. Normally in Classical Greek μή was used "with a circumstantial participle with the value of a conditional, otherwise οὐ" was used to negative a participle (Muraoka §83.bd; Robertson, 1137). In Koine Greek μή is normally used with participles (Robertson, 1136–39), but there are exceptions to that pattern (*GELS*, 511.c; BDF §426, 430; see also Muraoka §83.bd). It is interesting that in this context οὐ is employed with a conditional participle, suggesting the translator did not know the normal pattern for the use of negatives with participles in Classical and Koine Greek. Perhaps the best way to explain the use of οὐκ in this context is Robertson's general rule that in Koine "the presence of οὐ with the participle means that the negative is clear-cut and decisive" (1137–38), although the negative in the source text (here אֵין) may also have influenced the translator's choice of a negative (see the discussion in Robertson, 1138).

ἔχων. Pres act ptc nom masc sg ἔχω (conditional, modifying ἐρεύξεται and giving the condition for its occurrence). Muraoka (§31.dg) comments concerning this verse that this "circumstantial participle is parallel with a conditional clause" in the next sentence, and this construction is "semantically vague"; it is an example of stylistic variation on the part of the translator. Wallace (632) notes that this use of the participle is "almost always equivalent to the third-class condition [protasis formed by ἐάν + subjunctive]."

εἰ. See 3:3. The second question in the verse is very similar to the first one. Lions are the subjects of both questions, and both sentences refer to the fact that lions roar or make sounds when they have taken prey.

δώσει. Fut act ind 3rd sg δίδωμι. The future here is used instead of a subjunctive in a deliberative real question. The question is one of possibility (see Wallace, 465–67). This same language is used of the Lord, who "gives [his] voice" from Jerusalem in 1:2.

σκύμνος. Nominative subject of δώσει. The noun is indefinite, referring to "one member of a class, without specifying which member" (Wallace, 244), i.e., a lion "cub" (LEH, 560; LSJ, 1617). Here the "young lion" is old enough to capture prey.

φωνήν. Accusative direct object of δίδωμι; referring to the "roar" of the young lion (see *GELS*, 351, s.v. καθόλου).

αὐτοῦ. Possessive genitive.

ἐκ τῆς μάνδρας. Origin, modifying δώσει. The preposition ἐκ indicates the direction from which something comes (BDAG, 296.2); see the discussion of the parallel use of ἐκ earlier in this verse. "Almost invariably the article is used when a possessive pronoun is attached to the noun" (Wallace, 239). The object of the preposition refers to some sort of an "enclosed space" (LSJ, 1078), sometimes a "sheep fold" (BDAG, 615); here it must refer to the lion cub's "den."

αὐτοῦ. Possessive genitive.

καθόλου. Adverb, modifying δώσει, with the sense "in any way, if ever" (*GELS*, 351). See the discussion of this word in 3:3b; its presence there may have influenced the translator to add it here in 3:4b (see Arieti, 41; Park, 147; *pace* Tov and Polak, who do not call it an addition).

ἐὰν μή. See 3:3. The following phrase functions as the protasis of a conditional sentence.

ἁρπάσῃ. Aor act subj 3rd sg ἁρπάζω. Consummative aorist, focusing on the accomplishment of the activity; the subjunctive is normally used with ἐὰν μή and the sense is similar to the protasis of a third-class conditional sentence (Wallace, 696–99) or a more vivid future conditional (Smyth §2297, 2323). The subject ("it") is contained in the verbal.

τι. Accusative direct object of ἁρπάσῃ.

3:5 εἰ πεσεῖται ὄρνεον ἐπὶ τὴν γῆν ἄνευ ἰξευτοῦ; εἰ σχασθήσεται παγὶς ἐπὶ τῆς γῆς ἄνευ τοῦ συλλαβεῖν τι;

εἰ. See 3:3.

πεσεῖται. Fut mid ind 3rd sg πίπτω. The future is used instead of a subjunctive in a deliberative real question. The question is one of possibility; see Wallace, 465–67. The future of this verb is built off the stem πετ (*MBG*, 264). This is one of several verbs that arc always middle in the future tense (see BDF §77; Robertson, 356). The subject is clearly affected by the action of the verb, which is the general characteristic of the middle voice, but the reason why it has an active form in the present, aorist, and perfect is less clear (see the discussion in Muraoka §27.e).

ὄρνεον. Nominative subject of πεσεῖται. The noun is indefinite, referring to "one member of a class [i.e., a 'bird'], without specifying which member" (Wallace, 244).

ἐπὶ τὴν γῆν. Locative, modifying πεσεῖται; the preposition ἐπί "indicates a movement from a higher position on to something" (*GELS*, 266. III.1.b). The article is commonly used with the object of a preposition, and here it is used with a monadic noun (Wallace, 223–24); the object of the preposition (γῆν) has the sense "land, ground" in this verse (*GELS*, 129.4).

ἄνευ ἰξευτοῦ. Separation, modifying πεσεῖται. The preposition ἄνευ has the sense "with absence of" (*GELS*, 50). BDAG (78.a) suggests that it has the sense "not without the knowledge and consent of" when referring to persons. The genitive object of the preposition (ἰξευτοῦ) refers to a "fowler, bird catcher" (*GELS*, 341). This noun is only in Amos in the LXX (cf. 2x in 8:1).

εἰ. See 3:3.

σχασθήσεται. Fut pass ind 3rd sg σχάζω. The future here is used instead of a subjunctive in a deliberative real question. The question is one of possibility; see Wallace (465–67). This is a simple passive, and no agency is expressed. See the discussion of the verb's meaning in *GELS* (666), suggesting the sense "to move suddenly when there is no more constraint" and the meaning "spring" in this context; LSJ (1743.3) suggests the sense "let go" in this context. The verb is a LXX *hapax*.

παγίς. Nominative subject of σχασθήσεται. The noun is indefinite, referring to "one member of a class ('a trap'), without specifying which member" (Wallace, 244).

ἐπὶ τῆς γῆς. Locative, modifying σχασθήσεται. The preposition with the genitive refers to something "situated, moving, happening, or performed *on the surface of* [the ground]" (*GELS*, 263.I.2; emphasis original). The article is commonly used with the object of a preposition, and it is normal for a monadic noun (γῆς) to be articular (Wallace, 223–24); see the discussion above.

ἄνευ τοῦ συλλαβεῖν. Separation. See above.

τοῦ συλλαβεῖν. Aor act inf συλλαμβάνω; the infinitive is technically the object of the preposition ἄνευ (Muraoka §30.aba). The verb has the sense "to catch" when describing the action of a trap (*GELS*, 645.2). An infinitive is always articular in a prepositional phrase construction, indicating the case of the object of the preposition (ἄνευ always takes a genitive object). Wallace notes, "When the infinitive occurs after a preposition, the preposition combines with the infinitive for an adverbial force" (see Wallace, 588–89). See the discussion of this particular phrase in Muraoka (§30.abaa), where he suggests it is equivalent to a subordinate phrase.

τι. Accusative direct object of συλλαβεῖν.

3:6 εἰ φωνήσει σάλπιγξ ἐν πόλει καὶ λαὸς οὐ πτοηθήσεται; εἰ ἔσται κακία ἐν πόλει ἣν κύριος οὐκ ἐποίησεν;

εἰ. See 3:3.

Φωνήσει. Fut act ind 3rd sg φωνέω. The future is used here instead of a subjunctive in a deliberative real question. The question is one of possibility (see Wallace, 465–67), but it differs slightly from the other deliberative questions in the εἰ clauses in 3:3–6, since this clause functions like the protasis in the implied condition and thus the deliberation involves the complete sentence and not just whether the apodosis will occur. The verb has the general sense to "produce a sound or tone" (LSJ, 1967), and in this context it describes the sounding of a trumpet.

σάλπιγξ. Nominative subject of φωνήσει. The noun is indefinite, referring to "one member of a class [i.e., a 'trumpet'], without specifying which member" (Wallace, 244); see the similar idea in Hos 5:8.

ἐν πόλει. Locative, modifying Φωνήσει. The preposition ἐν indicates a place "in which some action takes place, or some state prevails" (*GELS*, 231.1.b). The dative object of ἐν (πόλει) is indefinite, referring to "one member of a class [i.e., a 'city'], without specifying which member" (Wallace, 244).

καὶ λαὸς οὐ πτοηθήσεται. Varying from the other sentences in this section (3:3–6), the second clause in this sentence functions like an apodosis in the implied conditional sentence. (See the discussion of εἰ in 3:3.) The relationship between the two parts of the sentence is difficult; it is conditional and temporal, and the καί here is probably best understood as introducing the apodosis (*GELS*, 354.11; BDAG, 494–95.1.b.δ), but the relationship between the two clauses in the sentence is also temporal (see MHT 2:422).

λαὸς. Nominative subject of πτοηθήσεται. This anarthrous noun is definite, since its referent is identified in the previous context by the city; they are the specific people in the city where the trumpet sounds.

οὐ πτοηθήσεται. Fut pass ind 3rd sg πτοέω. The future tense involves deliberation since the deliberative real question in the first clause of this sentence carries over to the second clause. See above in this verse on φωνήσει. The passive is a simple passive with no agency expressed. The understood cause of the people being terrified is the sounding of the trumpet. This is a stronger word for fear than the verb φοβέω in 3:8a; πτοέω has the sense "terrify, frighten" (BDAG, 895; *GELS*, 606.b). The negative particle οὐ is used here, as is the normal pattern, with an indicative verb.

εἰ. See 3:3.

ἔσται. Fut mid ind 3rd sg εἰμί. As is common in the questions in this context, the future is used instead of a subjunctive in a deliberative real question. The question is one of possibility (see Wallace, 465–67).

κακία. Predicate nominative. The sentence is simplest if the subject of the verb is understood to be contained in the verb ("there will be"), and κακία is understood as a predicate nominative; κακία is the normal Greek word for "evil," and if that is its meaning here it suggests the Lord is directly responsible for evil. Probably in this context it should be understood to mean "trouble," "distressing circumstances," or "misfortune" (BDAG, 500; *GELS*, 356.2; Dines 1991, 105; Glenny 2013b, 65–66; Glenny 2009, 194–96), although such a rendering does not resolve the theological questions concerning the Lord's relationship to evil and suffering.

ἐν πόλει. See the discussion of the prepositional phrase above in 3:6; here it modifies ἔσται.

ἣν. Accusative direct object of ἐποίησεν. The relative pronoun introduces the relative clause that serves as the protasis of the implied condition: "If the Lord did not do it, then will there be . . . ?" The antecedent of this relative pronoun is ambiguous in the LXX; it could be κακία or πόλις. If πόλις is the antecedent it removes the theological issues of the Lord being directly responsible for κακία. But it is most likely that κακία is the antecedent of the relative pronoun, or else it would not be necessary in the sentence. I have tried to reflect the ambiguity in the translation, and either way the emphasis is the Lord's sovereign control of all things.

κύριος. Nominative subject of οὐκ ἐποίησεν. Although anarthrous, it is definite because it is a monadic noun.

οὐκ ἐποίησεν. Aor act ind 3rd sg ποιέω. The verb should probably be understood as a consummative aorist, focusing on the accomplishment of the activity by the Lord who is sovereign over it, but the aorist could also be understood to be constative, viewing the action as a whole. The negative particle οὐ is normal with an indicative verb.

3:7 διότι οὐ μὴ ποιήσῃ κύριος ὁ θεὸς πρᾶγμα, ἐὰν μὴ ἀποκαλύψῃ παιδείαν αὐτοῦ πρὸς τοὺς δούλους αὐτοῦ τοὺς προφήτας.

διότι. This conjunction could be causal or inferential (*GELS*, 172.1 and 4; BDAG, 251.1 and 2; LEH, 117). Although some have understood its force to be causal (Dines 1991, 105–6, "because"; Arieti, 42–43, "since"; Brenton, "for"), "the logic of the passage requires the conjunction to be inferential here," rendered "wherefore, therefore" (see Glenny 2013b, 66, for a fuller discussion). The relationship between the revelation of the Lord to his prophets and his actions in 3:7–8 is not the cause of the previous connections between actions in 3:3–6. Rather, the relationship between the revelation of the Lord to his prophets and his actions in 3:7–8 is an inference the author draws on the basis of their analogy with the relationship between the actions described in 3:3–6. The Creator-Lord has established connections between events, many based on natural laws (3:3–6). The connections in the previous verses (3–6) illustrate the connection between the words of the prophets and the Lord's actions that is described in 3:7–8; that connection between the prophets' words and the Lord's actions is ordained by the Lord.

οὐ μὴ ποιήσῃ. Aor act subj 3rd sg ποιέω. Aorist subjunctive with οὐ μή for emphatic negation. MSS B, V, and Q have the future tense here (ποιήσει), which is apparently a confusion of the vowels in the ending of the verb; see Thackeray (§6, esp. §6.20, 21). There are variants throughout this section reflecting confusion of these vowels (ει and η), which could have resulted from difficulty in distinguishing them when spoken or from grammatical changes favoring one form or the other.

κύριος ὁ θεός. Nominative subject of ποιήσῃ. The proper noun κύριος is monadic when it refers to the Lord, and thus although it is anarthrous, it is definite. This is the first of seventeen occurrences of the title κύριος ὁ θεός in the R-H text of Amos; nine times it is part of the longer title κύριος ὁ θεὸς ὁ παντοκράτωρ. This full title is employed to translate several different Hebrew names for God, but the one thing they all have in common is that they contain the tetragrammaton (יהוה). The name ὁ θεός should probably be understood to be in apposition to and further describing κύριος. It is common to have an article with a monadic noun like θεός.

πρᾶγμα. Accusative direct object of ποιήσῃ. It is indefinite, not specifying a particular thing or matter, and thus rendered "anything."

ἐὰν μή. See 3:3. These two words introduce a clause that functions as the protasis of a conditional sentence (Smyth §2286; Muraoka §89.ab).

ἀποκαλύψῃ. Aor act subj 3rd sg ἀποκαλύπτω. This is probably a consummative aorist, focusing on the accomplishment of the activity by the one who is sovereign over it. The subjunctive is used here in the future more vivid (or third class) conditional sentence introduced by ἐὰν μή (Smyth §2297).

παιδείαν. Accusative direct object of ἀποκαλύψῃ. Abstract nouns are commonly anarthrous, but that does not mean they are indefinite. Robertson (794) writes, "[N]o vital difference was felt between articular and anarthrous abstract nouns" (see Wallace, 249, where this quotation is also found). This important word can have the sense of "chastisement, instruction, teaching," and even "culture, the result of teaching" (LSJ, 1286; LEH, 455; BDAG, 748-49.1 and 2; *NIDNTTE*, 3:584-90). Muraoka (*GELS*, 587.2) suggests that in this context it refers to a "body of knowledge to be inculcated." However, in the Septuagint the ideas of divine education and divine discipline are both expressed by this word, and the latter is suggested also by this context (see Pouchelle, 44-45). The Hebrew corresponding to παιδείαν αὐτοῦ is סודו ("his secret"); the translator may for some reason have read the Hebrew as a form from I יסר ("to instruct"), or perhaps he had a source text that differed from the MT. Compare the rendering of סוד by παιδεία in LXX Ezek 13:9.

αὐτοῦ. Subjective genitive. The Lord is the one who functions as the instructor of the παιδεία. This pronoun corresponds to a pronominal suffix in the MT, but it is not found in some manuscripts and versions (B, W, Ziegler); the correspondence with the Hebrew and its presence in the vast majority of manuscripts favors its inclusion.

πρὸς τοὺς δούλους αὐτοῦ. Direction, modifying ἀποκαλύψῃ. The preposition indicates the one spoken to or addressed "with verbs of speaking, addressing, etc." (*GELS*, 589.III.2). The article is commonly used with objects of prepositions, and it is consistently used with nouns that have possessive pronouns attached to them, pointing out particular objects.

αὐτοῦ. Possessive genitive.

τοὺς προφήτας. In simple apposition with τοὺς δούλους, giving a different designation of τοὺς δούλους that further clarifies who they are (Wallace, 96). The article here indicates they are particular prophets, in this context the Lord's.

3:8 λέων ἐρεύξεται, καὶ τίς οὐ φοβηθήσεται; κύριος ὁ θεὸς ἐλάλησεν, καὶ τίς οὐ προφητεύσει;

The logic or argument of the two sentences in this verse is that of conditional sentences, with each question containing two inseparable elements, like the sentences in 3:3-7. The first clause in both sentences functions rhetorically like the protasis in a conditional sentence, and the second clause in both functions like the apodosis. The καί in each sentence is probably best understood as introducing the apodosis, as it did in 3:6 (see above). The first sentence is an analogy from the natural realm, illustrating the truth in the second. See Glenny (2013b, 66-67) on the argument of the verse.

λέων. Nominative subject of ἐρεύξεται. It is anarthrous and indefinite (see the discussion of this noun in 3:4). The asyndeton at the beginning of this verse follows the Hebrew. However, often in Greek asyndeton is "used in contexts of close connection, such as moving from *generic* to *specific*" (Runge, 23), and that seems to be what is happening here; 3:8 is the climax of the section 3:1-8, and it is the most specific expression of the main point of the passage.

ἐρεύξεται. Fut mid ind 3rd sg ἐρεύγομαι. See 3:4, where the same noun and verb combination occurs; in 3:4 the logic of the sentence requires that these words were part of the implied apodosis of the sentence, but here they are the implied protasis. Here the future-tense verb is best understood as a gnomic future, true of any time and not referring to any specific event (Wallace, 571; BDF §349). The implied condition is best understood to be a "neutral condition," simply communicating that if the action in the protasis is fulfilled, then the action in the apodosis will follow (*CGCG* §49.5; Smyth §2297 calls it an "emotional future" condition). Roaring is communicated in Greek in the middle voice, apparently because the subject is acting in its own interests.

καί. See 3:6 on καὶ λαὸς οὐ πτοηθήσεται.

τίς. Nominative subject of φοβηθήσεται.

οὐ φοβηθήσεται. Fut mid ind 3rd sg φοβέω. In the question being asked in the sentence, the future tense invites deliberation, although in the implied condition, the answer to the question is understood to be positive (i.e., "If a lion roars, then everyone will be afraid"). As with the previous verb, the future tense here could be classified as a gnomic future, true of any time and not referring to any specific event (Wallace, 571; BDF §349). See the discussion of -θη- verbs in the Introduction to this volume. As expected, the negative particle οὐ is employed with the indicative mood. A stronger word for fear (πτοέω) is found in 3:6a.

κύριος ὁ θεὸς. Nominative subject of ἐλάλησεν. See the discussion of this title and the individual words in 3:7.

ἐλάλησεν. Aor act ind 3rd sg λαλέω. This is probably best understood to be a gnomic aorist, not referring to any particular event but rather to something that is timeless. The other three verbs in the implied conditions in 3:8 are future, and the proverbial nature of the statements in the verse, as well as the gnomic future tenses, points to a timeless event. (See Glenny 2013b, 67, on the problem of the time of the action in 3:7–8.) The aorist makes this action more definite than the events described by the three future-tense verbs in the verse, but it does not require it be past time from the perspective of the author. "The description of the Lord's revelation to the prophets as in 3:7, which is perhaps the contemporary application of what 'the Lord has spoken' (3:8b) through the biblical prophets, point[s] to the fact that the prophecy is relevant to the readers" (Glenny 2013b, 67).

τίς. Nominative subject of προφητεύσει.

οὐ προφητεύσει. Fut act ind 3rd sg προφητεύω. In this question the future tense involves deliberation, although in the implied condition the answer is understood to be positive, i.e., the prophets will prophesy. The future tense could be classified again as a gnomic future true of any time and not referring to a specific event (Wallace, 571; BDF §349).

Amos 3:9–15

⁹"Proclaim to the districts among the Assyrians and to the districts of Egypt and say, 'Assemble on the mountain of Samaria and see many marvelous things in the midst of her and the oppression in her. ¹⁰And she did not know what things will be before her,' says the Lord, 'those who are storing up unrighteousness and misery in their districts.'" ¹¹Therefore, thus says the Lord God, "Tyre, your land round about shall be made desolate, and he will bring down from you your strength and your districts will be spoiled." ¹²Thus says the Lord, "Just as when the shepherd pulls out of the mouth of the lion two legs or a lobe of an ear, so will the sons of Israel be pulled out who dwell in Samaria before the tribe and in Damascus." ¹³"Hear, O Priests, and bear witness to the house of Jacob," says the Lord, the God who is Almighty, ¹⁴"for in the day when I will punish the ungodly acts of Israel upon him, also I will bring

punishment upon the altars of Bethel, and the horns on the altar will be torn down and they will fall upon the ground. ¹⁵I will demolish and I will strike the colonnaded house in addition to the summerhouse, and ivory houses will perish and many other houses will be added," says the Lord.

This portion begins with a summons to the Assyrians and the Egyptians to gather together at Samaria, surprisingly not to be judged but to observe Israel's sins of "oppression" and the Lord's judgment of them.

3:9 Ἀπαγγείλατε χώραις ἐν Ἀσσυρίοις καὶ ἐπὶ τὰς χώρας τῆς Αἰγύπτου καὶ εἴπατε Συνάχθητε ἐπὶ τὸ ὄρος Σαμαρείας καὶ ἴδετε θαυμαστὰ πολλὰ ἐν μέσῳ αὐτῆς καὶ τὴν καταδυναστείαν τὴν ἐν αὐτῇ·

Ἀπαγγείλατε. Aor act impv 2nd pl ἀπαγγέλλω. The aorist points to a specific occurrence (Fanning, 326), and the plural command is from the Lord to heralds, apparently from Israel, who are to call the Assyrians and Egyptians to gather together in Mount Samaria to see what is going to happen there.

χώραις. Dative indirect object of Ἀπαγγείλατε (Muraoka §22.wb). The noun (χώρα) is definite because it is specified by the following PP. It occurs seven times in LXX Twelve and four of those times are in 3:9–11 (Glenny 2013b, 67), where it always renders ארמון. Here it refers to the "smaller districts within a country, region" (*GELS*, 739.1.b), which probably would have been thought of as administrative districts, especially in Egypt (LSJ, 2015.II.3); see the occurrence of χώρα later in the verse with reference to Egypt. The corresponding word in the MT, ארמון ("palace, fortress"), is a word that gave the Septuagint translators trouble because it is rare in postbiblical Hebrew. This Hebrew word occurs twelve times in Amos; for a discussion of its rendering as θεμέλια ("foundation") in the Oracles against the Nations in 1:3–2:16, see 1:4 and Glenny (2009, 78–79). In its five occurrences in Amos outside of the Oracles to the Nations (3:9–11 [4x]; and 6:8), it is always rendered with χώρα.

ἐν Ἀσσυρίοις. Locative, modifying the χώραις and indicating that the districts are "among" the Assyrians (*GELS*, 231.2). The dative object of the preposition, Ἀσσυρίοις, differs from the Hebrew "Ashdod" and makes sense with LXX readers' knowledge of the conquerors of the Northern Kingdom.

ἐπὶ τὰς χώρας. Direction, modifying Ἀπαγγείλατε; it is parallel to the dative indirect object χώραις (see above) and functions like a second indirect object. The preposition ἐπί here indicates "one to whom or that to which action, attention, thought, emotion, utterance, etc.

are directed"; here it is utterance (*GELS*, 266.III.4.d; see also BDAG, 366.14). In the Hebrew there are two parallel prepositional phrases at the beginning of this verse, but the translator varied the pattern, with a dative indirect object and a PP. The accusative article clarifies that the object of the preposition is definite. See the discussion of χώρας above in this verse.

τῆς Αἰγύπτου. Genitive of place, indicating where the districts are located. The genitive article is consistent with Apollonius' canon (Wallace, 239–40). Muraoka (§5.cb) notes that Αἴγυπτος is normally anarthrous when it is in the genitive and modifies the head noun; this is an exception to the normal pattern.

εἴπατε. Aor act impv 2nd pl λέγω. As in the first clause in the verse, the aorist command points to a specific occurrence (Fanning, 326), and the plural command is from the Lord to heralds, who are perhaps again, like in the first sentence in the verse, the recipients of the oracle. The rest of the verse contains the contents of what the heralds are commanded to say to the Assyrians and Egypt and functions as the direct object of the parallel commands Ἀπαγγείλατε and εἴπατε.

Συνάχθητε. Aor pass impv 2nd pl συνάγω. This aorist command ("assemble"), like the preceding one, also points to a specific occurrence (Fanning, 326), and the verb has a consummative idea, stressing the completion of the act. The passive of συνάγω is intransitive when the subjects are human, as here (see *GELS*, 651.1.c), and this is an example of a -θη- aorist passive form that has a middle meaning (see the Introduction).

ἐπὶ τὸ ὄρος Σαμαρείας. Locative, modifying Συνάχθητε, and ἐπί indicates "a surface on which some action takes place" (*GELS*, 266.III.3); here the action is the assembling of the people. The object of ἐπί (ὄρος) corresponds to a plural form in the Hebrew, but the LXX is referring to the mountain on which the capital of the Northern Kingdom was situated (LXX.E, 2349; see also Muraoka §21.c, who thinks this is a collective use of the singular).

Σαμαρείας. Genitive of apposition or, possibly, possessive genitive. Used with the singular noun, the genitive of apposition would provide a specific example of the category mentioned in the head noun (Wallace, 95–100).

ἴδετε. Aor act impv 2nd pl ὁράω. The plural command is addressed to the inhabitants of Assyria and the districts of Egypt. The aorist imperative seems to picture a specific command "to be done in a particular instance" (Fanning, 328); it is probably a constative aorist, looking at the specific action as a whole.

θαυμαστὰ πολλά. Accusative direct object of ἴδετε. Abstract substantives are commonly anarthrous and qualitative, as here. The neuter plural form of this word normally refers to the works of God on behalf of his people, for which he deserves praise (Exod 34:10; Josh 3:5; Tob 12:22; Sir 11:4). However, in the prophets the substantival use of the word refers to God's judgment, sometimes in an eschatological context (Isa 25:1; Mic 7:15; Dan 12:6; in Isa 3:3 it functions as an adjective; see also Dan Th 8:24). The use of the word elsewhere in the prophets suggests that it refers to the Lord's judgment of Samaria, perhaps at the hand of Antiochus (Dan 8:20–26; cf. 12:6 and Dan Th 8:24), which the Assyrians and the Egyptians are being summoned to view (see Glenny 2013b, 67–68).

ἐν μέσῳ. Locative, modifying the substantive θαυμαστά. The preposition ἐν "indicates a place . . . in which some action takes place or some state prevails" (*GELS*, 231.1.b); μέσῳ is a dative adjective functioning as a substantival object of ἐν. Although it is anarthrous, the object of the preposition is definite (Wallace, 247).

αὐτῆς. Genitive of possession, probably referring to Samaria.

καί. Coordinating conjunction, connecting the two direct objects of ἴδετε (*GELS*, 352.1.a).

τὴν καταδυναστείαν. Accusative direct object of ἴδετε. Abstract substantives are commonly anarthrous, but occasionally they are articular where the presence of the article contributes to the understanding (Wallace, 249); here the two articles clarify that the following prepositional phrase modifies this noun, but that is the natural understanding whether they are present or not. MSS B, V, L, C, Swete, and Ziegler do not have the article here, but A, Q, W, and Rahlfs include it. This noun, which refers to "oppression," is a neologism, occurring only in the LXX and literature based on it (LEH, 313). It occurs five times in the LXX, and in Exod 6:7 it describes the Egyptians' "oppression" of the Israelites.

τήν. The accusative article functions as an adjectivizer, changing the following PP (ἐν αὐτῇ) into an attributive modifier of τὴν καταδυναστείαν. Ziegler, L, and C do not include the article here, but B, A, V, W, Swete, and R-H all include it, and the evidence for it being included here seems strong.

ἐν αὐτῇ. Locative, modifying καταδυναστείαν, and the preposition ἐν "indicates a place . . . in which some action takes place or some state prevails" (*GELS*, 231.1.b); αὐτῇ is the dative object of ἐν.

3:10 καὶ οὐκ ἔγνω ἃ ἔσται ἐναντίον αὐτῆς, λέγει κύριος, οἱ θησαυρίζοντες ἀδικίαν καὶ ταλαιπωρίαν ἐν ταῖς χώραις αὐτῶν.

καὶ. Coordinating conjunction, connecting clauses; the following clause gives "parenthetical, supplementary information" (*GELS*, 354.1.b.7).

οὐκ ἔγνω. Aor act ind 3rd sg γινώσκω. Constative aorist. The third singular implied subject of the verb must be Samaria, which is also the reference intended by the following pronoun αὐτῆς; there is no other singular subject in the preceding context that is as suitable, since the references to Assyria and Egypt go together and they are not addressed individually. The corresponding Hebrew verb is third-person plural.

ἃ. Nominative subject of ἔσται. The relative clause, which is in the form of indirect speech, serves as the object of the verb ἔγνω.

ἔσται. Fut mid ind 3rd sg εἰμί. Predictive future.

ἐναντίον αὐτῆς. This adverb functions as a preposition with a genitive (BDAG, 330.1; Muraoka §26.f). See the discussion of this semi-preposition in Sollamo (21–28, 131–33, 151, 317); it generally means "in the presence of, before," as is most likely here, and it can be local or temporal (LSJ, 554); here it is likely temporal ("she did not know what was before her"). But it can also at times have the sense "opposed, hostile" (see *GELS*, 233–34), which would also be possible here. See Glenny (2009, 128) on the rendering of this phrase; the translator apparently did not know the Hebrew word נכחה ("right, straight," 4x in MT as a substantive and only this one time in MT Twelve) and took it as its homograph meaning "front, opposite" (see *HALOT*, 2:698–99).

λέγει. Pres act ind 3rd sg λέγω. Instantaneous present, a usage that is common with verbs of speaking since the action is often completed as soon as it is spoken (Wallace, 517); λέγει κύριος occurs thirty-nine times in LXX Amos with the verb in the aorist and present tenses (see 1:6).

κύριος. Nominative subject of λέγει; see 1:2 on the absence of the article with κύριος.

οἱ θησαυρίζοντες. Pres act ptc nom masc pl θησαυρίζω (substantival; i.e., "those who are storing up"). The antecedent of this articular participle is unclear (see the discussion in Glenny 2013b, 68). It is apparently in apposition to and describing further either (1) Samaria (i.e., "she" the implied subject of οὐκ ἔγνω and the referent of αὐτῆς ["her"]), (2) the "Assyrians" and "Egypt," who are called to witness the events in Samaria, or (3) the subject of the immediately preceding relative clause "what things will be before her" (ἃ ἔσται ἐναντίον αὐτῆς). Muraoka (§87.c) understands the plural articular participle construction to be specifying the preceding impersonal third singular verb (ἔγνω) and referring to Samaria. But the fact that Samaria is always third-person feminine singular in this context suggests this masculine plural participle does not refer to it. Furthermore, this understanding of the participle phrase makes no sense with διὰ τοῦτο at the beginning of 3:11. The mention of their "districts" (χώρα) later in 3:10 suggests this participle construction is connected with the "districts of Egypt" in 3:9 and the "districts" of Tyre in 3:11, and that in the LXX Assyria, Egypt, and Tyre are all to be understood as the group that is "storing up unrighteousness and misery in their districts" in 3:10b. However, there is no real connection of these groups in the passage except the word "districts" (χώρα). The simplest explanation, which also combines the strength of the previous option and makes sense of what follows in 3:11 (διὰ τοῦτο . . .) is that this participle construction in 3:10b is a description and specification of "what things will be before her [Samaria or Israel]" (ἃ ἔσται ἐναντίον αὐτῆς), i.e., "those who are storing up unrighteousness and misery in their districts" are "before her." And "those things which are before her" involve the people of Tyre, since as a result of the description in 3:10b Tyre will be brought down and destroyed (3:11).

ἀδικίαν καὶ ταλαιπωρίαν. Parallel accusative direct objects of θησαυρίζοντες, i.e., "unrighteousness and misery." Abstract substantives are commonly anarthrous and qualitative, as here.

ἐν ταῖς χώραις. Locative, modifying the participle θησαυρίζοντες; the preposition "indicates a place . . . in which some action takes place or some state prevails" (*GELS*, 231.1.b). It is normal to have an article with a noun when it is modified by a possessive pronoun. See the discussion of χώραις in 3:9.

αὐτῶν. Possessive genitive.

3:11 διὰ τοῦτο τάδε λέγει κύριος ὁ θεός Τύρος, κυκλόθεν ἡ γῆ σου ἐρημωθήσεται, καὶ κατάξει ἐκ σοῦ ἰσχύν σου, καὶ διαρπαγήσονται αἱ χῶραί σου.

διὰ τοῦτο. Inferential. See the discussion of this formula in 2:13. The causal idea, which is common for this formula, would not make sense in this verse; here it is inferential and indicates the result of the actions of the nations in 3:10b (i.e., "therefore"), a sense it has in the LXX (see the NETS rendering of 3:9 and LEH, 135). The words διὰ τοῦτο τάδε λέγει κύριος are also found at the beginning of 5:16 and 7:17, where they also introduce an announcement of judgment and διὰ τοῦτο has the sense "therefore."

τάδε λέγει κύριος. See 1:6. This introductory formula is found at the beginning of all the Oracles against the Nations in chapters 1–2, except the first one (see 1:3).

κύριος ὁ θεός. See 3:7.

Τύρος. Nominative for a vocative. Often even in the nominative masculine singular, the vocative has the same form as the nominative (Smyth §233, 249; Zerwick §33). The patristic interpreters bear witness to two different interpretations of Τύρος, which are discussed in Dines (1991, 108–9). It could either be understood to be a vocative, addressing Tyre in this verse, or it could be "involved in the grammar of κυκλόθεν," functioning as the object of κυκλόθεν, which would then function as a preposition (i.e., "your [Israel's] land around Tyre"); but then we would expect Τύρος to be a genitive (see BDAG, 1021). To complicate matters further, some manuscripts have a καί following Τύρος (see V and Ziegler), and if the coordinating conjunction would be included Τύρος and κυκλόθεν ἡ γῆ ("your [Israel's] land round about") would be parallel subjects in this clause, and κυκλόθεν would function as an adverb. In our text without καί, Τύρος is best understood to be a vocative addressing Tyre. This reading has the better manuscript support, and this understanding is simplest and is also consistent with the prophetic oracles against Tyre in 1:9–10, Jeremiah 29, and Ezekiel 28–29. The Hebrew word corresponding to Τύρος is "adversary" (צר), which has the same radicals as the Hebrew word for Tyre. The difference between the Hebrew and Greek texts changes the focus of the verse from the desolation of Samaria (Israel) by an adversary (in the MT) to the desolation of Tyre (in the LXX). It is possible the translator and the early readers of the LXX would have connected this verse with the destruction of Tyre by Alexander (Glenny 2009, 139, 160).

κυκλόθεν. Adverb, meaning "round about" (*GELS*, 417). This word can also function as a preposition with the genitive, and it is possible it could be functioning as a preposition with σου as its object (LEH, 359). But the order of words in the Greek, which follows the Hebrew, does not lend itself to this understanding. See the discussion above in this verse regarding Τύρος, which is a vocative and cannot serve as the object of κυκλόθεν.

ἡ γῆ. Nominative subject of ἐρημωθήσεται. It is normal to have an article modifying a noun modified by a possessive pronoun.

σου. Possessive genitive, modifying γῆ. This pronoun is apparently referring to Tyre, the subject that is being addressed in the Lord's statement. There is no corresponding word in the MT.

ἐρημωθήσεται. Fut pass ind 3rd sg ἐρημόω. Predictive future; simple passive, indicating the subject receives the action (Wallace, 439). The verb has the sense "lay waste," and it is an apparent plus in the LXX to make sense of the differences between the Hebrew and Greek (see above on Τύρος).

κατάξει. Fut act ind 3rd sg κατάγω. Predictive future. The subject of this verb is not given. If it was the Lord, it would be expected to be first-person singular ("I will bring down"), so it is apparently referring to a nation (perhaps known to the readers) or perhaps to Alexander the Great (see above on Τύρος), who will bring down Tyre.

ἐκ σοῦ. Separation, modifying κατάξει. The preposition indicates "dissociation" (*GELS*, 201.1).

ἰσχύν. Accusative direct object of κατάξει.

σου. Possessive genitive, modifying ἰσχύν.

διαρπαγήσονται. Fut pass ind 3rd sg διαρπάζω. Predictive future, i.e., "will be spoiled"; simple passive, indicating the subject receives the action (Wallace, 439; Thackeray §18.3.iii.a, calls this future passive form a Hellenistic guttural tense).

αἱ χῶραί. Nominative subject of διαρπαγήσονται. See the discussion of this word in 3:9. It is normal to have an article with a noun modified by a possessive pronoun.

σου. Possessive genitive, modifying χῶραί.

3:12 τάδε λέγει κύριος Ὃν τρόπον ὅταν ἐκσπάσῃ ὁ ποιμὴν ἐκ στόματος τοῦ λέοντος δύο σκέλη ἢ λοβὸν ὠτίου, οὕτως ἐκσπασθήσονται οἱ υἱοὶ Ισραηλ οἱ κατοικοῦντες ἐν Σαμαρείᾳ κατέναντι φυλῆς καὶ ἐν Δαμασκῷ ἱερεῖς.

The formula "Thus says the Lord" indicates that this verse is a new oracle. The verse compares the "rescue" of Israelites in Samaria and priests in Damascus to the rescue of body parts from the mouth of a lion. Thus, since the parts saved cannot survive, it is no rescue at all, but rather violent destruction.

τάδε λέγει κύριος. This introductory formula occurs thirteen times in LXX Amos; see the discussion at 1:3 and 1:6. It is employed seven times in the Oracles against the Nations (1:3–2:16) to introduce a new oracle, as it does here.

Ὃν τρόπον. See the discussion of this idiomatic adverbial accusative phrase (BDF §160; Smyth §1608) in 2:13; it has the sense "just as."

ὅταν. Conjunction introducing a clause preceding the main clause; here it is probably a doublet and "almost pleonastic" with the preceding Ὃν τρόπον (*GELS*, 510.2.b). This conjunction or particle has a temporal sense (BDAG, 730), and with a subjunctive verb it often approaches the meaning of ἐάν (BDAG, 730–31.1.a; see also *CGCG* § 47.9 and the use of ὅταν in 3:14). With Ὃν τρόπον the temporal sense of the conjunction is weakened.

ἐκσπάσῃ. Aor act subj 3rd sg ἐκσπάω. Constative aorist, viewing the action as a whole. The subjunctive here is what Wallace (479–80) calls the use of it in an indefinite temporal clause (here with ὅταν). The verb has the sense "pull out" (*GELS*, 216).

ὁ ποιμήν. Nominative subject of ἐκσπάσῃ. This generic noun (and article) distinguishes shepherds, as a class, from other classes.

ἐκ στόματος. Separation, modifying ἐκσπάσῃ; the preposition ἐκ indicates "dissociation" (*GELS*, 201.1). The noun (στόματος) is definite, as is often the case for an object of a preposition without an article, and the noun should be understood to be generic, not referring to a specific "mouth of a lion."

τοῦ λέοντος. Possessive genitive, modifying στόμα; it is a generic noun, referring to a class, not a specific "lion." The article with a generic noun distinguishes one class from another (Wallace, 227–30).

δύο σκέλη. Accusative direct object of ἐκσπάσῃ. This should probably be understood as generic also. The noun refers to "legs" of animals or humans (*GELS*, 623; LSJ, 1606; Prov 26:7).

ἤ. Disjunctive particle, marking alternatives, and found here between "related and similar terms, where one can take the place of the other or one supplements the other" (see BDAG, 432.1.a.α).

λοβόν. Accusative direct object of ἐκσπάσῃ. An indefinite, generic noun, a "lobe" of an ear.

ὠτίου. Partitive genitive; the lobe is part of the "ear." An indefinite generic noun.

οὕτως. Adverb "underlying the notion of comparability and analogy"; here with anaphoric reference (*GELS*, 515.A).

ἐκσπασθήσονται. Fut pass ind 3rd pl ἐκσπάω. Predictive future; simple passive with the subjects receiving the action. See its use earlier in the verse.

οἱ υἱοί. Nominative subject of ἐκσπασθήσονται. This is the basic individualizing use of the article pointing out a specific group (see Wallace, 216–17).

Ισραηλ. Genitive of relationship.

οἱ κατοικοῦντες. Pres act ptc nom masc pl κατοικέω (attributive). Customary present indicating an ongoing state (Wallace, 521–22). The participle with the article is adjectival, and the participial phrase is in apposition to the preceding subject, οἱ υἱοὶ Ισραηλ.

ἐν Σαμαρείᾳ. Locative, modifying κατοικοῦντες. The preposition ἐν "indicates a place in which some object is found or placed" (*GELS*, 231.1).

κατέναντι φυλῆς. Locative, modifying κατοικοῦντες; κατέναντι is an adverb, which functions as a preposition with a genitive object, as here (BDAG, 530–31.2.b). It can have the sense "against, in opposition to" (see Mic 2:8) or "before, in the presence of" (Amos 4:3; Joel 1:16; Zech 14:4; *GELS*, 388). The latter sense is required here. See also the discussion of ἐναντίον in 3:10.

Sawyer argues that φυλῆς should be understood as definite, and it does have the article in some manuscripts (B, V, and Swete's edition; A, Q, R-H, and Ziegler do not have the article; it is indefinite in NETS and definite in *LES*). Also it is common for anarthrous objects of prepositions to be definite (Wallace, 247). Sawyer argues further, "[F]rom the LXX point of view, 'the Tribe' par excellence was the tribe of Judah" (124). The use of φυλή elsewhere in the LXX offers support for this argument (see Mic 6:9; Ezek 12:13 [or 21:18]; and Ruth 3:11; and the discussion in Sawyer; and in Glenny 2013b, 69–70). Thus, there is good reason to understand φυλῆς to be definite, whether there is an article in the text or not. And if it is understood to be definite and Sawyer is right about referent of "the tribe" in the LXX, "it would mean that the devastation of Samaria takes place before Judah, or as Judah, Israel's neighbor, watches. This could be a reference to 722 BCE" (Glenny 2013b, 70; see also Dines 1991, 114–15). Brenton understands the noun to be anarthrous and renders the prepositional phrase "in the presence of *a* foreign tribe," apparently referring to some enemy of Israel. The LXX rendering κατέναντι φυλῆς differs substantially from our modern Hebrew texts (בפאת מטה—"with the corner of a couch," ESV, NRSV); for a discussion of these differences, see Glenny (2009, 134–35, 160–63).

καί. Coordinating conjunction, connecting parallel PPs (*GELS*, 352.1.a).

ἐν Δαμασκῷ ἱερεῖς. Locative, modifying κατοικοῦντες and parallel to the preceding PP. The preposition "indicates a place in which some object is found or placed" (*GELS*, 231.1). The rendering καὶ ἐν Δαμασκῷ differs from our modern Hebrew texts (ובדמשק—"and part," ESV, NRSV); see Glenny (2009, 128–29, 160–63).

ἱερεῖς. Vocative of address. The function of this word is debated; some think it should be understood as a vocative introducing 3:13 (LXX.D, 1180; LXX.E, 2349), and others connect it with 3:12 and understand it to be a nominative further explaining the second group in Israel that is "rescued" from the coming judgment (who are "in Damascus as priests"; see NETS). With the latter view "priests" is in apposition to those who dwell in Damascus. The first understanding, that the word is a vocative introducing verse 13, is supported by the patristic commentators (Dines 1991, 111–12), to whom this understanding apparently made good sense in view of 3:14; this is also the function of the word in Vaticanus (see Glenny 2013b, 20–22). The latter understanding, that ἱερεῖς is the last word in 3:12, is the preference of most MSS and modern editions (Swete, R-H, and Ziegler), and it also finds support in that ἱερεῖς (plural) is apparently the rendering of the last word in the Hebrew of 3:12 (ערש, "couch," sg). However, the obscurity and awkwardness of the latter view suggest it would not be the way an early reader would understand the text before it had verse divisions, as the evidence from the fathers indicates. Therefore, although the issue is difficult and complex, it is best to read ἱερεῖς as a vocative introducing 3:13. (See Glenny 2009, 160–63, on the difference of the LXX rendering [ἱερεῖς] from the Hebrew; the rendering is an apparent use of a Greek word "of similar sound to the Hebrew" [Thackeray §4 (p. 37)].) Dines (1991, 117) suggests that "the sons of Israel in Samaria . . . and in Damascus" who are the objects of judgment in 3:12 are "Samaritan rivals" or "Qumran-like sectaries" toward whom the translator felt strong animosity. However, it is impossible to clearly identify these groups, and it is likely that for the reader the application would change to different individuals and groups in different places and times (see Glenny 2013b, 70; and Dines 1991, 111–17).

3:13 ἀκούσατε καὶ ἐπιμαρτύρασθε τῷ οἴκῳ Ιακωβ, λέγει κύριος ὁ θεὸς ὁ παντοκράτωρ,

This oracle begins with a vocative and commands to the priests (see the discussion of ἱερεῖς in 3:12). The message—which is addressed to "the house of Jacob," apparently Judah, "the tribe" before whom the Samaritans are judged in 3:12—is that the punishment of Samaria will reach to the altars at Bethel and to the houses of the worshippers there.

This message (3:13–15) is a warning to Judah, which is addressed to the priests, who will deliver it to the nation. The vocative ἱερεῖς (3:12) should probably be understood to be a vocative introducing 3:13; see the discussion at 3:12.

ἀκούσατε. Aor act impv 2nd pl ἀκούω. Constative aorist, a specific command for the priests or prophets (Fanning 328, 334–35). On the use of genitive or accusative objects with ἀκούω, see 3:1 on ἀκούσατε.

ἐπιμαρτύρασθε. Aor mid impv 2nd pl ἐπιμαρτύρομαι. Constative aorist, a specific command for the priests or prophets (Fanning 328, 334–35; and 351–52 on aorist verbs of speaking). The understood direct object is the content of the testimony, which is summarized in 3:14–15.

τῷ οἴκῳ. Dative indirect object of ἐπιμαρτύρασθε. The individualizing use of the article points out something specific (Wallace, 216–17).

Ἰακωβ. Genitive of relationship, referring to the patriarch of the "house." See 6:8 on Ἰακωβ. The "house of Jacob" should probably be understood to include the whole nation (see also 9:8).

λέγει. Pres act ind 3rd sg λέγω; instantaneous present, completed at the moment of speaking (Wallace, 517–18). See the discussion of λέγει κύριος in 1:3.

κύριος ὁ θεὸς ὁ παντοκράτωρ. Nominative subject of λέγει. See 3:7, 8, 11. The title κύριος ὁ θεός ὁ παντοκράτωρ occurs thirteen times in the LXX (R-H text) and always in the Twelve. It occurs ten times in Amos in the R-H text (see also 4:13; 5:8, 14, 15, 16, 27; 9:5, 6, 15), and it corresponds to a number of different divine names in the MT. In this passage it corresponds to אדני יהוה אלהי הצבאות. It corresponds to יהוה in 5:8 and 9:6; it corresponds to הצבאות יהוה in 9:5 and יהוה אלוהך in 9:15; it normally corresponds to the Hebrew יהוה אלהי צבאות (4:13; 5:14, 15, 16, and 27). This was clearly a favorite title for the translator to use when referring to the Lord (see παντοκράτωρ below).

ὁ παντοκράτωρ is in apposition to κύριος ὁ θεός. In the LXX the title παντοκράτωρ emphasizes the Lord's universal sovereignty, especially over gentiles, and his creation of all things (see esp. 4:13; 5:5; 9:6, 15; see also Glenny 2009, 186–89). The article is used here with a monadic noun (Wallace, 223–24).

3:14 διότι ἐν τῇ ἡμέρᾳ, ὅταν ἐκδικῶ ἀσεβείας τοῦ Ισραηλ ἐπ' αὐτόν, καὶ ἐκδικήσω ἐπὶ τὰ θυσιαστήρια Βαιθηλ, καὶ κατασκαφήσεται τὰ κέρατα τοῦ θυσιαστηρίου καὶ πεσοῦνται ἐπὶ τὴν γῆν·

διότι. Subordinating conjunction, giving the reason for the commands in the previous verse.

ἐν τῇ ἡμέρᾳ. Temporal, modifying ἐκδικῶ. The preposition ἐν is marking a "point of time when something occurs" (BDAG, 329–30.10.b). The article is commonly used with the object of a preposition, and here it clarifies that the object of the preposition is definite.

ὅταν. This temporal particle functions as a subordinating conjunction (see *GELS*, 510). The Hebrew has a temporal clause, but ὅταν would not be necessary here to replicate the temporal idea in the Hebrew (see Garrett, 101), and it is somewhat repetitive and unnecessary in the LXX. Cf. the use of ὅταν in 3:12.

ἐκδικῶ. Pres act subj 1st sg ἐκδικέω. Use of the subjunctive in an indefinite temporal clause (see Wallace, 479; Muraoka §29.v). Wallace (518–19) suggests this use of the subjunctive "indicates a future contingency from the perspective of the time of the main verb"; the present subjunctive implies simultaneity with the following matrix (main) clause (*CGCG* § 47.9). The present tense is best understood as a progressive present, describing the action as continuing or in progress. See Glenny (2013b, 71–72) and the discussion above in 3:2 on the rendering of this verb.

ἀσεβείας. Accusative direct object of ἐκδικῶ. This noun is also found in each of the eight Oracles against the Nations in chapters 1–2 (where it is rendered "ungodly act") and in 5:14.

τοῦ Ισραηλ. Subjective genitive. The article with this indeclinable monadic noun indicates the case of the noun (see Muraoka §5.caa; Wallace, 240).

ἐπ' αὐτόν. Direction, modifying ἐκδικῶ. The preposition indicates "one to whom … action, attention, thought emotion, utterance, etc. are directed," and here the action is hostile (*GELS*, 266.III.4; see also 206.1.k, s.v. ἐκδικέω).

καὶ. Coordinating conjunction, introducing an apodosis, following a temporal clause (see *GELS*, 354.11). It has the sense "then," but it is probably best rendered "also."

ἐκδικήσω. Fut act ind 1st sg ἐκδικέω. Predictive future. See the discussion of this verb above in this verse.

ἐπὶ τὰ θυσιαστήρια. Direction, modifying ἐκδικήσω. See the same use of this preposition above in this verse. The article is commonly used with the object of a preposition, and here it clarifies that the object of the preposition is definite. In the LXX this noun is used mainly to refer to an altar of "the true God," contrasted with βωμός, which is normally used to refer to a pagan altar (LEH, 281).

Βαιθηλ. Genitive of place.

κατασκαφήσεται. Fut pass ind 3rd sg κατασκάπτω. Predictive future, and a simple passive in which the subject receives the action; the Lord is the implied agent, doing the action. The repeated *kappa* in the words καὶ κατασκαφήσεται τὰ κέρατα involves alliteration, and the translator created it by employing the verb κατασκάπτω ("tear down, raze to the ground," *GELS*, 382; BDAG, 526), which is not a close rendering of the corresponding Hebrew word (גדע "hack off," *HALOT*, 1:180) and is different than the way the translator rendered גדע in Zech 11:10, 14, the only other occurrences of this Hebrew verb in the MT Twelve; see Dines (2013, 402).

τὰ κέρατα. Nominative subject of κατασκαφήσεται.

τοῦ θυσιαστηρίου. Genitive of place, i.e., the horns "on the altar" (Muraoka §22.i). In genitive phrases it is normal for the head noun and the genitive noun to either both not have the article or to have it, as here (Wallace, 239–40). See the discussion of this noun above in this verse.

πεσοῦνται. Fut act ind 3rd pl πίπτω. Predictive future, "they will fall."

ἐπὶ τὴν γῆν. Locative, modifying the preceding verb, πεσοῦνται; ἐπί "indicates a movement on to the surface of" the earth, here from a "higher position" (*GELS*, 265.III.1.a–b). The article is normal with a monadic noun.

3:15 συγχεῶ καὶ πατάξω τὸν οἶκον τὸν περίπτερον ἐπὶ τὸν οἶκον τὸν θερινόν, καὶ ἀπολοῦνται οἶκοι ἐλεφάντινοι, καὶ προστεθήσονται οἶκοι ἕτεροι πολλοί, λέγει κύριος.

It is noteworthy that that translator did not render the *waw* at the beginning of the Hebrew in 3:15, resulting in asyndeton in the Greek. Perhaps he thought that there was a shift to a new topic at this point, moving from the judgment on the holy sites to the judgment on the homes of the wealthy (on asyndeton, see Runge, 20–23).

συγχεῶ. Fut act ind 1st sg συγχέω. Predictive future, "I will demolish" (*GELS*, 644.3).

πατάξω. Fut act ind 1st sg πατάσσω. Predictive future ("I will strike," LEH, 474–75; see also *GELS*, 538–39.1); this word is always used in a context of judgment in LXX Amos, as it is often elsewhere. This verb and the preceding (συγχεῶ) form a doublet in the LXX joined by καί and rendering one Hebrew verb (נכה). Ziegler does not include καὶ πατάξω, and his decision not to include it is surprising (it is found in B, A, and W), because πατάσσω, which occurs over four hundred times in the LXX, usually renders נכה *hiphil* (see its other three occurrences in LXX Amos in 4:6; 6:11; 9:1; and Glenny 2013b, 20).

τὸν οἶκον τὸν περίπτερον. Accusative direct object of συγχεῶ and πατάξω. This is a generic noun referring to a "house" as a class of buildings, and with the modifier it refers to a specific kind of house. This is the use of the article with a generic noun to distinguish the class from others.

τὸν περίπτερον suggests a house "with a row of columns all around" (LSJ, 1384), thus "colonnaded"; it is used to describe sparks or fire "flying about" in Song 8:6 (*GELS*, 552). The article is used with the adjective in the second attributive position (see Muraoka §37.bbb; Wallace, 239).

ἐπὶ τὸν οἶκον τὸν θερινόν. Addition, modifying συγχεῶ; ἐπί has the sense "in addition to, along with" (*GELS*, 267.III.9.a). The preposition could have the sense "onto" (*GELS*, 644.3, s.v. συγχεῶ; *GELS*, 265–66. III.1, s.v. ἐπί); however, this latter understanding of the passage is not as straightforward and requires the addition of assumed words, resulting in a rendering something like, "I will smite the colonnaded house [and make it collapse] onto the summerhouse."

The generic noun refers to a "house" as a class of buildings, and with the modifier it refers to a specific kind of house. The article serves two functions: with a generic noun it distinguishes the class from others, and it clarifies that the object of the preposition is definite. The adjective θερινόν refers to something that is "of summer" (LEH, 274; BDAG, 453). The article denotes the second attributive position of the adjective (see Muraoka §37.bbb; Wallace, 239).

ἀπολοῦνται. Fut mid ind 3rd pl ἀπόλλυμι. Predictive future. The future middle of this verb is intransitive, and the subject is affected by the action of the verb; this form is often rendered "perish" (see *GELS*, 78–79).

οἶκοι ἐλεφάντινοι. Nominative subject of ἀπολοῦνται. This generic noun is anarthrous, but it probably should be understood as definite, based on the context and since the houses are further specified by the following adjective; however, without the article the emphasis here is on the quality of the houses, and it allows that not all the "ivory houses" perished (see the discussion in Wallace, 227–30, 243–45). This is the third category of "houses" in the verse, and they all suggest affluence and prosperity.

προστεθήσονται. Fut pass ind 3rd pl προστίθημι. Predictive future, and a simple passive with the subject receiving the action of the verb, i.e., many other houses "will be added" to the demolition. The Lord is the understood agent, performing the action.

οἶκοι ἕτεροι πολλοί. Nominative subject of προστεθήσονται. See the discussion of anarthrous use of this noun in the previous clause. The adjectives show that the noun οἶκοι does not include all the houses.

λέγει κύριος. See the discussion of this divine speech formula above in 1:3 and 1:5. It encloses this oracle (see 3:13).

Amos 4:1–3

¹Hear this word, heifers of Bashan who [are] in the mountain of Samaria, who oppress the poor and trample underfoot the needy, who say to their lords, "Give to us, so that we may drink." ²The Lord swears by his holy ones, "Behold, days are coming upon you, and they will take you with weapons, and fiery destroyers will throw those with you into heated caldrons, ³and you will be carried out naked before one another, and you will be cast away onto Mount Remman," says the Lord God.

The command to "hear" (see also 3:1) combined with a vocative address to the "heifers of Bashan" introduces a new section. The asyndeton at the beginning of 4:1 supports this (Runge, 21–23). The section concludes with a repetition of the divine speech formula "says the Lord" at the end of 4:3.

4:1 Ἀκούσατε τὸν λόγον τοῦτον, δαμάλεις τῆς Βασανίτιδος αἱ ἐν τῷ ὄρει τῆς Σαμαρείας αἱ καταδυναστεύουσαι πτωχοὺς καὶ καταπατοῦσαι πένητας αἱ λέγουσαι τοῖς κυρίοις αὐτῶν Ἐπίδοτε ἡμῖν ὅπως πίωμεν·

Ἀκούσατε. Aor act impv 2nd pl ἀκούω; see 3:1 (cf. 3:13; 5:1). On the use of genitive or accusative objects with ἀκούω, see ἀκούσατε in 3:1.

τὸν λόγον τοῦτον. Accusative direct object of Ἀκούσατε. The demonstrative pronoun construction refers to the Lord's oath in 4:2–3 (i.e., cataphoric, Muraoka §12.c).

δαμάλεις. Vocative of address, clarifying the addressees, the "heifers." This word is apparently used metaphorically to refer to the rich women of Israel.

τῆς Βασανίτιδος. Genitive of place, indicating place or location. The Greek word renders and refers to Bashan, "the fertile area of upper Transjordan east of the Sea of Galilee and mainly north of the Yarmuk river" (see *ABD*, 1:623–24). This place-name (Hebrew בשן) occurs sixty times in the LXX, and it is rendered Bashan (Βασαν) in the great majority of its occurrences (eighteen of nineteen times in the Pentateuch and the single time it differs it is rendered "bulls" [Deut 32:14]); in only thirteen occurrences is בשן rendered Βασανίτις, and those are the only occurrences of Βασανίτις in the LXX. In its four occurrences in LXX Twelve, it is always rendered Βασανίτις (see also Mic 7:14; Nah 1:4; Zech 11:2). The article may designate Βασανίτις as being well known, although the use of articles with different proper nouns in the LXX is "commonplace . . . , albeit not compulsory" (see Muraoka §5.cb–cba; see also BDF §261).

αἱ. The vocative article functions as a nominalizer, changing the following PP (ἐν τῷ ὄρει) into an attributive modifier of δαμάλεις. This is the first of three adjectival phrases modifying and describing δαμάλεις. These words describe the location of the "heifers." A relative pronoun and a linking verb are required in the English translation ("who [are] . . .").

ἐν τῷ ὄρει. Locative, nominalized by the preceding article and describing the place where the δαμάλεις are found (*GELS*, 231.1.a). The article is often used with a monadic noun.

τῆς Σαμαρείας. Genitive of apposition, describing the mountain and clarifying what mountain it is (Wallace, 94–97). The article is commonly employed with a well-known substantive (Muraoka §5.c–cbh); its use also follows Apollonius' canon.

αἱ καταδυναστεύουσαι πτωχοὺς καὶ καταπατοῦσαι πένητας. This is the second of three phrases modifying the δαμάλεις. The asyndeton leaves the relationship between the phrases unspecified, but since they all modify δαμάλεις, it is understood that they have a coordinate relationship.

αἱ καταδυναστεύουσαι. Pres act ptc nom fem pl καταδυναστεύω (attributive, modifying δαμάλεις). The present tense signifies customary or habitual action. In English the article modifying the participle is translated as a relative pronoun. In this context the verb has the sense "to cause unjust hardship" to someone (*GELS*, 370–71.1). In Exod 21:17 this strong word has the sense of treating a fellow Israelite like a slave, after kidnapping them (see Wevers 1990, 330–31).

πτωχούς. Accusative direct object of καταδυναστεύουσαι. This abstract adjective is functioning as a substantive. This word is often used to refer to a beggar or someone who is so destitute they have nothing (Glenny 2013b, 56). This anarthrous generic substantive is definite (see Muraoka §1.d, on the optional use of the article with definite generic substantives).

καί. Coordinating conjunction, connecting the two parallel participial phrases, which are both controlled by the preceding αἱ and together comprise one of the three main parallel phrases modifying δαμάλεις.

καταπατοῦσαι. Pres act part nom fem pl καταπατέω (attributive, modifying δαμάλεις). The most basic sense of this word is "to tread underfoot," but here it has the sense "to deal harshly and oppressively with" (*GELS*, 379.2). The present tense signifies customary or habitual action. This participle is parallel with the preceding one (καταδυναστεύουσαι; see καί above), and they have rhyming endings, like the corresponding Hebrew participles (העשקות and הרצצות); also, they both start with κατα, giving an alliterative effect (Dines 2013, 403).

πένητας. Accusative direct object of καταπατοῦσαι. This is another class of poor people (see Glenny 2013b, 55–56), and they are not as destitute as the πτωχός mentioned earlier in the verse; this word (πένης) often refers to a day-laborer, who is not a beggar or destitute (*TDNT*, 6:38–40). This anarthrous generic substantive is definite (see Muraoka §1.d, on the optional use of the article with definite generic substantives).

αἱ λέγουσαι τοῖς κυρίοις αὐτῶν Ἐπίδοτε ἡμῖν ὅπως πίωμεν. This is the third phrase modifying δαμάλεις. The asyndeton leaves the relationship between the phrases unspecified, but since they all modify δαμάλεις, it is understood that they have a coordinate relationship.

αἱ λέγουσαι. Pres act ptc nom fem pl λέγω (attributive, modifying δαμάλεις). The present tense signifies customary or habitual action. In

English the article modifying the participle is translated as a relative pronoun.

τοῖς κυρίοις. Dative indirect object of λέγουσαι. This word is used for those with authority or power, like gods, masters, husbands, and here the context suggests it refers to the latter (LEH, 361; GELS, 419–20). The Hebrew has לאדניהם ("to their lords [husbands]"). It is normal to have an article with a noun when a possessive pronoun is modifying it (Wallace, 239).

αὐτῶν. Genitive of relationship. The emphasis seems to be on the husband/wife relationship rather than the possession of a spouse (i.e., possessive genitive). The pronoun refers to δαμάλεις.

Ἐπίδοτε. Aor act impv 2nd pl ἐπιδίδωμι. Imperatives "can express a variety of nuances: peremptory commands, polite requests, suggestions, etc.," depending on the context and content of the command (*CGCG* §34.20). The use of κύριος to refer to the husbands suggests a request from a superior here, but the other actions of the δαμάλεις indicate they exercise a degree of authority also. In the written text it is difficult to discern the speaker's exact tone (Wallace, 487–88). The aorist portrays the action as a whole (constative). The direct speech that begins here functions as the object of the participle λέγουσαι; and the following purpose clause, "so that we may drink," is understood to be the direct object of ἐπίδοτε.

ἡμῖν. Dative indirect object of ἐπίδοτε.

ὅπως. Conjunction with the subjunctive case marking purpose (BDAG, 718).

πίωμεν. Aor act subj 1st pl πίνω. Subjunctive with ὅπως in a purpose clause; the aorist is constative, viewing the action as a whole (Wallace, 557–58).

4:2 ὀμνύει κύριος κατὰ τῶν ἁγίων αὐτοῦ Διότι ἰδοὺ ἡμέραι ἔρχονται ἐφ' ὑμᾶς, καὶ λήμψονται ὑμᾶς ἐν ὅπλοις, καὶ τοὺς μεθ' ὑμῶν εἰς λέβητας ὑποκαιομένους ἐμβαλοῦσιν ἔμπυροι λοιμοί,

The asyndeton here is consistent with a change of topic (Runge, 21–23), switching from the "heifers of Basanitis" to the Lord's oath. See 6:8 and 8:7 for other oath formulas in Amos, emphasizing the inevitability of the thing sworn.

ὀμνύει. Pres act ind 3rd sg ὀμνύω; instantaneous use of the present tense in which the action ("swears") is completed at the moment it is spoken (Wallace, 517).

κύριος. Nominative subject of ὀμνύει. The Hebrew has the longer title אדני יהוה.

κατὰ τῶν ἁγίων. Oath formula. The preposition κατά with a genitive object is used in oaths to invoke someone or something (*GELS*, 404.2 and 495.1, s.v. ὀμνύω; LEH, 331; Gen 22:16; see the discussion in Glenny 2013b, 73); the preposition is usually rendered "by" (LEH, 308). The Hebrew has "by his holiness" (בקדשו).

If τῶν ἁγίων is neuter it refers to "his sacred objects," and if it is masculine it refers to "his holy ones"; the latter seems more likely in view of the following context (see Glenny 2013b, 73, 76). The article confirms that the object of the preposition is definite. It is common to have an article with a noun when a possessive pronoun is attached to the noun (Wallace, 239).

αὐτοῦ. Possessive genitive.

Διότι. This conjunction could introduce the noun clause that comprises the content of the oath (Brenton; *GELS*, 172.2; LSJ, 435), be causal (NETS; Dines 1991, 120), or be inferential (BDAG, 251.2). A conjunction is not needed to introduce the content of an oath, and when one is used, the conjunction normally employed is ὅτι. This conjunction (διότι) occurs ten times in LXX Amos, and besides this occurrence and the parallel construction in 6:8, it is always causal or inferential. However, in the parallel oath formulas here and in 6:8 (see also LXX Jer 28:14 and other examples of διότι introducing a noun clause in *GELS*, 172.2), it is simplest to understand it to be introducing the contents of the oath. It could be left untranslated when used in this manner, as I have done.

ἰδοὺ. A presentative particle that draws "attention to what follows" (*GELS*, 377; BDAG, 468); here it is introducing a prophetic, "eschatological pronouncement" (*GELS*, 377.b; see the similar phrase in eschatological contexts in 8:11 and 9:13). See 2:13 on ἰδού.

ἡμέραι. Nominative subject of ἔρχονται.

ἔρχονται. Pres mid ind 3rd pl ἔρχομαι. Indirect middle in which the subject acts in her own interest (Wallace, 419–21); Kemmer (269) classifies this verb as a verb of translational motion, which typically has middle-voice morphology. The present tense is a futuristic present (Wallace, 535–37); for Muraoka (§28.b.iv) the present tense is here a "statement of destiny, of what is destined to happen."

ἐφ᾽ ὑμᾶς. Direction, modifying ἔρχονται. The preposition ἐπί "indicates a movement towards, or aimed at, an object" (*GELS*, 266.III.2).

καὶ. Coordinating conjunction, connecting the clauses and introducing a consequence that will follow if (or when) the preceding clause is realized (*GELS*, 354.9).

λήμψονται. Fut mid ind 3rd pl λαμβάνω. Predictive future. λαμβάνω is one of a number of verbs that form their future in the middle voice (see BDF §77, which notes that many of these verbs, like λαμβάνω, do not have an "active sigma-aorist" [1st aorist] form either, which is formed with the addition of a *sigma* to the stem, like the active and middle future form).

ὑμᾶς. Accusative direct object of λήμψονται.

ἐν ὅπλοις. Instrumental, modifying λήμψονται. The preposition ἐν shows the "means or instrument," more specifically introducing the things that "accompany someone to secure an objective" (BDAG, 328.5.a; see also *GELS*, 232.7.a). The noun ὅπλον is a general word for a "tool, instrument" (LSJ, 1240), which often refers to an instrument for war, a "weapon," as it does here (*GELS*, 501.1). The Hebrew has בְּצִנּוֹת ("with hooks"). This noun (צֵן) occurs only three times in the LXX (see also Job 5:5 and Prov 22:5), and the translator apparently did not know it, taking it for צִנָּה ("shield"), which has the same form in the plural; then he rendered it more generically, as "instrument" (see the fuller discussion in Glenny 2009, 129).

καὶ. Coordinating conjunction, connecting the following with the preceding parallel clause and giving a second consequence that will follow if (or when) the eschatological days announced early in the verse (ἡμέραι ἔρχονται) are realized (*GELS*, 354.9).

τοὺς. The accusative article functions as a nominalizer, changing the following PP (μεθ᾽ ὑμῶν) into the accusative direct object of ἐμβαλοῦσιν (BDF §266).

μεθ᾽ ὑμῶν. Association. The preposition μετά has the sense "in the company of" someone (*GELS*, 451.I.1).

εἰς λέβητας ὑποκαιομένους. Spatial, modifying ἐμβαλοῦσιν. The preposition εἰς indicates "extension involving a goal or place" and means "into" (BDAG, 288–89.1.a.ε). *GELS* (196.1) describes this usage as "towards a goal which is inside an area." See the discussion of this phrase in Glenny (2013b, 74–75). This Greek phrase, which I have rendered "into heated caldrons," corresponds to the Hebrew בְּסִירוֹת דּוּגָה ("with fishhooks"). See the discussion of this phrase in Glenny (2009, 120–21 and 163–65).

The noun λέβητας occurs in the Septuagint as an instrument of torture in contexts describing Antiochus' persecution of the seven brothers (2 Macc 7:3; 4 Macc 8:13; 12:1; 18:20); it apparently refers to a "cooking utensil," like a "cauldron" that would be used to cook meat (*GELS*, 427). The Hebrew corresponding to this word is סִירָה ("hook"), and the translator apparently read it as סִיר, which has the same plural form and means "pot, tub" (see Glenny 2009, 120–21, for more details on this translation).

ὑποκαιομένους. Pres pass ptc acc masc pl ὑποκαίω (adjectival, modifying λέβητας). Progressive present, describing continuous but not constant action. The middle/passive form is best understood as passive (see *GE*, 2221, which glosses it "to be burned from underneath," thus the caldrons are being heated by a fire below them). For other uses of this verb in the LXX, see Jer 1:13, where it is used with λέβης; see also Ezek 24:5; Dan 3:25 and 46; and 4 Macc 11:18. The Hebrew corresponding with this word is דוגה (meaning something like "fish" or "fishhook"); it is not clear what the translator read to render it as he did (see Glenny 2009, 120–21).

ἐμβαλοῦσιν. Fut act ind 3rd pl ἐμβάλλω. Predictive future. This word is a LXX plus with nothing corresponding to it in the Hebrew; the translator was scrambling to make sense of this difficult verse (Glenny 2009, 121).

ἔμπυροι λοιμοί. Nominative subject of ἐμβαλοῦσιν. The adjective ἔμπυροι, which occurs only twice in the LXX (see also Ezek 23:37, where it refers to fire or flames), has the sense "possessing fire" (*GELS*, 230) and means "fiery" in this context. This word seems to have no equivalent in the Hebrew, unless it is somehow connected with the rendering of ὑποκαιομένους above (see Glenny 2009, 104–5). It is difficult to know whether λοιμοί is the noun or adjective of λοιμός, but it is apparently a substantival use of the adjective (see BDAG, 602; and HR, 887; *GELS*, 435, lists only the adjective, and the three occurrences classified as the noun in HR [3 Kgdms 8:37; Ezek 36:29; and 4 Macc 15:32] all appear to be a mistake). The word is used in 1 Macc 10:61; 15:3 and 21 to describe a subversive element, people who are enemies of the rulers, and in Ezekiel 28–32 it describes terrible foreigners whom the Lord sends against Tyre and Egypt to judge them (see Glenny 2013b, 76). In this verse these "destroyers" are personal agents who cast people into the caldrons, but they are indefinite, and it is difficult to identify them further. Dines (1991, 133) summarizes, concerning the use of this word in the LXX, "In every case it [λοιμός] has the derived sense of a pernicious, harmful person ('a pest'), one who flouts standards of public decency, political integrity or religious orthodoxy, at least from the writer's point of view." See the fuller discussion of this term in Glenny (2009, 75–77). This term seems to correspond with the Hebrew word פרץ ("breach") at the beginning of 4:3 in the Hebrew. Apparently, the translator was having trouble making sense of verse 2, and he rendered פרץ with what comes before it (i.e., 4:2) and read it as פריץ ("violent one") to try to make sense out of verse 2. See the rendering of פריץ by λοιμόν in Ezek 18:10 and the discussion in Glenny (2009, 105).

4:3 καὶ ἐξενεχθήσεσθε γυμναὶ κατέναντι ἀλλήλων καὶ ἀπορριφήσεσθε εἰς τὸ ὄρος τὸ Ρεμμαν, λέγει κύριος ὁ θεός.

ἐξενεχθήσεσθε. Fut pass ind 2nd pl ἐκφέρω. Predictive future. The passive voice is used without the agent being expressed, and the subjects who are acted upon are expressed by the verb, i.e., "you will be carried out." *GELS* (219.1) suggests the subjects are being carried out of their houses (see 3:15).

γυμναί. Nominative adjective modifying the subject expressed by the verb, "you." The feminine form is used, because the subjects in view are still the δαμάλεις ("heifers") addressed in verse 1. The verb forms and the pronominal suffix in the Hebrew are feminine also.

κατέναντι ἀλλήλων. Locative, modifying ἐξενεχθήσεσθε; κατέναντι is an adverb, which functions as a preposition with a genitive object, as here (BDAG, 530–31.2.b). It can have the sense "against, in opposition to" (see Mic 2:8) or "before, in the presence of" (Amos 3:12; Joel 1:16; Zech 14:4; *GELS*, 388.2). The latter sense is required here. See also the discussion of ἐναντίον in 3:10. The gender of the reciprocal pronoun depends on the antecedent, and I understand it to refer to the δαμάλεις in 4:1 and perhaps others with them also. See Muraoka (§9.a) on the reciprocal pronoun in this passage with reference to the second person.

ἀπορριφήσεσθε. Fut pass ind 2nd pl ἀπορίπτω. Predictive future. The use of the passive voice with the actions of judgment and punishment in verses 2–3 emphasizes that these things will be done to the recipients against their will (see Muraoka §27.ba on the difference between the "tolerative passive" and the use of the passive to describe things experienced under duress). As with ἐξενεχθήσεσθε, no agent is expressed. Muraoka (*GELS*, 81) suggests the idea of the verb in this context is that the heifers will be "cast away" as useless.

εἰς τὸ ὄρος τὸ Ρεμμαν. Locative, modifying ἀπορριφήσεσθε; the preposition εἰς signifies movement "towards a goal which is inside an area or in the direction of it" (*GELS*, 196.1). The articles in this construction serve to clarify the appositional relationship between ὄρος (neut acc) and Ρεμμαν (indeclinable but probably gen) (see LEH, 447, s.v. ὄρος). "Remman" (Ρεμμαν; spelled Ρομμαν in MS B and Ραμμαν in MS W) is perhaps "another name for the Canaanite storm god [Ramman, 'thunderer'] also known as Baal, who was head of the Aramean pantheon" (Glenny 2013b, 77). This supposition is supported by "the mourning of Hadadrimmon in the valley of Megiddo" referred to in Zech 12:11 MT (see also J. K. Palmer, 63–64). The reference to "Remman" here in Amos is probably to "the place where Baal dwells or his homeland of Syria" (Glenny 2013b, 77); thus, the "heifers" will be cast away into the mountain of this Syrian god. The corresponding Hebrew is ההרמונה ("to Harmon"), which the translator apparently read as הר and רמונה. See the fuller discussion of this phrase in Glenny (2009, 165–66).

λέγει κύριος ὁ θεός. See 1:3, 1:5, and 3:11 on this divine speech formula. It concludes this oracle (see 4:3, 5; 8:9; and 9:12 also). See also the discussion of λέγει κύριος in 1:3 and 1:5. The Hebrew has the shorter נאם יהוה, which corresponds to λέγει κύριος, the reading in MS B and Ziegler. But the longer LXX reading has good support (MSS A, W, Q; see also 4:5).

Amos 4:4–13

⁴"You entered Bethel and you broke the Law, and in Gilgal you frequently committed sin, and you brought your sacrifices in the morning, on the third day your tithes. ⁵They read a law outside, and they called for votive offerings. Proclaim that 'The sons of Israel loved these things,'" says the Lord God. ⁶"And I myself will give you aching of teeth in all your cities and want of bread in all your places. Yet you did not return to me," says the Lord. ⁷"Also I myself withheld the rain from you three months before the harvest; and I will send rain upon one city, and upon another city I will not send rain; one part will be rained upon, and the part upon which I do not send rain, it will be dried up. ⁸And two or three cities will be gathered together into one city to drink water, and they will not be satisfied. Yet you have not returned to me," says the Lord. ⁹"I smote you with fever and with jaundice. You multiplied your gardens; the caterpillar devoured your vineyards and your fig yards and your olive groves. Yet, even so, you have not returned to me," says the Lord. ¹⁰"I sent death to you in the way to Egypt, and I slew with the sword your young men along with captive bands of your horses, and I sent your encampments up with fire in my anger; yet, even so, you have not returned to me," says the Lord. ¹¹"I overthrew you just as God overthrew Sodom and Gomorrah, and you were like a brand snatched out of the fire; yet, even so, you have not returned to me," says the Lord. ¹²"For this reason, I will do such a thing to you, Israel; however, because I will do such a thing to you, prepare to call upon your God, Israel. ¹³For behold, I [am the one] strengthening thunder and creating wind and proclaiming to people his anointed, making dawn and misty darkness and treading upon the high places of the earth; the Lord, the God, the Almighty One, [is] his name."

This next major section, 4:4–13, is made up of at least three units. The first unit in 4:4–5 is marked by the divine speech formula in 4:3 that ends the preceding section and by ironic descriptions of Israel's sinful worship in 4:4–5. The second unit in 4:6–12 is placed in the Lord's mouth and describes the Lord's attempts to capture Israel's attention by means of the catastrophes he sent them; it is intermixed with the refrain "Yet you have not returned to me" (4:6, 8, 9, 10, and 11). The third unit is the first of three doxologies in Amos (see also 5:8–9; 9:5–6), praising the Lord for his work of creation. Thus, the large section moves from a description of Israel's insincere worship (4:4–5) to a description of the Lord's warnings and Israel's lack of response to him (4:6–12) to a description of the greatness of the Lord with whom Israel will have to contend (4:13), if they do not repent and call upon him (4:12).

4:4 Εἰσήλθατε εἰς Βαιθηλ καὶ ἠνομήσατε καὶ εἰς Γαλγαλα ἐπληθύνατε τοῦ ἀσεβῆσαι καὶ ἠνέγκατε εἰς τὸ πρωὶ θυσίας ὑμῶν, εἰς τὴν τριημερίαν τὰ ἐπιδέκατα ὑμῶν·

The asyndeton at the beginning of this section suggests a new topic (Runge, 20–23). The tone of the verse differs markedly from the Hebrew because the four ironic imperatives in 4:4 in the Hebrew are rendered as indicatives in the LXX.

Εἰσήλθατε. Aor act ind 2nd pl εἰσέρχομαι. Consummative aorist, summarizing the action and connoting it is completed (Fanning, 263–64; Wallace, 559 n. 12).

εἰς Βαιθηλ. Locative, modifying εἰσήλθατε. The repetition of the preposition in the verb and in the phrase following it emphasizes the idea of entering Bethel, more than just going there, as the command in the Hebrew (באו בית אל). The preposition εἰς has the sense "at the place of" (*GELS*, 197.8; BDAG, 288–89.1.a.δ). "Bethel" (Βαιθηλ) is the site of the main altar in the Northern Kingdom (see Glenny 2013b, 77).

ἠνομήσατε. Aor act ind 2nd pl ἀνομέω. Consummative aorist, summarizing the action and connoting it is completed, i.e., "you broke the Law" (Fanning, 263–64; Wallace, 559 n. 12).

εἰς Γαλγαλα. Locative, modifying ἐπληθύνατε; the preposition εἰς has the sense "at the place of" (*GELS*, 197.8; BDAG, 288–89.1.a.δ). "Gilgal" (γαλγαλα) was an important sanctuary site in the Northern Kingdom (see Glenny 2013b, 77–78).

ἐπληθύνατε. Aor act ind 2nd pl πληθύνω. Consummative aorist, summarizing the action and connoting it is completed (Fanning, 263–64; Wallace, 559 n. 12). Muraoka (*GELS*, 563.1.b) discusses this use of πληθύνω, and he advocates the sense "to do something frequently or over a long time" in this context; he suggests the gloss "(you) frequently committed sin" for the verb and following infinitive.

τοῦ ἀσεβῆσαι. Aor act inf ἀσεβέω (complementary; so Muraoka §30.bg, 31.e; see also *GELS*, 563.1.b; Wallace, 607, 610, notes that genitive articular infinitives can be epexegetical, but epexegetical infinitives qualify a noun or an adjective rather than completing the idea of a verb). The aorist is a constative aorist, looking at the action as a whole.

ἠνέγκατε. Aor act ind 2nd pl φέρω. Consummative aorist, summarizing the action and connoting it is completed (Fanning, 263–64; Wallace, 559 n. 12).

εἰς τὸ πρωὶ. Temporal. Idiomatic PP indicating time (*GELS*, 196.4; and 604.II.c, s.v. πρωΐ) and modifying ἠνέγκατε. The preposition εἰς sometimes points to the time at which something takes place (BDAG, 289.2.a.γ). The article is idiomatic with the adverb πρωΐ, and in the prepositional phrase it nominalizes πρωΐ (*GELS*, 604.II.b and c; Muraoka §6.ea comments that there is no functional difference between the articular of anarthrous use of the adverb πρωΐ); πρωΐ can function as a noun (indeclinable), but the PP is adverbial here with the sense "in the morning" and can indicate "eagerness" (Muraoka 2002, 495.II.2).

θυσίας. Accusative direct object of ἠνέγκατε.

ὑμῶν. Possessive genitive.

εἰς τὴν τριημερίαν. Temporal. Idiomatic PP indicating time (*GELS*, 196.4; and 604.I, s.v. πρωΐ), modifying ἠνέγκατε, and parallel to the preceding PP εἰς τὸ πρωί. The preposition εἰς is sometimes employed to indicate "an extent of time" (*GELS*, 196.4). The asyndeton here, which follows the Hebrew, is probably because the parallelism of the two temporal prepositional phrases beginning with εἰς and modifying ἠνέγκατε is obvious (see Runge, 20), and no conjunction is needed. The article clarifies that the accusative object of the preposition (τριημερίαν) is definite, and the presence of the article gives the noun, which means "period of three days" (LSJ, 1819; *GELS*, 686), more the sense "on the third day" (NETS).

τὰ ἐπιδέκατα. Accusative direct object of ἠνέγκατε, parallel to θυσίας and meaning "tithes." It is very common for an article to be attached to a noun that is modified by a possessive pronoun.

ὑμῶν. Possessive genitive.

4:5 καὶ ἀνέγνωσαν ἔξω νόμον καὶ ἐπεκαλέσαντο ὁμολογίας· ἀπαγγείλατε ὅτι ταῦτα ἠγάπησαν οἱ υἱοὶ Ισραηλ, λέγει κύριος ὁ θεός.

ἀνέγνωσαν. Aor act ind 3rd pl ἀναγινώσκω. Consummative aorist, summarizing the action and connoting it is completed (Fanning, 263–64; Wallace, 559 n. 12). The translator read the first two ironical imperatives in the Hebrew in 4:5 as indicatives, as he did with the four imperatives in 4:4. In the LXX the verb means "to read aloud" (*GELS*, 37; for an interesting survey of its background, see *NIDNTTE* 1:278).

ἔξω. Adverb of place (BDAG, 354), modifying the preceding verb. It has been suggested that this construction refers to a reading of the Samaritan Pentateuch "outside the cultic community" by the leaders of the Samaritan cult (Dines 1991, 146 n. 43) or to the reading of the Torah outdoors, mimicking the worship in the time of Ezra (2 Esd 18:8 [Neh 8:8 MT]). It is impossible to be certain what it refers to (Glenny 2013b, 79–80). On the rendering of the first words in this verse, see Glenny 2009, 87–89; the MT has וקטר מחמץ תודה ("and offer an unleavened sacrifice of thanksgiving"), but the LXX translator read something like וקרא מחוץ תורה (LXX.E, 2350).

νόμον. Accusative direct object of ἀνέγνωσαν. It is difficult to know if the "law" here refers to the Hebrew Torah or Scriptures, in which case it would be monadic and would not require an article to be definite, or if it refers to "a law," like the Samaritan Pentateuch; see the discussion above on various possible meanings of ἔξω. I translated "law" in the lowercase here, because it is unclear that it refers to the Hebrew Scriptures (cf. 2:4 and 4:4 where "Law" is part of the rendering of ἀνομέω). The corresponding word in the MT is תודה ("sacrifice of thanksgiving"), but the LXX rendering reflects תורה ("law"). *Dalet* and *resh* were difficult for the translator to distinguish.

ἐπεκαλέσαντο. Aor mid ind 3rd pl ἐπικαλέω. Constative aorist, looking at the action as a whole. This is probably an indirect middle (Wallace, 419–23), and the subjects are affected by the action of the verb. The subjects of the verb are apparently the same as the subjects of ἀνέγνωσαν.

ὁμολογίας. Accusative direct object of ἐπεκαλέσαντο. In this context, which mentions sacrifices and tithes (4:4), the word probably refers to "an offering made in accordance with a vow or promise" (Glenny 2013b, 78–79; Deut 12:17; Ezek 46:12).

ἀπαγγείλατε. Aor act impv 2nd pl ἀπαγγέλλω. The aorist imperative should probably be understood to be a specific command referring to a specific occasion (see Fanning, 334), and the aorist is a constative aorist, summarizing the action. The word can mean to "tell in the way of explaining or interpreting" or "to announce" or "to proclaim," and the last two ideas are more the sense here (*GELS*, 62.1, 2, 5; see also its use in 4:13). This command is apparently not addressed to the sinners described in 4:1–3; it is natural to take the subject of the verb to be the prophets, who would (supposedly) speak for the Lord. The context suggests that this clause should be taken negatively, perhaps sarcastically.

MSS B and C have the synonym ἀναγγέλλω, but it does not have enough support to be accepted by R-H or Ziegler.

ὅτι. Conjunction, marking discourse content; here it is indirect discourse (BDAG, 731.1.a; *GELS*, 511.2).

ταῦτα. Accusative direct object of ἠγάπησαν. This pronoun apparently refers to the ritual described in the preceding verses (4:4–5a).

ἠγάπησαν. Aor act ind 3rd pl ἀγαπάω. Gnomic aorist, here referring to a customary, timeless fact (Wallace, 562).

οἱ υἱοί. Nominative subject of ἠγάπησαν. The article is employed here with a well-known entity that has not been referred to in the immediate context (cf. 2:11; 3:12; 9:7; Wallace, 225).

Ισραηλ. Genitive of relationship.

λέγει κύριος ὁ θεός. See 1:3, 3:11, and 3:13. The two nouns stand in apposition to each other. The divine speech formula λέγει κύριος occurs forty times in LXX Amos, and it often begins or concludes an oracle. It is repeated several times in this section (4:5, 6, 8, 9, 10, 11), emphasizing the divine source of these words.

4:6 καὶ ἐγὼ δώσω ὑμῖν γομφιασμὸν ὀδόντων ἐν πάσαις ταῖς πόλεσιν ὑμῶν καὶ ἔνδειαν ἄρτων ἐν πᾶσι τοῖς τόποις ὑμῶν· καὶ οὐκ ἐπεστρέψατε πρός με, λέγει κύριος.

καί. Coordinating conjunction, connecting two independent clauses (*GELS*, 352.1.b). The following is actually the result of the hypocritical and insincere worship described in 4:4–5.

ἐγώ. Nominative subject of δώσω. An emphatic personal pronoun.

δώσω. Fut act ind 1st sg δίδωμι. This probably should be understood as a predictive future, but the translator's use of tenses in 4:6 is difficult to understand. He returns to the aorist in the following refrain. The translator now includes his readers in those threatened by judgment.

ὑμῖν. Dative indirect object of δώσω.

γομφιασμόν. Accusative direct object of δώσω. There is some question about the meaning of this *hapax* in the biblical corpus. The cognate verb occurs in Sir 30:10 and Ezek 18:2; in the former it refers to the grinding or gnashing of teeth, and in the latter passage it refers to teeth that ache. In this context LEH (123) favors the former idea, and Dines (1991, 146) and Muraoka (*GELS*, 135) favor the latter; either idea is fitting in the warning of judgment in this passage, and the ideas are similar and overlap. However, the Greek word suggests the translator was emphasizing the "aching" more than the gnashing or dullness of teeth (*GELS*, 135; LSJ, 356). The corresponding word in the MT has the sense "cleanness" (נִקָּיוֹן), i.e., "cleanness of teeth," a figure for lack of food. The translator apparently rendered it as קִהְיוֹן (Wolff, 209) from the root קהה ("become blunt"; *HALOT*, 2:1078), which is used to describe aching teeth in Jer 31:29–30 and Ezek 18:2.

ὀδόντων. Subjective genitive.

ἐν πάσαις ταῖς πόλεσιν. Locative. The preposition ἐν "indicates a place" in which an action takes place (*GELS*, 231.a.b). The PP is best understood to modify the preceding direct object (γομφιασμόν), showing where the described state prevails, although it could modify δώσω, indicating where the Lord will give this judgment. See Muraoka (§38.b.i) for this construction with πᾶς and the article; it has the sense "all the . . ."

ὑμῶν. Possessive genitive.

καί. Coordinating conjunction, connecting two direct objects (*GELS*, 352.1.a).

ἔνδειαν. Accusative direct object of δώσω. This word refers to "want, lack," and of its nineteen occurrences in the LXX, many are in the context of divine judgment (*GELS*, 234; see Deut 28:20, 57; Job 30:3; Prov 6:11; Ezek 4:16; 12:19).

ἄρτων. Objective genitive. The MT has the collective singular here, and the LXX renders it as a plural.

ἐν πᾶσι τοῖς τόποις. Locative. The preposition ἐν "indicates a place" in which an action takes place (*GELS*, 231.1.b). The PP is best understood to modify the preceding direct object (ἔνδειαν), showing where the described state prevails, although it could modify δώσω, showing where the Lord will give this punishment. See Muraoka (§38.b.i) for this construction with πᾶς and the article; it has the sense "all the . . ."

ὑμῶν. Possessive genitive.

καί. Coordinating conjunction, connecting two independent clauses (*GELS*, 352.1.b); this use of καί "indicates contrast" (*GELS*, 353.4) or an element of "surprise" or the "unexpected" (*GELS*, 353.5). A very similar clause is repeated in 4:8, 9, 10, and 11, and the repetition serves to unite this section of the book.

οὐκ ἐπεστρέψατε. Aor act ind 2nd pl ἐπιστρέφω. "Consummative or effective aorist," which emphasizes "the endpoint of the action" (Fanning, 263–64); in the end they did "not return."

πρός με. Direction, modifying οὐκ ἐπεστρέψατε. The preposition πρός with the accusative object here has the sense of "in the direction of, towards" (*GELS*, 589.III.1) and could be rendered "to" with the consummative aorist verb.

λέγει κύριος. See the discussion of this divine speech formula above in 1:3, 1:5, and 4:5.

4:7 καὶ ἐγὼ ἀνέσχον ἐξ ὑμῶν τὸν ὑετὸν πρὸ τριῶν μηνῶν τοῦ τρυγήτου· καὶ βρέξω ἐπὶ πόλιν μίαν, ἐπὶ δὲ πόλιν μίαν οὐ βρέξω· μερὶς μία βραχήσεται, καὶ μερίς, ἐφ᾽ ἣν οὐ βρέξω ἐπ᾽ αὐτήν, ξηρανθήσεται·

ἐγώ. Nominative subject of ἀνέσχον. Emphatic first-person personal pronoun, parallel with the construction at the beginning of 4:6 (καὶ ἐγώ) and introducing the Lord's further warning to Israel, continuing the theme of 4:6.

ἀνέσχον. Aor act ind 1st sg ἀνέχω. Constative aorist, looking at the action as a whole (see Muraoka §52.c on this verb). The variation in verb tenses and moods in this section is noteworthy (see also 4:6); this aorist is followed by future tenses and a subjunctive in 4:8, and then there is another aorist in the last clause in 4:8. This variation "gives the readers the impression they are in the midst of the judgment and warnings being described; the Lord has withheld the rain, but he will cause it to rain and not to rain in the future (4:7)" (Glenny 2013b, 81).

ἐξ ὑμῶν. Separation, modifying ἀνέσχον, and the preposition ἐκ "indicates dissociation" (*GELS*, 201.1). Muraoka (§52.c) notes that this is the first attestation of ἐκ with ἀνέχω (see also *GELS*, 50, s.v. ἀνέχω), and it is likely that is because of the Hebrew source text (מכם). However, as Muraoka (§52.c) demonstrates, the LXX translators did not always follow the basic meaning of the prepositions in their Hebrew and Aramaic source texts, and often chose a pattern of rection which appeared best to them in the context.

τὸν ὑετόν. Accusative direct object of ἀνέσχον. Article with this monadic noun, "rain."

πρὸ τριῶν μηνῶν τοῦ τρυγήτου. Temporal, also modifying ἀνέσχον. The preposition πρό is means "prior to, before." Here the preposition is "followed by the genitive of a noun denoting a period of time at the end of which an event denoted by another, immediately following, genitive takes place" (*GELS*, 583.1.b; see the same construction in 1:1). This construction, placing the preposition before the time period rather than before its object, is a Hellenistic Greek idiom commonly employed to indicate duration of time (MHT, 3:260; see also Robertson [423–24], who calls this unusual word order hyperbaton); μηνῶν ("months") is an idiomatic use of the genitive to indicate a period of time in this construction (*GELS*, 583.I.b, s.v. πρό), τριῶν ("three") is an adjective modifying μηνῶν, and τρυγήτου ("harvest") functions as the object of πρό. The article before τρυγήτου clarifies that the object of the preposition is definite, referring to a specific "harvest."

βρέξω. Fut act ind 1st sg βρέχω. Predictive future: "will send rain."

ἐπὶ πόλιν μίαν. Locative, modifying βρέξω. With the accusative object the preposition "indicates a movement from a higher position on to something" (*GELS*, 266.III.1.b). The adjective εἷς (here accusative μίαν), modifying the object πόλιν, has the sense "a certain, unspecified" (*GELS*, 197.b),

ἐπὶ δὲ πόλιν μίαν οὐ βρέξω. This clause is similar to the preceding clause (see above) with the exceptions of the addition of the negative particle (οὐ) and the use of the connective δέ rather than καί. (This is one of only five time the translators employed δέ in Amos.) Both of these differences serve to create a contrast between this clause and the preceding one.

μερὶς μία βραχήσεται. The asyndeton before this clause follows the Hebrew and leaves its connection with the preceding clause unmarked; here the asyndeton does not indicate a change in topic, but it is consistent with the move from more general to more specific details (i.e., from no rain to dry up; Runge, 20, 22-23).

μερὶς μία. Nominative subject of βραχήσεται. Anarthrous generic noun representing all places that will receive rain; generic nouns may be articular or anarthrous (see Muraoka §1.d). In this passage the adjective μία has the sense "a certain, unspecified" (*GELS*, 197.b).

βραχήσεται. Fut pass ind 3rd sg βρέχω. Predictive future and simple passive. There is no agent expressed, but the Lord is the understood agent. Muraoka (§58.h) notes that this is one of two instances in the LXX where a substantive denoting physical space serves as the subject of the passive of this verb (see also Ezek 22:24). This same verb occurs three times in the verse in the future active "will send rain."

καί. Coordinating conjunction, connecting two independent clauses (*GELS*, 352.1.b), and here introduces a contrast with the preceding clause (*GELS*, 353.4). One might expect δέ here, as in the contrast earlier in the verse, but as mentioned there δέ occurs only five times in Amos, and the LXX translators usually rendered *vav* (ו) with καί.

μερίς. Nominative subject of ξηρανθήσεται. Anarthrous generic noun, representing all places that will not receive rain; here the anarthrous noun is definite, "the part" (see Muraoka §1.d on anarthrous definite generic nouns).

ἐφ᾽ ἥν. Locative, modifying μερίς. Here the preposition ἐπί "indicates a movement from a higher position on to something" (*GELS*, 266.III.1.b), as it does throughout this verse.

οὐ βρέξω. Fut act ind 1st sg βρέχω. Predictive future with the negative particle.

ἐπ᾽ αὐτήν. Locative, modifying βρέξω. The preposition ἐπί "indicates a movement from a higher position on to something" (*GELS*, 266.III.1.b), as it does throughout this verse. The accusative object of the preposition (αὐτήν) is anaphoric referring back to the preceding relative pronoun ἥν, which in turn refers back to the "part" (μερίς) that is the subject of the last clause in the verse. This prepositional phrase is repetitious in Greek and is not reflected in the translation. This prepositional phrase is found in MSS A, Q, and R-H and Ziegler, and it is absent from B, W, *C*, and *L*; it corresponds closely to the Hebrew עליה and could well be the original reading, which was deleted because of its repetition in the LXX.

ξηρανθήσεται. Fut pass ind 3rd sg ξηραίνω. Predictive future and a simple passive with no agent expressed, "it will be dried up."

4:8 καὶ συναθροισθήσονται δύο καὶ τρεῖς πόλεις εἰς πόλιν μίαν τοῦ πιεῖν ὕδωρ καὶ οὐ μὴ ἐμπλησθῶσιν· καὶ οὐκ ἐπεστρέψατε πρός με, λέγει κύριος.

συναθροισθήσονται. Fut pass ind 3rd pl συναθροίζω. Predictive future and simple passive voice without the agent expressed. This verb has the sense "to come together, assemble" (*GELS*, 651.1). The translator apparently read the corresponding verbal (נוע; here in the *qal* stem, ונעו) "and they trembled, wandered" (*HALOT*, 1:681) as ונועדו, a *niphal* form of יעד (*HALOT*, 1:419; "they gather together").

δύο καὶ τρεῖς πόλεις. This phrase is the subject of the clause. The two nominative cardinal numbers are modifying the nominative plural noun πόλεις, which is the subject of συναθροισθήσονται, and the coordinating conjunction καί indicates "an approximate quantity by joining two consecutive cardinal numbers" (*GELS*, 353.1.j), i.e., "two or three cities."

εἰς πόλιν μίαν. Locative, modifying συναθροισθήσονται. The preposition εἰς indicates "extension involving a goal or place" and in this context "with focus on the area within the point reached" (BDAG, 28–29.1.a.β). The anarthrous accusative object of εἰς (πόλιν) with the cardinal number modifying it do not refer to a specific city; the number (μίαν) indicates "a certain, unspecified" city (*GELS*, 197.b).

τοῦ πιεῖν. Aor act inf πίνω (purpose). The category of purpose may seem unusual for the genitive + infinitive construction (see Burk, 63). However, Smyth (§1408) mentions the association of the genitive of cause, which is "partly true genitive, partly ablatival," with the genitive of purpose in the genitive articular infinitive construction. Ehorn (224) explains that "purpose (which emphasizes the *end* of an action) and cause (which emphasizes the *beginning* of an action) are conceptually similar" (emphasis in original). Thus, the explanation of the τοῦ +

infinitive construction denoting purpose may be the ablative sense of the genitive case (see Burk, 63–67)

ὕδωρ. Accusative direct object of πιεῖν.

καί. This coordinating conjunction introduces a clause giving the consequences or results of the actions in the first clause (*GELS*, 352.1.b).

οὐ μὴ ἐμπλησθῶσι. Aor pass subj 3rd pl ἐμπίπλημι. This construction with the subjunctive and the two negative particles communicates emphatic negation. The passive is a simple passive, and the aorist is a consummative aorist (Fanning, 263–65). This verb has the sense of "fill" or "have one's fill" in the active, but in the passive voice it often has the sense of being satisfied or "sated" (*GELS*, 227–28.6).

καί. This use of καί "indicates contrast" (*GELS*, 353.4) or an element of "surprise" or the "unexpected" (*GELS*, 353.5).

οὐκ ἐπεστρέψατε πρός με. See 4:6.

λέγει κύριος. See the discussion of this divine speech formula in 1:3, 1:5, and 4:5.

4:9 ἐπάταξα ὑμᾶς ἐν πυρώσει καὶ ἐν ἰκτέρῳ· ἐπληθύνατε κήπους ὑμῶν, ἀμπελῶνας ὑμῶν καὶ συκῶνας ὑμῶν καὶ ἐλαιῶνας ὑμῶν κατέφαγεν ἡ κάμπη· καὶ οὐδ᾽ ὣς ἐπεστρέψατε πρός με, λέγει κύριος.

The asyndeton before this clause follows the Hebrew and suggests in Greek that the relationship between what follows and what preceded it is clear and does not need a conjunction to clarify it (see Runge, 20–23); the topic of the Lord's warnings continues from the preceding verses, but it progresses to a different warning. There is also some question on where to divide the clauses in this verse (see Glenny 2013b, 81–82), and the division here reflects the critical texts (R-H and Ziegler). The message and vocabulary of this verse are similar to Hag 2:17.

ἐπάταξα. Aor act ind 1st sg πατάσσω. Constative aorist ("I smote"), looking at the action as a whole. After several predictions about the future (predictive futures) in 4:7–8, the verb tenses in this verse are aorist; the change in tenses gives the impression the recipients (readers) are in the midst of the warnings described in these verses.

ὑμᾶς. Accusative direct object of ἐπάταξα.

ἐν πυρώσει. Means, modifying ἐπάταξα. The preposition ἐν has the sense "by means of, using as instrument" (*GELS*, 231.6.a). It has been suggested that the dative object of ἐν (πυρώσει) refers to a "forest fire" (*GELS*, 609.1), "rust (disease of cereal plants)" (LEH, 539), and "fever" (NETS). The word occurs only one other time in the LXX (Prov 27:21), where it refers to "the testing of gold in the fire" (*TDNT* 6:951). Although this judgment could refer to the burning up of crops from heat and drought, the idea of "fever" or "inflammation" of people is most consistent with the parallel phrase (ἐν ἰκτέρῳ) that follows (see *TDNT* 6:951 for examples of this usage of πύρωσις). This understanding also parallels the first judgment ("aching of teeth") in 4:6.

ἐν ἰκτέρῳ. Means, modifying ἐπάταξα in a second parallel PP that is connected by καί (*GELS*, 352.1.a); the preposition ἐν has the sense "by means of, using as instrument" (*GELS*, 231.6.a). The dative object of ἐν (ἰκτέρῳ) refers to jaundice outside of the LXX (LSJ, 827), it refers to human sickness or jaundice in Lev 26:16 and Jer 37:6, and in 2 Chr 6:28 it refers to a blight on crops. Here it likely refers to a human illness of some sort, as the first punishment mentioned in 4:6, "aching of teeth" (γομφιασμόν); see Glenny (2013a, 81).

ἐπληθύνατε. Aor act ind 2nd pl πληθύνω. Constative aorist, looking at the action as a whole. This common word means "to increase, multiply, fill" (LEH, 497). The lack of a connector (asyndeton) follows the Hebrew; there is a continuation of the theme of the Lord's warnings, but there is a change to a new topic in the development of that theme. The listing of the Lord's warnings without connectors has a staccato-like effect and gives the impression that they are coming one after another in rapid succession.

κήπους. Accusative direct object of ἐπληθύνατε. The following context (ἀμπελῶνας, συκῶνας, ἐλαιῶνας) suggests that these "gardens" are similar to orchards (see *GELS*, 396–97). Normally a noun with a possessive pronoun attached to it has an article, but that is not true of the nouns in this verse; this is probably because of Hebrew (and Aramaic) influence (Muraoka §3.b; also, BDF §259).

ὑμῶν. Possessive genitive.

ἀμπελῶνας. Accusative direct object of κατέφαγεν. This is the first of three coordinate direct objects, all modified by personal pronouns and joined by καί. On the lack of an article with this noun, see κήπους above. This word could refer to "vineyards" or the "fruit of vineyards" (*GELS*, 33), but the parallel words suggest "vineyards" here.

ὑμῶν. Possessive genitive.

συκῶνας. Accusative direct object of κατέφαγεν. This word, which occurs in the LXX only here and in Jer 5:17, refers to "fig-yards" (*GELS*, 645). On the lack of an article with this noun, see κήπους above.

ὑμῶν. Possessive genitive. Brenton's translation divides the clauses in this verse after this pronoun, taking the "vineyards" (ἀμπελῶνας) and "fig yards" (συκῶνας) to be part of what the people multiplied (ἐπληθύνατε), but Dines (1991, 148), Ziegler, Swete, R-H, and NETS understand these words to be objects of the following word "devoured" (κατέφαγεν), along with the following "olive groves" (ἐλαιῶνας); the punctuation of the critical editions is more fitting for this context, which describes the Lord's judgments for the purpose of turning the people back to him as well as their lack of response, as is repeatedly described in this section "[even so] you did not return to me" (see 4:6, 8, 9, 10, and 11).

ἐλαιῶνας. Accusative direct object of κατέφαγεν. On the lack of an article with this noun ("olive groves"), see κήπους above.

ὑμῶν. Possessive genitive.

κατέφαγεν. Aor act ind 3rd sg κατεσθίω. Constative aorist, looking at the action as a whole. The translator's choice of a compound verb here creates alliteration in the words κατέφαγεν ἡ κάμπη (Dines 2013, 403). See Joel 1 for another description of the devastation caused by caterpillars and locusts.

ἡ κάμπη. Nominative subject of κατέφαγεν. A generic noun referring to a class of insects ("the caterpillar," LEH, 305); it is common to have an article with a generic noun (Muraoka §1.d).

οὐδ' ὡς. In this combination ὡς functions as an adverb, "so." The combination means "even so... not" (GELS, 749.VII, s.v. ὡς; LSJ, 2038.A.2, s.v. ὡς); the same combination is found in 4:9, 10, and 11, and it strengthens the refrain, making it a more intense negation than the simple negative (οὐ) found in 4:6 and 4:8 (Muraoka §83.fe), suggesting that the judgments in verses 9–11 are more severe than those in verses 6 and 8.

ἐπεστρέψατε πρός με, λέγει κύριος. See 4:6.

4:10 ἐξαπέστειλα εἰς ὑμᾶς θάνατον ἐν ὁδῷ Αἰγύπτου καὶ ἀπέκτεινα ἐν ῥομφαίᾳ τοὺς νεανίσκους ὑμῶν μετὰ αἰχμαλωσίας ἵππων σου καὶ ἀνήγαγον ἐν πυρὶ τὰς παρεμβολὰς ὑμῶν ἐν τῇ ὀργῇ μου· καὶ οὐδ' ὡς ἐπεστρέψατε πρός με, λέγει κύριος.

ἐξαπέστειλα. Aor act ind 1st sg ἐξαποστέλλω. Consummative aorist stressing the completion or accomplishment of the action of sending death.

εἰς ὑμᾶς. Direction, modifying ἐξαπέστειλα. The preposition εἰς indicates a "target" of the action, and the action is hostile (GELS, 196.3.a).

θάνατον. Accusative direct object of ἐξαπέστειλα. Dines (1991, 148) renders this noun "plague," and Brenton renders it "pestilence," but there seems to be no reason to render it other than with its normal meaning "death." The MT has "pestilence" (דבר), and the translator changed the sense slightly; the translator of Exodus also employed θάνατος to render "pestilence" (דבר) in Exod 5:3, and Muraoka (GELS, 324.b) suggests the sense "fatal illness" for θάνατος in that context, a rendering that includes death.

ἐν ὁδῷ. Locative, modifying ἐξαπέστειλα. The preposition indicates a place in which the action took place (*GELS*, 231.1.b). On the meaning of this phrase, see its use in Isa 10:24; 19:23; Jer 2:18 and the discussion in Van der Kooij (146); the translator apparently read the Hebrew idiom בדרך, meaning "after the manner" (*HALOT*, 1:232.4, s.v. דרך) as "in the way." Egypt would have had special connotations for early readers of LXX Amos if it was translated there for them. On the absence of the article in this phrase and the use of the article with the proper noun Αἴγυπτος, see Muraoka (§22.v.iii).

Αἰγύπτου. Genitive of destination, i.e., "to Egypt" (Wallace, 100–101).

ἀπέκτεινα. Aor act ind 1st sg ἀποκτείνω. Consummative aorist; the lexical nature of this verb requires that the stress be on the completion or accomplishment of the slaying or killing (Wallace, 559–61).

ἐν ῥομφαίᾳ. Instrumental, modifying ἀπέκτεινα. The preposition ἐν has the sense "by means of, by using [the 'sword'] as instrument" (*GELS*, 231.6). The object of the preposition is definite and generic.

τοὺς νεανίσκους. Accusative direct object of ἀπέκτεινα. It is common to have an article with a noun that is modified by a possessive pronoun.

ὑμῶν. Possessive genitive.

μετὰ αἰχμαλωσίας. Accompaniment, modifying ἀπέκτεινα, i.e., the killing of the young men with the sword took place along with the captivity of their horses. The preposition μετά indicates a "common fate or lot" (*GELS*, 452.5). The object of the preposition, αἰχμαλωσίας, may be used concretely in the LXX for a group of captives (see 1:6, 9; 9:14), and here it is applied to horses (*GELS*, 18.2).

ἵππων. Objective genitive.

σου. Possessive genitive. This is the only singular second-person pronoun in this verse, and it does not follow the plural in the Hebrew; it is a collective singular. All five second-person pronominal suffixes in Hebrew in this verse are plural.

ἀνήγαγον. Aor act ind 1st sg ἀνάγω. Consummative aorist. Muraoka (*GELS*, 38.1.a) suggests the rendering "sent up" for this verb in this context.

ἐν πυρί. Means, modifying ἀνήγαγον. The preposition ἐν has the sense "by means of, by using as instrument" (*GELS*, 231.6.a). באש ("stench") in the MT is read as its homograph, "with fire."

τὰς παρεμβολὰς. Accusative direct object of ἀνήγαγον. Nouns modified by possessive pronouns are commonly articular.

ὑμῶν. Possessive genitive.

ἐν τῇ ὀργῇ. Stative, modifying ἀνήγαγον. The preposition ἐν has the sense "being found in a certain state or condition" (*GELS*, 232.14). Nouns modified by a possessive pronoun are commonly articular.

The translator apparently read II אף in the Hebrew as "anger" rather than "nose"; the word has both senses (*HALOT*, 1:76–77), but with the rendering of באש ("stench") as ἐν πυρί (see above), the context requires that אף be read as "anger."

μου. Possessive genitive. The MT has the second-person plural pronoun, followed by MSS B, W, Swete, and Ziegler; the first-person pronoun is in A, Q, L, and R-H. The second-person plural pronoun, which must be understood as an objective genitive (so Muraoka §22.v.xiii), does not make sense unless a first-person pronoun is also understood ("in [my] anger against you"; see Glenny 2013b, 22, 82).

οὐδ' ὥς. See 4:9.

ἐπεστρέψατε πρός με, λέγει κύριος. See the end of 4:9 and the discussion of these words at the end of 4:6.

4:11 κατέστρεψα ὑμᾶς, καθὼς κατέστρεψεν ὁ θεὸς Σοδομα καὶ Γομορρα, καὶ ἐγένεσθε ὡς δαλὸς ἐξεσπασμένος ἐκ πυρός· καὶ οὐδ' ὡς ἐπεστρέψατε πρός με, λέγει κύριος.

κατέστρεψα. Aor act ind 1st sg καταστρέφω. Consummative aorist. This verb means "overturn, overthrow" (LEH, 327), and often it has the sense "ruin, destroy," as here (*GELS*, 384–85.3).

ὑμᾶς. Accusative direct object of κατέστρεψα.

καθώς. This adverb, indicating "similarity and comparison," introduces a clause (*GELS*, 352.1.c; *GELS* calls this word a conjunction, but BDAG, LSJ, and *GE* all classify it as an adverb).

κατέστρεψεν. Aor act ind 3rd sg καταστρέφω. Consummative aorist. See the discussion of this word above; the use with Sodom and Gomorrah echoes Gen 13:10.

ὁ θεός. Nominative subject of κατέστρεψεν in a dependent clause. The actions of God are here described by the Lord, who is speaking. This is the use of the article with a monadic noun.

Σοδομα καὶ Γομορρα. These two indeclinable proper nouns function as coordinate accusative direct objects of κατέστρεψεν, joined by the coordinating conjunction καί (*GELS*, 352.1.a). Σόδομα is a neuter plural form, and there is some debate whether Γόμορρα is feminine singular or neuter plural. In the LXX Γόμορρα is inflected as a first-declension feminine singular noun in the nominative and genitive (Gen 10:19; 14:2, 8, 10 [2x]; 18:16, 20; 19:28; Deut 32:32; Odes 2:32; Zeph 2:9; Isa 1:9, 10; Jer 23:14), and when it is in the accusative it is inflected as a neuter plural (Gen 13:10; 19:24; Deut 29:22; Amos 4:11; Isa 13:19; Jer 27:40; 30:12). Thackeray (§11.10) helpfully explains, "Names of *towns* as a rule end in -α and are declined like *neuters* of Declension II, with occasional transition (metaplasmus) to Declension I, especially where the nom. [inative] ends in–(ρ)ρα" (emphasis in original). Because of its function here as a direct object and the fact that the neuter form is always used for this function in the LXX, it is best to understand it as a neuter plural accusative form (see the discussion in BDF §57; Thackeray §11.10; BDAG, 205). Blomqvist's study of the gender of place-names of Boeotian toponyms has demonstrated "that feminine gender is not automatically linked with settlement names" (8), and the assignment of gender to place-names may be "pure coincidence" (18).

ἐγένεσθε. Aor mid ind 2nd pl γίνομαι. Constative aorist, looking at their existence in this state. On the middle form and function of γίνομαι, see 1:1 on ἐγένοντο.

ὡς. Relative adverb (BDAG, 1103), which here "introduces the predicate in an equational sentence" (*GELS*, 748.7.a).

δαλὸς. Predicate nominative in an equative sentence. The anarthrous noun is indefinite, "a brand" or "piece of burning wood" (*GELS*, 139).

ἐξεσπασμένος. Prf pass ptc masc sg nom ἐκσπάω. The basic sense of this compound verb is "to pull out" (*GELS*, 216); note its use in 3:12 (2x) and in 9:15. It is an intensive perfect emphasizing "the results or present state produced by a past action" (Wallace, 574–76). The participle is adjectival, modifying the preceding noun; see Muraoka (§31.ce) on the absence of the article with an adjectival participle.

ἐκ πυρός. Separation, modifying ἐξεσπασμένος. The preposition ἐκ indicates dissociation (*GELS*, 201.1). The object of the preposition, πυρός, is generic, and it is definite, as are many anarthrous objects of prepositions.

καὶ οὐδ᾽ ὡς ἐπεστρέψατε πρός με, λέγει κύριος. See the discussion of this same phrase at the end of 4:6 and 4:9.

4:12 διὰ τοῦτο οὕτως ποιήσω σοι, Ισραηλ· πλὴν ὅτι οὕτως ποιήσω σοι, ἑτοιμάζου τοῦ ἐπικαλεῖσθαι τὸν θεόν σου, Ισραηλ.

διὰ τοῦτο. Causal. See the discussion of this phrase in 2:13. The PP could be rendered "therefore" or "for this reason," but the latter brings out the causal idea more clearly. The object of the preposition (τοῦτο) refers to the preceding verses describing Israel's rejection of the Lord's warnings (4:6–11); that rejection is the reason for the judgment referred to in the next words.

Οὕτως. The function of this adverb in 4:12 is debatable, and Muraoka lists three possible ways to understand it (see *GELS*, 515.A.a: anaphoric; 515.A.c: equal to τάδε; or 515.b: cataphoric). I take it to be a Hebraism, meaning "such a thing" (LSJ, 1277.V; see also Gen 29:26) and equal to τάδε; thus, it functions like a direct object of ποιήσω (*GELS*, 515.A.c) and refers to the coming judgment described previously in 3:2, 11-12, 13-15, and 4:2-3.

ποιήσω. Fut act ind 1st sg ποιέω. Predictive future.

σοι. Dative indirect object of ποιήσω with the understood direct object οὕτως (see above). The singular pronoun (3x in this verse and always following the Hebrew) is collective, referring to Israel, and is a change from the preceding pattern of plural pronouns and subjects.

Ισραηλ. Vocative of simple address. Indeclinable proper noun (having no distinct vocative form).

πλὴν ὅτι. These two words often function as a unit meaning "except that, save that" (LSJ, 1419.II.4). This combination occurs nine times in the LXX with a variety of meanings. In its other occurrence in the Prophets in Amos 9:8, the words function as a unit meaning "however" and introduce "a parenthetical after-thought" (*GELS*, 564.A.4). That understanding of the words does not make sense here. I have argued elsewhere that the two words function independently here and the first conjunction, πλήν, introduces the following clause, which qualifies the preceding statement, and the second conjunction, ὅτι, is functioning as a causal participle (see Glenny 2013b, 84, and the translation above where they are rendered "however, because..."). The causal idea seems necessary in this context; Muraoka (§76.d) mentions this as an example of "a fronted causal clause."

οὕτως ποιήσω σοι. These words repeat a clause in the first sentence in the verse; see the discussion there.

ἑτοιμάζου. Pres mid impv 2nd sg ἑτοιμάζω. This is a direct or reflexive middle with the sense "make yourself ready" (*GELS*, 296.II.1). The present imperative is a specific command, aimed at a single response. The singular verb form fits with the collective description of the recipients as "Israel" and with the repetition of the second-person singular pronoun three times in this verse.

τοῦ ἐπικαλεῖσθαι. Pres mid inf ἐπικαλέω (purpose). Infinitive showing purpose with a genitive neuter article (i.e., "prepare yourself [Israel] for the purpose of calling upon your God"). The direct or reflexive middle with the accusative of person following indicates that the subject is to appeal to the person [Lord] for help (*GELS*, 273.B.b). The present tense should probably be understood to be iterative in force; Israel is to prepare (once and for all) to call upon its God (repeatedly). The Hebrew reads "to meet" (II קרא), and the translator read it more positively as "to call upon" (I קרא). The infinitive constructs of these homographs are pronounced slightly differently, and apparently the translator read it as the latter.

τὸν θεόν. Accusative object of ἐπικαλεῖσθαι. The article is employed with a monadic noun; it is also customary to employ an article with a noun that is followed by a possessive pronoun.

σου. Possessive genitive.

4:13 διότι ἰδοὺ ἐγὼ στερεῶν βροντὴν καὶ κτίζων πνεῦμα καὶ ἀπαγγέλλων εἰς ἀνθρώπους τὸν χριστὸν αὐτοῦ, ποιῶν ὄρθρον καὶ ὁμίχλην καὶ ἐπιβαίνων ἐπὶ τὰ ὕψη τῆς γῆς· κύριος ὁ θεὸς ὁ παντοκράτωρ ὄνομα αὐτῷ.

This verse is the first of three doxologies in Amos (see also 5:7–9 [8–9 MT]; and 9:5–6). They all contain participles extolling the Lord's actions and an identification of the Lord ("His name is . . ."). The LXX contains some important differences from the Hebrew in its description of the Lord's actions (on this verse see Glenny 2013b, 84–87; and Glenny 2009, 177–78 and 184–86).

διότι. Causal. This conjunction reinforces the connection between 4:12 and 4:13 by giving the reason why ("for, because"); see *GELS* (172.1).

ἰδού. Presentative particle drawing attention to what follows, which is here a verbal clause (*GELS*, 337.a and f; BDAG, 468). See 2:13 on ἰδού.

ἐγώ. Nominative subject of an understood copula (see Muraoka §94.d). There is no personal pronoun in the Hebrew, and the Greek pronoun is not so much emphatic as supplying a subject of the sentence who is doing the action described by the five participles. Likely the translator understood the pronoun to refer to the Lord. The fact that the Lord describes himself in the first (ἐγώ) and third person (κύριος ὁ θεὸς ὁ παντοκράτωρ ὄνομα αὐτῷ) in this verse seems to be inconsistent. But in 4:11 and 4:12 the Lord (God) also refers to himself in the first and third persons in the LXX and Hebrew (see above). The title "God" (θεός) is especially employed to describe the Lord as the one who judges, and in the refrain at the end of 4:13 "Lord" and "God" are linked as names of the one God of Israel.

στερεῶν. Pres act ptc nom masc sg στερεόω (substantival). Gnomic present. This verb has the sense "to make firm, solid" (*GELS*, 635.1), and it is the first of five anarthrous (in agreement with the Hebrew) present participles in this verse, which must all be understood to function as substantives (predicate nominatives) and refer to the Lord. The same form of this verb occurs in what is likely a LXX addition in Hos 13:4; the context there is very similar to that of this verse, and both passages likely involve anti-Baal polemic (see Glenny 2013b, 85 on this verb).

βροντὴν. Accusative direct object of στερεῶν. This is a monadic noun without the article. The reference to "thunder" in the LXX likely involves anti-Baal polemic, since Baal was known as Hadad ("the thunderer"); the Hebrew has "mountains" (הרים). LXX readers could have understood the first two participle phrases to be polemic against the thunderbolts of Zeus (see Glenny 2013b, 85).

κτίζων. Pres act ptc nom masc sg κτίζω (substantival). Gnomic present and functioning as a predicate nominative. The sense of this verb is "to bring into being" (*GELS*, 416–17), and it is often rendered "create."

πνεῦμα. Accusative direct object of κτίζων. This is a monadic noun without the article. Here where it is parallel to thunder, it refers to "wind," not the Spirit. In the early church in the debates about the full deity of the Holy Spirit, this verse was used to argue that that Spirit was created. The orthodox countered this argument by appealing to the Scriptures as a whole, the difference between the Greek and Hebrew in this verse, and careful analysis of the text (see Dines 1991, 152–54; and Kelly, 255–58).

ἀπαγγέλλων. Pres act ptc nom masc sg ἀπαγγέλλω (substantival). Gnomic present and functioning as a predicate nominative. See the discussion of this verb in 3:9 and 4:5.

εἰς ἀνθρώπους. Direction, modifying ἀπαγγέλλων. The preposition εἰς has the sense "in the direction" of a goal, used here with a verb of verbal communication (*GELS*, 196.1). The anarthrous object of the preposition (ἀνθρώπους) is qualitative, emphasizing the traits of being human; it has "no particular reference to maleness," but it refers to "human beings" (*GELS*, 52.1.a). In 9:12 it refers to gentiles, and they would apparently be included in the referents of the word here; in view of the emphasis on gentiles in 9:12, they could be the exclusive intended referent here also.

τὸν χριστὸν. Accusative direct object of ἀπαγγέλλων. This word could refer to a priest, a king, or to the anticipated eschatological messiah (see Dines 1991, 155). Instead of the Hebrew words מה שחו ("what is his thought"), the LXX translates it as משיחו ("his Christ"). See Glenny (2009, 229–40) on this rendering and on messianism in LXX Amos; see also Glenny (2018) for a survey of some different views of this rendering and an argument that there is evidence of messianism in LXX Amos 4:13. The article is employed with this monadic noun; it is also normal to use an article with a noun that is modified by a possessive pronoun.

αὐτοῦ. Possessive genitive, referring to κύριος ὁ θεὸς ὁ παντοκράτωρ, who is identified at the end of the verse.

ποιῶν. Pres act ptc nom masc sg ποιέω (substantival). Gnomic present and functioning as another predicate nominative. The asyndeton between this participle phrase and the preceding (in Hebrew and LXX) is apparently a simple variation in style since there is a coordinating conjunction (καί) between the other participle phrases in the verse.

ὄρθρον καὶ ὁμίχλην. Accusative direct objects of ποιῶν. There is no article with these qualitative nouns. I have rendered ὁμίχλην "misty darkness" (so also Dines 1991, 150; cf. Job 38:9; Isa 29:18; Zeph 1:15); thus, together with the coordinate object (ὄρθρον, "dawn") they form a merism, indicating the Lord creates not only these two contrasting aspects of creation but also everything between.

ἐπιβαίνων. Pres act ptc nom masc sg ἐπιβαίνω (substantival). Gnomic present and functioning as another predicate nominative. With the following PP modifying it, it has the sense "treading upon."

ἐπὶ τὰ ὕψη. Locative, modifying ἐπιβαίνων. The preposition ἐπί "indicates a surface on which some action takes place" (*GELS*, 266.3.a). The articles with the head noun ὕψη and its genitive modifier (τῆς γῆς) follow Apollonius' canon, and the article is normal with the monadic noun γῆς.

τῆς γῆς. Partitive genitive, i.e., the high places that are a part of the earth.

κύριος ὁ θεὸς ὁ παντοκράτωρ. This phrase recurs ten times in LXX Amos (3:13; 4:13; 5:8, 14, 15, 16, 27; 9:5, 6, 15) and three other times in LXX Twelve (Hos 12:6; Nah 3:5; Zech 10:3); see the discussion of it in 3:13. Here it corresponds to יהוה אלהי צבאות.

ὄνομα αὐτῷ. This construction occurs three other times in Amos (5:8, 27; 9:6), always, as here, with the title κύριος ὁ θεὸς ὁ παντοκράτωρ. The occurrences of these words in 5:8 and 9:6 are in the other two hymns describing the Lord in Amos. On the awkwardness of the change from the Lord speaking in the first person to the description of the Lord in the third person, see ἐγώ above in this verse.

ὄνομα. Predicate nominative in the clause with an implied copula verb ("the Lord, the God, the Almighty One, [is] his name"). This name is not only that by which God is called (*GELS*, 498.1.a), but also "it captures the essence of his person and describes his attributes and character" (Glenny 2013b, 87).

αὐτῷ. Dative of possession.

Amos 5:1–17

¹Hear this word of the Lord, which I am taking up for you as a funeral dirge, O house of Israel: ²"She has fallen, never again to arise, the maiden

Israel; she has fallen upon her land; there is no one who will raise her up." ³For thus says the Lord God, "The city, out of which a thousand used to go out, a hundred will be left, and the one out of which a hundred used to go out, ten will be left for the house of Israel." ⁴Therefore thus says the Lord to the house of Israel, "Seek me and you will live, ⁵but do not continue to seek Bethel, and do not continue to enter in to Gilgal, and do not continue to cross over to the well of the oath, because Gilgal, by being taken captive, will be taken into captivity, and Bethel will be as though not existing." ⁶Seek the Lord and live, so that the house of Joseph may not flame up like a fire; and it will devour it, and there will be no one to quench [it] for the house of Israel. ⁷The Lord [is] the one who executes judgment on high, he also established justice with respect to the earth, ⁸who makes all things and transforms [them], he also changes the shadow of death into the morning, and he darkens day into night. He who summons the water of the sea and pours it out on the surface of the earth, the Lord, the God, the Almighty One, [is] his name. ⁹He who dispenses ruin upon strength and brings distress upon a fortress. ¹⁰They hated him who reproves in the gateways, and they loathed pious speech. ¹¹Therefore, because you were buffeting the poor and you received choice gifts from them, you have built houses of polished stones, but you will never settle down and be at home in them; you have planted desirable vineyards, but you will never drink the wine from them, ¹²for I know your many ungodly deeds, and your sins are weighty, trampling upon the just man, taking bribes, and doing injustice to the poor in the gateways. ¹³Therefore, the prudent man will be silent at that time, for it is an evil time. ¹⁴Seek the good and [seek] not the evil, so that you may live, and then in this way the Lord, the God, the Almighty One, will be with you. In the same way as you say, ¹⁵"We hate the evil things, and we love the good things." Also restore judgment in the gateways so that the Lord, the God, the Almighty One, may have mercy on the survivors of Joseph. ¹⁶Therefore, thus says the Lord, the God, the Almighty One, "In all the streets there will be lamentation, and in all the roadways it will be said, Woe! Woe! The farmer will be summoned to mourning and lamentation and to those knowing a funeral dirge. ¹⁷And in all the roadways there will be mourning, because I will pass through the midst of you," says the Lord.

This section is a parody or imitation of a "funeral dirge" or "lament" (θρῆνος). The lament is over the nation of Israel (see also Lamentations 1–4), who has died (5:2) and whose army has been decimated (5:3). There is a combination of lament (5:1–3, 16–17), announcements of judgment (5:10–13), and exhortations to repent and seek the Lord (5:4–6, 14–15).

This combination of messages in the dirge seems to be contradictory, but the mention of the "remnant" in 5:15 is the solution to the seeming contradiction. Although the nation has died, there is a future for the remnant who will seek God and live (5:4). The offer of repentance and life in the section is real. Although the lament pronounces judgment and doom on the nation, which from the perspective of the original LXX reader has already been accomplished, the passage also contains a real invitation to the reader to repent and live; this invitation is marked by imperatives to seek the Lord in 5:4–6 and to seek good in 5:14.

5:1 Ἀκούσατε τὸν λόγον κυρίου τοῦτον, ὃν ἐγὼ λαμβάνω ἐφ᾽ ὑμᾶς θρῆνον, οἶκος Ισραηλ.

Ἀκούσατε. Aor act impv 2nd pl ἀκούω. This command to "hear" is an attention-getting device (see also 3:1, 13; 4:1; 7:16; 8:4). On the use of genitive or accusative objects with ἀκούω, see 3:1 on ἀκούσατε. The asyndeton, imperative verb commanding the recipients to listen, and announcement of a funeral dirge all signal the beginning of a new section.

τὸν λόγον ... τοῦτον. Accusative direct object of ἀκούσατε. The article is used with the noun modified by a demonstrative pronoun that refers to something in close proximity, the following oracle (i.e., cataphoric).

κυρίου. Genitive of source. This Greek word, which seems out of place between the preceding noun and the demonstrative pronoun modifying it, is not in the Hebrew (MT).

ὅν. Accusative direct object of λαμβάνω. The antecedent of the relative pronoun is λόγον.

ἐγώ. Nominative subject of λαμβάνω. The pronoun gives prominence to or emphasizes the subject (Young, 72). Throughout this section the Lord's speeches in the first person are mixed with his speeches and references to himself in the third person (e.g., 5:1a, 3; see the discussion in 4:13).

λαμβάνω. Pres act ind 1st sg λαμβάνω. Instantaneous or punctiliar present, completed at the moment the Lord "takes up" the speech. The verb has the sense "pronounce, utter" (*GELS*, 424.10), a sense that is not attested for it before the LXX.

ἐφ᾽ ὑμᾶς. Direction, modifying λαμβάνω. The preposition ἐπί indicates the ones to whom the utterance is directed (*GELS*, 266.4.d). In this context, with an accusative object (ὑμᾶς referring to the "house of Israel"), the preposition could have the sense of "for," "over," or "against"

(Dines 1991, 157); in keeping with the parody in the context, it makes more sense to understand it as "for" or "over" rather than "against."

θρῆνον. Accusative in simple apposition with the previously mentioned "word" (λόγον) and thus further describing it as a "lament, dirge" (*GE*, 950; *GELS*, 332; Lam 1:1; Amos 5:16; 8:10).

οἶκος. Nominative for a vocative, designating the addressees (see esp. 3:1; also see 5:25; 6:14, for the same use of this phrase).

Ισραηλ. Genitive of apposition (see 3:1). There is debate whether the address "house of Israel" at the end of 5:1 goes with 5:1, identifying the recipients of the lament (so NETS and apparently R-H and Ziegler [although neither R-H nor Ziegler has a punctuation mark at the end of 5:1] and Dines 1991, 157); or if it goes with 5:2, serving as the subject of the first verb in that verse (so Arieti, 64; Johnson, 33; Brenton; Swete; and B, which clearly has two clauses in 5:2: "the house of Israel is fallen" and "the maiden Israel has fallen"; see the discussion of this issue in Glenny 2013b, 88). The first option is preferred for three reasons: it follows the Hebrew, the second option would leave the recipients of the lament announced in 5:1 unspecified, and a vocative type address is employed with similar exhortations to "hear" in 3:1 and 4:1.

5:2 Ἔπεσεν οὐκέτι μὴ προσθῇ τοῦ ἀναστῆναι παρθένος τοῦ Ισραηλ· ἔσφαλεν ἐπὶ τῆς γῆς αὐτῆς, οὐκ ἔστιν ὁ ἀναστήσων αὐτήν.

Ἔπεσεν. Aor act ind 3rd sg πίπτω. Consummative aorist, indicating in this context the cessation or completion of the action of falling. The subject of this verb is best understood to be "the house of Israel," addressed at the end of 5:1, but at this point simply identified by the subject implied in the verb, "she," and later further identified as "the maiden Israel."

οὐκέτι μή. This double negative construction has the sense "no more, never again" (Muraoka §83.cb-cc; BDAG, 736.1). The combination of this double negation (10x in the Twelve) with προστίθημι followed by an infinitive reinforces the idea of "no-repetition, non-recurrence" (Muraoka §83.cb n. 1); this construction with the verb is a calque, a literal rendering of the Hebrew idiom (לֹא תוֹסִיף).

προσθῇ. Aor act subj 3rd sg προστίθημι. Constative aorist, looking at the action as a whole; the subjunctive with the negative is a calque (see previous entry), and with the double negative it is best understood as a subjunctive indicating emphatic negation. The subject of this verb is also best understood to be the "the house of Israel" (see also ἔπεσεν above), addressed at the end of 5:1 and later further identified as "the maiden Israel." MSS B, C, and Swete have προσθήσει (future indicative), but the aorist subjunctive "is consistent with the negative particle μή; cf. 7:8, 13; 8:2" (Glenny 2013b, 22) and is found in MSS A, Q, R-H, and Ziegler.

τοῦ ἀναστῆναι. Aor act inf ἀνίστημι (complementary). See Muraoka (§30.bg) and also Coneybeare and Stock (§60.d). This verb can have the nuance of resurrection, although here in a national context it is not likely (see its use later in the verse and in 8:14).

παρθένος. Nominative in simple apposition to the implied subject in ἔπεσεν and προσθῇ. Thus, "she" (NETS) is "the maiden Israel." Brenton and Swete, following the punctuation in MS B, understand this noun to be the subject of the following verb (ἔσφαλεν); however, R-H and Ziegler have the punctuation division after παρθένος τοῦ Ισραηλ and understand this noun to go with what precedes it in the verse (see the discussion in Glenny 2013b, 88, and above in this verse). This noun could be rendered "virgin" or "young woman, maiden." The breadth of its meaning and its metaphorical application to unfaithful Israel suggest "maiden, young woman" is the best rendering (so NETS; GELS, 535.a, suggests the sense here is a marriageable "young woman").

τοῦ Ισραηλ. Genitive of apposition, further describing and identifying the παρθένος as "Israel"; the head noun is metaphorical in meaning, and the genitive "brings the metaphor down to earth" (Wallace, 95). The article in this construction is very unusual. Perhaps it was employed here to clarify the case of the following noun. The phrase παρθένος τοῦ Ισραηλ occurs four other times in the LXX (translating the same Hebrew phrase all five times); however, in all the other occurrences of it there is no article (Deut 22:19; Jer 18:13; 38:4, 21). *HALOT* (1:167.2, s.v. בתולה) asserts that the Hebrew corresponding to παρθένος τοῦ Ισραηλ (בתולת ישראל) means "the virgin [maiden] Israel" not "the virgin [maiden] of Israel" in the Hebrew Bible (although Paul [160 n. 9] demurs). "The maiden of Israel" does not make sense when addressing Israel, and it is better to render it "maiden Israel" (so NETS). The phrase "maiden Israel" is parallel to the address at the end of 5:1, "house of Israel" (see *GELS*, 535, s.v. παρθένος), although here in 5:2 the head noun is not functioning as a vocative, since the verbs in 5:2 are all third person, describing Israel rather than addressing it.

ἔσφαλεν. Aor act ind 3rd sg σφάλλω. Consummative aorist ("she has fallen"), indicating the cessation or completion of the action. The subject of this verb is best understood to be the "the house of Israel," addressed at the end of 5:1 and identified further in this clause as "the maiden Israel." This form could be first or second aorist (Conybeare and Stock §23; Thackeray §24 [p. 286]).

ἐπὶ τῆς γῆς. Locative, modifying ἔσφαλεν. The preposition ἐπί is employed here to describe something that is occurring "on the surface of" the land (*GELS*, 263.2). The article with the object of the preposition (τῆς γῆς) is normal with a noun that is also modified by a possessive pronoun.

αὐτῆς. Possessive genitive.

οὐκ ἔστιν. Pres act ind 3rd sg εἰμί. The copulative verb has the sense "to exist," and with the negative it communicates nonexistence (*GELS*, 193.1.a); see the same sense of the verb in 5:6. With this sense of the verb it is best to understand the subject to be supplied by the verb, i.e., "there is not [i.e., no one]."

ὁ ἀναστήσων. Pres act ptc nom masc sg ἀνίστημι (substantival). Predicate nominative following the copulative verb. The article clarifies that the following participle has a substantival function, rather than periphrastic (Muraoka §1.c). This verb can have the nuance of resurrection from the dead (*GELS*, 54.4); here in a national context it refers to the raising up again of fallen Israel (*GELS*, 53.1; see its use earlier in the verse and in 7:2 and 5).

αὐτήν. Accusative direct object of ἀναστήσων, referring to "maiden Israel."

5:3 διότι τάδε λέγει κύριος κύριος Ἡ πόλις, ἐξ ἧς ἐξεπορεύοντο χίλιοι, ὑπολειφθήσονται ἑκατόν, καὶ ἐξ ἧς ἐξεπορεύοντο ἑκατόν, ὑπολειφθήσονται δέκα τῷ οἴκῳ Ισραηλ.

διότι. Causal conjunction, giving the reason or cause of the preceding (*GELS*, 172.1).

τάδε λέγει κύριος. See 1:3 and 1:6 on this phrase.

κύριος. The repetition of κύριος in R-H is based on MSS B and W; Ziegler, following L, does not repeat the divine name (see Glenny 2013b, 24). I have rendered the title "Lord God," following R-H. Every time κύριος is repeated like this in Amos, it is rendering the Hebrew words אדני יהוה (see also 7:2, 5; 9:5); however, the translator felt free to render these Hebrew words, which occur in this combination twenty-one times in Amos, by a variety of other divine names in the Greek translation (κύριος ὁ θεός, κύριος θεός, or κύριος; except in 9:5, which has κύριος κύριος ὁ θεός).

Ἡ πόλις. Pendent nominative, which is the "logical rather than syntactical subject at the beginning of a sentence" (Wallace, 51–53; BDF §466.2–4). The city is a "population center" in which people live (not metonymy for the people; *GELS*, 573.a). The article with the substantive is cataphoric, pointing to and anticipating the following descriptions of the city (see BDF §258 and Wallace, 220–21).

ἐξ ἧς. Origin, modifying ἐξεπορεύοντο. The preposition ἐκ (ἐξ before vowels) indicates origin or point of departure (*GELS*, 201.5). The repetition of the preposition in the following compound verb, which it modifies, emphasizes it. The antecedent of the genitive relative pronoun is πόλις.

ἐξεπορεύοντο. Impf mid ind 3rd pl ἐκπορεύομαι. Iterative imperfect, which is likely meant to be distributive, indicating "individual acts of multiple agents" (Wallace, 546). The middle is what Kemmer (269) calls "translational motion"; it is easy to see how the action of these kinds of verbs affects the subject. In the Hebrew the "going out" is apparently for a military operation, but in the LXX it is not clear, and perhaps the going out of cities here would be understood as going into captivity (see Glenny 2013b, 89).

χίλιοι. Nominative subject of ἐξεπορεύοντο. The plural form of the word is used to represent "one thousand" (LEH, 664), except with collective nouns (LSJ, 1992.2; Muraoka §21.c). χίλιοι is representative of the "city" described above in the verse. The numbers in this section, which serve as the subjects of the verbs, follow the verbs and are at the end of their clauses (except for the last clause, where the number is followed by the PP "for the house of Israel"), and the rhetorical effect is to emphasize the numbers.

ὑπολειφθήσονται. Fut pass ind 3rd pl ὑπολείπω. Predictive future, and the passive is a simple passive. The subject of the plural verb is ἑκατόν. The verb has the sense of "an amount remaining after removing a part" (*GELS*, 703.1), and it has connotations of a remnant here (see Glenny 2013b, 89; Amos 6:9; and the mention of a remnant in 5:14–15).

ἑκατόν. This adjective is an indeclinable number (*GELS*, 203), functioning as a nominative masculine, and the singular is used collectively and is plural in meaning (Muraoka §21.c). The role of this adjective is debatable. It could be the retained accusative direct object of the passive verb (BDF §159; i.e., "they will be left a hundred," which is the passive of "I will leave them a hundred"). But since in the preceding clause (and likely in the rest of the clauses giving numbers in the verse), the number following the verb is its subject, it is better to understand this number as the nominative subject of the preceding verb ("a hundred will be left").

ἐξ ἧς. Origin. See the parallel clause above (ἐξ ἧς ἐξεπορεύοντο χίλιοι) in the verse. It is repeated here with smaller numbers to emphasize further the extent of death in Israel.

ἐξεπορεύοντο ἑκατόν. See the parallel use of these words above in the verse.

ὑπολειφθήσονται. See the parallel use of this verb form above in the verse.

δέκα. This adjective is an indeclinable number (*GELS*, 142), functioning as the nominative subject of ὑπολειφθήσονται. See the discussion concerning ἑκατόν above in the parallel clause (ὑπολειφθήσονται ἑκατόν).

τῷ οἴκῳ. Dative of advantage or interest, here indicating the one who is especially interested or benefited by the action of the verb. The article is expected with "house of Israel," since it is a monadic noun.

Ισραηλ. This indeclinable noun is functioning as a genitive of apposition (see 3:1). The "house of Israel" is the addressee in the dirge in this section of Amos (see 5:1), and the designation occurs also in 5:4 and 6.

5:4 διότι τάδε λέγει κύριος πρὸς τὸν οἶκον Ισραηλ Ἐκζητήσατέ με καὶ ζήσεσθε·

διότι. The conjunction functions inferentially here: "therefore" (*GELS*, 172.4). The commands in 5:4–6 give hope after the devastation predicted in 5:1–3; the seeming contradiction of hope being contained in a funeral dirge is alleviated by the mention of and implications of a remnant in the context.

τάδε λέγει κύριος. See 1:3, 6; and 5:3 for discussion of this phrase.

πρὸς τὸν οἶκον Ισραηλ. Direction, modifying λέγει. The preposition gives the direction of or that toward which the Lord speaks (*GELS*, 589. III.2). See the discussion of "the house of Israel" above in 5:1 and 5:3.

Ἐκζητήσατέ με καὶ ζήσεσθε. This phrase and the similar one in 5:6 bracket verses 4–6, marking a subsection in the dirge. The parallel construction at the beginning of 5:6 has two aorist imperatives. This compound clause should be understood to function like a conditional sentence, with the first verb (a command) serving as the protasis and the second (future indicative) serving as the apodosis (see the discussion in Glenny 2013b, 90).

Ἐκζητήσατέ. Aor act impv 2nd pl ἐκζητέω. Conditional imperative (Porter 1994, 226–27; Wallace, 489–92; BDF §387). The fact that it is a conditional imperative does not remove the semantic force of the imperative (Porter 1993, 352–53), and the conditional idea should not be emphasized (see ζήσεσθε below). The action of the aorist verb is presented as a whole, and the aorist is best understood to be constative (cf. Wallace, 720, on what he calls the "pure ingressive" aorist imperative); the aorist imperative here also has a sense of urgency. The plural command directed to the collective "house of Israel" should be understood to stress the individuals in Israel, who are being commanded to respond. The seeking here is not for something that is lost; the verb has the idea "to engage oneself earnestly and devotedly in or with" (Muraoka §63.d.n2; *GELS*, 207.2).

με. Accusative direct object of Ἐκζητήσατέ, referring to the Lord.

καί. Coordinating conjunction, connecting parallel verbs (*GELS*, 352.1.a); here the conjunction "introduces an apodosis and indicates a consequence to follow when a request or command is acted upon" (*GELS*, 354.10).

ζήσεσθε. Fut mid ind 2nd pl ζάω. Muraoka (§28.ge–gea, esp. ge n. 2) calls this a future of "theoretical possibility," which deals with "a *theoretical* possibility of a situation or condition becoming a reality" (emphasis in original). Muraoka (§28.gea n. 2) is hesitant to give this sentence the force of a conditional construction; he contends Greek could express that explicitly, and in this case "the author or translator was content with leaving the matter vague and unspecified," i.e., "seek me and then you could live." It is easy to see how the action of this middle-voice verb affects the subjects (see Thackeray §24 [p. 269], on the forms of this verb in the LXX); the middle use is probably best classified as a spontaneous event of an animate being (Kemmer, 269). The plural verb, like the previous one, stresses the individuals in Israel.

5:5 καὶ μὴ ἐκζητεῖτε Βαιθηλ καὶ εἰς Γαλγαλα μὴ εἰσπορεύεσθε καὶ ἐπὶ τὸ φρέαρ τοῦ ὅρκου μὴ διαβαίνετε, ὅτι Γαλγαλα αἰχμαλωτευομένη αἰχμαλωτευθήσεται, καὶ Βαιθηλ ἔσται ὡς οὐχ ὑπάρχουσα·

καί. Coordinating conjunction, connecting coordinate clauses: the first clause in the verse, as well as the two following it, contains negative commands in contrast to the preceding positive one (*GELS*, 352.1.a; 352.4), and for that reason it is rendered "but." However, the juxtaposition of positive and negative provides explanation and expansion of what precedes as well as contrast with it.

μὴ ἐκζητεῖτε. Pres act impv 2nd pl ἐκζητέω. The plural prohibition stresses individual responsibility, and the present tense has an iterative sense, indicating something they are not to continue to do; in this context it could be rendered "stop seeking" (so NETS). This command is a correlative of seeking the Lord (5:4). The negative particle μή is normally used with nonindicative verbals; this is the first time in LXX Amos it is used with an imperative.

Βαιθηλ. Indeclinable proper noun, functioning as the accusative direct object of ἐκζητεῖτε (see below in this verse). On Βαιθηλ as the center of the idolatrous and corrupt alternative religion in Israel, see 3:14; 4:4; 7:10–17; (Glenny 2013b, 90).

καί. Coordinating conjunction, connecting clauses with coordinate prohibitions (*GELS*, 352.1.a).

εἰς Γαλγαλα. Locative, modifying μὴ εἰσπορεύεσθε. Here the preposition εἰς is synonymous with ἐν (*GELS*, 197.8) or as BDAG explains it "indicates a position within a certain area" (289.1.a.δ). The indeclinable proper noun Γαλγαλα functions as the accusative object of εἰς.

μὴ εἰσπορεύεσθε. Pres mid impv 2nd pl εἰσπορεύομαι. See the discussion of the preceding parallel present prohibition. This middle-voice verb involves what Kemmer (269) calls "translational motion." The compound verb with the prepositional prefix emphasizes the idea of the preceding preposition. This verb is appropriate for describing sexual or idolatrous activity (see Glenny 2013b, 90). See μὴ ἐκζητεῖτε above on the negation.

καί. Coordinating conjunction, connecting clauses with coordinate prohibitions (*GELS*, 352.1.a).

ἐπὶ τὸ φρέαρ. Direction, modifying μὴ διαβαίνετε. The preposition ἐπί "indicates a movement towards, or aimed at, an object" (*GELS*, 266. III.2). The translator rendered "Beersheba" according to its constituent parts ("the well of the oath"). See also Gen 21:14, 31–33; 26:31; in 8:14 "Beersheba" is transliterated "Bersabee."

τοῦ ὅρκου. Genitive of description. According to Apollonius' canon we should expect that a head noun and its genitive modifier either both have the article or do not.

μὴ διαβαίνετε. Pres act impv 2nd pl διαβαίνω. See the discussion of the two preceding parallel present prohibitions. This verb has the sense "to traverse" for the purpose of reaching another place (*GELS*, 148), and I have rendered it "cross over" (see also 6:2).

ὅτι. Causal conjunction, introducing coordinate causal clauses giving the reasons or causes of the preceding commands (*GELS*, 511.1).

Γαλγαλα. Indeclinable proper noun, functioning as the subject of a clause.

αἰχμαλωτευομένη αἰχμαλωτευθήσεται. The participle and finite future indicative construction (both from αἰχμαλωτεύω) corresponds to an infinitive absolute with an imperfect in Hebrew (see the discussion of this phenomenon in LXX Amos in Glenny 2009, 54). With this verb and its preceding participle, the translator was apparently trying to reproduce the striking effect of the corresponding Hebrew: הגלגל גלה יגלה (Dines 2013, 401); the assonance of the Greek corresponds to assonance in the source text. However, it is doubtful that Greek readers would have understood the Greek the same way the Hebrew was understood, and the translation ("Gilgal, by being taken captive, will be taken into captivity") attempts to reflect the way Greek readers would have understood the construction. For these reasons it is difficult to describe the two verb forms. The present tense of the participle is what Wallace calls a "perfective present," emphasizing that the "results of a past action are still continuing" (Wallace, 532–33), and the future finite form is predictive. Both passive verb forms are simple passives without agency expressed.

αἰχμαλωτευομένη. Pres pass nom masc sg αἰχμαλωτεύω (circumstantial). This is what Muraoka (§31.db) calls a participle "reflecting *figura etymologica* in Hebrew." He understands this use (see above) to be circumstantial, and I have rendered it as a circumstantial participle of means. It could also be attributive, modifying Γαλγαλα (i.e., "Gilgal, taken captive, will be taken").

αἰχμαλωτευθήσεται. Fut pass ind 3rd sg αἰχμαλωτεύω.

καί. Coordinating conjunction, connecting the two coordinate clauses that follow ὅτι and giving the reason for the preceding (*GELS*, 352.1.a).

Βαιθηλ. Indeclinable proper noun, functioning as the nominative subject of ἔσται. There would not have been a sanctuary in Bethel in the second century BCE when Amos was translated into Greek, so its nonexistence would have seemed appropriate to the translator.

ἔσται. Fut act ind 3rd sg εἰμί. Predictive future. The last clause in the verse corresponds to the Hebrew יהיה לאון ("shall come to nothing"); the translator read לאון ("to nothing") as לאין ("to non-existence") and rendered the following words accordingly.

ὡς. This comparative particle "introduces the predicate in an equational sentence" (*GELS*, 748.7.a); it has the sense "as if" here (see Dines 1991, 158).

οὐχ ὑπάρχουσα. Pres act ptc nom fem sg ὑπάρχω (predicate). This is an adjectival participle in the predicate position after the copulative verb; such participles never have an article (Wallace, 617–19). The negative particle μή is normally used with nonindicative verbals in Koine Greek, but this is an example of the Classical pattern in which μή was used with circumstantial participles and οὐ was used otherwise with participles (Muraoka §83.bd).

5:6 ἐκζητήσατε τὸν κύριον καὶ ζήσατε, ὅπως μὴ ἀναλάμψῃ ὡς πῦρ ὁ οἶκος Ιωσηφ, καὶ καταφάγεται αὐτόν, καὶ οὐκ ἔσται ὁ σβέσων τῷ οἴκῳ Ισραηλ.

The asyndeton here does not signal any specific relationship between this verse and the preceding, but the repetition of ideas from 5:4 in the first clause communicates emphasis and continuity. Yet there is also change from the preceding, since the Lord is not speaking here (see the discussion of κύριον below).

ἐκζητήσατε. See the discussion of the same verb form in 5:4. Muraoka (§28.gea) notes that the first clause is parallel to the command to seek the Lord in 5:4 (although it is not identical).

τὸν κύριον. Accusative direct object of ἐκζητήσατε. The prophet is understood to be talking here; compare the parallel command at the end of 5:4 where the Lord is speaking and says, "Seek me." The article is common with a monadic noun, since they are naturally definite.

καὶ. Coordinating conjunction, connecting parallel verbs (*GELS*, 352.1.a); here the conjunction "introduces an apodosis and indicates a consequence to follow when a request or command is acted upon" (*GELS*, 352.10; see the parallel usage at the beginning of 5:4).

ζήσατε. Aor act impv 2nd pl ζάω. Constative aorist, looking at the action as a whole; the imperative could be a rare example of a potential imperative in the apodosis of an implied conditional sentence (Wallace, 492, mentions this category). However, Muraoka (§28.gea) questions whether the construction in 5:4 and 6 should be called a conditional sentence; he thinks there is "ambiguity inherent in this syntagm," suggesting potential more than condition. The future forms in MS A and *L* were perhaps influenced by 5:4; MS B has ζῆτε (which could be pres act ind or subj 2nd pl) and seems awkward in this context. The plural verb stresses the individuals in Israel.

ὅπως μὴ. Introduces a purpose clause, clarifying that the warning in 5:6 is so that the house of Joseph might not perish (Glenny 2013b, 91). The ὅπως μή construction has the sense "lest, so that not" (Smyth §2193); the negative particle μή with the subjunctive is commonly employed after warnings.

ἀναλάμψῃ. Aor act subj 3rd sg ἀναλάμπω. The verb has the sense "shine brightly" (*GELS*, 42), but in this context must mean "flame up" (see LEH, 40); the aorist is ingressive, stressing the beginning of the action. The verb is always used in a positive context elsewhere in the LXX (Job 11:15; 2 Macc 1:22; Wis 3:7; Isa 42:4).

ὡς. Introduces a comparative clause, involving ellipsis: "The house of Joseph may not flame up *like* a fire [flames up]." The comparative particle and following noun make up a simile, and "in similes the noun following ὡς is usually anarthrous" (*GELS*, 748.6).

πῦρ. Nominative subject of an implied form of ἀναλάμπω.

ὁ οἶκος. Nominative subject of ἀναλάμψῃ. The article with "house of Joseph" is expected, since it is monadic.

Ιωσηφ. Genitive of apposition. The "house of Joseph" is simply "Joseph" in 5:15 and 6:6; it originally referred to the Joseph tribes,

Ephraim and Manasseh, but the meaning was extended to refer to all of Israel (Obad 18; Zech 10:6).

καί. The coordinating conjunction καί "introduces a consequence that would ensue if what is denoted by the preceding clause is realized" (*GELS*, 354.9).

καταφάγεται. Fut mid ind 3rd sg κατεσθίω. Predictive future; the future-tense verb connected by καί to the preceding subjunctive verb purpose clause, designates "some further consequence" that is related to the main purpose (BDF §369; see also Isa 6:10; Rom 3:4). Muraoka (§77.f) uses this verse as an example of a construction in which the subjunctive-mood verb expresses "what might or could happen," and the indicative indicates a situation that will follow, if what is expressed in the subjunctive occurs. The subjunctive form of this verb in MSS B V and *L* is apparently an attempt to smooth out the differences in moods. The future of ἐσθίω is formed from a different verb (BDF §74), and it is in the middle voice; this is what Kemmer (268) calls a reflexive use of the middle. The πῦρ in the preceding context must be the understood subject of the verb (confirmed in the final clause).

αὐτόν. Accusative direct object of καταφάγεται. The masculine pronoun agrees with its immediate antecedent (οἶκος), but the context also describes Israel as a παρθένος (5:2; see the feminine pronouns there). There is no corresponding pronoun in the Hebrew.

καί. Coordinating conjunction, connecting parallel clauses (*GELS*, 352.1.b); the clauses give consequences that will follow if the preceding purpose clause is realized (*GELS*, 354.9).

οὐκ ἔσται. Fut act ind 3rd sg εἰμί. The negative particle with the verb indicates "there does [will] not exist" (*GELS*, 193.1); here the sense seems to be "there will not emerge, make an appearance" (*GELS*, 193.1.b). On the transition of εἰμί to the middle forms, see Thackeray (§23.11) and BDF (§98). The future is predictive; see above on the parallel καταφάγεται for the function of the future in this context.

ὁ σβέσων. Pres act ptc nom masc sg σβέννυμι (substantival). Predicate nominative. The article removes any syntactical ambiguity concerning whether the participle is periphrastic or substantival following ἔσται (Muraoka 1.c).

τῷ οἴκῳ. Dative of interest. There will be no one to act in the interest of or for the benefit of "the house of Israel." The article is employed with the monadic noun.

Ισραηλ. Indeclinable proper noun functioning as a genitive of apposition, further defining the house. See the reference to the house of Israel in 5:3 and 5:4; the designation would probably have had a broad meaning for LXX readers, referring to the nation as a whole. The

Hebrew reading לבית אל ("Bethel") is rendered "house of Israel" (τῷ οἴκῳ Ισραηλ) in the LXX.

5:7 κύριος ὁ ποιῶν εἰς ὕψος κρίμα καὶ δικαιοσύνην εἰς γῆν ἔθηκεν,

Verses 7–9 make up the second of three hymns or doxologies in LXX Amos (see also 4:13 and 9:5–6). The description of the Lord's actions, the main focus of the hymns, is communicated by participles, with the single exception of ἔθηκε in 5:7. In the Hebrew, 5:7 is a description of the sins of Israel, but in the LXX it is part of the hymn in 5:8–9 (see Glenny 2009, 80).

κύριος. Nominative subject of an equative sentence with a supplied copulative verb. Some MSS (B and V) do not contain this word; MS A has κύριος ὁ θεός, and MSS Q and *L* are among the manuscripts with this word only, which is the reading preferred in both Ziegler and R-H (see Glenny 2013b, 24). There is nothing corresponding to this word in the MT.

ὁ ποιῶν. Pres act ptc nom masc sg ποιέω (substantival). Gnomic present. The substantival participle construction functions as the predicate nominative in the equative sentence with an implied copula; the article functions as a substantive for this participle, and it also continues to have this function with the first four participles in 5:8. The verb here has the sense "to engage oneself in and effect" (*GELS*, 569.6), and I have rendered it "execute." Since it is done "on high," it apparently especially refers to the Lord's jurisdiction over judgment on earth from his vantage point in heaven.

εἰς ὕψος. Locative. PP modifying ποιῶν. Here εἰς is synonymous with ἐν, with the sense "at the place of" (*GELS*, 197.8; see also *GELS*, 708.2.a, s.v. ὕψος). The accusative object of the preposition, ὕψος, can have the sense "exalted status" (*GELS*, 708.4; BDAG, 1045.2), with the resulting rendering "who exalts judgment" in the phrase ποιῶν εἰς ὕψος κρίμα (see the discussion in Dines 1991, 159; Job 5:11). But the sense "who executes judgment on high" is preferred here for several reasons. The abstract idea of exalting judgment is out of place in this hymn, since most of the actions of the Lord in the hymns in Amos are related to creation; the adjective ὕψος is found in the previous hymn (4:13) in the phrase "high places" and does not have the sense "exalted status" there; and the verse is comparing the Lord's actions "on high" and his actions "with respect to the earth" (see further Glenny 2009, 92). The translator apparently read the Hebrew ללענה ("to wormwood") as למעלה ("to the ascent," "to the height," *HALOT* 1:613–14); see Glenny 2009, 80.

κρίμα. Accusative direct object of ποιῶν. This abstract noun and the following one (δικαιοσύνην) are anarthrous but not indefinite (see Wallace 249–50). "No vital difference was felt between articular and anarthrous abstract nouns," and the focus is on quality (Robertson, 794). Muraoka's (*GELS*, 412.3) suggested rendering, "acts justly," does not seem to make sense with the PP εἰς ὕψος (see the discussion of it above).

δικαιοσύνην. Accusative direct object of ἔθηκεν. See the preceding word. I have rendered this word as "justice" (LEH, 154; *GELS*, 169.3).

εἰς γῆν. Locative, modifying ἔθηκεν. The sense of the preposition εἰς is difficult; one would expect a phrase like "on the earth," but there is no normal category of meaning for εἰς with that sense. It is more likely it should be understood to mean "for, with respect to, with reference to" (BDAG, 291.5); this also makes sense since justice has not been established on the earth. The accusative object (γῆν) is a monadic noun and does not need an article to be definite.

ἔθηκεν. Aor act ind 3rd sg τίθημι. Consummative aorist, "emphasizing the endpoint of the action described, the Lord's establishment of a fixed standard of justice that does not vary" (Glenny 2009, 92–93). This aorist contrasts with the present participles in the rest of the hymn, describing the Lord's nature and character.

5:8 ποιῶν πάντα καὶ μετασκευάζων καὶ ἐκτρέπων εἰς τὸ πρωὶ σκιὰν θανάτου καὶ ἡμέραν εἰς νύκτα συσκοτάζων, ὁ προσκαλούμενος τὸ ὕδωρ τῆς θαλάσσης καὶ ἐκχέων αὐτὸ ἐπὶ προσώπου τῆς γῆς, κύριος ὁ θεὸς ὁ παντοκράτωρ ὄνομα αὐτῷ·

ποιῶν. Pres act ptc nom masc sg ποιέω (substantival). Gnomic present. This participle connects the following with the hymnic description of the Lord that began in 5:7 (see intro to 5:7 and 4:13), and the participle is parallel with the same form found there. Some manuscripts and texts (B, *L*, Qᵃ, and Swete) have an article with this participle (see Glenny 2013b, 24), but the four nominative participles at the beginning of verse 8 are understood to be connected to the article at the beginning of 5:7 and must modify the Lord, who is named at the beginning of 5:7 and is the subject of the hymn (see the similar grammatical construction in 9:5–6); the Hebrew, R-H, and Ziegler do not have the article, nor do W, A, and Qʼ. The asyndeton here indicates there was no need to specify any kind of relationship between the clauses (Runge, 20); the coordinate nature of the clauses is clear.

πάντα. Accusative direct object of ποιῶν. This word corresponds to the Hebrew word for the constellation Pleiades (כימה), a word that the translator probably did not know (only elsewhere in MT in Job 9:9 and

38:31) and rendered either as כל ("all") or as best he could according to the context and his worldview.

μετασκευάζων. Pres act ptc nom masc sg μετασκευάζω (substantival). Gnomic present. This participle could form a compound construction with the following one (ἐκτρέπων), but its meaning ("transform, refashion"; LEH, 397) seems repetitive with the specific descriptions that follow of how the Lord transforms his creation. It is better to connect it with the preceding general action (ποιῶν), which is connected to it with a coordinating καί, so the two give a summary of the Lord's actions: he creates all things and transforms what he creates (see the discussion of ποιῶν above in 5:8). The object of the first participle in the verse (πάντα) is also understood to be the object of this one. This verb and the καί preceding it correspond to the Hebrew words "and Orion" (וכסיל), which were apparently thought to be parallel to the following καὶ ἐκτρέπων and rendered as a doublet (Glenny 2009, 49–50). This word (II כסיל) occurs only three times elsewhere in the MT (Job 9:9; 38:31; and Isa 13:10, where it is plural referring to "Orion and its constellations"; see *HALOT*, 1:489), and it is likely the translator did not know it. His confusion accounts for the difficult grammar at the beginning of this verse.

καί. Coordinating conjunction, introducing material that explains what precedes (*GELS*, 354.13). Three examples follow of the Lord's ability to change and transform the forces of nature. The first two, describing the change between day and night (see also 4:13), form a chiasm, and the third describes the Lord's control of the waters of the earth (see also 8:9).

ἐκτρέπων. Pres act ptc nom masc sg ἐκτρέπω (substantival). See the discussion of ποιῶν above in 5:8. Gnomic present. In the active voice this verb has the sense (1) "turn aside, divert, deflect, cause to deviate" or (2) "turn, change" (*GE*, 649.1). Here with an εἰς τι construction following, it has the latter sense.

εἰς τὸ πρωί. Direction or goal, modifying ἐκτρέπων. The preposition εἰς indicates the aim or focus of the transformation: "into the morning" (*GELS*, 196.1). Compare 4:4 and 8:4, where this phrase functions as an idiomatic PP indicating time: "in the morning" (*GELS*, 196.4 and 5, s.v. εἰς; and 604.II.c, s.v. πρωΐ; BDAG, 289.2.a.γ). The article is idiomatic with the adverb of time πρωΐ (BDAG, 892) and required after the preposition to "nominalize" the adverb, which functions as the object of the preposition (*GELS*, 604.II.b and c, s.v. πρωΐ).

σκιάν. Accusative direct object of ἐκτρέπων. The figure "shadow of death" is found at least thirteen times in the LXX (see also Pss 22:4;

43:20; 87:7; 106:10, 14; Job 3:5; 12:22; 24:17 [2x]; 28:3; Isa 9:1; and Jer 13:16), and it often has the sense of a dark, grim, or trying situation that threatens death or seems near to it. It is possible that the translator read the Hebrew צלמות as two words, צל ("darkness, shade") and מות ("death"), but it is also possible he rendered the Hebrew metaphorically employing the popular figure "shadow of death." Every time the phrase "shadow of death" (σκιὰν θανάτου) occurs in the LXX, it is rendering the Hebrew word צלמות, and it seems the rendering of it elsewhere influenced his rendering here. *HALOT* (2:1029) suggests this rendering of צלמות may come from a "popular folk etymology."

θανάτου. Descriptive genitive. This is the most general genitive classification, and it should be avoided whenever a more specific genitive relationship is possible. Here it seems to be the only resort, and when the head noun in a genitive construction is figurative, i.e., "shadow" (σκιάν), "the genitive can frequently be described as descriptive" (Wallace 79 n. 24). MSS W, Q^{mg}, as well as *L*, R-H and Ziegler, incorporate this word in their texts (see support above in the discussion of σκιάν); MSS B, A, and Q omit it. The addition of this word in the margin of MS Q suggests it may have come to be considered original.

ἡμέραν. Accusative direct object of συσκοτάζων.

εἰς νύκτα. Direction or goal, modifying συσκοτάζων. The preposition εἰς indicates the aim or focus of the transformation, i.e., "day into night" (see the preceding PP in 5:8).

συσκοτάζων. Pres act ptc nom masc sg συσκοτάζω (substantival). See the discussion of ποιῶν above in 5:8. Gnomic present. The verbal συσκοτάζων is transitive, "to darken" (as also in Ezek 32:7) in this context; however, it is always intransitive ("to become dark") before the time of the LXX and often in the LXX (*GELS*, 663).

ὁ προσκαλούμενος. Pres mid ptc nom masc sg προσκαλέομαι (substantival). The article functions as a substantive for this participle, and it also continues to have this function with ἐκχέων. Gnomic present. There are no active forms of this verb in the LXX (BDAG, 881; *GELS*, 595), and the middle idea ("summons") here is apparently one of interaction between the subject and object; in this context it has the sense of summoning "to charge with a task" (*GELS*, 595.1.b; BDAG, 881). The object of the summoning is not a person but a thing ("water"), and Muraoka (§27.db, n. 4) uses this clause as an example of the fact that there is no "*syntactic* opposition" (emphasis in original) between personal and nonpersonal objects concerning the value of the middle voice. This use of the article with the nominative attributive participle again (see ὁ ποιῶν at the beginning of 5:7), after several participles without it in 5:7–8, further indicates that all the participles in the hymn should be understood to be substantival; the long string of participles in 5:7–8 functions as a predicate nominative, modifying the Lord (see ποιῶν in 5:7). The asyndeton before this participle signals the beginning of a new thought. The last half of 5:8, beginning with this participle construction, is repeated exactly in 9:6 in the third hymn in LXX Amos.

τὸ ὕδωρ. Accusative direct object of ἐκχέων.

τῆς θαλάσσης. Genitive of source, the water comes from the "sea." The article with the head noun and genitive modifier follows Apollonius' canon.

ἐκχέων. Pres act ptc nom masc sg ἐκχέω (substantival). Gnomic present. This verb can refer to a profuse pouring out (LSJ, 526), and it could have a negative connotation here; this same phrase is repeated in 9:6 where the context describes the Lord's destructive powers (esp. 9:5, 8).

αὐτὸ. Accusative direct object of ἐκχέων, referring back to τὸ ὕδωρ.

ἐπὶ προσώπου τῆς γῆς. Locative, modifying ἐκχέων. The preposition ἐπί indicates the surface on which this action takes place (*GELS*, 263.I.2), and the object of the preposition (προσώπου) does not need an article to be definite (Wallace, 247); furthermore, προσώπου is a monadic noun in this construction with the monadic noun τῆς γῆς modifying it. The partitive genitive, τῆς γῆς, has the sense "the face [surface] which is a part of the earth" (Wallace, 84–86), and in this Hebrew idiom the noun "face" is redundant (pleonasm) and could be omitted without losing the sense of the phrase.

κύριος ὁ θεὸς ὁ παντοκράτωρ ὄνομα αὐτῷ. This exact phrase is found in 4:13; 5:27; and 9:6. This divine title recurs ten times in LXX Amos (3:13; 4:13; 5:8, 14, 15, 16, 27; 9:5, 6, 15) and three other times in the LXX Twelve (Hos 12:6; Nah 3:5; Zech 10:3); see the discussion of it in 3:13. Here the divine title is not at the end of the hymn as in 4:13 and 9:6, and here it corresponds to יהוה. MS B has the simple reading κύριος here, corresponding more closely to the Hebrew.

5:9 ὁ διαιρῶν συντριμμὸν ἐπ᾽ ἰσχὺν καὶ ταλαιπωρίαν ἐπὶ ὀχύρωμα ἐπάγων.

The hymn continues in this verse. There are two more participle phrases further describing the Lord, who was named at the beginning of the hymn (5:7) and further identified at the end of 5:8.

ὁ διαιρῶν. Pres act ptc nom masc sg διαιρέω (substantival). Gnomic present. This participle continues the string of participles in 5:7–9 functioning as predicate nominatives. In 5:9 the descriptions of the Lord's activities move from his control over the natural realm to his guidance in the moral realm, preparing for the return to the theme of judgment in 5:10. Although most of the substantival participles in the hymn that refer to the Lord do not have an article, this is the third one that does (see the discussion in 5:7 and 8). This verb means "divide" or "dispense," and here it must have the latter sense (LEH, 138; GELS, 151.2).

συντριμμὸν. Accusative direct object of διαιρῶν. This is an abstract, qualitative noun without an article (see Robertson, 794, and the discussion of κρίμα καὶ δικαιοσύνην in 5:7). It means "ruin, destruction" here (GELS, 662.1) and is parallel the following noun ταλαιπωρίαν ("wretched miserable condition," GELS, 669).

ἐπ' ἰσχύν. Direction, modifying διαιρῶν. The preposition ἐπί indicates those to whom hostile action is directed (GELS, 266.III.4.a). The abstract noun ἰσχύν ("strength") probably refers to those who feel secure in their own strength and see no need to seek him (5:4, 6). Muraoka (GELS, 345.1.b) suggests it has the sense "physical strength" here and is parallel to the following ὀχύρωμα ("fortress") and the opposite of the preceding συντριμμόν.

ταλαιπωρίαν. Accusative direct object of ἐπάγων. This is another abstract, qualitative noun without an article (see συντριμμόν above).

ἐπὶ ὀχύρωμα. Direction, modifying ἐπάγων. The preposition ἐπί indicates those to whom hostile action is directed (GELS, 266.III.4.a). The "fortress" (ὀχύρωμα) represents (by metonymy) those who depend on it for their security. This anarthrous noun is qualitative.

ἐπάγων. Pres act ptc nom masc sg ἐπάγω (substantival). Gnomic present and substantival, parallel to the participle in the first clause and modified by the article at the beginning of the verse.

5:10 ἐμίσησαν ἐν πύλαις ἐλέγχοντα καὶ λόγον ὅσιον ἐβδελύξαντο.

Amos 5:10–12 returns abruptly to the themes of justice and judgment. The asyndeton at the beginning of 5:10 suggests the change in topic, and the subjects of the verbs change at 5:10 from the singular participles, referring to the Lord in 5:7–9, to third-person plural indicative forms, referring to those who oppress the poor. The subjects of the two verbs in 5:10 (third-person plural) are further distinguished from Israel, who is addressed in the second-person plural in 5:11–12; Israel was also addressed in the second-person plural in 5:1–7. Thus, the oppressors addressed in 5:10 may be a minority in Israel or foreigners (see Glenny 2013b, 94). The sins of the oppressors in 5:10 involve their feelings and emotions, which they express in their sinful actions.

ἐμίσησαν. Aor act ind 3rd pl μισέω. Constative aorist, describing the sin as a whole.

ἐν πύλαις. Locative, modifying ἐλέγχοντα. The preposition ἐν "indicates a place" where the reproving (ἐλέγχοντα) takes place (*GELS*, 231.1.b). The object of a preposition does not require an article to be definite. The phrase ἐν πύλαις is common in the LXX (5:12, 15; Hag 2:14; Prov 12:13; 22:22; 31:23, 31; Isa 29:21), with πύλαις referring to "a forum for public gatherings, a public square" where business took place and legal matters were settled (*GELS*, 607.b; LEH, 412). Here it probably refers to court or government proceedings (see Glenny 2013b, 95). The noun is singular in Hebrew.

ἐλέγχοντα. Pres act ptc acc masc sg ἐλέγχω (substantival). Direct object of ἐμίσησαν. In the LXX this verb, translated "reprove," is associated with various aspects of judicial proceedings (Isa 11:3, 4; 29:21; Job 13:3; 32:12; see LSL, 531; and Glenny 2013b, 95). The present tense describes customary action; it is common for substantival participles to be anarthrous in LXX Greek (Muraoka §30.ba). See the long LXX plus in Hag 2:14 with language similar to this clause.

λόγον ὅσιον. Accusative direct object of ἐβδελύξαντο. Here λόγος refers to "that which is said or uttered" (*GELS*, 434.1.a); it is apparently something spoken by the upright that conflicts with or opposes the plans of the oppressors. This anarthrous noun is qualitative, referring to speech in general. It corresponds to the verb דבר in Hebrew, which the translator took to be a noun. For a helpful discussion of the meaning of ὅσιος in the Greco-Roman world, see BDAG (728). In that world "this term for the most part described that which helps maintain the delicate balance between the interests of society and the expectations of the transcendent realm." In the LXX when the subject is humans, it has the sense "pious" (*GELS*, 508.2). "When a substantive has no article, its attributive adjective usually follows" (Muraoka §37.ba). This Greek noun corresponds to the Hebrew noun תמים, which is often rendered "truth," in this context referring to speech. However, the Hebrew word has a wide range of meanings (*HALOT*, 2:1748–49), and this is not a bad rendering.

ἐβδελύξαντο. Aor mid ind 3rd pl βδελύσσω. Constative aorist, describing the sin as a whole. This verb occurs four times in the Twelve (see also Hos 9:10; Amos 6:8; and Mic 3:9), and in Lev 20:23 it describes God's attitude concerning the sinful customs and deeds of the Canaanites. In the middle voice it means "to detest something because it is utterly offensive or loathsome" (BDAG, 172); it is what Kemmer (269) classifies as an "emotion middle" involving two participants.

5:11 διὰ τοῦτο ἀνθ᾽ ὧν κατεκονδυλίζετε πτωχοὺς καὶ δῶρα ἐκλεκτὰ ἐδέξασθε παρ᾽ αὐτῶν, οἴκους ξυστοὺς ᾠκοδομήσατε καὶ οὐ μὴ

Amos 5:10–11

κατοικήσητε ἐν αὐτοῖς, ἀμπελῶνας ἐπιθυμητοὺς ἐφυτεύσατε καὶ οὐ μὴ πίητε τὸν οἶνον ἐξ αὐτῶν.

See Glenny (2009, 53–56) for further discussion of some of the differences between the Hebrew and Greek in 5:11.

διὰ τοῦτο. Inferential. See the discussion of this formulaic PP in 2:13. The PP (corresponding to לכן) points to the consequence of the sinful attitudes and values of the oppressors in in 5:10, i.e., "therefore"; the following phrase (see below) refers to the cause or reason for the judgment announced in 5:11, i.e., "for this reason." The antecedent of the accusative object of the preposition (τοῦτο) is the description of the attitudes and values of the oppressors in 5:10.

ἀνθ' ὧν. Causal. This construction corresponds to the Hebrew יען, which is causal. It is technically composed of the contracted form of the preposition ἀντί that is used before a rough breathing mark (Decker, 157) and its genitive object. It occurs several times in chapters 1–2 in the Oracles against the Nations (1:3, 9, 13; 2:1, 6), where the translator alternated this phrase and ἕνεκα. This construction (ἀνθ' ὧν) indicates the reason or cause for something (BDAG, 88). *GELS* (58.3.b) describes ἀνθ' ὧν as "introducing a clause the verb of which is in the past and specifies a commendable or (mostly) punishable deed, and such a clause usually follows the main clause"; here it introduces two causal subordinate clauses in the first part of 5:11, which are followed by the main statement in the latter part of the verse.

κατεκονδυλίζετε. Impf act ind 2nd pl κατακονδυλίζω. Customary imperfect, referring to a recurring activity in past time. *GELS* (373) suggests it means "to maltreat"; but with the intensifying prepositional prefix, it is better to understand it to mean "to punch, hit" (the related noun κατακονδυλίστος has the sense "punched"; see *GE*, 1058 on both of these words). I have followed NETS in rendering the imperfect tense "you were buffeting." This compound verb is a LXX *hapax*; its simple form is found in LXX pluses in Amos 2:7 and Mal 3:5. The related verbal noun (κονδυλισμός) occurs one time in the LXX (Zeph 2:8), where it has the sense "reviling, insult" (NETS; see *GELS*, 406); it is a LXX neologism. The corresponding Hebrew verb (בשׁס) is also a hapax, meaning something like "crush" (*HALOT*, 1:165) and perhaps read as שׁסה ("plunder, spoil"; *HALOT*, 2:1608, s.v.). The shift from the third-person subjects, apparently the oppressors, in 5:10 to the second person in 5:11 suggests the nation is the subject in 5:11. Some manuscripts (B, A, Q, W) have a third-person plural form of κατακονδυλίζω here (see Glenny 2013b, 24, 96), which disagrees with the Hebrew second person and does not make sense with the apparent change in subject here and the following second-person verbs; thus, R-H and Ziegler follow MS L and the Hebrew with their second-person readings.

πτωχούς. Accusative direct object of κατεκονδυλίζετε. This is a substantival use of the adjective, and the substantive has a generic idea, here without the article (Wallace, 253). This word can refer to a person who is extremely poor and has nothing (see the discussion of it in 2:7 and 4:1). The form is a singular generic noun in Hebrew.

καί. Coordinating conjunction, connecting parallel clauses (*GELS*, 352.1.b), which are the reasons for the judgment in the two main clauses at the end of the verse.

δῶρα ἐκλεκτά. Accusative direct object ἐδέξασθε. The adjective has the sense "elect, select, chosen," and in this context modifying δῶρα ("gifts"), it has the idea of "choice" (see LEH, 183–84, s.v. ἐκλεκτός; see also Isa 22:7, 8). Note the similar language (πᾶν ἐκλεκτὸν τῶν δώρων ὑμῶν) used to describe the gifts the Israelites were commanded to bring to the Lord when they enter the land (Deut 12:11). "When a substantive has no article, its attributive adjective usually follows" (Muraoka §37.ba), as is the case here.

ἐδέξασθε. Aor mid ind 2nd pl δέχομαι. Constative aorist. This is an indirect middle with a verb of "coming into possession" (Kemmer, 268), i.e., "you received." Muraoka (*GELS*, 145–46.a; see also BDAG, 221; LSJ, 382–83) suggests the sense "to receive approvingly or willingly" in this context and gives no instances of the idea "take," as NETS and *LES* render the verb in this context. The sense of the verb does not suggest taking something by force from the poor, as the Hebrew לקח does.

παρ' αὐτῶν. Source, modifying ἐδέξασθε. The preposition παρά with the genitive here "indicates origin, source, starting point of physical movement" (*GELS*, 522.I.1). It is difficult to know to what αὐτῶν refers; it could refer to the oppressors who bribe the Jews with gifts, or it could refer to the poor from whom the oppressing Israelites take gifts. The description of the gifts as ἐκλεκτός and the sense of the preceding verb suggest the former (see discussion in Glenny 2013b, 96), and this pronoun suggests the latter, apparently referring to the preceding πτωχούς, but not necessarily so. The corresponding pronoun in Hebrew is singular, consistent with the generic singular Hebrew noun referring to the "poor" (דל).

οἴκους ξυστοὺς. Accusative direct object of ᾠκοδομήσατε. The anarthrous plural noun is indefinite, referring to members of this class ("houses"). The adjective ξυστούς, modifying οἴκους, has the sense "polished, smoothed" (*GELS*, 482; LEH, 425; see 1 Chr 22:2; 1 Esd 6:8, 24; Sir 22:17 [in R-H]); this reading is found in MSS A, Q, and R-H. The similar-sounding adjective ξεστούς ("hewn [of stone]"; *GELS*, 480) is the reading in MSS B, L, Swete, and Ziegler (see Glenny 2013b, 24). In 1 Macc 13:27 ξεστός describes polished stones used in a monument. These two words are very close in meaning, as indicated by the fact that they are variant readings in this verse and in Sir 22:17, referring to a hewn or smooth wall, and I have used the R-H reading in my text for consistency. This word begins the last two parallel clauses in the verse; they are the main clauses and describe the judgment, which is the fulfillment of the covenant curse (Deut 28:30, 39; Isa 18:5; Mic 6:15; cf. Amos 9:13).

ᾠκοδομήσατε. Aor act ind 2nd pl οἰκοδομέω. This is apparently a consummative aorist, stressing the end or completion of the action of building.

καί. Coordinating conjunction, indicating contrast (*GELS*, 352.4).

οὐ μὴ κατοικήσητε. Aor act subj 2nd pl κατοικέω. This is the subjunctive with οὐ μή communicating emphatic negation. BDAG (646.4, s.v. μή) says "οὐ μή is the most decisive way on negativing something in the future." The verb has the sense "settle in" (LSJ, 928) or "live as permanent resident" (*GELS*, 391.1) and does not mean they could never inhabit the houses. Thus, it is a constative aorist, looking at the action as a whole.

ἐν αὐτοῖς. Locative, modifying κατοικήσητε. The preposition ἐν indicates a place in which an action takes place (*GELS*, 231.1.b), and its object, αὐτοῖς, refers to the οἴκους ξυστούς.

ἀμπελῶνας ἐπιθυμητούς. Accusative direct object of ἐφυτεύσατε. The anarthrous plural noun ἀμπελῶνας is indefinite, referring to members of this class ("vineyards"). The adjective ἐπιθυμητούς has the sense "desirable"; it is used in Greek literature for the cravings of pregnant women (LSJ, 634). Seven of the fifteen times it occurs in the LXX, it modifies the noun σκεῦος ("vessel, object"; see Glenny 2013b, 97). There is continuity of thought between the last two clauses in the verse, and the asyndeton at the beginning of the last clause indicates that the continuity is understood (Runge, 20).

ἐφυτεύσατε. Aor act ind 2nd pl φυτεύω; consummative aorist, emphasizing the completion or end of the action of planting.

καί. Coordinating conjunction, here indicating contrast (*GELS*, 352.4).

οὐ μὴ πίητε. Aor act subj 2nd pl πίνω. This is the subjunctive with οὐ μή communicating emphatic negation. See the discussion of this construction in the previous clause.

τὸν οἶνον. Accusative direct object of πίητε. The article is one of simple identification, perhaps pointing to the wine from each vineyard (Wallace, 216–17).

ἐξ αὐτῶν. Source, modifying τὸν οἶνον. The preposition ἐκ indicates origin or source (*GELS*, 201–2.5).

5:12 ὅτι ἔγνων πολλὰς ἀσεβείας ὑμῶν, καὶ ἰσχυραὶ αἱ ἁμαρτίαι ὑμῶν, καταπατοῦντες δίκαιον, λαμβάνοντες ἀλλάγματα καὶ πένητας ἐν πύλαις ἐκκλίνοντες.

ὅτι. This conjunction introduces two main clauses giving further reasons for the judgment in the last two clauses of 5:11. The first part of 5:11 also gives two reasons for the judgment in the latter part of that verse (introduced by ἀνθ᾽ ὧν; see 5:11).

ἔγνων. Aor act ind 1st sg γινώσκω. Gnomic aorist, describing something that is timeless.

πολλὰς ἀσεβείας. Accusative direct object of ἔγνων. This is a favorite noun in Amos (10x); it is employed in each of the oracles in chapters 1–2 to describe the sins of the nations addressed. "In general, ἀσέβεια is understood vertically as a lack of reverence for deity and hallowed institutions as displayed in sacrilegious words and deeds" (BDAG, 141), thus "ungodly deeds." The quantifying adjective πολλάς ("many") tends to precede its nominal head, often against the Hebrew (Muraoka §37. baaa), although here it follows the Hebrew order.

ὑμῶν. Possessive genitive.

ἰσχυραί. Predicate adjective in a new clause; the reader must supply the understood equative verb. This adjective, which normally has the sense "strong," means "grave, serious" in this context, describing sins (*GELS*, 345.2).

αἱ ἁμαρτίαι. Nominative subject of the understood equative verb. It is normal to have an article with a head noun that is modified by a possessive pronoun.

ὑμῶν. Possessive genitive. The repetition of the possessive pronoun in the first part of this verse accentuates the responsibility of the recipients for their sins.

καταπατοῦντες. Pres act ptc nom masc sg καταπατέω (causal). The present tense suggests actions that are regular or characteristic. The participle is causal, giving the first reason or ground for the preceding equative statement. In MSS B, W, and Swete the participle is feminine, modifying αἱ ἁμαρτίαι; it is masculine in A, Q*, R-H, and Ziegler, modifying the subjects of the preceding equative sentence, which seems to be required (see the discussion of difficult and imprecise texts in the LXX in Muraoka §77.n)

δίκαιον. Accusative direct object of καταπατοῦντες. Substantival use of the adjective; here it is generic and should be understood as definite, even though it is anarthrous (Wallace, 253–54; Muraoka [§1.d] gives examples of generic nouns without the article). "In Greco-Roman tradition a δίκαιος person is one who upholds the customs and norms of behavior, including especially public service, that make for a well-ordered, civilized society" (BDAG, 246); in the LXX this word describes the Lord, who is "just and upright" (Deut 32:4; Ps 10:7), the Messiah (Jer 23:5–6), and people who are "innocent" and "do the will of the Lord" (Sir 16:3) (Spicq, 1:322). Both times the word occurs in Amos, it is parallel to the "poor" (see also 2:6 and the discussion there).

λαμβάνοντες. Pres act ptc nom masc pl λαμβάνω (causal). The present tense suggests actions that are regular or characteristic. The participle gives the second reason or ground for the preceding equative statement.

ἀλλάγματα. Accusative direct object of λαμβάνοντες. This noun should also be understood as generic, even though it is anarthrous (Wallace, 253–54; Muraoka §1.d gives examples of generic nouns without the article). Muraoka (*GELS*, 27) gives the following overview of this word's meaning in the LXX. In Lev 27:10 and 33 this word refers to a sacrificial animal that is exchanged for or replaces another; it can also refer to a "payment made for service rendered or in return for something purchased" (Deut 23:8; Lam 5:4; Isa 43:3; Job 28:17; Ps 43:13), and sometimes that payment is virtually a bribe, as in Amos 5:12; or it can have the sense "changing" or turning (Sir 2:4). The prefixed form of the noun (ἀνταλλάγματα), which emphasizes further the idea of exchange found in "ransom" in the MT and suggests this idea was understood here, is found in some MSS (B, W, and in Swete; see the discussion in Glenny 2013b, 26), but R-H and Ziegler have the simple form of the noun, which is probably original. For a discussion of the prefixed form, see Glenny 2013b, 98.

καὶ. Coordinating conjunction, connecting parallel phrases (*GELS*, 352.1.a); here it introduces the third of three coordinate participle phrases, although there was no connector between the first two.

πένητας. Accusative direct object of ἐκκλίνοντες. This noun should also be understood to be definite and generic, even though it is anarthrous (Wallace, 253–54; Muraoka §1.d gives examples of generic nouns without the article). See 2:6 for a discussion of this word for "the poor."

ἐν πύλαις. Locative, modifying ἐκκλίνοντες. The preposition ἐν indicates a place where the action described by the following participle takes place, "in the gateways" (*GELS*, 231.1.a); it is singular in the Hebrew. On the meaning of this phrase see 5:10 and 15.

ἐκκλίνοντες. Pres act ptc nom masc pl ἐκκλίνω (causal). The present tense suggests actions that are regular or characteristic. The participle is causal, giving the third reason for the preceding equative statement. See the use of this verb in 2:7 in a similar context (see also LSJ, 509); there it seems to have the sense "pervert, turn aside," but here with the accusative of person, the context suggests the sense "wrong, do injustice to" (so *GELS*, 209.2; perhaps it has this same sense in Job 34:20); Dines (1991, 161) suggests the translation "ignore."

5:13 διὰ τοῦτο ὁ συνίων ἐν τῷ καιρῷ ἐκείνῳ σιωπήσεται, ὅτι καιρὸς πονηρός ἐστιν.

διὰ τοῦτο. Inferential. See the discussion of this formulaic PP in 2:13. Here it indicates the following is an inference from 5:12 ("therefore").

ὁ συνίων. Pres act ptc nom masc sg συνίημι (substantival). With the article, the participle makes a generic reference to the class of those who are "prudent" or "understand."

ἐν τῷ καιρῷ ἐκείνῳ. Temporal, modifying σιωπήσεται. The preposition ἐν "indicates a point in time" (*GELS*, 231.3.a). This expression can refer to the "day of the Lord" in the prophets (Mic 3:4; Joel 3:1; Zeph 3:16, 19, 20), but it normally refers to a designated or specific period of time, as it does here. An article is required with the head noun (τῷ καιρῷ) when the noun is modified by a demonstrative pronoun (ἐκείνῳ).

σιωπήσεται. Fut mid ind 3rd sg σιωπάω. Predictive future. Eight of the ten times this verb is found in the future tense in the LXX it is in the middle voice (Job 30:27; 41:4; Amos 5:13; Isa 42:14; 62:1, 6; Jer 4:19; Lam 3:28); the other two uses in the future in the LXX are active voice (Job 16:6; Isa 65:6). There does not seem to be any difference between the sense of the two voices of this verb (*GE*, 1919.1).

ὅτι. The subordinating conjunction ὅτι "introduces a causal clause" (*GELS*, 511.1), giving the cause or reason for the preceding clause.

καιρὸς πονηρός. Predicate nominative, anarthrous and indefinite with a nominative adjective. MS B has the genitive plural form of the adjective resulting in the sense "a time of evil deeds."

ἐστιν. Pres act ind 3rd sg εἰμί. The equative verb has the sense "be present, exist" (*GELS*, 193.1.a), and its subject is understood, i.e., "it."

5:14 ἐκζητήσατε τὸ καλὸν καὶ μὴ τὸ πονηρόν, ὅπως ζήσητε· καὶ ἔσται οὕτως μεθ᾽ ὑμῶν κύριος ὁ θεὸς ὁ παντοκράτωρ, ὃν τρόπον εἴπατε

The word order in 5:14 is somewhat awkward, because the translator was following the order in the Hebrew.

ἐκζητήσατε. Aor act impv 2nd pl ἐκζητέω. Simple general command to "seek" (cf. 5:4 and 5:6 where the same verb form has more of a conditional idea); the aorist could be understood as constative. There is asyndeton here at the beginning of a new thought (Runge, 23).

τὸ καλὸν. Accusative direct object of ἐκζητήσατε. It is normal for neuter adjectives to "be applied to an intangible, general notion or concept" (Muraoka §20.ea), but they can also "refer to a more concrete entity, a concrete deed or phenomenon bearing a character denoted by the adjective" (§20.eb), and Muraoka uses this passage as an example of the latter. The parallel articles with "good" and "evil" may have an anaphoric sense, referring back to the earlier admonitions and descriptions of "good" and "evil" in the chapter, and they tend to emphasize the difference between "good" and "evil," sharpening the quality of both.

καὶ μὴ. Coordinating conjunction, connecting contrasting parallel clauses (GELS, 352.4); the verb in the first clause is understood to be repeated with the second object. One might also understand the conjunction to be marking contrast between parallel direct objects of ἐκζητήσατε (GELS, 353.4), but the negative particle μή suggests that there is an elided imperative verb, i.e., "seek not" (Muraoka §82.b.i; 83 .bg), since οὐ is employed for negativing a substantive (Muraoka §83.h.i).

τὸ πονηρόν. Accusative direct object of the understood verb (ἐκζητήσατε). See the discussion with the preceding parallel abstract noun (τὸ καλόν) with an article.

ὅπως. This subordinating conjunction indicates purpose here with the subjunctive verb (GELS, 502.4.a); it indicates more explicitly the logical relationship between the clauses than the similar statements in 5:4 and 5:6 without it (Muraoka §28.gea).

ζήσητε. Aor act subj 2nd pl ζάω. Used with ὅπως to indicate a purpose. This verb is also found in the parallel ideas in 5:4 and 5:6, giving the motivation to seek the Lord. The logical relationship is more explicit in this purpose clause with a subjunctive verb than in the parallel clauses in 5:4 (with a potential future-tense verb) and in 5:6 (with an aorist indicative verb) (Muraoka §28.gea).

καί. Coordinating conjunction, connecting parallel clauses (GELS, 352.1.b). This καί almost has the sense "then"; the following clause with a future-tense verb apparently designates "some further consequence" that has a "kind of independence" but is related to the main purpose (BDF §369; see also Isa 6:10; Rom 3:4).

ἔσται. Fut act ind 3rd sg εἰμί. Predictive future.

οὕτως. This adverb has the sense "in this manner, accordingly" and refers to the preceding (BDAG, 741.1; GELS, 515.A.b; BDF §453). The correlation of "the Lord ... will be with you" is not with the following sentence (see below) but rather with the preceding "you may live." "The purpose of seeking the Lord is presented as correlative to a promise that the Lord will be present with those who seek him (cf. Deut 30:20), and the presence of the Lord with them is part of the life that they may find, if they seek him" (Glenny 2013b, 100).

μεθ' ὑμῶν. Association, modifying ἔσται. The preposition μετά "indicates a relationship which is forged" (*GELS*, 452.I.4).

κύριος ὁ θεὸς ὁ παντοκράτωρ. Nominative subject of ἔσται. See the discussion of this name at 3:13; it recurs in 4:13; 5:8, 15, 16, 27; 9:5, 6, 15. Here it corresponds to יהוה אלהי צבאות.

ὃν τρόπον εἴπατε. In Hebrew the corresponding words must be retrospective, referring back to the first part of 5:14, since 5:15 begins with two second-person plural imperatives directed at the recipients. However, in the LXX, 5:15 begins with two first-person plural verbs, and this phrase (ὃν τρόπον εἴπατε) is prospective, introducing the direct speech found in the first part of 5:15 (Dines 1991, 161 n. 9).

ὃν τρόπον. This is an idiomatic adverbial accusative phrase (BDF §160; Smyth §1608). This phrase has the sense "just as, exactly as," and it introduces a clause that emphasizes comparability and analogy (*GELS*, 688.1.b, s.v. τρόπος); Muraoka (§26.f n. 1) calls it "a pseudo-subordinating conjunction." See 3:12 on ὃν τρόπον.

εἴπατε. Aor act impv 2nd pl λέγω. Constative aorist.

5:15 Μεμισήκαμεν τὰ πονηρὰ καὶ ἠγαπήκαμεν τὰ καλά· καὶ ἀποκαταστήσατε ἐν πύλαις κρίμα, ὅπως ἐλεήσῃ κύριος ὁ θεὸς ὁ παντοκράτωρ τοὺς περιλοίπους τοῦ Ιωσηφ.

The beginning of 5:15 is the content of the formula at the end of 5:14 ("in the same way as you say"; see the discussion there). Thus, the people are describing their conduct in direct speech in the first two clauses of 5:15.

μεμισήκαμεν. Prf act ind 1st pl μισέω. Present use of the perfect (Porter 1994, 41; Wallace, 579–80). The context suggests that the speakers are not talking about something they did in the past, and thus it seems best to understand these stative verbs to be emphasizing the existence of hate and love (see ἠγαπήκαμεν below).

τὰ πονηρά. Accusative direct object of μεμισήκαμεν. The article with the abstract noun focuses on quality, but it can also refer to concrete deeds or phenomena; see the discussion of πονηρός and and καλός in 5:14.

ἠγαπήκαμεν. Prf act ind 1st pl ἀγαπάω. Present use of the perfect (see μεμισήκαμεν above).

τὰ καλά. Accusative direct object of ἠγαπήκαμεν. See the discussion of the article with the abstract noun above and in 5:14 (πονηρός and καλός).

καί. Coordinating conjunction, used here in the second member of a comparison, "reinforcing the comparison" (*GELS*, 353.2.c; see also BDAG, 496.2.c).

ἀποκαταστήσατε. Aor act impv 2nd pl ἀποκαθίστημι. This is a general command for the community to "restore judgment," and the aorist should be understood to be ingressive, emphasizing the change from the previous state or the beginning of the commanded condition (see Fanning, 368).

ἐν πύλαις. Locative, modifying κρίμα and describing the "judgment." The preposition ἐν "indicates a place" (*GELS*, 231.1). The "gateways" (πύλαις) refer to the courts that were convened there (5:10, 12); the noun is definite, but it is anarthrous, as is often the case with definite objects of prepositions. The noun is singular in Hebrew.

κρίμα. Accusative direct object of ἀποκαταστήσατε. In this context, with the location of the "gates" given, the noun probably refers to "a court" (*GELS*, 412.1).

ὅπως. This word, functioning as a conjunction, indicates the purpose of the preceding clause ("so that").

ἐλεήσῃ. Aor act subj 2nd sg ἐλεέω. This is a subjunctive in the purpose clause after ὅπως; the aorist tense is ingressive, emphasizing the change from the previous condition and the beginning of the reception of mercy.

κύριος ὁ θεὸς ὁ παντοκράτωρ. See Amos 3:13. This title occurs also in 4:13; 5:8, 14, 16, 27; 9:5, 6, and 15; here it corresponds to יהוה אלהי צבאות.

τοὺς περιλοίπους. Accusative direct object of ἐλεήσῃ. The article clarifies that the noun "survivors" refers to a definite group.

τοῦ Ιωσηφ. Indeclinable noun functioning as a partitive genitive and referring to the "house of Joseph" (see 5:6 and 6:6 on this word); the article follows Apollonius' canon.

5:16 διὰ τοῦτο τάδε λέγει κύριος ὁ θεὸς ὁ παντοκράτωρ Ἐν πάσαις πλατείαις κοπετός, καὶ ἐν πάσαις ὁδοῖς ῥηθήσεται Οὐαὶ οὐαί· κληθήσεται γεωργὸς εἰς πένθος καὶ κοπετὸν καὶ εἰς εἰδότας θρῆνον,

διὰ τοῦτο. Inferential. See the discussion of this formulaic PP in 2:13. Here it indicates the following is an inference from 5:15 (i.e., "therefore"). The words διὰ τοῦτο τάδε λέγει κύριος are similarly found at the beginning of 3:11 and 7:17, where they also introduce an announcement of judgment.

τάδε λέγει κύριος. See the discussion of this formula in 1:6.

κύριος ὁ θεὸς ὁ παντοκράτωρ. This is a favorite divine title in this section (5:14, 15, 27). See the discussion of this title in 3:13. Here it corresponds to יהוה אלהי צבאות אדני, and there is nothing in the LXX corresponding to אדני.

ἐν πάσαις πλατείαις. Locative, modifying the implied verb "will be." The preposition ἐν "indicates a place" in which an action takes place or a state prevails (*GELS*, 231.1.b). See Muraoka (§38.b.i) on this adjectival construction with πᾶς (rendered "in all the streets"); the object of the preposition (πλατείαις) can be definite, even though it is anarthrous (Wallace, 247).

κοπετός. Nominative subject of implied equative verb "lamentation will be . . ." or predicate nominative of the verb, if another subject is understood (i.e., "there will be lamentation . . ."). Abstract nouns are commonly anarthrous with accent on quality or nature.

ἐν πάσαις ὁδοῖς. Locative, modifying ῥηθήσεται. The preposition ἐν "indicates a place" in which an action takes place or a state prevails (*GELS*, 231.1.b). See Muraoka (§38.b.i) on this adjectival construction with πᾶς (rendered "in all the roadways"); ὁδοῖς, the object of the preposition, can be definite, even though it is anarthrous (Wallace, 247).

ῥηθήσεται. Fut pass ind 3rd sg εἶπον. Predictive future. This is a simple passive with no agency expressed ("it will be said"), corresponding with the active, "they will say," in the Hebrew.

Οὐαὶ οὐαί. This interjection is a "transcription of the Hebrew" (BDF §4), denoting pain, grief, or horror (LEH, 449–50; BDAG, 734). The doubling of the exclamation (found in Hebrew and Greek) is for emphasis (LEH, 449–50).

κληθήσεται. Fut pass ind 3rd sg καλέω. Predictive future. This is a simple passive with no agency expressed ("will be summoned"), corresponding to the active voice in Hebrew ("they shall call"). With this word the description of the Lord's judgment moves from a general description to specific examples, and asyndeton is common for such transitions (Runge, 23).

γεωργός. Nominative subject of κληθήσεται. This is an anarthrous generic noun, which is understood to be definite, "the farmer."

εἰς πένθος καὶ κοπετόν. Purpose, modifying κληθήσεται. The preposition εἰς indicates the purpose (*GELS*, 196.3, calls it "target, aim, or focus"). Abstract nouns like "mourning" (πένθος) and "lamentation" (κοπετόν) are commonly anarthrous with accent on quality or nature. The coordinating conjunction (καί) connects parallel accusative objects of the preposition (*GELS*, 352.1.a).

καί. Coordinating conjunction, connecting parallel PPs.

εἰς εἰδότας. Direction, modifying κληθήσεται (coordinate with the preceding PP). The preposition εἰς indicates the goal toward which or in the direction to which the "farmer" is called ("to, towards"; *GELS*, 196.1); he is apparently called to join the community of those who know how to mourn. The coordinate PPs are connected by καί (*GELS*, 352.1.a).

εἰδότας. Prf act ptc acc masc pl οἶδα (substantival). This anarthrous participle functions as the object of εἰς, and thus it is substantival ("those knowing"). It is common in the LXX for anarthrous participles to function in this way (Muraoka §31.ba), and objects of prepositions are often definite without an article. The perfect tense focuses on the state of knowing, resulting from a past action (Muraoka §28.ec). The knowledge described by the verb is "knowledge of something through experience or learning" (*GELS*, 486–87.2).

θρῆνον. Accusative direct object of εἰδότας. θρῆνον ("lament, lamentation") is employed in 5:1 to describe the content of 5:1–17 (see also 8:10). The repetition of it in this verse forms an *inclusio* around the section. The indefinite θρῆνον refers to any one of a number of funeral dirges.

5:17 καὶ ἐν πάσαις ὁδοῖς κοπετός, διότι διελεύσομαι διὰ μέσου σου, εἶπε κύριος.

καὶ. Coordinating conjunction, connecting parallel clauses (*GELS*, 352.1.b). The following clause is parallel to the first statement of the Lord in 5:16, describing the results of Israel's sin, and gives another parallel description of the results of that sin. The use of the words πάσαις ὁδοῖς in both clauses (and ἐν πάσαις πλατείαις in 5:16) reinforces the connection between the statements.

ἐν πάσαις ὁδοῖς. Locative, modifying the implied verb "will be." See the discussion of the same phrase in 5:16. The noun corresponding to ὁδοῖς in Hebrew is כרמים ("vineyards"; 92x in the MT), which the translator read as דרכים, apparently influenced by the language of 5:16 and his use of this Greek word there.

κοπετός. Nominative subject of implied equative verb "will be" or predicate nominative of the verb, if another subject is understood (i.e., "There will be..."). See the same noun in 5:16 translating the same Hebrew noun.

διότι. Cause, marking the reason for the mourning and lamentation described in 5:16–17 (BDAG, 251.1; *GELS*, 172.1; see 5:3).

διελεύσομαι. Fut mid ind 1st sg διέρχομαι. Predictive future. The middle category is "translational motion" (Kemmer, 269). The Lord, who is speaking in this verse, is the subject of the verb, and his presence is not connected here with life and blessing, as in 5:14, but it is the source of judgment.

διὰ μέσου. Locative, modifying διελεύσομαι. The repetition of the preposition διά (see διελεύσομαι above) emphasizes its force, but it is not repeated in the translation; it has the sense "through [a passable space]" (*GELS*, 147.1.a). The genitive adjective μέσου functions as a substantive here, and it is definite, as is common for anarthrous objects of prepositions and for nouns modified by possessive pronouns. See Sollamo (238) on this phrase.

σου. Possessive genitive.

εἶπε. Aor act ind 3rd sg λέγω. The aorist tense refers to a present time, and it might best be understood to be what Fanning (275–81) and Porter (1994, 36–37) call a dramatic aorist.

κύριος. Nominative subject of εἶπε. This anarthrous, monadic noun is definite.

Amos 5:18–27

[18]"Woe to those who desire the day of the Lord! What is the purpose of this day of the Lord to you? Whereas it is darkness and not light, [19]just as when someone flees from a lion, and a bear attacks him, and he rushes into his house, and he places his hands upon the wall, and a snake bites him. [20]Is not the day of the Lord darkness and not light, and blackness without brightness in it? [21]I hate, I reject your religious festivals, and I will not smell the savor in your festal gatherings. [22]Because even if you bring to me your whole-burnt-offerings and sacrifices, I will not accept them, and I will not regard your ostentatious peace offerings. [23]Take away from me the sound of your hymns, and I will not listen to the music from your instruments. [24]And judgment will roll as water and righteousness as an impassable wadi. [25]You did not offer to me sacrificial victims and sacrifices for forty years in the wilderness, did you, O house of Israel? [26]And you took up the tent of Moloch and the star of your God Raiphan, the images of them, which you made for yourselves. [27]And I will lead you away captive beyond Damascus," says the Lord; his name is the God, the Almighty One.

This section contains three units. The transitions between the units are marked by asyndeton (Runge, 22–23). The first unit (5:18–20) is a woe oracle, and it warns of judgment on the day of the Lord. It is announced by the interjection Οὐαί, and it is enclosed by rhetorical questions describing the day of the Lord as darkness and not light (5:18 and 20). The second unit (5:21–24) is a classic description of the Lord's desire for righteousness and justice and his abhorrence of outward expressions of worship without righteousness and justice. And in the third unit (5:25–27) the Lord again says he will send Israel into exile (see also 5:4–7) because of their sins; Israel's sins in the wilderness, which are described in 5:25–26, are prototypical of their later sins (see Acts 7:41–43), which are the reason for their exile (5:27).

5:18 Οὐαὶ οἱ ἐπιθυμοῦντες τὴν ἡμέραν κυρίου· ἵνα τί αὕτη ὑμῖν ἡ ἡμέρα τοῦ κυρίου; καὶ αὐτή ἐστιν σκότος καὶ οὐ φῶς,

Οὐαί. This interjection begins a new section and connects this section with the preceding and the following (see 5:16; 6:1). It is an "exclamation of pain, grief, or horror" (LEH, 449–50).

οἱ ἐπιθυμοῦντες. Pres act ptc nom masc pl ἐπιθυμέω (substantival). The substantival participle signals direct address, identifying the objects of the preceding interjection; therefore "to" may be added to the translation ("woe *to* those who desire...."; see 6:1). The article functions as a substantiver, and the participle construction functions like a nominative used as a vocative (Muraoka §22.yb; Wallace, 56–58). The present-tense participle should be understood to refer to a customary or continual attitude.

τὴν ἡμέραν. Accusative direct object of ἐπιθυμοῦντες. The same expression ("day of the Lord"), which refers to a time of the Lord's distinct intervention in the affairs of the world (Glenny 2013b, 102), occurs again in 5:18 and 5:20 with an article modifying κυρίου. There is no difference in the Hebrew phrases in 5:18 (2x) and 5:20 that explains the variation in the use of articles, and in the LXX the phrase "day of the Lord" occurs with and without an article modifying κύριος and ἡμέρα. These variations in the use of the article seem to be stylistic. The article (τήν) with ἡμέραν, the accusative object of ἐπιθυμοῦντες is expected with this monadic noun.

κυρίου. Possessive genitive.

ἵνα τί. The interrogative phrase is the predicate of the equative clause and has the idea "for what reason or purpose...?, why...?" (*GELS*, 341.3; see also LSJ, 830.II.3.c). Muraoka (*GELS*, 341) notes that the phrase usually occurs with "an overtone of discontent, displeasure, incredulity," and here the sense is incredulity. In the 141 times it occurs in the LXX, it is almost always rendered "why?" in NETS (see also LEH, 288, which suggests the rendering "to what end, why?"). Here, with the threatening description of the day of the Lord following the question, the context suggests the phrase should have the sense "what is the reason or purpose" that you desire this previously mentioned day of the

Lord, since it is "darkness and not light"? (See Dines 1991, 163, who renders the question "For what is it for you, the Day of the Lord"?)

αὕτη. This nominative demonstrative pronoun could be "enclitically attached to an interrogative [ἵνα τί] so as to reinforce the latter" (Muraoka §12.ga, who renders the clause "of what use is the Lord's day for you?"); in such cases the demonstrative is usually neuter, and its sense ("this, that") is not normally communicated in the translation. However, the demonstrative could also grammatically modify the following ἡ ἡμέρα τοῦ κυρίου since its gender is attracted to it and to the use of this same noun phrase earlier in the verse; thus, it would be rendered something like "for what purpose is this day of the Lord to you"? A Greek reader would likely sense both ideas in the construction: this demonstrative pronoun definitely has an enclitic force, emphasizing the interrogative, but its gender, number, and case, which agree with the following ἡ ἡμέρα τοῦ κυρίου, strongly suggest it is modifying that phrase, from which it is separated by one word.

ὑμῖν. Dative of reference or, more likely, dative of advantage. Thus, the question for the reader is, what is the benefit or advantage for you of this day of the Lord that you desire?

ἡ ἡμέρα τοῦ κυρίου. Here the construction follows Apollonius' canon. See the discussion of this phrase above in this verse where there is no article before κύριος.

καί. This connecting particle "highlights a logical contradiction with what precedes" (*GELS*, 353–54.6; see 2 Kgdms 11:11; Judg 9:2), and it has the sense "since, when, whereas." The καί has nothing corresponding to it in the Hebrew. The καί in the LXX explicitly connects and marks a relationship between the preceding and following clauses (Runge, 22–23); the significance of καί is intensifying, and as mentioned above, in this context it also signifies contradiction or correction (see *GE*, 1010.4.B).

αὐτή. Nominative subject of ἐστιν. Substantival use of the demonstrative pronoun, referring back to "the day of the Lord."

ἐστιν. Pres act ind 3rd sg εἰμί. The verb has the sense "to possess a certain characteristic, to be identical with (so-called copula)" (*GELS*, 193.2). The present tense is used here to describe a future event, and it adds a connotation of certainty (Wallace, 535–36).

σκότος καὶ οὐ φῶς. Predicate nominatives connected by καί (*GELS*, 352.1.a); the negative particle οὐ is positioned immediately before φῶς ("light") to negate it, thus emphasizing the "darkness" of this day (*GELS*, 511.b; Muraoka §83.b.i).

5:19 ὃν τρόπον ὅταν φύγῃ ἄνθρωπος ἐκ προσώπου τοῦ λέοντος καὶ ἐμπέσῃ αὐτῷ ἡ ἄρκος, καὶ εἰσπηδήσῃ εἰς τὸν οἶκον αὐτοῦ καὶ ἀπερείσηται τὰς χεῖρας αὐτοῦ ἐπὶ τὸν τοῖχον καὶ δάκῃ αὐτὸν ὁ ὄφις.

ὃν τρόπον ὅταν. The construction ὃν τρόπον has the sense "just as, exactly as" and emphasizes "comparability and analogy" (*GELS*, 688.b, s.v. τρόπος); it is followed by the conjunction or particle of condition ὅταν (*GELS*, 688.d, s.v. τρόπος; see also Ὃν τρόπον ὅταν in 3:12). MSS B and Q, *L*, Swete, and Ziegler have ἐάν in 5:19, and MSS A, W, V, and R-H have ὅταν; the meaning is essentially the same with either one. The construction with ἐάν is found only in Isaiah (17:5; 24:13; 31:4; and 33:4), and the construction with ὅταν is the norm in the LXX Twelve (see also Amos 3:12; Mic 5:7; Zech 4:1; Isa 7:2; and Ezek 10:10) and thus preferred here. The corresponding Hebrew is כאשר, which is elsewhere rendered with the simple ὃν τρόπον in Amos (2:13; 3:12; 5:19; and 9:9). Thus, there is no word corresponding to ὅταν in Hebrew in 5:14. The temporal particle ὅταν is employed here with three aorist subjunctive verbs, and in this construction it is "almost pleonastic" (*GELS*, 688.2.c); with the subjunctive verb, ὅταν "approaches the meaning of ἐάν, since the time reference also indicates the conditions under which the action of the main clause takes place" (BDAG, 730.1.a, s.v. ὅταν). The aorist subjunctive is used following the preceding temporal particle of condition (ὅταν) to describe the hypothetical examples that make up the conditional idea in the verse, i.e., "if someone flees." The temporal particle gives the verse the sense of a conditional sentence; in fact, the whole verse should probably be understood to have the sense of a protasis of a probable conditional sentence, with the implied apodosis being the comparison the verse is making: "then that would be like the day of the Lord." However, with the indefinite temporal particle there is also a trace of a temporal idea. The verse is a general description with many generic nouns, meant to illustrate the danger and death that will characterize the day of the Lord.

φύγῃ. Aor act subj 3rd sg φεύγω. Subjunctive following ὅταν.

ἄνθρωπος. Nominative subject of φύγῃ. Indefinite generic noun not specifying the referent in mind and with weakened force so that it is "almost equal to τις"; this usage is common "in a conditional or associated clause" (*GELS*, 52.3; cf. BDAG, 81.4). This noun can refer to a person (i.e., human being without reference to maleness), but the masculine pronouns referring to this word later in the verse (3x) and the activity described suggest a male is in view.

ἐκ προσώπου. Separation, modifying φύγῃ. The preposition ἐκ indicates "dissociation" (*GELS*, 201.1.a) or "separation" (BDAG,

295–96.1). The phrase ἐκ προσώπου is based on a Hebrew idiom that has the idea "away from" with verbs of fleeing (*GELS*, 601.6.d, s.v. πρόσωπον); the two words are a rendering of the Hebrew semi-preposition מִפְּנֵי (see Sollamo, 81–94), and thus, although προσώπου is technically the object of the preposition ἐκ, the two words function as a preposition equal to ἐκ.

τοῦ λέοντος. Functions as the object of the preposition ἐκ (see the previous entry). If προσώπου is understood to refer to a literal "face," λέοντος would be a genitive of possession. The article (τοῦ) with λέοντος is probably best understood to be the use of the article with a generic noun, singling out "a typical case as representative of that species and as against some other species" (Muraoka §1.d).

καί. Coordinating conjunction, connecting independent clauses (*GELS*, 352.1.b); here it introduces another description of the day of the Lord, which is part of the compound protasis of the general, conditional idea in the verse.

ἐμπέσῃ. Aor act subj 3rd sg ἐμπίπτω. Subjunctive following ὅταν. The verb has the sense "fall upon, attack" in this context (*GELS*, 228.3).

αὐτῷ. Dative complement of ἐμπέσῃ (LSJ, 545, s.v. ἐμπίπτω).

ἡ ἄρκος. Nominative subject of ἐμπέσῃ. The article used with the generic noun, "a bear" (see τοῦ λέοντος above).

καί. Coordinating conjunction, connecting independent clauses (*GELS*, 352.1.b). It is introducing another description of the day of the Lord, which is part of the compound protasis of the general, conditional idea in the verse.

εἰσπηδήσῃ. Aor act subj 3rd sg εἰσπηδάω. Subjunctive following ὅταν. This intransitive verb has the sense "move in rapidly" (*GELS*, 200).

εἰς τὸν οἶκον. Location, modifying εἰσπηδήσῃ. The preposition εἰς has the sense of extension toward and into a goal (*GELS*, 196.1; in BDAG, 288.1.a.β, to "focus on the area within the point reached," which is the sense here). The accusative object of the preposition (τὸν οἶκον) is generic, even though modified by αὐτοῦ, since the referent of the pronoun is generic, "a man, someone." This phrase and the following words develop the generic situation in some detail.

αὐτοῦ. Possessive genitive.

καί. Coordinating conjunction, connecting independent clauses (*GELS*, 352.1.b); here it is introducing another description of the day of the Lord, which is part of the compound protasis of the general, conditional idea in the verse.

ἀπερείσηται. Aor mid subj 3rd sg ἀπερείδω. Subjunctive following ὅταν. The verb has the sense "position firmly" (*GELS*, 67) or "to put upon" (LEH, 63); it is always in the middle voice in the LXX, and it is easy to see how the subject is affected by the action in this middle-voice verb. This is best classified as a middle of "nontranslational motion" (Kemmer, 268).

τὰς χεῖρας. Accusative direct object of ἀπερείσηται. The "hands" of the representative person are in view. In Hebrew the word corresponding to χεῖρας (יד) is singular.

αὐτοῦ. Possessive genitive.

ἐπὶ τὸν τοῖχον. Locative, modifying ἀπερείσηται; the preposition ἐπί "indicates a surface on which something is situated" (*GELS*, 266.III.3.b), and its accusative object (τοῖχον, "wall") is definite, referring to a specific wall of the house of the generic individual being described.

καὶ. Coordinating conjunction, connecting independent clauses (*GELS*, 352.1.b); here it is introducing another description of the day of the Lord, which is part of the compound protasis of the general, conditional idea in the verse.

δάκῃ. Aor act subj 2nd sg δάκνω. Subjunctive following ὅταν. The verb has the meaning "bite" (*GELS*, 139.1); in 9:3 this verb describes the "bite" of a dragon.

αὐτὸν. Accusative direct object of δάκῃ.

ὁ ὄφις. Nominative subject of δάκῃ. Generic noun, representing a class, "a snake." It is not necessary to use an article with generic nouns (Ziegler's text does not include one here), and even when articular a generic noun can be translated as indefinite (Muraoka §1.d; Wallace, 228).

5:20 οὐχὶ σκότος ἡ ἡμέρα τοῦ κυρίου καὶ οὐ φῶς; καὶ γνόφος οὐκ ἔχων φέγγος αὐτῇ.

The description of the day of the Lord in this verse builds on and completes the description in 5:18–19. It repeats much of the language in 5:18 (ἡ ἡμέρα τοῦ κυρίου and σκότος καὶ οὐ φῶς), forming an *inclusio* around the small section.

οὐχὶ. This strengthened form of οὐ can function as a simple negative, but here it is an interrogative word in a question that expects an affirmative answer (BDAG, 742.3; *GELS*, 515.1). Its position with a noun at the beginning of the sentence emphasizes the expected affirmative answer and the noun, i.e., "it is darkness."

σκότος. Predicate nominative of the understood equative clause.

ἡ ἡμέρα τοῦ κυρίου. See the same form of this phrase in 5:18; here it serves as the nominative subject of a verbless equative clause.

καὶ. Coordinating conjunction, connecting compound predicate nominatives (*GELS*, 352.1.a).

οὐ φῶς. The second predicate nominative (φῶς) is negative; see these words in 5:18.

καί. Coordinating conjunction, connecting independent clauses (*GELS*, 352.1.b); here it is introducing another rhetorical question describing the day of the Lord. The subject and verb in this sentence are elided and understood from the previous parallel sentence ("Is not the day of the Lord . . .").

γνόφος. Predicate nominative. This word, which is a "later form for the earlier and poetic δνόφος (on which see LSJ, 441, s.v. δνόφος)," has the sense "darkness" (BDAG, 202; LEH, 122; LSJ, 354); of its twenty-seven occurrences in the LXX, it most often describes a manifestation of God (Exod 20:21; Deut 4:11) or the atmosphere where he lives (2 Kgdms 22:10; 3 Kgdms 8:53; 2 Chr 6:1; Pss 17:10; 96:2; see also Heb 12:18), although it often describes the day of the Lord (Joel 2:2; Zeph 1:15; Isa 60:2; Ezek 34:12). See the discussion of this word in Glenny (2013b, 103).

οὐκ ἔχων. Pres act ptc nom masc sg ἔχω (result). The result is logical and simultaneous with the existence of the darkness (Wallace, 638). The participle modifies the understood equative verb (i.e., the day of the Lord is without brightness in it); if it were adjectival modifying γνόφος (i.e., the day of the Lord is blackness that is without brightness in it), it would mean there is no brightness in the darkness, and the following modifying pronoun (αὐτῇ) would then be masculine (referring to γνόφος), rather than feminine (referring to the day of the Lord). Muraoka (§31.ce; 83.bd) seems to forget about the gender of this pronoun, and he translates the phrase here "darkness having no brightness for it," taking the participle to be attributive and the pronoun "it" (αὐτῇ) to be apparently referring to the "darkness" (γνόφος), which is masculine. (If he is taking the pronoun to be referring to the day of the Lord, the resulting meaning is awkward.) The negative particle οὐ is used in the LXX to negate a circumstantial or non-circumstantial participle (see Muraoka §31.bd). This participle phrase is a Greek idiom, and there is nothing corresponding to the participle in the Hebrew.

φέγγος. Accusative direct object of ἔχων. The absence of the article puts the stress on the quality of "brightness, light." See the discussion of φέγγος in Glenny (2013b, 103).

αὐτῇ. Dative of place or sphere, modifying ἔχων and referring back to ἡ ἡμέρα τοῦ κυρίου.

5:21 μεμίσηκα, ἀπῶσμαι ἑορτὰς ὑμῶν καὶ οὐ μὴ ὀσφρανθῶ ἐν ταῖς πανηγύρεσιν ὑμῶν·

The asyndeton marks a transition to a new topic, moving from the description of the day of the Lord in 5:18–20 to a focus on Israel's empty religious ritual and idolatry and their coming captivity in 5:21–27.

μεμίσηκα. Prf act ind 1st sg μισέω. The perfect focuses on the present state, i.e., "I hate" (BDF §341).

ἀπῶσμαι. Prf mid ind 1st sg. The perfect focuses on the present state (BDF §341). The subject is affected by involvement volitionally, and the middle voice is what Kemmer (269) calls an emotional middle involving two participants. This verb is almost always middle voice in LXX; the only exception I found out of seventy occurrences was in Job 18:18. It has the literal sense "push aside," and the figurative extension of that meaning, required in this context, is "reject, repudiate" (BDAG, 126–27; GELS, 88.1). The absence of a connector between the two first-person verbs intensifies the feelings and makes them more emphatic.

ἑορτάς. Accusative direct object of the two preceding verbs. In accord with the Hebrew, the noun is anarthrous, but with the pronoun (ὑμῶν) it is definite. The noun refers to a "feast" or "festival" (LEH, 219), and in the LXX it is often further defined by a genitive that identifies the feast to which it refers (e.g., Exod 23:15, 16; 34:18, 22, 25; Spicq, 3:4–8; Glenny 2013b, 104).

ὑμῶν. Possessive genitive.

οὐ μὴ ὀσφρανθῶ. Aor pass subj 1st sg ὀσφραίνομαι. This passive θη- form replaced the earlier middle/passive forms in many verbs (Conrad 2015). It has a middle force, and it has the sense "to smell the odor of, to sniff" (*GE*, 1497); the middle force is what Kemmer (269) calls a perception middle. The double negation with the aorist subjunctive is emphatic (see BDF §365; Smyth §2754–55), sometimes rendered "never," and adds intensity to the condemnation. The imagery is that of a god savoring the smell of a sacrifice (*GELS*, 510.I), indicating the sacrifice is accepted (1 Kgdms 26:19; see also Gen 8:21; Lev 26:31). This imagery is found in early Greek literature (Homer, *Il.* 8.48; 23.148; *Od.* 8.363; Hesiod, *Theog.* 557), and it should not be limited to meat offerings, as Brenton does in his translation (cf. Lev 2:2; Num 15:7). See Glenny (2013b, 104). Anthropomorphic language is used throughout this section to describe the Lord's response to Israel's worship ("smell" in 5:21; "look upon" ["respect"] in 5:22; and "listen" in 5:23).

ἐν ταῖς πανηγύρεσιν. Locative, modifying ὀσφρανθῶ. The preposition ἐν is probably best understood to refer to "a place in which some action takes place or some state prevails" (*GELS*, 231.1.b), rather than a time (*GELS*, 231.3). The dative object of the preposition (πανηγύρεσιν) occurs only four times in the LXX, and it is always parallel to ἑορτή (see Glenny 2013b, 104); it refers to "a major gathering of people to celebrate a formal occasion" (Spicq, 3:5). The article is normal with a noun modified by a possessive pronoun (ὑμῶν).

ὑμῶν. Possessive genitive.

5:22 διότι καὶ ἐὰν ἐνέγκητέ μοι ὁλοκαυτώματα καὶ θυσίας ὑμῶν, οὐ προσδέξομαι αὐτά, καὶ σωτηρίου ἐπιφανείας ὑμῶν οὐκ ἐπιβλέψομαι.

διότι. This conjunction often indicates a causal relationship between statements ("because, since"; see *GELS*, 172.1; BDAG, 251.1), but here it introduces an inference from or explanation of the preceding statement (BDAG, 251.2; NETS renders it "for").

καὶ ἐάν. The connector καί is adverbial and invites comparison; the combination of words has the sense "even if" (*GELS*, 354.8.b); ἐάν is a conditional particle, introducing the protasis of a future more vivid condition (Smyth §2321–25). There is good support for καί here (MSS A, Q, W, and R-H), but Ziegler follows B in not including it. There is nothing in the Hebrew source text corresponding to καί.

ἐνέγκητέ. Aor act subj 2nd pl φέρω. Subjunctive following ἐάν in a conditional sentence. The aorist tense refers to the action as a whole. This verb is an example of suppletion; the root φερ- is only found in the present and imperfect tenses, and the roots οἰ- (future tense) and ἐνεκ- (aorist tense) supplement gaps in its paradigm (*TDNT*, 9:56).

μοι. Dative indirect object of ἐνέγκητε.

ὁλοκαυτώματα καὶ θυσίας. Compound accusative direct objects of ἐνέγκητε connected by the coordinating conjunction καί (*GELS*, 352.1.a). The general word for sacrifice in the LXX is θυσία, and ὁλοκαυτώματα is usually rendered "wholly [whole] burnt offering" (*GELS*, 493). Muraoka (*GELS*, 334.1) suggests θυσία here, combined with ὁλοκαύτωμα, refers to animal sacrifices; however, the word can also refer to "cultic offering in general" (*GELS*, 334.2), and that could be the meaning here. See Wevers' discussion (1997, 484–87) of the rendering of Hebrew words for sacrifice in the LXX and the discussion of the verb ὀσφρανθῶ in 5:21.

ὑμῶν. Possessive genitive, modifying both ὁλοκαυτώματα and θυσίας.

οὐ προσδέξομαι. Fut mid ind 1st sg προσδέχομαι. It is the future tense in the apodosis of a future more vivid condition, "I will not accept" (Smyth §2321–25). This is probably best seen as an "indirect middle" with a verb of "coming into possession" (Kemmer, 268).

αὐτά. Accusative object of προσδέξομαι. Although the object of προσδέξομαι is understood in all texts, it is not included in B and *L*.

σωτηρίου ἐπιφανείας ὑμῶν οὐκ ἐπιβλέψομαι. This clause is the second part of the apodosis of the conditional sentence connected to the preceding apodosis clause by καί (*GELS*, 352.1.b). It is in many ways parallel to the preceding clause (negated parallel future-tense verbs with references to sacrifices as their objects).

σωτηρίου. Genitive of apposition, modifying ἐπιφανείας. Daniel suggested that σωτήριον should be read as an accusative here, and MS B and the Armenian version have an accusative plural form (see also Ezek 45:15 [where A has the accusative reading in a context discussing sacrifices]; and the discussion in Dines 1991, 164 n. 12, following Daniel, 282–85). But modern critical editions (both R-H and Ziegler) have the genitive singular form in this verse (and in Ezek 45:15), and it can make good sense as a genitive, if one takes ἐπιφανείας as the object of the verb (*GELS*, 269.1.b, s.v. ἐπιβλέπω, suggests the predicate of the clause be rendered "your ostentatious thank-offerings for deliverance"). The noun σωτηρίου could function as a genitive of purpose or direction (Muraoka §22.v.xiv; Wallace, 100–101), meaning something like "deliverance," i.e., "conspicuous acts for deliverance" (so NETS); or it could be understood to be a genitive of apposition (Wallace, 94–100), meaning something like "deliverance [peace] offering" and rendered with ἐπιφανείας as "ostentatious acts, which are deliverance offerings." The function of this noun depends on its meaning, and the meaning of σωτήριον is somewhat ambiguous in the LXX when describing sacrifices, especially the "peace offering" (see Lev 3 and 7; and the discussion in Wevers 1997, 23, where he suggests it refers to a "sacrifice for deliverance"). The focus on sacrifices in this verse and the use of this noun to render the various forms of the "peace offering" in Leviticus 3, 7, and elsewhere make it likely that it refers to a sacrifice here (so Dines 1991, 164; *GELS*, 668.2.b, s.v. σωτήριον). Wevers felt that the LXX translator often understood it to refer to an offering that was based on deliverance (Wevers 1997, 23); the basic idea of the offering is that the eating of it enacts the worshippers' fellowship with the Lord. The noun σωτήριον is normally plural when it refers to "peace offerings" in the LXX (see Glenny 2013b, 28, 105), but it is singular here, as is the corresponding Hebrew word (שלם). Although it is not the norm, the singular σωτήριον seems to be used to refer to "peace offerings" in Ezek 45:15, 17; 46:2 (see *GELS*, 668.2.b; in those contexts, which are describing various sacrifices, the corresponding Hebrew word [שלם] is plural). Thus, σωτηρίου should probably be understood here as a genitive of apposition, telling more about the ostentatious acts: they are "peace offerings" or "deliverance offerings," and the offerors presume the offerings enact their fellowship with the Lord.

ἐπιφανείας. Accusative direct object of ἐπιβλέπω. The word has the sense "manifestation" or better "outward show" in this context where the language is pejorative (*GELS*, 286.2); with the preceding genitive of apposition, which serves to define this ambiguous word, the phrase probably should be understood to have the sense "outward acts of [or show of] peace offerings." The point of the clause is that the Lord has no respect for their outward, superficial acts consisting of peace offerings. The corresponding word in Hebrew is מריא ("fattened animals"), which the translator apparently read as מראה, meaning "appearance" (*HALOT*, 1:630).

ὑμῶν. Subjective genitive, modifying ἐπιφανείας. The recipients are the ones performing the ostentatious acts (ἐπιφανείας).

οὐκ ἐπιβλέψομαι. Fut mid ind 1st sg ἐπιβλέπω. Future tense in the apodosis of a future more vivid condition (Smyth §2321–25). Muraoka (*GELS*, 269.1.b) suggests the verb here has the sense of look or watch "approvingly." The middle voice is what Kemmer (269) calls an "emotional middle" involving one participant or a "perception middle," depending on how literally one understands the verb. I have rendered the verb "regard," following Dines (1991, 164).

5:23 μετάστησον ἀπ' ἐμοῦ ἦχον ᾠδῶν σου, καὶ ψαλμὸν ὀργάνων σου οὐκ ἀκούσομαι·

The sense of the connection with the previous verse seems to be that the command continues the preceding condemnation of Israel's empty ritual and idolatry, and it advances the rhetoric by commanding Israel's proper response to the Lord's abhorrence of their behavior.

μετάστησον. Aor act impv 2nd sg μεθίστημι. The sense of this word is to "transfer from one place to another," and here it has the sense "remove"; it is transitive in the present, future active, and aorist (BDAG, 625.1.a; *GELS*, 446.1). This aorist imperative beginning the sentence with asyndeton gives the sense of an urgent request. The second-person singular forms in 5:23 (cf. the plurals in 5:21–22) should be understood to be collective, addressing the community as a whole (see Deut 6:4; see also the discussion in Glenny 2013b, 105).

ἀπ' ἐμοῦ. Separation, modifying μετάστησον. The preposition ἀπό has the sense of "removal or dissociation," and it is spatial (*GELS*, 69.1). ἐμοῦ is "emphatic in form only [with an *epsilon* prefix]," because its "selection is due to morphologically conditioned, complementary distribution" (Muraoka §7.c). In other words, the combination of ἀπό with the first-person personal pronoun as its object only occurs in the LXX with the emphatic form of the pronoun.

ἦχον. Accusative direct object of μετάστησον. This word is used elsewhere in the LXX to describe "tumult" or "noise" of battle (1 Kgdms 14:19; Joel 3:14), the sound of sea waves (Ps 64:8; Jer 28:42), the "howling" of owls (Isa 13:21), as well as music (e.g., Dan 3:7, 10, 15) (see Glenny 2013b, 105–6).

ᾠδῶν. Genitive of source, providing the source of the "sound" (ἦχον), i.e., ἦχον refers to the sound of the "hymns," not their words.

σου. Possessive genitive. The singular form pronoun is collective, addressing the community as a whole.

καὶ. Coordinating conjunction, connecting compound clauses (*GELS*, 352.1.b). The conjunction could be understood to be introducing a clause that "explicates" the first clause (*GELS*, 354.13), "introduces a consequence which would ensue" if the preceding is realized (*GELS*, 354.9), or perhaps gives the cause of the preceding clause; however, none of these explanations is totally convincing, and the force of the parallelism with the preceding clause indicates it has a coordinate relationship with it.

ψαλμὸν. Accusative direct object of ἀκούσομαι. The singular noun ψαλμόν probably refers to "music made with an instrument," rather than the more common sense of the word: "song of praise" (LEH, 672).

ὀργάνων. Genitive of source (or perhaps a genitive of production, Wallace, 104–6).

σου. Possessive genitive. The singular form is collective, addressing the community.

οὐκ ἀκούσομαι. Fut mid ind 1st sg ἀκούω. Predictive future with a negative particle. Kemmer (269) calls this use of the middle voice "perception middle." On the use of genitive or accusative objects with ἀκούω, see 3:1 on ἀκούσατε.

5:24 καὶ κυλισθήσεται ὡς ὕδωρ κρίμα καὶ δικαιοσύνη ὡς χειμάρρους ἄβατος.

καὶ. Coordinating conjunction, connecting compound clauses (*GELS*, 352.1.b). The exact sense of the conjunction here is difficult to classify, since it introduces a new idea.

κυλισθήσεται. Fut pass ind 3rd sg κυλίω. This verb is a later form of κυλίνδω (LSJ, 1008, s.v. κυλίνδω). The verb κυλίω has the general sense of rolling, or to move by rolling (*GE*, 1191; BDAG, 574), and here, referring to water, it communicates the idea "to flow along with great speed" (*GELS*, 418.2); in keeping with the general sense of the verb, I have rendered it "roll." The θη- middle/passive form (see Conrad) should probably be understood to be what Kemmer (269) calls a middle of translational motion. The future tense could be understood as a jussive future or imperatival future, following the MT (Conybeare and Stock §74; BDF §362; Smyth §1917; see for example Lev 19:20–22), but it is more likely that it would be read as a predictive future (so NETS; Dines 1991, 165; Glenny 2013b, 106). The Lord was the subject in the last clause in 5:23, and it is natural that he continues to be the one acting in 5:24. Also, the compound subjects in 5:24 (κρίμα and δικαιοσύνη) are the same words used in 5:7 to describe the social justice the Lord will bring to the earth.

ὡς. Here the particle ὡς communicates similarity, not identity, and indicates manner (BDAG, 1103.1); it introduces a subordinate clause in the comparison (Muraoka §26.n).

ὕδωρ. Nominative subject of the implied verb in the subordinate clause ("roll"; i.e., "as *water* rolls"). Often in comparisons with ὡς missing words can be supplied (*GELS*, 748.3). As with most similes in the LXX, the noun following ὡς is anarthrous (*GELS*, 748.6).

κρίμα. Nominative subject of κυλισθήσεται, which together form the main clause of the comparison. This noun is highlighted by its location at the end of the comparison.

δικαιοσύνη. Nominative subject of the implied repeated verb (κυλισθήσεται), which together form the main clause of the second comparison in the verse. Often in comparisons with ὡς missing words can be supplied (*GELS*, 748.3). The subjects of the two main clauses in the two comparisons in this verse are joined by the coordinating conjunction καί (*GELS*, 352.1.b); their location together serves to connect and stress these two abstract ideas (see 5:7, where the same two terms occur). The article is often absent with abstract nouns (BDF §258), but that does not mean they are indefinite; when they are anarthrous the stress is often on the quality, as here.

ὡς. See ὡς ὕδωρ above for a discussion of the parallel comparative article.

χειμάρρους ἄβατος. Nominative subject of the implied verb in the subordinate clause ("roll"; i.e., "as an impassable wadi rolls"); often in comparisons with ὡς missing words can be supplied (*GELS*, 748.3). χειμάρρους (alternatively χείμαρρος) refers to "a stream of water that flows abundantly in the winter" or rainy season (BDAG, 1082). Here it is modified by ἄβατος, which means "impassable," or in this context "unfordable" (*GELS*, 1). The corresponding Hebrew word (איתן) has the sense "ever flowing" (*HALOT*, 1:45). As with most similes in the LXX, the noun following ὡς is anarthrous (*GELS*, 748.6).

5:25 μὴ σφάγια καὶ θυσίας προσηνέγκατέ μοι ἐν τῇ ἐρήμῳ τεσσαράκοντα ἔτη, οἶκος Ισραηλ;

Amos 5:25-27 is a unit in the larger paragraph (5:18-27). It is an important passage, because 5:26-27 is quoted by Stephen in his sermon in Acts 7:42-43 and in the Damascus Document (CD VII, 13-19). The interpretation in CD is unique, "describing the historical genesis of the Qumran sect and applying the text to the community's sectarian interests" (see the summary in Glenny 2013b, 108).

μὴ. The negative particle at the beginning of this question requires the answer "no" and clarifies the translator's understanding of the question. It is less clear in the MT.

σφάγια καὶ θυσίας. Compound accusative direct objects of προσηνέγκατε, joined by a coordinating conjunction (*GELS*, 352.1.α). The noun σφάγιον ("sacrificial victims") refers to "animal victim[s] slaughtered for sacrifice" (*GELS*, 664.2; see also LSJ, 1737; Ezek 21:15, 20, 33) parallel with θυσία, a common word for a "sacrifice."

προσηνέγκατέ. Aor act ind 2nd pl προσφέρω. Constative aorist, viewing the forty-year period as a whole and summarizing the activity during that period. This verb has the sense "bear toward, present" (*GE*, 1831-32) and is used often for offering sacrificial gifts (BDAG, 886.2). See ἐνέγκητέ in 5:22 on the suppletion of φέρω verbs.

μοι. Dative indirect object of προσηνέγκατε.

ἐν τῇ ἐρήμῳ. Locative, modifying προσηνέγκατέ. Most MSS have the phrase "in the wilderness" (ἐν τῇ ἐρήμῳ) in this verse, following the Hebrew, and so the time period referred to is specified (see Glenny 2013b, 28; and Dines 1991, 165-66, for discussion of the textual issues). However, the phrase ἐν τῇ ἐρήμῳ is not found in "a significant and varied number of witnesses," most importantly W (Dines 1991, 165), and its position varies in the manuscripts in which it is found (esp. B, V, and L). Therefore, Ziegler considered the phrase a later addition in the LXX, and he did not include it in the Göttingen LXX edition. Its presence in different places in important manuscripts supports its inclusion. Dines suggests several possibilities for the historical background of the forty years. In light of the description of the activities during this time in 5:25, it could refer to a period in the Northern Kingdom after it was conquered by Assyria, Judah during its exile (if "Israel" in 5:25 is taken inclusively), or perhaps the state of the Jerusalem cultus closer to the time of the translation of Amos (Dines 1991, 166). However, the only other time "forty years" occurs in Amos is in 2:10, where it clearly refers to the wilderness period in Israel's history, and it is likely that was the period intended here also; that is the time period it refers to in its use in Stephen's speech in Acts 7:39–44.

τεσσαράκοντα ἔτη. Accusative of extent of time, functioning adverbially and modifying προσηνέγκατε (BDF §161.2; Smyth §1582–87, 1609; Muraoka §22.xd); the adjective τεσσαράκοντα ("forty") modifies the noun ἔτη ("years"). Wallace (201) suggests that with this use of the accusative the reader should supply "for the extent of" or "for the duration of" before the accusative. The time period that the "forty years" refers to here is discussed in the previous entry.

οἶκος Ισραηλ. Nominative for a vocative and a genitive of apposition. See the discussion of the same construction in 3:1 and 5:1 (see also 6:14; the two words in this designation occur nine times in LXX Amos, but five times [5:3, 4, 6; 7:10; 9:9] they have a different case or use than they do here). In light of the discussion of "forty years" above in this verse, it seems "Israel" is used here to refer to the nation, not the Northern Kingdom; that seems to be the way it is used in 3:1 also.

5:26 καὶ ἀνελάβετε τὴν σκηνὴν τοῦ Μολοχ καὶ τὸ ἄστρον τοῦ θεοῦ ὑμῶν Ραιφαν, τοὺς τύπους αὐτῶν, οὓς ἐποιήσατε ἑαυτοῖς.

καί. Coordinating conjunction, connecting compound clauses (*GELS*, 352.1.b); it could function like an intensifying adverb here (e.g., "even" NETS; see also BDAG, 495–96.2.b). The main clause that this καί introduces is apparently parallel with the rhetorical question in 5:25. The aorist verb in 5:25 describes what they did not do in the wilderness, and the aorist verb in the main clause of 5:26 describes what they did do during that time; thus, the idolatry in 5:26 replaced the sacrifices not offered in the wilderness in 5:25 (see Dines 1991, 167; Glenny 2013b, 107). The Hebrew describes the wilderness period in 5:25, but it moves on to a later situation in the Northern Kingdom in 5:26.

ἀνελάβετε. Aor act ind 2nd pl ἀναλαμβάνω. Constative aorist, summarizing iterative actions during the time in the wilderness. The verb has the sense "to take up in order to carry" (BDAG, 66.2). Dines (1991, 169) comments that the aorist tense here, which allows a past time for this action in the LXX, is very important, and the context of 5:26 as well as Stephen's use of this passage from the LXX in Acts 7 connect it with the forty years in the wilderness and, specifically, with the golden calf incident (7:38–44).

τὴν σκηνὴν. Accusative direct object ἀνελάβετε. The "tent" (σκηνή) that housed Moloch is usually understood to be a reference to the tabernacle (Glenny 2013b, 108), although the picture could be one of "a procession with images carried in shrines" (Dines 1991, 167).

τοῦ Μολοχ. The indeclinable proper noun Μόλοχ is a possessive genitive, i.e., there is a sense in which this tent belongs to this god. It could also be a genitive of content in the sense that Moloch was housed in the tent, but the sense seems to be broader than that. The articles with the head noun and its genitive modifier correspond with Apollonius' canon, and the article with the head noun is an individualizing article. The worship of Moloch involved child sacrifice (see 4 Kgdms 23:10; Jer 39[32 MT]:35; and the discussion in Glenny 2009, 107). The Greek phrase τὴν σκηνὴν τοῦ Μολοχ renders the Hebrew סכות מלככם ("Sikkuth your king"); סכות (Sikkuth) is apparently read as סכת (tent). See the discussion of the translation in Glenny (2009, 136).

τὸ ἄστρον. Accusative direct object of ἀνελάβετε. This word indicates that Raiphan, the god this star represents, is an astral deity; see Deut 4:19; 17:2–5 for prohibitions against worshipping stars. In the histories of the northern (4 Kgdms 17:16, 17) and southern tribes (4 Kgdms 23:5, 10, 24; see also Ezek 20 in MT), the worship of stars was connected with the worship of Moloch. The article is an individualizing article. In Stephen's use of Amos 5:26–27 in Acts 7:38–44, he connects the gods Moloch and Raiphan with the golden calf and suggests they are both astral deities.

τοῦ θεοῦ. Possessive genitive, modifying ἄστρον. The "star" (ἄστρον) belongs to the god. The article with θεοῦ is consistent with Apollonius' canon.

ὑμῶν. Genitive of subordination, making it clear that Israel worshipped Raiphan in the wilderness; he was their god.

Ραιφαν. This indeclinable proper noun is functioning as a genitive in simple apposition to τοῦ θεοῦ, further clarifying who the god is. BDAG (903) mentions that the spelling of this god's name varies in the LXX manuscripts; the Hebrew has the star god כיון, referring to Saturn (*HALOT*, 1:472), although the word order differs in the LXX.

τοὺς τύπους. Accusative in apposition to the preceding descriptions of the gods. The word τύπος only occurs three other times in the LXX (3 Macc 3:30; 4 Macc 6:19; Exod 25:40); in secular Greek it is a common word for "statue" or "image," and Dines (1991, 169) notes that the use of the word here "suggests that these images were prototypes for subsequent idols." The article is normal with a head noun followed by a possessive pronoun.

αὐτῶν. Objective genitive or, better, representative (or "representation," Muraoka §22.v.xxiii), indicating that the images represented the gods; either way it clarifies in the Greek rendering that the τύπους are of Moloch and Raiphan. The order of some of the words in this verse in the LXX differs from the Hebrew, and τοὺς τύπους αὐτῶν and their corresponding Hebrew (צַלְמֵיכֶם, "your images") are an example of that.

οὕς. Accusative direct object of ἐποιήσατε, introducing a relative clause that modifies τύπους and explains that the τύπους ("images") were the creation of people (see the similar clause also referring to idols in 2:4).

ἐποιήσατε. Aor act ind 2nd pl ποιέω. Constative aorist, summarizing the action.

ἑαυτοῖς. Dative of advantage. The subjects of the verb are the people involved in the reflexive relationship communicated by this pronoun.

5:27 καὶ μετοικιῶ ὑμᾶς ἐπέκεινα Δαμασκοῦ, λέγει κύριος, ὁ θεὸς ὁ παντοκράτωρ ὄνομα αὐτῷ.

καί. Coordinating conjunction, connecting compound clauses (*GELS*, 352.1.b). Although the clauses are compound or parallel, the clause in 5:27 introduced by καί contains the consequences of the previous actions (see *GELS*, 354.9).

μετοικιῶ. Fut act ind 1st sg μετοικίζω. Predictive future. This verb has the sense "to cause to move to a new abode, resettle" (*GELS*, 456), and NETS renders it "deport."

ὑμᾶς. Accusative direct object of μετοικιῶ.

ἐπέκεινα Δαμασκοῦ. Locative. Adverb referring to time or place, functioning here as an "improper preposition" with the genitive case (Muraoka §26.d) meaning "beyond, on the other side of" (see *GELS*, 261.1; BDAG, 361; LSJ, 616; Robertson, 642). The quotation of this passage in Acts 7:43 has "Babylon," and early LXX readers as well as readers of the NT probably understood the passage to refer to the captivity of the Southern Kingdom in Babylon.

λέγει κύριος. See the discussion of Καὶ εἶπεν κύριος in 1:3; also see 1:6 and 5:3 for discussion of this oath-like confirmation formula. It occurs about fifty times in LXX Amos with the aorist and present-tense verb forms, and it is often found in the form τάδε λέγει κύριος (1:2 has the words in this order, but as parts of different phrases).

κύριος ὁ θεὸς ὁ παντοκράτωρ ὄνομα αὐτῷ. This phrase occurs four times in the LXX, all in Amos (see also 4:13; 5:8; 9:6). See the discussion of it at 4:13. The divine title κύριος ὁ θεὸς ὁ παντοκράτωρ occurs ten times in Amos; see the discussion of it at 3:13. Here it corresponds to יהוה אלהי צבאות. The oath-like confirmation formula at the end of 5:27 strengthens the promise of captivity earlier in the verse.

Amos 6:1-14

[1]"Woe to those who scorn Zion and to those who trust in the mountain of Samaria; they have plucked the heads of the nations, and they have entered in. House of Israel, [2]all of you cross over and see and pass through from there to Hamath Rabba and go down to Gath of the foreigners, the best out of all these kingdoms; notice whether their borders are greater than your borders. [3]Those who are moving toward a bad day, who are drawing near and adopting false Sabbaths, [4]who sleep upon ivory beds and behave lewdly upon their couches; and who eat kids out of the flocks and little suckling calves from among the herds, [5]who clap to the sound of the instruments—they considered [them] to be permanent and not fleeting things. [6]Who drink the strained wine and anoint themselves with the finest ointment, and they were not suffering anything on account of the destruction of Joseph. [7]Therefore now, they will be captives from among the head of princes; and the neighing of horses will be removed from Ephraim." [8]For the Lord swore by himself, "I myself loathe all the arrogance of Jacob, and I hate his regions, therefore I will remove a city with all of those inhabiting it." [9]And it shall be if ten men are left in one household, then they shall die but the survivors will be left, [10]and their kinsmen will take [them], and they will endeavor to carry away their bones out of the house, and someone will say to the heads of this household, "Is there still [anyone] with you?" And someone will say, "Not any longer." And he will say, "Be silent, so as not to name the name of the Lord." [11]For, behold, the Lord has commanded, and he will strike the great house with bruises and the little house with lacerations. [12]Will horses run among the rocks? Will [stallions] remain silent among mares? For you yourselves have perverted judgment into wrath and the fruit of righteousness into bitterness. [13]You who rejoice in what amounts to nothing, you who say, "Did we not have horns by our own power?" [14]"Therefore, behold, I will raise up a nation against you, house of Israel, and they will oppress you so that you will not enter into Hamath and as far as the wadi of the west."

Amos 6 begins with another woe oracle (6:1-7; cf. οὐαί in 5:18 and 6:1). The oracle begins with the scorning of Mount Zion by an unnamed group who are trusting in the "mountain of Samaria" (6:1), and then it moves to an address to the house of Israel (6:2). This is followed with a description of the activities of the idle rich in Israel (6:3-6), who are likely the same group described in 6:1. The imperfective aspect of the verbs and participles in 6:3-6 (present and imperfect tenses) marks off this section and implies that the activities described are customary or characteristic (the only exception is ἐλογίσαντο in 6:5). The woe oracle concludes (διὰ τοῦτο) with an announcement of captivity (6:7). The second half of the chapter contains the Lord's oath (6:8–14), and it could be divided into several subunits (6:8, 9–10, 11, 12–14). Verse 8 is the oath proper, and the contents of the oath are repeated in 6:14: the Lord will raise up a nation to oppress Jacob, so they cannot enter the land. Verses 9–13 give details supporting the oath and explaining further what the fulfillment of this oath involves. Distinct to this chapter is the address to "the house of Israel" at the beginning and end.

6:1 Οὐαὶ τοῖς ἐξουθενοῦσι Σιων καὶ τοῖς πεποιθόσιν ἐπὶ τὸ ὄρος Σαμαρείας· ἀπετρύγησαν ἀρχὰς ἐθνῶν, καὶ εἰσῆλθον αὐτοί. οἶκος τοῦ Ισραηλ,

Οὐαὶ. This interjection ("woe!") is a "transcription of the Hebrew" (BDF §4), denoting pain, grief, or horror (LEH, 449–50; BDAG, 734). It begins a new section and connects this section with the preceding and the following (see 5:16 and 5:18).

τοῖς ἐξουθενοῦσι. Pres act ptc dat masc pl ἐξουθενέω (substantival). The dative indicates the people "over whose condition the [woe] utterance is made" (GELS, 512.I.b); here the present participle describes the ongoing attitude and action of the people. This verb (ἐξουθενέω/ ἐξουθενόω = ἐξουδενέω/ἐξουδενόω, GELS, 254–5; BDAG, 352) has the sense "to consider to be of no account and treat as such" (GELS, 254); BDAG (352, s.v. ἐξουδενέω/ἐξουδενόω) gives the literal rendering "to make an οὐδείς/οὐδέν of someone/something." The use of the two verb forms ἐξουθεν- and ἐξουδεν- follows the development from οὐθείς to οὐδείς in the third and second centuries BCE. The former was predominant in the third century, and then by about 132 BCE the latter forms began to reassert themselves (Thackeray §5.1, 7.16). The verbals follow the same pattern (see the chart of the use of the different verb forms in the LXX in Thackeray §7.16; see also BDF §33, §108.2; MHT 2:111–12, 310, 396). The corresponding Hebrew is הַשַּׁאֲנַנִּים ("those who are at ease"), and it is possible that the translator was doing his best here with a word he did not know (Glenny 2013, 169; see pp. 167–69 for a survey of explanations of this rendering). Dines (1991, 180) lists several possible groups the translator may have had in mind with this translation: Israel, Hellenizers, and liberal priests; but the following substantival participle (τοῖς πεποιθόσιν) apparently refers to the same people and suggests they are Samaritans or at least people connected with Samaria. That interpretation makes sense in 6:1a (so Cripps, 202 n. 2), even if it is not clear in the rest of the verse (see below).

"It is clear that the translator connects hostility against Zion with those who are trusting in Samaria" (Glenny 2009, 169).

Σιων. Indeclinable noun functioning as the accusative direct object of ἐξουθενοῦσι.

καὶ. Connecting compound substantives (*GELS*, 352.1.a).

τοῖς πεποιθόσιν. Prf act ptc dat masc pl πείθω (substantival). This dative participle, like the preceding one, indicates the people "over whose condition the [woe] utterance is made" (*GELS*, 512.I.b, s.v. οὐαί); the perfect participle describes the state of the people, who "trust in" the mountain of Samaria. It is possible that this participle describes a group that is different than the people described by the first participle, since both participles have an article. However, it is also possible that both participles describe the same people, who are the recipients of the woe. The third-person plural verb (ἀπετρύγησαν) that describes these people in the next clause suggests they should be understood as one group rather than two.

ἐπὶ τὸ ὄρος. Direction, modifying τοῖς πεποιθόσιν. The preposition here indicates "one to whom or that to which action, thought, emotion, utterance, etc. are directed" (*GELS*, 266.III.4). The verb πείθω is often followed by ἐπί with an accusative object, having the sense "to rely on and trust in with confidence" (*GELS*, 541.1.a, s.v. πείθω). The article (τό) is to be expected with the monadic object "mountain of Samaria," although it could be more stylistic than anything else. The same construction (ἐπὶ τὸ ὄρος Σαμαρείας) is also found in 3:9. Other similar constructions are found in the LXX in Sir 50:26 and Jer 38[31 MT]:5, but in both of those places ὄρος is dative and has no article following the preposition ἐν. The invective against Samaria in Sir 50:26 has "Samaria" (Σαμαρείας) in Greek and "Seir" (שעיר Geniza MS B) in Hebrew, suggesting that Samaria is a later reading, perhaps coming from the time when Sirach was translated into Greek (ca. 132 BCE, close to the time Amos was probably translated into Greek; see ABD, 5:932). The LXX rendering of Amos 6:1 (see also Sir 50:25–26) suggests the translator possibly meant to draw his readers' attention to Samaritans, who worshipped on Mount Gerizim, and who "scorned" Jerusalem and would not worship there (see the discussion of Amos 6:1 in Glenny 2009, 167–73; and Dines 1991, 178).

Σαμαρείας. Genitive of description.

ἀπετρύγησαν. Aor act ind 3rd pl ἀποτρυγάω. Constative aorist, summarizing the action. This LXX *hapax* has the sense "pluck" and is used metaphorically or figuratively here with the picture of a "harvest" (so NETS; see LSJ, 224; *GELS*, 87; Dines 1991, 181–83; Glenny 2009, 170). This Greek verb corresponds with the Hebrew *qal* passive participle נִקְבֵי ("notable men," ESV), which the translator may have read as a form of the verb נָקַף ("cut down, tear," *HALOT*, 1:722); see Dines (1991, 181–83); Park (168); and Arieti (60), on this problematic rendering. The asyndeton at the beginning of this clause is consistent with the transition to more specific examples of the actions of the people who are the recipients of the "woe" (Runge, 23).

The subject of this Greek verb seems to be the same group addressed by the participles in the first clause. If those who "trust in Samaria" are also the same people who "pluck" or "harvest" the "heads of the nations," they are apparently a larger group than the Samaritans, who worshipped on Mount Gerizim. These descriptions likely refer to the Seleucid Hellenizers and their sympathizers. The Seleucids had defeated some of the surrounding nations and were connected to and controlled Samaria in the second century BCE (see Glenny 2013b, 110; *ABD* 4:93, 919). Josephus refers to the capture of Samaria by Antiochus the Great in 198 BCE (*Ant*. 12.133) and the close connection of the leaders in Shechem with the Seleucids (*Ant*. 11.340–5; 12.257–64). He mentions specifically that the Samaritans identified with the Jews when it was to their advantage and with the Sidonians when that was to their benefit; at the time of the Maccabean revolt they identified with the Greeks, calling Antiochus "god," naming their temple after Zeus Hellenios, and saying they chose to live after the customs of the Greeks (see esp. *Ant*. 12.257–64). Thus, the people described in 6:1 are likely the Seleucids and their sympathizers, including some Samaritans.

ἀρχὰς. Accusative direct object of ἀπετρύγησαν. This noun can have the sense "beginning, origin" or that which is in "first place, power, sovereignty" (LSJ, 252); here it must have the latter sense, "ruler, head."

ἐθνῶν. Objective genitive (i.e., the "rulers" rule over the "nations").

καί. Connecting two clauses (*GELS*, 352.1.b).

εἰσῆλθον. Aor act ind 3rd pl εἰσέρχομαι. Constative aorist, summarizing the action. The subject of this verb could be the Seleucid Hellenizers, described earlier in the verse or the leaders of the nations, who were "plucked." With the καί it is more natural to understand the continuation of the same subject as in the previous clause, the Hellenizers who remove the leaders of the nations and then enter into them. The verb could refer to the Seleucids' entrance into other countries or, perhaps, into Samaria (Josephus, *Ant*. 12.133), Bethel (1 Macc 9:50), or Jerusalem and Judea (Josephus, *Ant*. 12.133). This verb is employed in 6:14 describing the inability of the people of Israel to enter their land (see 6:14).

αὐτοί. Nominative subject of εἰσῆλθον. The pronoun is an emphatic nominative personal pronoun in MSS B, V, W, A, Q; Ziegler, consistent with the Hebrew and a few Lucianic manuscripts, prefers the reflexive pronoun ἑαυτοῖς; the personal pronoun has better support.

οἶκος τοῦ Ισραηλ. In the LXX this address is syntactically linked with 6:2, but it is part of 6:1. The same address is found in the last verse of the chapter, enclosing the unit (see also 9:9).

οἶκος. Nominative (substituting for vocative) in apposition to πάντες (6:2), clarifying for whom the utterance is addressed (Muraoka §22. ya–yb). Here the οἶκος refers to the clan of people descended from a common ancestor, thus the idea here is "descendants," or better "nation" (BDAG, 699.3).

τοῦ Ισραηλ. Indeclinable noun functioning as a genitive of apposition, and thus the construction has the sense the people or members of the house or nation, which is Israel (see Wallace, 95–100); it is possible to call it a genitive of source if the emphasis is on the fact that the nation is made up of the descendants of Israel. The article clarifies the case of the indeclinable noun. This singular noun is the subject of the four plural verbs at the beginning of 6:2; Muraoka (§77.ba) calls this "*ad sensum* concord," where the "form is selected by taking the meaning into account," i.e., this "substantive refers to an entity consisting of multiple members," and thus it can agree with the plural verbs following it.

6:2 διάβητε πάντες καὶ ἴδετε καὶ διέλθατε ἐκεῖθεν εἰς Εμαθ Ραββα καὶ κατάβητε ἐκεῖθεν εἰς Γεθ ἀλλοφύλων, τὰς κρατίστας ἐκ πασῶν τῶν βασιλειῶν τούτων, εἰ πλέονα τὰ ὅρια αὐτῶν ἐστι τῶν ὑμετέρων ὁρίων.

διάβητε πάντες καὶ ἴδετε καὶ διέλθατε. This verse is direct address to the "house of Israel" in the second-person plural; it begins with four aorist imperatives (the first three are from διαβαίνω, ὁράω, and διέρχομαι) that summarize the action of the verbs and refer to the action as a whole (Wallace, 485). The commands are connected by the coordinating conjunction (καί), and "all" (πάντες) is the nominative subject of the four imperatives; πάντες corresponds to the Hebrew place-name "Calneh" (כלנה), which the translator probably did not know and rendered as "all" (כל); see Glenny (2009, 90). This rendering changed the sense of the first part of the verse.

ἐκεῖθεν. Adverb of place, meaning "from there" (BDAG, 301) and modifying διέλθατε; here it indicates "a place from which a physical movement starts" (*GELS*, 207.a). The translator had some unnamed location in mind from which the addressees are to pass over to Hamath Rabba; perhaps it is from Judah or Samaria.

εἰς Εμαθ Ραββα. Direction, modifying διέλθατε. The preposition εἰς has the sense "*towards* a goal which is inside an area or in the direction of it" (*GELS*, 196.1). The indeclinable proper noun Εμαθ Ραββα functions as the accusative object of εἰς. This city in central Syria (Hamath) was the idealized northern border of Israel (3 Kgdms 8:65; 1 Chr 13:5; see the discussion in Amos 6:14).

κατάβητε. Aor act impv 2nd pl καταβαίνω. As with the three preceding parallel aorist imperatives, this one is also a summary command referring to the action as a whole (Wallace, 485).

ἐκεῖθεν. See the previous occurrence in the verse; this adverb modifies κατάβητε. Ziegler thought that the preceding occurrence of this adverb in 6:2 led to it being added here; there is nothing corresponding to this occurrence of it in the Hebrew. MSS B, V, and A are among the manuscripts that support its inclusion in the LXX.

εἰς Γεθ. Direction, modifying κατάβητε; on the use of εἰς, see εἰς Εμαθ Ραββα above. This indeclinable proper noun is functioning as the accusative object of εἰς and refers to a Philistine city that was not mentioned in the oracle against Philistia in 1:6–8.

ἀλλοφύλων. Possessive genitive, Gath belonging to the foreigners. This word means "of another race," but in the LXX it is "used especially with reference to Philistines" (*GELS*, 29.b). See 1:8.

τὰς κρατίστας. Accusative in apposition to Εμαθ Ραββα and Γεθ, further describing the two cities. The adjective κράτιστος is the superlative form of the comparative adjective κρείττων, "best, most powerful" (also spelled κρείσσων; see BDAG, 566). Muraoka (§23.bb) notes this is a "true superlative" and also comments (652) that "the translator is possibly representing Gath as the chief among the powerful Philistine pentapolis, which is historically accurate during the reign of David, whether or not the translator was aware of it." The individualizing article is functioning as a substantiver for the adjective.

ἐκ πασῶν τῶν βασιλειῶν τούτων. Partitive, modifying κρατίστας. The preposition ἐκ "indicates an entity out of which a component or part is singled out" (*GELS*, 201.2). The object of the preposition, τῶν βασιλειῶν, has the article, because it is modified by the demonstrative pronoun τούτων in the predicate position. The genitive adjective πασῶν, which also modifies βασιλειῶν and has nothing corresponding to it in the Hebrew, has the meaning "all the . . ." when preceding and modifying a plural articular noun (Muraoka §38.b.i).

εἰ. Conditional particle introducing an indirect question (*GELS*, 190.3.b; Muraoka §88). NETS renders the following sentence "See if their borders are greater than your borders." The indirect question asks the house of Israel to compare the size of the other nations with their territory.

πλέονα τὰ ὅρια αὐτῶν ἐστι. The nominative neuter plural predicate adjective πλέονα is the comparative form of the adjective πολύς (i.e., πλείων), meaning "greater." The subject of the clause is the nominative ὅρια "borders," which is modified by the possessive genitive αὐτῶν.

ἐστι. Pres act ind 3rd sg εἰμί. The singular form is used with the neuter plural noun. The copulative verb is understood in the Hebrew but made explicit by its addition in the LXX.

τῶν ... ὁρίων. Genitive of comparison. The article is common in constructions with a head noun modified by a possessive pronoun.

ὑμετέρων. Possessive genitive, formed from the adjectival pronoun ὑμέτερος. This word is rare in the LXX (4x); it was replaced by the second-person personal pronoun. Muraoka (§11.a) notes the contrasting use of possessive pronouns in this verse.

6:3 οἱ ἐρχόμενοι εἰς ἡμέραν κακήν, οἱ ἐγγίζοντες καὶ ἐφαπτόμενοι σαββάτων ψευδῶν,

οἱ ἐρχόμενοι. Pres mid ptc nom masc pl ἔρχομαι (substantival). This is the first of nine masculine plural substantival participles in 6:3–6 that describe the sinful actions of a group of people (ἑστῶτα and φεύγοντα in 6:5 are neuter and have a different function; see 6:5). In the LXX the participles in 6:3–6 could be in apposition to the participles in 6:1 and have the same referents, those who "scorn Zion" and "trust in the mountain of Samaria," or the participles in 6:3–6 could further describe the "house of Israel," which is addressed with second-person plural imperatives in 6:2 (see Glenny 2013b, 111–15). In the LXX Israel seems to be addressed only in 6:2, and the participles in 6:1 and 3–6 and the third-person finite verbs in 6:1 and in 6:5b, 6:6b, and 6:7a, which alternate with the participles in those verses, all seem to refer to the actions of another group, which is distinct from Israel, perhaps Seleucid Hellenizers and their sympathizers (Glenny 2013, 109–14). This use of the middle voice is the middle of "translational motion" (Kemmer, 269). MSS A and Q, followed by Ziegler, have εὐχόμενοι ("pray for"), a difficult reading in this context. Most manuscripts have ἐρχόμενοι, which is preferred because it is better attested and fits better conceptually. The explanation for either of these readings seems to be that the translator did not know the corresponding Hebrew *piel* participle from נדה ("put away, push out, postpone"), and he rendered it based in the parallel verb in the next clause (נגשׁ, "bring near"; see Glenny 2009, 97–98).

εἰς ἡμέραν κακήν. Direction, modifying ἐρχόμενοι. The preposition εἰς with a verb of movement points "*towards* a goal" (*GELS*, 196.1; emphasis original). The accusative ἡμέραν is the object of the preposition, and the accusative adjective κακήν modifies the object. The idea of κακήν is "bad in effect," resulting in the idea "a day of misfortune" (*GELS*, 57.1.a); they thought they were moving toward something good, but it will turn out to be bad for them.

οἱ ἐγγίζοντες. Pres act ptc nom masc pl ἐγγίζω (substantival). On the function of the participle, see οἱ ἐρχόμενοι above. The article modifies the two participles following it, which are a doublet: both translate the same Hebrew word (Glenny 2009, 49–50). The present tense probably indicates customary action: "drawing near."

ἐφαπτόμενοι. Pres mid ptc nom masc pl ἐφάπτω (substantival). On the function of the participle, see οἱ ἐρχόμενοι above. This middle-voice verb, in its various senses, refers to actions that affect the subject (it can mean "hold fast, apply oneself to, take hold of, touch, possess, participate in, adopt"); it is probably an "indirect middle," with a verb of "coming into possession" (Kemmer, 268). I render it "adopt" (see Glenny 2013b, 111).

σαββάτων ψευδῶν. Genitive complement of ἐφαπτόμενοι. Often verbs describing sensory perception take their objects in the genitive. Josephus mentions the issue of Sabbaths in describing the Samaritans in *Ant.* 12.257–64; apparently, they adopted the Jewish Sabbath and later adapted it when they no longer wanted to be identified with the Jews (see 6:1). "False Sabbaths" could refer to things like the syncretistic worship of the Samaritans (*Ant.* 12.257–64) or the profanation of the Sabbath described in 1 Macc 1:43. The genitive adjective ψευδῶν, modifying σαββάτων, could mean the Sabbaths were "false" in the sense of being "deceptive" or "giving false security" (Dines 1991, 187 n. 15) or different from what they were purported to be (*GELS*, 741.1). The Hebrew has "seat of violence" (שבת חמס), with "seat" being figurative for reign or rule. The translator read שבת ("seat") as the noun "sabbath," which has the same consonants, and made it plural (see Glenny 2009, 130–31).

6:4 οἱ καθεύδοντες ἐπὶ κλινῶν ἐλεφαντίνων καὶ κατασπαταλῶντες ἐπὶ ταῖς στρωμναῖς αὐτῶν καὶ ἔσθοντες ἐρίφους ἐκ ποιμνίων καὶ μοσχάρια ἐκ μέσου βουκολίων γαλαθηνά,

οἱ καθεύδοντες. Pres act ptc nom masc pl καθεύδω (substantival). On the function of the participle, see οἱ ἐρχόμενοι in 6:3. The one article modifying the three substantival participles in 6:4 and the use of the coordinating conjunction καί (*GELS*, 352.1.a) before the second and third participles in this verse require that they all have the same referent; they refer to the same group as the two substantival participles in 6:3.

ἐπὶ κλινῶν ἐλεφαντίνων. Locative, modifying καθεύδοντες. The preposition ἐπί has the sense "on the surface of" (*GELS*, 263.I.2). The "beds" (κλινῶν) are the object of the preposition, and the adjective "ivory" (ἐλεφαντίνων) modifies κλινῶν.

κατασπαταλῶντες. Pres act ptc nom masc pl κατασπαταλάω (substantival). On the function of the participle, see οἱ ἐρχόμενοι in 6:3. This verb occurs elsewhere in the LXX only in Prov 29:21 ("he who lives wantonly") and is rare in Hellenistic Greek. Here with στρωμνή ("bed covering, bed") it has sexual connotations, as the Targum (rendering it "there are stains upon their couches"; see Cathcart and Gordon, 88 n. 6) and Talmud (understanding the verse to describe "people who eat and drink together, join their couches, exchange their wives, and make their couches foul with semen that is not theirs"; b. Shab, 62b; Jastrow, 1025, s.v. סרח) understood it. See the discussion in Glenny (2013b, 111–12). The translator apparently did not know the Hebrew adjective (סרוח, "stretched out") corresponding to this participle, since it occurs only four times in the LXX (see also Amos 6:7; Exod 26:13; Ezek 23:15), and likely by being sensitive to the context, he did pretty well in rendering it.

ἐπὶ ταῖς στρωμναῖς αὐτῶν. Locative, modifying κατασπαταλῶντες. The preposition ἐπί has the sense "on the surface of" (*GELS*, 264. II.2). The object of the preposition (στρωμναῖς) refers to a prepared bed (LSJ, 1656; *GELS*, 640) or the covering for the bed (Esth 1:6). It has sexual connotations in Gen 49:4, although it does not always have such in the LXX. It is common to have an article with a head noun that is modified by a possessive pronoun (i.e., the possessive genitive αὐτῶν).

ἔσθοντες. Pres act ptc nom masc pl ἐσθίω (substantival). On the function of the participle, see οἱ ἐρχόμενοι in 6:3. This is the last of three substantival participles in this verse that go with the article at the beginning of the verse.

ἐρίφους. Accusative object of ἔσθοντες, referring to the "kids, young of goats" (*GELS*, 291) and parallel with μοσχάρια.

ἐκ ποιμνίων. Partitive, modifying ἐρίφους. The preposition ἐκ "indicates an entity out of which a component or part is singled out" (*GELS*, 201.2).

καὶ. Coordinating conjunction, connecting compound objects of ἔσθοντες (*GELS*, 352.1.a).

μοσχάρια . . . γαλαθηνά. Accusative object of ἔσθοντες; it is parallel to ἐρίφους. This noun (μοσχάριον) is the diminutive of μοσχος (with -άριον see BDF §111.3); thus, it has the meaning "little calf" (LEH, 408). The separation of the neuter adjective from its governing noun is a good example of hyperbaton. The adjective γαλαθηνός, with only three occurrences in the LXX, refers to a suckling and emphasizes the youth of the calves (LEH, 115).

ἐκ μέσου βουκολίων. Source, modifying μοσχάριον. The preposition ἐκ "indicates origin, point of departure, source" (*GELS*, 201.5). The adjective μέσου functions as a neuter substantive here (object of preposition; see BDAG, 634–35.1.b; BDF §264.4); as the object of the preposition, it is understood to be definite. The genitive βουκολίων ("herds of cattle"; *GELS*, 121) is partitive: "from among the herds."

6:5 οἱ ἐπικροτοῦντες πρὸς τὴν φωνὴν τῶν ὀργάνων ὡς ἑστῶτα ἐλογίσαντο καὶ οὐχ ὡς φεύγοντα·

Dines (1991, 308) suggests this verse may be a place where the translator paraphrased his source text, rather than following his normal pattern of struggling "with the individual items of the text."

οἱ ἐπικροτοῦντες. Pres act ptc nom masc pl ἐπικροτέω (substantival). On the function of the participle, see οἱ ἐρχόμενοι in 6:3. This verb occurs five times in the LXX with different senses (see *GELS*, 275). The simple verb κροτέω has the sense "to clap" in the LXX (*GELS*, 415), and that is apparently the meaning of the compound form in this context describing people responding to music (LEH, 230).

πρὸς τὴν φωνὴν. Reference, modifying ἐπικροτοῦντες. The preposition πρός probably has the sense "with regard to, concerning" (*GELS*, 590.III.9; see also BDAG, 875.III.e). The accusative object of πρός (φωνήν) has the sense "sound" (*GELS*, 725.1), and the use of articles with the head noun and genitive modifier follows Apollonius' canon.

τῶν ὀργάνων. Genitive of source (i.e., the sound comes from "the instruments"). The more specific word in Hebrew, "harp" (נבל), corresponding with ὀργάνων, is a generic singular; the same rendering of "harp" (נבל) is found in 5:23.

ὡς. This relative adverb is used here (it occurs 2x in 6:5), prefixed to predicates, to introduce "the perspective from which a person, thing or activity is viewed or understood" (BDAG, 1104–5.3). Muraoka (*GELS*, 748.9.e) explains that the two instances of ὡς in 6:5 with λογίζομαι are situations in which "one can detect a subtle shift from the notion of similarity to that of identity"; they might be rendered "to be." (See the related discussion in Muraoka [§22.ba] and BDF §145 on the use of εἰς and ὡς in predicates.) The clause beginning with ὡς should probably be understood to be causal, giving the reason why the people being described in 6:3–5a live as they do (NETS adds "since . . ."). The asyndeton at the beginning of this clause is consistent with the change from the preceding participle constructions (in 6:3–5a) to a finite verbal clause, which is parenthetical, and a change in topic.

ἑστῶτα. Prf act ptc acc neut pl ἵστημι (substantival) (the alternative form of the perfect, ἑστηκότα, is found in B and V; see Glenny 2013b, 28). The neuter participle functions like a predicate nominative (see Muraoka §31.ba on anarthrous substantival participles). The perfect-tense participle suggests a state of being; the verb in this context has the idea "permanent" or "enduring" (*GELS*, 343.I.1.b). The form of this participle and the one following in the verse could also be accusative, masculine, singular. If that were the case, they would refer to a person who was not standing but was fleeing. If they are neuter plural, they refer to things, apparently the pleasures described by the preceding participles in 6:3–5a, which the referents mistakenly think are permanent (i.e., permanent things). The context supports understanding the participles to be neuter plural, because there is nothing in this context to suggest a person who is established as permanent and not fleeting. See also the discussion below on the word φεύγοντα. The corresponding Hebrew word "David" (דויד) is perhaps read here as the participle עמוד ("standing"); perhaps the *Vorlage* was difficult to read or damaged.

ἐλογίσαντο. Aor mid ind 3rd pl λογίζομαι. Constative aorist summarizing the action as a whole. The aorist tense, which points back to the previous cause of the activities in this verse, interrupts the string of imperfective-aspect verbs and participles in 6:3–6 describing the characteristic activities of the subjects. The middle voice is normal with cognitive verbs; Kemmer (269) calls this the "cognition middle." The return to the third-person plural verb (after 6:1) identifies the referent(s) of the substantival participles in 6:3–5a. To clarify the meaning it is best to supply the implied direct object of this verb: "them."

καὶ οὐχ ὡς. The coordinating conjunction connects antonymous terms, ἑστῶτα and φεύγοντα (*GELS*, 352.1.k). The negative particle with ὡς introduces the opposite perspective in comparison with the first ὡς phrase (see above on ὡς). These words correspond to the Hebrew "instruments" (כלי), which the translator may have read as כלא, something like "as not."

φεύγοντα. Pres act ptc acc neut pl φεύγω (substantival). Functioning like a predicate nominative (see ἑστῶτα above). This verb normally means "to flee some danger, run away from [an] undesirable situation" (*GELS*, 713.a), but Muraoka suggests it can also mean "fleeting (as against 'permanent')," as seems to be required in this context (*GELS*, 713.b). This participle could be understood to be masculine, accusative, singular, referring to a person "running away," or it could be neuter, accusative, plural, referring to pleasures that are "fleeting" (see Dines 1991, 188–96). Perhaps the best example elsewhere in biblical literature of φεύγω with the sense of "fleeting, ephemeral" is Rev 16:20: "And every island fled (φεύγω), and the mountains were not found." It also has this sense in Jer 26[46 MT]:15, and φεύγω has the idea "vanish, disappear" (BDAG, 1052.4) in Ps 67:2; Deut 28:7; and Josh 8:5 (see the discussion in Glenny 2013b, 112–13). The source of this reading is difficult to know; the corresponding Hebrew is שִׁיר ("music, song"), and perhaps this rendering was intended to contrast with ἑστῶτα above (Gelston 2010, 85*).

6:6 οἱ πίνοντες τὸν διυλισμένον οἶνον καὶ τὰ πρῶτα μύρα χριόμενοι καὶ οὐκ ἔπασχον οὐδὲν ἐπὶ τῇ συντριβῇ Ιωσηφ.

οἱ πίνοντες. Pres act ptc nom masc pl πίνω (substantival). On the function of the participle, see οἱ ἐρχόμενοι in 6:3. The text now returns to the participial sequence of 6:3–5a, and the article modifies the two substantival participles following it, which are connected by the coordinating conjunction καί (*GELS*, 352.1.a).

τὸν διυλισμένον οἶνον. Pres pass ptc acc masc sg διϋλίζω (substantival). This adjectival participle, with the article, is in the first attributive position, modifying the following noun, οἶνον, which is the object of πίνοντες. The article and the noun are generic, describing a class. The passive participle communicates what has been done to the wine ("strained"; LSJ, 438), and the present tense has a perfective sense (see Wallace, 532–33, on the perfective present). This "strained" wine is purified and refined, suggesting that "an elite group of people indulged in the best quality of wine, a kind which encouraged more consumption than would unfiltered wine" (Theocharous, 150; see her discussion of wine drinking in the Greek and Roman worlds on pp. 146–50). The Hebrew במזרקי ("in bowls"), corresponding to τὸν διυλισμένον was apparently read as זקק ("filtered"; *HALOT*, 1:279), or the translator had a different source text.

τὰ πρῶτα μύρα. Accusative direct object of χριόμενοι. The article and adjective preceding the noun are in the first attributive position, modifying the noun. The article and the noun it modifies are generic, describing a class. The adjective πρῶτα has the sense "choice, top quality" (*GELS*, 605.d; see Ezek 27:17).

χριόμενοι. Pres mid ptc nom masc pl χρίω (substantival). On the function of the participle, see οἱ ἐρχόμενοι in 6:3. The middle voice is a direct, or reflexive, middle, i.e., they "anoint themselves."

καί. The coordinating conjunction connects the following finite verb clause with the preceding participial construction.

οὐκ ἔπασχον. Impf act ind 3rd pl πάσχω. The imperfect tense describes a pattern of activity ("they were not suffering") in the past and gives background information. The indicative verb clause at the end of 6:6, as the one in 6:5b, serves as a parenthetical summary of the description of the people in 6:3–6 and as a transition to the announcement of judgment in 6:7.

οὐδὲν. Accusative direct object of ἔπασχον. The double negative emphasizes that they did not suffer anything. There is no corresponding Hebrew word; it is an emphasis found in the LXX.

ἐπὶ τῇ συντριβῇ. Causal, modifying ἔπασχον. The preposition ἐπί has the sense "on account of" here indicating the "cause" or "grounds" of the action of the verb (*GELS*, 265.II.6). The article (τῇ) is an individualizing article, pointing to a specific event, and the dative object of the preposition (συντριβῇ) often refers to a state of ruin resulting from disaster or calamity (Prov 14:28; 17:16; Nah 3:19; Lam 2:13; 3:47). Early LXX readers may have understood this noun to refer to the state of the Northern Kingdom after its defeat by Assyria.

Ιωσηφ. The indeclinable proper noun Ιωσηφ functions as an objective genitive and refers to the northern tribes, who were the objects of the destruction; see 5:6, 16; and Zech 10:6. Ephraim in 6:7 is another name for these tribes.

6:7 διὰ τοῦτο νῦν αἰχμάλωτοι ἔσονται ἀπ᾽ ἀρχῆς δυναστῶν, καὶ ἐξαρθήσεται χρεμετισμὸς ἵππων ἐξ Εφραιμ.

διὰ τοῦτο. Inferential. See the discussion of this formulaic PP in 2:13. Here the focus is on the consequences of Israel's action; this is supported by the following adverb (i.e., "therefore now").

νῦν. Adverb of time, modifying the main verb in the clause (ἔσονται). Here the temporal idea is not emphasized; it has more the idea "under the present circumstances, this being the case" (*GELS*, 478.5). LSJ (1185.4) mentions that the adverb can also introduce the opposite of what might have been under different circumstances, and that idea is present in this context also. Muraoka (*GELS*, 478) comments that νῦν is usually placed as close as possible to the beginning of a clause when it is used as a pure adverb.

αἰχμάλωτοι. Predicate adjective (see also Amos 7:11, 17; *GELS*, 18.2), meaning "captives." It is possible, but unlikely, that αἰχμάλωτοι could function as the subject of ἔσονται, especially if the verb is understood to mean something like "to emerge, make appearance" (*GELS*, 193.1.b) or "to come from somewhere" (BDAG, 285.8). However, it is unlikely the verb has either of these meanings here; it is more likely it has the basic sense "to exist, be present" (*GELS*, 193.1). Also, it makes sense, with the third-person plural verb describing the decadence of a group of people in 6:6b, which is the cause of this clause that contains another third-person plural verb, that this clause refers to that same group and describes the punishment of that group (i.e., "they will be captives").

ἔσονται. Fut ind 3rd pl εἰμί. Predictive future. There is no future active form of εἰμί, and often no voice is given when identifying the future middle forms of this verb (Decker, 316). See the preceding entry on possible translations of this verb.

ἀπ' ἀρχῆς δυναστῶν. Partitive. This PP is very difficult, and what it modifies depends on how one understands it. Dines (1991, 196–97) gives four different ways it could be understood, and NETS has another. The most likely options are: (1) ἀπό has partitive force (*GELS*, 70.3.b), ἀρχή refers to "head, first" (see Exod 6:25 where it refers to the "heads" of the families), and δυναστῶν is a partitive genitive, resulting in a rendering something like "from among the first of princes"; (2) ἀπό shows "place of origin, starting place" (*GELS*, 70.2.a), ἀρχή refers to "domain, realm, rule" (*GELS*, 94.2.b; LSJ, 252.II.2), and δυναστῶν is a subjective genitive, resulting in the idea that they will be captives "from the realm over which the princes (the powerful) reign"; (3) the preposition has partitive force (*GELS*, 70.3.b), ἀρχή refers to "rule, sovereignty, office" (LSJ, 252. II.3; see also Herodotus, *Hist*. 3.180; 4.147), and δυναστῶν is a subjective genitive, resulting in the idea that the subjects will be captives "coming (or taken) from the office of the princes (or powerful)," i.e., they will be princes; or (4) NETS takes ἀπ' ἀρχῆς as temporal ("from the beginning") and understands δυναστῶν to be a subjective genitive modifying αἰχμάλωτοι ("captives of the powerful"), resulting in "captives of the powerful from the beginning," which requires δυναστῶν to modify a word four words away as well as a rearrangement of the words. The first and third options seem most likely in the context, and I have opted for the first in my translation, thinking it has the fewest problems. With this rendering ("captives from among the head of princes"), the PP modifies the preceding predicate nominative (αἰχμάλωτοι). See Glenny (2013b, 114). This noun occurs in 6:1 in the plural, where it refers to "rulers" (so *GELS*, 94.2.c); it has two basic meanings: (1) first in time, beginning, and (2) first in power, rule, ruler (LSJ, 252); the latter is required in this context. The basic meaning of the partitive genitive δυναστῶν is "one who is in a position of power" (*GELS*, 179), and thus it can refer to princes, rulers, or the powerful. The first clause in LXX Amos 6:7 seems to be based on a source text very similar to, or the same as, the MT, but the sense of the rendering differs slightly from the MT. The Hebrew בראש ("at the head, beginning") corresponds with ἀπ' ἀρχῆς ("from the beginning"), and the Hebrew גלים ("captives") was apparently read as גדלים ("great, mighty ones") and rendered δυναστῶν.

καὶ ἐξαρθήσεται χρεμετισμὸς ἵππων ἐξ Εφραιμ. This clause continues the announcement of exile, completing what was started in the first clause of the verse. The imagery in this clause is fairly clear (see ἵππων below), but the referents intended are not (see Dines 1991, 197–99; Glenny 2009, 171–73). The sense of the Greek in this clause differs from the sense of the MT, and it is likely that the translator was confused, especially with two main words. The first word that differs is χρεμετισμὸς ("neighing"), which corresponds with the rare Hebrew מרזח ("revelry, cultic celebration," *HALOT*, 1:634; it only occurs elsewhere in the MT in Jer 16:5), which the translator read as צרח ("shout, scream"; *HALOT*, 2:1055) or חזר ("shout, screech"; see the discussion in Glenny 2009, 171). The second word that differs from the *Vorlage* is ἵππων ("horses"), which corresponds with the MT's סרוחים ("one's stretched out"; *HALOT*, 1:769; see 6:4, where this rare word was rendered with κατασπαταλῶντες), and which the translator read as סוסים ("horses"). The Greek words ἐξ Εφραιμ are a LXX plus. Seeligmann (78) suggests there was a lost tradition concerning the destruction of the army of Ephraim behind this verse and Isa 28:2–3. Another verse that could be important for understanding this verse is Zech 9:10. Van der Kooij (62) suggests the royal figure in Zech 9:10, who delivers Israel from its enemies by destroying chariots from Ephraim and horses from Jerusalem, "fits the picture of Maccabean leaders as presented in 1Maccabees. This applies in particular to Simon, because he is depicted as the leader who saved Israel from the enemies in the land, including the occupants of the citadel in Jerusalem" (see 1 Macc 13–14, esp. 14:36). In light of these LXX passages from Isa and Zech, it is likely that LXX Amos 6:7b is referring not to the situation of Israel in 722 BCE but rather to the situation in the time of the Hasmoneans under Simon (ca. 142–134 BCE), and the subjects of the third-person verbs in 6:6b and 6:7a are Seleucids and their Hellenistic sympathizers, who have likely been the referents in 6:1 and in all of 6:3–7 (see above on these verses).

ἐξαρθήσεται. Fut pass ind 3rd pl ἐξαίρω. Predictive future, "will be removed."

χρεμετισμὸς ἵππων. Nominative subject of ἐξαρθήσεται, modified by a subjective genitive. "Horses" signify power and military might, which often leads to self-reliance, rather than trust in God (Deut 17:16; Isa 2:7; Hos 14:4; Mic 5:10; Zech 9:10).

ἐξ Εφραιμ. Dissociation, modifying ἐξαρθήσεται. The preposition ἐκ "indicates dissociation," i.e., "from" (*GELS*, 201.1.a). The indeclinable proper noun Εφραιμ functions as the genitive object of ἐξ and refers to the northern tribes or their territory; see Ιωσηφ in 6:6 and Glenny 2013a, 99, 103. Εφραιμ occurs thirty-nine times in LXX Hosea, mostly as a title for the Northern Kingdom, as it is also elsewhere in Scripture (e.g., Zech 9:10, 13; Isa 7:2, 8, 9, 17). There is nothing corresponding to these words in the MT, and they were apparently added in the LXX to complete the sense of this clause (see above).

6:8 ὅτι ὤμοσεν κύριος καθ' ἑαυτοῦ Διότι βδελύσσομαι ἐγὼ πᾶσαν τὴν ὕβριν Ιακωβ καὶ τὰς χώρας αὐτοῦ μεμίσηκα, καὶ ἐξαρῶ πόλιν σὺν πᾶσι τοῖς κατοικοῦσιν αὐτήν·

This verse contains the oath proper. The contents of the oath are repeated in verse 14.

ὅτι. Causal conjunction, introducing a clause giving the reason or cause of the preceding, esp. 6:7 (*GELS*, 511.1). There is no counterpart to this conjunction in the Hebrew, and in the LXX it clarifies the sense of the connection between the verses.

ὤμοσεν. Aor act ind 3rd sg ὀμνύω. This verb is a "by-form of ὄμνυμι which is predominant in Hellenistic Greek" (BDAG, 705; see BDF §92 on the declension of -μι verbs). Constative aorist, viewing the action as a whole. The verb means "to swear" in the sense "to affirm the veracity of one's statement by invoking a transcendent entity" (BDAG, 705). Here God swears by himself because there is no one greater; see also Gen 22:16; Isa 45:23; Jer 22:5; and Deut 9:27.

κύριος. Nominative subject of ὤμοσεν.

καθ' ἑαυτοῦ. Oath formula, modifying the preceding verb with the genitive reflexive pronoun ἑαυτοῦ as the object of the preposition. The preposition κατά is used here to indicate that, or the one by whom, the Lord is swearing (*GELS*, 364.2). Several words in the MT (נאם יהוה אלהי צבאות) are not included in the LXX after καθ' ἑαυτοῦ, and the LXX may preserve the original reading (LXX.E, 2355).

Διότι. See the discussion of this conjunction at 4:2. There is no counterpart to this conjunction in the Hebrew, and it is possible it was added by the translator to match the parallel construction in 4:2.

βδελύσσομαι. Pres mid ind 1st sg βδελύσσομαι. Gnomic present, a "general, timeless fact" (Wallace, 523). Verbs of emotion are often in the middle voice; Kemmer (269) classifies such verbs as an "emotion middle." This is a strong word with the sense "to detest something because it is utterly offensive or loathsome" (BDAG, 172). This verb and the parallel verb that follows (μισέω) are used to describe the feelings of the leaders of Israel in 5:10, and here they are used to describe the Lord's feelings for them.

ἐγώ. Nominative subject and emphatic use of the personal pronoun.

πᾶσαν τὴν ὕβριν. Accusative direct object of βδελύσσομαι. In the predicate position modifying the following articular singular noun, the adjective πᾶσαν has the sense "the entire, all" (Muraoka §38.b.i); without the article it would refer to "every arrogance of Jacob," which would not make sense. The article is necessary with the abstract noun modified by the adjective πᾶς (Muraoka §38.b.i).

Ιακωβ. Subjective genitive ("all the arrogance Jacob expresses"). The sense of a possessive genitive is very similar to a subjective genitive, but "a subjective genitive takes precedence over possession when a verbal noun is involved" (Wallace, 82 n. 29). In LXX Amos, "Jacob" and "the house of Jacob" seem to refer to the patriarch or his descendants, ethnic Israel, including the northern and southern tribes (see references to "Jacob" in 3:13; 7:2, 5, 16; 8:7; 9:8).

τὰς χώρας αὐτοῦ. Accusative direct object of μεμίσηκα. This noun often refers to administrative districts (*GELS*, 739.1.b), and that is likely the sense it should have here; in 3:9, 10, and 11 it is parallel to γῆ and has this same sense. The pronoun αὐτοῦ is a possessive genitive, and it is normal to have an article with a head noun modified by a possessive pronoun (Wallace, 239). The Hebrew corresponding to χώρας is ארמון (stronghold, citadel), a word the translator did not seem to know (see the discussion of it in 1:4 under θεμέλια).

μεμίσηκα. Prf act ind 1st sg μισέω. The perfect is intensive, emphasizing "the results or present state produced by a past action" (Wallace, 574; BDF §342 calls this a perfect "used to denote a continuing effect").

καὶ ἐξαρῶ πόλιν σὺν πᾶσι τοῖς κατοικοῦσιν αὐτήν. There is a sense in which this clause brings out the result of the Lord's feelings that are described in the preceding two clauses. The future tense here logically follows the present and perfect in the first two clauses, and while the Lord describes his feelings in the first two clauses, in this clause he describes the resulting action. (BDAG, 495.1.b.ζ, explains that καί can "introduce a result from what precedes"; *GELS*, 354.9, notes καί can introduce a "consequence" of the preceding.) Thus, I have rendered the καί "therefore" at the beginning of the last clause in 6:8.

ἐξαρῶ. Fut act ind 1st sg ἐξαίρω. Predictive future, describing what the Lord is going to do. In this context the verb has the sense "remove, get rid of, efface, obliterate" referring to "objects considered undesirable" (*GELS*, 244.4); see the use of it in 6:7.

πόλιν. Accusative direct object of ἐξαρῶ. A πόλις is a "large population centre" (*GELS*, 573.a). This anarthrous noun could be definite (so Dines 1991, 199) or indefinite (NETS), I have taken it to be indefinite, an anarthrous generic, referring to cities as a class and not just one important city (see Muraoka §1.d; and Wallace, 253–54, on anarthrous generics).

σὺν πᾶσιν τοῖς κατοικοῦσιν αὐτήν. Accompaniment, modifying πόλις. The preposition σύν has the sense "along with, including" (*GELS*, 650.2).

πᾶσιν. Dative adjective in the predicate position modifying the following articular participle; it has the sense "all" (Muraoka §38.b.i).

κατοικοῦσιν. Pres act ptc dat masc pl κατοικέω (substantival). The participle construction functions as the object of the preposition σύν. The verb has the sense "dwell, inhabit" (*GELS*, 391.1; see its use in 5:11).

αὐτήν. Accusative direct object of κατοικοῦσιν, referring to πόλιν.

6:9 καὶ ἔσται ἐὰν ὑπολειφθῶσι δέκα ἄνδρες ἐν οἰκίᾳ μιᾷ, καὶ ἀποθανοῦνται, καὶ ὑπολειφθήσονται οἱ κατάλοιποι,

καὶ ἔσται. This construction (see also 5:14; 7:2; 8:9) always with this form of εἰμί, with or without the coordinating conjunction καί, is often used Hebraistically to "introduce an utterance indicating that which may or ought to happen, with a temporal clause or phrase or a conditional clause intervening" (*GELS*, 193.5, s.v. εἰμί; also 354.12, s.v. καί); see the similar construction in Zech 13:3. What follows gives details about the total destruction of a city mentioned in 6:8, and perhaps about those who are left after the deportation into captivity alluded to in 6:6.

ἔσται. Fut ind 3rd sg (εἰμί). Predictive future.

ἐάν. Conditional conjunction, marking a vivid future conditional sentence (Smyth §2323–28). The following account is presented as an open possibility at some indefinite time in the future. The first clause of 6:9 is the protasis of the condition, and the apodosis begins with the second clause (see below).

ὑπολειφθῶσι. Aor pass subj 3rd pl ὑπολείπω. Constative aorist and a subjunctive in a conditional sentence following ἐάν. There is no agent expressed with this passive verb, perhaps to emphasize the subject, the ten men who remain; in this verse and 5:3 the verb refers to "an amount remaining after removing a part" (*GELS*, 703.1.a); it has the sense "leave remaining" (BDAG, 1039; passive has the sense "to be left behind, remain or stay behind," *GE*, 2224.3).

δέκα ἄνδρες. Nominative subject of ὑπολειφθῶσι. The noun is generic, referring to a class, and the adjective δέκα is indeclinable. B, V, and W do not include the noun ἄνδρες; however, ἄνδρες is in the Hebrew and the majority of Greek manuscripts.

ἐν οἰκίᾳ μιᾷ. Locative, modifying ἄνδρες. The dative object of the preposition, οἰκίᾳ ("household"), is indefinite and generic, and the anaphoric article with the same noun in 6:10 will refer back to it, continuing the account of this representative household. Here the οἰκία could be a "structure used as a dwelling" or "a social unit within a dwelling" (BDAG, 695). Muraoka (*GELS*, 488.3) takes it as the latter ("household, family"), and it is best to distinguish it from the οἶκος in 6:10, which is most naturally understood to be an edifice (see below). The social unit described here should be understood to be living in close proximity to others, perhaps even in adjoining structures. It is described as "one" (μιᾷ).

καί. Introduces the apodosis of a conditional construction (*GELS*, 354, 11). It is difficult to know where the apodosis ends, but it likely continues to the end of 6:10; the string of future-tense verbs through verse 10 and the causal connector (διότι) at the beginning of 6:11 support this.

ἀποθανοῦνται. Fut mid ind 3rd pl ἀποθνῄσκω. Future tense in the apodosis of a vivid future conditional sentence (see Smyth §2323–28); the middle voice is regularly used with spontaneous events (Kemmer, 269).

καὶ ὑπολειφθήσονται οἱ κατάλοιποι. These words are not in the Hebrew, and the translator may have added them for emphasis or clarification. The repetition of the verb ὑπολείπω, which only occurs four times in Amos (2x in 5:3 and 2x in 6:9), is noteworthy; the ones "left" in 5:3 may represent the remnant of Israel. Here they apparently represent the family members who remain to bury the dead (see Glenny 2013b, 116). The coordinating conjunction καί connects the parallel clauses in the apodosis of the conditional sentence (*GELS*, 352.1.b); there is a contrast between the preceding clause and this one, so καί is rendered "but" (*GELS*, 353.4).

ὑπολειφθήσονται. Fut pass ind 3rd pl ὑπολείπω. Future tense in the apodosis of a vivid future conditional sentence (see Smyth §2323–28). See the same verb earlier in the verse. There is no agent expressed with this passive verb, perhaps to emphasize the subject, the people remaining.

οἱ κατάλοιποι. Nominative subject of ὑπολειφθήσονται. This is a generic use of the noun, referring to a class of people.

6:10 καὶ λήμψονται οἱ οἰκεῖοι αὐτῶν καὶ παραβιῶνται τοῦ ἐξενέγκαι τὰ ὀστᾶ αὐτῶν ἐκ τοῦ οἴκου· καὶ ἐρεῖ τοῖς προεστηκόσι τῆς οἰκίας Εἰ

ἔτι ὑπάρχει παρὰ σοί; καὶ ἐρεῖ Οὐκέτι· καὶ ἐρεῖ Σίγα, ἕνεκα τοῦ μὴ ὀνομάσαι τὸ ὄνομα κυρίου.

καί. Coordinating conjunction, connecting parallel clauses (*GELS*, 352.1.b). The following sentences continue the apodosis of the conditional sentence, which began in 6:9b.

λήμψονται. Fut mid ind 3rd pl λαμβάνω. Future tense in the apodosis of a vivid future conditional sentence (see Smyth §2323–28); indirect use of the middle voice, used with "verbs of coming into possession" (Kemmer, 268). The direct object "them" has been supplied to complement this verb, as seems required by the following context.

οἱ οἰκεῖοι αὐτῶν. Nominative adjective functioning as the subject of the clause. This adjective (οἰκεῖος) is only used as a substantive in early Christian literature, and it refers to "persons who are related by kinship or circumstances and form a closely knit group" (BDAG, 694), here a "family member" (*GELS*, 487.a), apparently some of the "survivors" of the original remnant mentioned in 6:9 (Glenny 2013b, 116). The article with the substantival adjective is expected, and its presence is normal with a head noun modified by a possessive pronoun (αὐτῶν). In Hebrew the corresponding noun and pronoun are singular.

παραβιῶνται. Fut mid ind 3rd pl παραβιάζομαι. Future tense in the apodosis of a vivid future conditional sentence (see Smyth §2323–28); this word is difficult, and it could be translated a number of ways (see Dines 1991, 200–206; Glenny 2013b, 116–17). The construction here with παραβιάζομαι and the genitive articular infinitive following it is parallel to Jonah 1:13, and the sense in both places is similar, "to endeavor, strive" (*GELS*, 524.1). This rendering, which is adopted here, suggests force and struggle are involved in carrying the bones out of the house; perhaps there was a struggle because the Lord had cursed the house because of idolatry or syncretistic worship in it (see 6:10; and Glenny 2013b, 117). The middle-voice verb in the intransitive construction fits best in Kemmer's category of the intentional middle, a subset of the "perception middle" (269). The translator did not know the Hebrew *hapax* סרף ("anoint," *HALOT*, 1:770), which corresponds with this verb, and read it as סרב ("obstinate," *HALOT*, 1:768) or פצר ("urge, coerce," *HALOT*, 2:954–55).

τοῦ ἐξενέγκαι. Aor act inf ἐκφέρω. Genitive articular infinitive construction, functioning as an accusative complement (Muraoka §30.bef); see also the construction with this verb in 4 Kgdms 5:16. In the LXX the uses of the articular infinitive construction are broader than in the NT, where it is limited primarily to indicating result or purpose (see Muraoka §30.b-d).

τὰ ὀστᾶ. The accusative object of the infinitive has the lexical form ὀστέον (also spelled ὀστοῦν). Here the "bones" probably refer to corpses (*GELS*, 510). It is normal to have an article with a head noun modified by a possessive pronoun.

αὐτῶν. Possessive genitive.

ἐκ τοῦ οἴκου. Source, modifying the infinitive ἐξενέγκαι. The preposition ἐκ indicates "source," communicating the place from which the bones are carried (*GELS*, 201–2.5). The object of the preposition, "house" (οἴκου), may be used here to distinguish the structure from the "household" (family), which is referred to twice in 6:9–10 using οἰκία. The article is not necessary with a definite object of a preposition, but it clarifies the definiteness.

ἐρεῖ. Fut act ind 3rd sg λέγω. This phrase continues the apodosis of the conditional sentence, which began in 6:9b, and this is another future tense in the apodosis of a vivid future conditional sentence (see Smyth §2323–28). This verb is repeated two more times in the remainder of the verse. "It is apparently used of two indefinite speakers, who are conversing in this verse" (Glenny 2013b, 117; see Dines 1991, 207–8, for discussion of the last half of 6:10), and since no speaker is mentioned to function as the subject of the verb, the verb provides the subject. I have tried to render the three occurrences of the verb accordingly: "someone will say," "someone will say," and "he will say," referring to the response of the first speaker. The subject of this verb (3x) in this verse is a "personal, but unspecified subject" (Muraoka §87.cb).

τοῖς προεστηκόσι. Prf act ptc dat masc pl προΐστημι (substantival). This articular, substantival participle serves as the indirect object of the preceding ἐρεῖ. The following statement is the complement, or direct object, of the verb. This word is often used of leaders (those who "stand in front of" in the LXX; *GELS*, 586–871 [see also BDAG, 870.1]), and here it apparently refers to the leaders of the family, who are presumably from among the "survivors" mentioned in 6:9.

τῆς οἰκίας. Objective genitive. The noun refers to the "household" that the "heads" or "rulers" (τοῖς προεστηκόσι) exercise authority over. The article is anaphoric (article of previous reference), referring to the household first mentioned in 6:9 and discussed throughout 6:9–10.

Εἰ. The conditional particle introduces a direct question (see 6:12).

ἔτι. Based on the answer that follows this question (οὐκέτι), this adverb apparently has the temporal sense "still" rather than "more" (*GELS*, 295–96.3 states that the word "denotes an additional amount"), although with either rendering the meaning is ultimately the same in this sentence.

ὑπάρχει. Pres act ind 3rd sg ὑπάρχω. Progressive present tense, indicating a continuous state. Here the verb has the sense "to exist" (*GELS*, 695–96.1, a). There is an implied predicate nominative with the verb, "anyone," or perhaps "another."

παρὰ σοί. Spatial, modifying ὑπάρχει. The preposition παρά "indicates proximity" and could have the sense "at your place" (*GELS*, 523. II, 1). The singular second-person personal pronoun (σοί), which serves as the object of the preposition, indicates that the question is addressed to one individual, the person who responds to this question in the next statement.

καί. Coordinating conjunction, connecting clauses that continue the apodosis of the conditional sentence that began in 6:9b.

ἐρεῖ. Fut act ind 3rd sg λέγω. See the discussion of this verb above in 6:10. The short sentence, of which this is the main verb, is a response to the preceding question. The subject is personal but unspecified (Muraoka §87.cb).

Οὐκέτι. This negative "indicates that a certain condition does *not* repeat itself *any longer*, mostly with reference to the future"; it is used here "in reply to ἔτι" (*GELS*, 513; emphasis in original).

καὶ ἐρεῖ. Fut act ind 3rd sg λέγω. See the discussion of this verb form above in 6:10; this is the third time it is employed in this verse. Here the unspecified person who spoke first in 6:10 (the first use of ἐρεῖ) responds to the answer to his question and speaks for the second time (see Muraoka §87.cb on the unspecified personal subject of this verb). This sentence concludes the lengthy apodosis in 6:9b–10 and the dialogue in 6:10.

Σίγα. Pres act impv 2nd sg σιγάω. Muraoka (§28.ha.iii n. 2) suggests the present imperative here "may mean 'Keep quiet' rather than 'Shut up.'" Wallace (721–22) comments that specific present tense commands, as this seems to be, are usually ingressive-progressive, stressing the inception and the progress of the action, which suggests this command has more the latter sense, "Shut up," or stop talking.

ἕνεκα τοῦ μὴ ὀνομάσαι τὸ ὄνομα κυρίου. Purpose. PP phrase with the genitive articular infinitive as its object (*GELS*, 237.3; Conybeare and Stock §59). This PP modifies the preceding command and explains it. See LSJ (563) for other spellings of this preposition; see also Thackeray (§9.8) and the use of this preposition in the Oracles against the Nations, 1:6, 11; 2:4, 6.

τοῦ μὴ ὀνομάσαι. Aor act inf ὀνομάζω (purpose). Genitive articular infinitive functioning as the object of ἕνεκα (*GELS*, 237.3;). The aorist is constative, summarizing the action as a whole. The reason for the prohibition to not "name the name of the Lord" is debated (see Glenny 2013b,

117–18). It could be because to do so is to curse, resulting in death, as in the blasphemy trial in Lev 24:10–23. However, it seems there is a closer parallel in Jer 51[44 MT]:24–30. In that passage Jewish exiles in Egypt, especially women, have promised to fulfill their vows to the Queen of Heaven, and they are told not to speak the Lord's name anymore (saying, "as the Lord lives"), because the Lord is going to destroy them. The syncretistic worship in the Jeremiah passage is similar to that depicted in Amos 8:14, which the Lord also condemns. Thus, it seems likely that the reason for the prohibition not to "name the name of the Lord" in 6:10 was because the invocations and worship referred to were syncretistic, applying sacred invocations to other gods. The negative μή is normally used with non-indicative verbs.

τὸ ὄνομα. Accusative object of the infinitive ὀνομάσαι. The article should probably be understood to be a simple, identifying article, pointing out a particular name; the monadic modifier κυρίου makes the "name" monadic also.

κυρίου. Possessive genitive. The noun κύριος in the genitive in the LXX is anarthrous almost eight times as often as it is articular (Muraoka §5.b); it is definite here, even though it is anarthrous. (See BDF §254 on the absence of the article with κύριος: "in the LXX literalistic translators like to render anarthrous יהוה with anarthrous κύριος" [as here].)

6:11 διότι ἰδοὺ κύριος ἐντέλλεται καὶ πατάξει τὸν οἶκον τὸν μέγαν θλάσμασιν καὶ τὸν οἶκον τὸν μικρὸν ῥάγμασιν.

διότι. This conjunction is functioning as a causal connector. It could be rendered "because, since, for" (*GELS*, 172.1), and indicates that what follows explains why what was stated in the preceding can be considered valid (BDAG, 251.3).

ἰδού. Aor mid impv 2nd sg εἶδον. See the discussion of this form in 2:13. Here it is functioning as a presentative particle drawing attention to what follows, which is here a verbal clause (*GELS*, 337.a and f; BDAG, 468).

κύριος. Nominative subject of ἐντέλλεται. This appellative, or name, is a monadic noun and definite (see BDF §254 and the discussion of this noun in 6:10).

ἐντέλλεται. Pres mid ind 3rd sg ἐντέλλω. The present tense here describes an action that was begun in the past and continues in the present; thus, it is rendered "as an *English present perfect*" (i.e., "has commanded"; Wallace, 519–20; emphasis original). The middle ("command, order") seems to be an indirect middle in that the will of the commander is expressed in the command (Kemmer, 268; the verb is exclusively middle in biblical literature, BDAG, 339).

καί. Coordinating conjunction, connecting clauses (*GELS*, 352.1.b). The Lord's command (see ἐντέλλεται) "is expressed in the following co-ordinate clause with a verb in a finite tense" (*GELS*, 241.1, s.v. ἐντέλλομαι; see also Muraoka, 699, and the similar construction in 9:3, 4, 9).

πατάξει. Fut act ind 3rd sg πατάσσω. Predictive future, "will strike."

τὸν οἶκον τὸν μέγαν. Accusative direct object of πατάξει. The referent intended by the "house" (2x) in this verse is not transparent. It seems that in 6:10 οἶκος is best understood to refer to a building or edifice, and οἰκία seemed to be employed to refer to a household or family (see 6:9–10). In verse 11 it is likely that the "houses" that receive the "bruises" and "lacerations" are more than edifices, although that would be figuratively possible. Furthermore, οἶκος is employed fourteen times (of its twenty-seven occurrences) in Amos to refer to the "descendants of a prominent ancestor in the sense of a dynasty or kingdom" (Glenny 2013b, 118; see 1:4; 3:1, 13; 5:1, 3, 6, 25; 6:1, 14; 7:9, 10, 16; 9:8, 9), and οἰκία in the LXX never has the sense of descendants of a prominent ancestor, as in a dynasty or kingdom. Thus, it seems likely that the LXX is changing the referent here from a structure or building (as in Hebrew) to dynasties or kingdoms, apparently referring to the judgment on the Northern and Southern Kingdoms. The "great" (μέγας) and "little" (μικρός) language with reference to the "houses" in this verse is seemingly more than a merism; the adjectives apparently are meant to contrast the Northern and Southern Kingdoms. The articles here with the head noun and modifier follow Apollonius' canon.

θλάσμασιν. Dative of means. This noun is a LXX *hapax*, and it likely refers to a bruise (*GELS*, 330). This is figurative language referring to the judgment of the Northern and Southern Kingdoms. This word rhymes with the following parallel dative of means ῥάγμασιν (homoioteleuton), which is also a rare word in the LXX; it is likely the translator was trying to match the rhyme of רסיסים and בקעים in Hebrew with his choice of words in Greek (see Dines 2013, 399). The corresponding Hebrew II רסיס ("fragments, ruins," *HALOT*, 2:1249) is an MT *hapax*; the translator probably did not know it and guessed at its meaning, based on the context.

τὸν οἶκον τὸν μικρὸν. This construction is identical to the preceding parallel direct object of the verb, except that the adjectives are different. The objects are connected by the coordinating conjunction καί (*GELS*, 352.1.a).

ῥάγμασιν. Dative of means. This noun is a LXX *hapax*, and it is likely an alternative Hellenistic spelling for ῥῆγμα (Conybeare and Stock §9b; Dines 1991, 211 n. 40); it is a LXX neologism (LEH, 540). It refers to a "laceration" (*GELS*, 611), a rend or a breakage (LSJ, 1568), or a "crack, fissure" (LEH, 540). This is figurative language describing the judgment of the Northern and Southern Kingdoms. The corresponding Hebrew word בקיע ("breach, rubble," *HALOT*, 1:149) occurs also in Isa 22:9, and it is likely that the translator knew it; see θλάσμασιν above for possible motives for this rendering.

6:12 εἰ διώξονται ἐν πέτραις ἵπποι; εἰ παρασιωπήσονται ἐν θηλείαις; ὅτι ὑμεῖς ἐξεστρέψατε εἰς θυμὸν κρίμα καὶ καρπὸν δικαιοσύνης εἰς πικρίαν,

Verses 12–14 form the last unit in chapter 6. These verses continue the theme of Israel's defeat from 6:8–11. In verse 12a absurdities from the natural realm illustrate the absurdity of Israel's behavior and beliefs, and then 6:12b-13 offers several examples of their actions and thoughts. Verse 14 concludes the unit and explains what the preceding context means for Israel.

εἰ. This conditional particle often introduces direct questions in biblical Greek (Conybeare and Stock §100; BDAG, 278; *GELS*, 190.3; Muraoka §88), and in the first half of 6:12 it is twice employed to introduce direct rhetorical questions (see 3:3–8 and the discussion at 3:3). These questions present absurd situations to emphasize the absurdity of Israel's behavior. The implied answer to both questions is "no."

διώξονται. Fut mid ind 3rd pl διώκω. The intransitive use of διώκω can have the sense "run" or "gallop" (Dines 1991, 211; *GELS*, 173.II, 1, suggests the meaning "to move with speed"). Translational motions, like running, affect the subject and are often middle voice (Kemmer, 269). The future tense here is gnomic, referring to a generic event that could take place at any time.

ἐν πέτραις. Locative, modifying διώξονται. The preposition ἐν is indicating a place ("among") in which the action of the verb takes place (*GELS*, 231.1.b), and the object of the preposition is probably indefinite here, referring to "rocks" as members of the class of objects, without any specific referents in mind; the noun is generic in this proverbial context.

ἵπποι. Nominative subject of the interrogative clause. The noun is generic here without an article (cf. the horses in 6:7).

εἰ. See above in 6:12.

παρασιωπήσονται. Fut mid ind 3rd pl παρασιωπάω. The future tense here is gnomic, referring to a generic event that could take place at any time. The verb has the sense "remain quiet" or "pass over in silence" (LEH, 467; see Hos 10:11, 13; Hab 1:13). The subject of this question must be supplied from the preceding question, and the context suggests it refers to "stallions," not just horses; perhaps ἵππος should have this sense in the first question also.

ἐν θηλείαις. Locative, modifying παρασιωπήσονται. The preposition ἐν has the sense "among" (*GELS*, 231.2, a). The basic sense of the object of the preposition is "female," but here it clearly refers to "mares" (LEH, 275; *GELS*, 329).

ὅτι. The connector is difficult here and could be left untranslated; the translator was following closely the Hebrew, which has כי. BDF (456 §2) notes a special use of ὅτι corresponding to כי and suggests with this usage the Hebrew particle is consecutive and ὅτι could have the sense "for what reason, why." Aejmelaeus (2007, esp. p. 14) helpfully explains the Septuagint use of ὅτι "in connection with *indirect causality*" (emphasis in original) introducing a motivation or explanation, the latter of which is the case in this usage. This use, which has a "loose connection with the preceding context," is found in expressions which should be governed by γάρ. In this context, because the actions of horses described in the two preceding questions are absurd, so are Israel's actions. BDAG (723.4.b) comments that the subordination in such causal relationships is often so loose "that the translation 'for' recommends itself [rather than because]." I have so rendered it, thinking that the explanatory connection between the actions of the horses and the Israelites is clear, and the causal connection is indirect.

ὑμεῖς. Nominative subject of ἐξεστρέψατε. The pronoun is emphatic in the LXX: "you yourselves."

ἐξεστρέψατε. Aor act ind 2nd pl ἐκστρέφω. Constative aorist, summarizing the action. The verb has the sense "to cause to turn aside from what is considered true or morally proper" (BDAG, 309).

εἰς θυμὸν. Spatial, modifying ἐξεστρέψατε. The preposition εἰς "indicates transformation," specifically the "transitive transform of the preceding" (*GELS*, 197.6.b). The anarthrous accusative object (θυμόν) is qualitative, emphasizing the quality of "wrath." The Hebrew has II ראש ("poison"), which occurs thirteen times in the MT and is also rendered with θυμός in Deut 32:33 and Job 20:16; the LXX is close to the MT, and apparently the translator expanded the meaning of the noun in his source text.

κρίμα. Accusative direct object. This anarthrous, abstract noun is qualitative, emphasizing the trait or essence of "justice" or "judgment."

καρπὸν. Accusative direct object. This object is coordinate with the preceding object and connected to it by καί (*GELS*, 352.1.a); although it is anarthrous, it is definite and generic.

δικαιοσύνης. Genitive of apposition, the "fruit" is more specifically "righteousness." This anarthrous, abstract noun is qualitative, emphasizing the quality it describes.

εἰς πικρίαν. Spatial, modifying ἐξεστρέψατε (the verb is understood to control the second direct object, καρπόν). The preposition εἰς "indicates transformation," specifically the "transitive transform of the preceding" (*GELS*, 197.6.b). The anarthrous, abstract object of the preposition, "bitterness" (πικρίαν), is qualitative, emphasizing the quality described by the noun. "Wrath" (θυμόν) and "bitterness" (πικρία) are only found here in LXX Amos; they suggest the deep feelings and emotions of those in Israel who are oppressing the poor and unjust. (For more details on the injustice and unrighteousness of the people of Israel, see 2:6–8; 3:9–10; 4:1; 5:10–15, 21–24.) The Hebrew corresponding to πικρίαν is לענה ("wormwood"), which is always metaphorical in the MT, having the sense "bitterness" (*HALOT*, 1:533).

6:13 οἱ εὐφραινόμενοι ἐπ᾽ οὐδενὶ λόγῳ, οἱ λέγοντες Οὐκ ἐν τῇ ἰσχύι ἡμῶν ἔσχομεν κέρατα;

οἱ εὐφραινόμενοι. Pres act ptc nom masc sg εὐφραίνω (substantival). The participle derives its subject from the second-person plural verb ἐξεστρέψατε in 6:12 and is grammatically in apposition to the subjects of that verb. The mention of another absurdity in 6:13 provides the thematic connection with 6:12.

ἐπ᾽ οὐδενὶ λόγῳ. Causal. This PP modifies εὐφραινόμενοι, and the preposition ἐπί has the sense "on account of," giving the "cause" or "ground" (*GELS*, 265.II.6; see also 1:3). The dative object of the preposition, λόγῳ, with the negative adjective modifying it has the negative sense "nothing, no matter" (BDAG, 600.1.a.ε; *GELS*, 434.6; on οὐδενί see BDAG, 735.1; and Muraoka §35; §39.ac). Whereas in the MT לא דבר is a place-name for a city they have defeated, in LXX οὐδενὶ λόγῳ ("what amounts to nothing") is a cynical reference to the matter under discussion (Park, 167; see *GELS*, 434.4). The city Lo-debar (see Josh 13:26; 2 Kgdms 9:4–5; 17:27) was a border town in Gilead about twelve miles south of the Sea of Galilee and 3 miles east of the Jordan. The MT makes a pun on the name of the city; the LXX translates the name and has no reference to a geographical location.

Οἱ λέγοντες. Pres act ptc nom masc sg λέγω (substantival). The participle functions as the subject of ἔσχομεν. See the discussion of the parallel substantival participle (οἱ εὐφραινόμενοι) at the beginning of the verse. The verb of speaking introduces the direct speech that follows it and functions as the object of the verb.

οὐκ. This negative particle marks the expectation of a positive answer to the following question (Smyth §2651; BDAG, 734.3).

ἐν τῇ ἰσχύι ἡμῶν. Instrumental. The PP modifies ἔσχομεν, and the preposition ἐν has the sense "by means of" and is used in reference to human agency (*GELS*, 231.6.b). It is normal for nouns modified by personal pronouns to be articular; ἡμῶν is a possessive genitive.

ἔσχομεν. Aor act ind 1st pl ἔχω. Constative aorist.

κέρατα. Accusative direct object of ἔσχομεν. Generic and figurative use of the noun, referring to "power, status, or military might" (Glenny 2013b, 119; 1 Sam 2:1). MT has "Karnaim," a city over halfway from Samaria to Damascus, which Jeroboam II had recaptured for Israel from Syria when God enabled him to extend Israel's control far to the north (4 Kgms 14:25–28). "Karnaim" means "might" or "a pair of horns," and the LXX translator interpreted the place-name literally ("horns"); as a result, there is no pun in the LXX. The translator again changed a reference to a place-name (see ἐπ' οὐδενὶ λόγῳ above) and a historical situation that might have been meaningless to his readers and perhaps did not make sense to him either.

6:14 διότι ἰδοὺ ἐγὼ ἐπεγείρω ἐφ' ὑμᾶς, οἶκος τοῦ Ισραηλ, ἔθνος, καὶ ἐκθλίψουσιν ὑμᾶς τοῦ μὴ εἰσελθεῖν εἰς Εμαθ καὶ ἕως τοῦ χειμάρρου τῶν δυσμῶν.

This verse seems to have to be direct speech from the Lord, and it is clearly attributed to the Lord in MT and in B, V, and Swete (see the rendering in *LES* and the discussion below under οἶκος τοῦ Ισραηλ).

διότι. The conjunction is inferential, "therefore" (*GELS*, 172.4; BDAG, 251.2; Smyth §2578). Although NETS seems to take διότι as causal ("for"), it is better to understand the circumstances in 6:14 as inferential, i.e., being inferred or deduced from the preceding, rather than being the cause of the preceding. Here the conjunction introduces the conclusion to the section that explains what the preceding means for Israel.

ἰδού. Aor mid impv 2nd sg εἶδον. See 2:13. Presentative particle drawing attention to what follows, which is here a verbal clause (*GELS*, 337.a and f; BDAG, 468).

ἐγώ. Nominative subject. The personal pronoun is redundant, repeating the noun embedded in the verb and perhaps signifying the switch to a new subject.

ἐπεγείρω. Pres act ind 1st sg ἐπεγείρω. Futuristic present, probably emphasizing the certainty of the event.

ἐφ' ὑμᾶς. Spatial, modifying the compound verb ἐπεγείρω, which repeats the preposition. The preposition indicates the ones to whom the action is directed, here referring to hostile action, i.e., "against" (*GELS*, 266.III.4.a). The accusative object of the preposition refers to the "house of Israel."

οἶκος τοῦ Ισραηλ. See 6:1 and also 5:25. The nominative οἶκος functions like a vocative of address (nominative for a vocative), clarifying for whom the utterance is addressed (Muraoka §22.ya and yb). B, L, and C do not have the article, as in 3:1; 5:1, 25; A, Q, and W include it, as in 6:1; it seems consistent to include it here, corresponding with 6:1, as R-H does. There is nothing corresponding to the MT's נאם יהשה אלהי הצבאות ("says the Lord of hosts") in R-H or in Ziegler at this point (see Glenny 2013b, 30).

ἔθνος. Accusative object of ἐπεγείρω. The translator was following the order in the Hebrew, and the separation of the object from the verb serves to put more emphasis on it.

καὶ. Coordinating conjunction, connecting independent clauses (*GELS*, 352.1.b); here it seems the conjunction is introducing "a consequence which would ensue if what is denoted in the preceding clause is realised" (*GELS*, 354.9). The change to a future-tense verb in the following clause supports this understanding.

ἐκθλίψουσιν. Fut act ind 3rd pl ἐκθλίβω. Predictive future. This verb can have the sense "press, squeeze" (Gen 40:11), "force" (Judg 1:34), or "afflict, oppress," as here and in Judg 2:15; see LEH, 181; *GELS*, 208.

ὑμᾶς. Accusative object of ἐκθλίψουσιν and referring to the "house of Israel." This accusative is in a sense also the subject of the following infinitive, but since it directly follows the finite verb, it is better to understand its main function as the object of the verb and to understand it as the implied subject of the following infinitive (see the discussion in Muraoka §69A.aa, af, ag).

τοῦ μὴ εἰσελθεῖν. Aor act inf εἰσέρχομαι (result). Constative aorist and result (or consequence) infinitive. The infinitive construction with the genitive neuter article (τοῦ) to indicate result or purpose is common in the Septuagint (Conybeare and Stock §60; Muraoka §30. baa); here it is modified by μή, which is the normal negative particle with non-indicative verbs. This rendering differs from the Hebrew, which has "from Lebo-Hamath" (מלבוא חמת), the first part of which the translator rendered as a *mem* and *lamed* with the infinitive construct of בוא (i.e., τοῦ μὴ εἰσελθεῖν εἰς Εμαθ). This rendering changes the sense from the Hebrew, which refers to the extent of the oppression, to the impossibility of entering into the land (see Glenny 2009b, 245–46).

εἰς Εμαθ. Spatial, modifying εἰσελθεῖν and repeating the preposition in that verbal; the preposition has the sense "toward a goal which is inside an area or in the direction of it: with verbs of movement" (*GELS*,

196.1). See 6:2 on the object of the preposition, Εμαθ; this city in central Syria (Hamath) was the idealized northern border of Israel (3 Kgdms 8:65; 1 Chr 13:5), and this verse describes the borders from the perspective of one outside the land.

καί. Coordinating conjunction and Hebraistically pleonastic use of καί (*GELS*, 353.1, i; see also *GELS*, 311.A.d, s.v. ἕως).

ἕως τοῦ χειμάρρου τῶν δυσμῶν. Spatial, modifying εἰσελθεῖν and parallel to the preceding PP, εἰς Εμαθ; the preposition ἕως is used here with a verb of movement (*GELS*, 311.A.b) and "with two extreme points given" (*GELS*, 311.A.d; see also 8:12). The two extreme points are the idealized northern border of Israel at Εμαθ (see above in 6:14 and in 6:2) and the "wadi of the west." The genitive χειμάρρου ("wadi") is the object of the preposition (see also 5:24), and δυσμῶν ("west") is probably a descriptive or general use of the genitive. This latter noun is always plural; in its three occurrences in the Twelve, it refers to the direction "west," as it does here (*GELS*, 180.2; Zech 8:7), or the setting, going down, of the sun (*GELS*, 180.1; Mal 1:11). The Hebrew "wadi [brook] of the Arabah" is only found here in the MT, and it is probably "in the vicinity of the northern end of the Dead Sea, often called the 'Sea of the Arabah'" (Paul, 221); thus, the Hebrew phrase probably refers to the southern border of the Northern Kingdom (see also 2 Kings 14:25; and the discussion in Paul, 220–21). The LXX rendering of the Hebrew ערבה ("desert"; *HALOT*, 1:881.3) as "west" is not unusual, but neither is it the consistent rendering of ערבה. The LXX's "wadi of the west," a phrase that occurs only this once in the LXX, is apparently the western border of Israel by the land of Egypt. The description of the land of Israel in this LXX verse, which approximates the borders before the kingdoms were divided, is from the perspective of someone outside of the land who cannot enter any part of the land from the northern border (Εμαθ) to the southern border (τοῦ χειμάρρου τῶν δυσμῶν), and this description makes the passage especially apt for readers in Egypt, who are not able to return to the land described, and suggests the originally intended readers (or the translator) may have been there (see Glenny 2013b, 120, and 2009, 245–46). The articles in this phrase are consistent with Apollonius' canon.

CHAPTER 7

Chapter 7 is closely connected with what follows in 8:1–9:7. The large section 7:1–9:7 is made up of five visions (7:1–3; 7:4–6; 7:7–9; 8:1–3; and 9:1–4). The first three visions follow each other in succession, and the third and fourth visions are further developed in the verses following each (7:7–9 is developed in 7:10–17, and 8:1–3 is developed in 8:4–14).

The first four visions all begin with the same introductory words: "So the Lord showed me, and behold" (Οὕτως ἔδειξέ μοι κύριος καὶ ἰδού), but in the last vision Amos states that he "saw the Lord standing upon the altar" (ἴδον τὸν κύριον ἐφεστῶτα ἐπὶ τοῦ θυσιαστηρίου) and the Lord spoke to him (9:1). Following the introductory words, the first two visions have a similar structure, describing an object (locusts and judgment by fire, respectively), giving further observations about the described object, relating a brief conversation between Amos and the Lord, and finally presenting the Lord's decision. There are no prophecies of judgment at the end of these visions because the Lord relents. (Nogalski's helpful discussion of the structure of the visions [1:336] influenced my descriptions of them.)

The third and fourth visions are also similar in structure. Following the introductory words, both visions describe an object that Amos saw (someone standing by a wall and a basket of summer fruit, respectively), a brief conversation between the Lord and Amos, and the Lord's decision with his explanation of it. The Lord's decision is given in the form of an oracle of judgment in 7:8b-9 and 8:2b-3.

The narrative of the confrontation involving Amos and Amaziah in 7:10–17 builds off Amos' message in 7:9, and Amaziah's description in 7:11 of what Amos was saying is a paraphrase of 7:9. The narrative in 7:10–13 includes the report of Amaziah to Jeroboam concerning Amos (7:10–11) and Amaziah's message to Amos (7:12–13). In 7:14–17, Amos defends himself and prophesies judgment against Amaziah and his house and against Israel. The development in 8:4–14, after the fourth vision, repeats themes found earlier in the book, including mistreatment of the poor, pride, idolatry, and judgment, providing a summary of the book's theology to this point.

The final vision in 9:1–4 is distinctive. It begins with a simple statement of the fact that Amos sees the Lord (see above), and in the rest of the vision the Lord gives a "monologue" describing the destruction of the Temple and the people. What is most important and unique in this vision is the centrality of the Lord; Amos is merely a passive observer reporting what he saw and what the Lord says (Nogalski, 1:348). Because of its uniqueness, one might question whether the last vision should be included with the others or instead be a separate unit. However, its unique structure contributes to its function, which seems to be to emphasize the Lord's absolute control and his decision to judge the nation.

The doxology near the end of this section (9:5–6) is the third and final doxology in the book (see 4:13; and 5:8–9). Each doxology contains participles describing "the Lord, the God, the Almighty One" (κύριος ὁ θεὸς ὁ παντοκράτωρ), who alone has the power to create, judge, and destroy creation.

Amos 7:1–3

¹So the Lord showed me, and behold early offspring of locusts coming, and behold one locust grub was Gog the king. ²And it will come to pass when he finishes devouring the grass of the land, then I said, "O Lord, O Lord, be merciful! Who will raise up Jacob, for he is very small in number? ³Repent, O Lord, concerning this!" "And so, this shall not be," says the Lord.

There is much discussion about the LXX rendering of this vision, which differs substantially from the Hebrew, most interestingly in its reference to "Gog" (see Bruce, 18–21; Dines 1991, 213–21; Gelston 2002, 497–98; Glenny 2013b, 121–23; Glenny 2007, 539–40; Glenny 2009, 91–93, 139–40, 202–7; and Park, 157).

7:1 Οὕτως ἔδειξέν μοι κύριος καὶ ἰδοὺ ἐπιγονὴ ἀκρίδων ἐρχομένη ἑωθινή, καὶ ἰδοὺ βροῦχος εἷς Γωγ ὁ βασιλεύς.

Οὕτως ἔδειξέν μοι κύριος καὶ ἰδού. This formula introduces each of the first four visions (7:1, 4, 7; 8:1), separating them from each other much like τάδε λέγει κύριος introduces prophetic speech. The prophetic vision is found in 7:1–2a, and the prophet's response in the apodosis of the conditional sentence in 7:2b.

Οὕτως. Adverb ("so, in this way") referring to what follows (i.e., cataphoric) and functioning as the direct object of ἔδειξέν, equal to τάδε (see *GELS*, 515.A.c).

ἔδειξέν. Aor act ind 3rd sg δείκνυμι. Constative aorist summarizing the action, "showed."

μοι. Dative indirect object.

κύριος. Nominative subject of ἔδειξέν. The corresponding name in Hebrew is אדני יהוה, and some Greek manuscripts add another name (Κύριος ὁ θεός in B and V; κύριος κύριος in C; see also the parallel readings in 7:4, 6; and 8:1). It is most likely the shorter reading, which is found in many manuscripts and is the preferred reading in R-H and Ziegler, is best. The translator apparently rendered two Hebrew words with one Greek word.

καὶ ἰδού. This phrase, which occurs nineteen times in the Twelve, is often used to introduce the content of visions (5x in Amos and 10x in Zech [cf. Zech 1:11; 7:5; 11:6; and Mal 4:4]); here the content of the vision is apparently summarized in 7:1, and 7:2 contains specific details of the vision and the prophet's response to them. This phrase is found at the beginning of all of the first four visions in Amos (see also 7:4, 7; and 8:1). The coordinating conjunction καί connects independent clauses (*GELS*, 352.1, b); the verb is implied in the clause following καί (i.e., "there was" or "I saw").

ἰδού. Aor mid impv 2nd sg εἶδον. See 2:13. Here it follows "a verb of seeing or showing in the past tense" (ἔδειξέν) and introduces "a report of the vision or sight" (*GELS*, 337.c).

ἐπιγονή. Predicate nominative (or possible subject) of an implied linking verb. This word is in apposition to οὕτως, explaining what the Lord showed the prophet. This word occurs only three times in the LXX (see also 2 Chr 31:16, 18). It can have the sense of "increase, growth" (LSJ, 628.I.1), but it has more the sense "offspring" or "descendant" in the LXX (LEH, 226; *GELS*, 270); Dines suggests it perhaps has the nuance "plentiful" in this context (Dines 1991, 213, where she renders it "swarm"), but the nuance "plentiful" is linked with the word in all its uses and is a more general than necessary idea in this context. The word often functions as a collective noun, and it need not be limited to one offspring or descendant but apparently refers to many; the further reference in the following clause to "one locust grub" apparently distinguishes that one from the many referred to by the "offspring of locusts" in this clause. It is worth noting that in the time the LXX was translated, the word was used in Egypt to refer to "descendants of foreign military leaders" or mercenaries (LSJ, 628.2; Dines 1991, 213 n. 1), a sense that might have been in the mind of the translator.

ἀκρίδων. Genitive of material; the ἐπιγονή consists of "locusts." The locusts represent an army, as becomes clear in the next clause, describing Gog as their king. Such an understanding is also consistent with the function of the locusts in Joel, a book that may have been influential in the connection of Gog with locusts in this verse (see the discussion below concerning "Gog").

ἐρχομένη. Pres mid ptc nom fem sg ἔρχομαι (attributive). It modifies ἐπιγονή, i.e., "offspring . . . coming"; see Muraoka (§31.ce) on the attributive participle without the article. The middle category is "translational motion" (Kemmer, 269).

ἑωθινή. Nom fem sg adjective ἑωθινός. This adjective has the sense "of very early morning, daybreak" and is normally taken to be modifying the noun ἐπιγονή (*GELS*, 311.a; so NETS "early offspring"), but some understand it to be adverbial, modifying the adjectival participle ἐρχομένη (*GELS*, 311.b; so Dines 1991, 213 "coming at dawn"). When it is adverbial it tends to be in the dative with no noun to modify (1 Macc 5:30) or neuter (*Hist*. 3.104.2; see also *GE*, 888). Thus, the natural understanding of the adjective here is that it modifies the noun ἐπιγονή and has the sense "early, early morning." It occurs eight times in the LXX and elsewhere always has the meaning "early morning, dawn" (see Exod 14:24; Jud 12:5; 1 Macc 5:30; Ps 21:1; Odes 14:0; Sir 50:6; and Jonah 4:7).

καὶ ἰδοὺ. See above in 7:1; here the phrase introduces further details of the vision.

βροῦχος. Nominative subject of the implied equative verb. This noun can refer to locust larva or the locust (LSJ, 331); whether it is to be distinguished from ἀκρίς (see above), which apparently refers to common desert locusts (*EDB*, 818, s.v. locust), is not clear, but the fact that the "offspring of locusts" are characterized as "early" or "early morning" (ἑωθινός) suggests understanding βροῦχος as locust larva (so NETS) or "grub" (Dines 1991, 213). The translator apparently rendered the second occurrence in the verse of לקש ("latter growth, spring growth") as ילק ("locust"; see *HALOT*, 1:413, where the entry says, "a creeping locust but without wings"). The translator's Hebrew *Vorlage*, if it read לקש, would have been very difficult. This word occurs only twice in the MT, and its previous occurrence is earlier in this verse, where the translator apparently skipped it (see Glenny 2009, 92; H-R, 592). Here following גבי ("locusts"), which the translator apparently rendered with ἀκρίς, he apparently read לקש as ילק; thus employing another word for locusts (cf. ἀκρίς earlier in the verse).

εἷς. Attributive adjective modifying βροῦχος. The cardinal number attached to a noun here serves "to refer to a non-particularised entity, [with] the notion of unity or oneness only in the background" (Muraoka §10.db). The translator has apparently read אחר ("latter, after") as אחד ("one").

Γωγ. Predicate nominative in the equative sentence. The translator's rendering of the Hebrew גזי ("mowings" from גזם) with גוג ("Gog") is interesting, because the other three times the word occurs in the Hebrew (Deut 18:4; Job 31:20; Ps 72[71]:6), it is always rendered by the translator as "fleece" (which is a good translation in Deut 18 and Job 31), even though it clearly refers to mown grass in Psalm 72, as it does in Amos 7:1. It is likely that the translator had some problems with this word, but "eschatological expectations associated with Gog were strong at the time when the LXX translation was being made" (Gelston 2002, 498), and it is likely they also influenced the translator's rendering of this word. The most important references to Gog elsewhere in the LXX are in Ezek 38–39 (9x in the MT in various forms) and in Num 24:7, and it seems clear from these passages that in the LXX Gog was understood to be an eschatological character who leads his army against Israel. It is impossible to say whether the LXX translator would have connected this figure with a specific historical character, like Antiochus Epiphanes. (See Glenny 2013b, 121–22, for more detail on the references to Gog in the LXX and other related works from the second century BCE.)

ὁ βασιλεύς. Nominative in apposition to and further defining Γωγ as "the king." This description of "Gog" requires that it be a definite character, and the singular verb that follows in 7:2 (συντελέσῃ) confirms that. The article functions to point out a well-known substantive.

7:2 καὶ ἔσται ἐὰν συντελέσῃ τοῦ καταφαγεῖν τὸν χόρτον τῆς γῆς, καὶ εἶπα Κύριε κύριε, ἵλεως γενοῦ· τίς ἀναστήσει τὸν Ιακωβ; ὅτι ὀλιγοστός ἐστι·

καὶ ἔσται. See 6:9. Following the Hebrew, the Greek is "mechanically beginning with καὶ ἔσται" (*GELS*, 183.III.a, s.v. ἐάν). This phrase often "introduces an utterance indicating that which may or ought to happen, with a temporal clause or phrase or a conditional clause intervening" (*GELS*, 193.5, s.v. εἰμί; 354.12, s.v. καί). The construction in 7:2 does not follow exactly that pattern; the intervening conditional clause is clear in 7:2a, and the apparent apodosis in 7:2b indicates what happens as a result of the details of the vision described in 7:2a. There is a sense in which the καί at the beginning of 7:2 is functioning as a coordinating conjunction, connecting independent clauses (*GELS*, 352.1, b). This verse continues the eschatological tone established in 7:1 and probably is a look at specific details in the vision, after its summary in 7:1. It is the details in 7:2a that bring about the prophet's response in 7:2b.

ἔσται. Fut ind 3rd sg εἰμί. Predictive future.

ἐάν. Conditional particle introducing a third-class condition (open possibility), reflecting typical Hebrew syntax (*GELS*.III.a; see above on καὶ ἔσται). Muraoka (§89.ab) notes that when conditional sentences are introduced by ἐάν "the premise presents what one can or must consider as probable." In this conditional sentence the protasis and apodosis have a cause and effect relationship to each other; if or when the prophet observes that the locust has finished devouring the grass (7:1a), then he will respond with the words in the apodosis in 7:2b (see Wallace, 682–83). The context suggests that the conditional particle has a temporal sense; BDAG (268.2) suggests it approaches the sense of ὅταν here.

συντελέσῃ. Aor act subj 3rd sg συντελέω. Subjunctive with ἐάν. The implied singular subject of the verb is apparently Gog in 7:1. This compound form of the verb may have had an intensive function, but it came to be an ordinary term to "express the concept of completion" (*NIDNTTE* 4:472).

τοῦ καταφαγεῖν. Aor act inf κατεσθίω. Complementary infinitive. In LXX Greek the infinitive preceded by a genitive neuter article can have many functions and need not be limited to purpose/result (see the lengthy discussion in Muraoka §30.baa, d; Muraoka [§30.d] concludes that there is "functional opposition recognizable between a bare infinitive and a τοῦ infinitive"). This is the tenth of twelve occurrences of this compound verb in Amos, where it is always employed to describe the Lord's judgment. Although it always renders אכל it has a more intensive sense than the simple form of ἐσθίω; it is often rendered "devour, consume."

τόν χόρτον. Accusative. Direct object of καταφαγεῖν.

τῆς γῆς. Genitive of place, referring to "the land" of Israel. The article is used here with what could be classified as a well-known noun. But since Israel is considered to be the best land, this is better understood to be the use of the article in a "par excellence" manner; i.e., with a noun that is "in a class by itself" (see Wallace, 222–25; emphasis in original). The article with the head noun and its genitive modifier follows Apollonius' canon.

καί. Here καί introduces the apodosis of the conditional sentence, and it should be rendered "then" (*GELS*, 354.11.a). The NETS translation renders the verse as if there is aposiopesis ("And it will be, if they finish to devour the grass of the land—and I said . . ."). This rendering understands the apodosis of the conditional sentence to be left unspoken in the verse, and the prophet's speech in 7:2b follows the unspoken apodosis. There are similar constructions in 6:9 and in Zech 13:3; NETS renders the latter passage as a complete conditional sentence, and Amos 6:9 also seems to be a complete conditional sentence (see above). See also the discussion in *GELS* (183.III.a, s.v. ἐάν), which seems to support reading the second clause of 7:2 beginning with καί as the apodosis of the conditional sentence in 7:2.

εἶπα. Aor act ind 1st sg λέγω. This should probably be understood as a constative aorist, summarizing the action. At first the aorist tense here seems awkward, and it could be used in various time contexts, which might seem to ease the awkwardness (see Porter 1994, 35–39); but it makes sense to take it as past time. This aorist takes the reader back to the time of the aorist verb in 7:1a at the beginning of the vision, "the Lord showed me," and the action of this aorist ("I said") follows the vision. Furthermore, what the prophet "said" in 7:2b-3 is a consequence of the details he saw concerning Israel's future in 7:2a (see Glenny 2013b,

123). The speech here is direct, reporting the words that were spoken, as all the reported speeches are in this chapter (see the discussion of direct and indirect speech in Muraoka §79).

Κύριε κύριε. The double vocative of direct address renders two divine names in Hebrew: אדני יהוה. See 5:3. These Greek words begin the direct speech of the prophet.

ἵλεως. Predicate adjective. This word is only used to describe an attribute of God in the LXX (BDAG, 474). See the use of this adjective in the similar requests for mercy in 2 Macc 2:7, 22; 4 Macc 6:28; 12:17.

γενοῦ. Aor mid imp 2nd sg γίνομαι. This exact expression (ἵλεως γενοῦ) occurs three other times in the LXX: Exod 32:12; Deut 21:8; and 4 Macc 6:28. See also the discussion in Glenny 2013b, 123. The verb γίνομαι is always middle; the semantics of the middle voice should probably be categorized as a spontaneous event (Kemmer, 269). The aorist imperative here is used to express a specific command, or more precisely a request, in response to the vision. Imperatives often express requests when the speaker addresses a superior (Wallace, 487–88).

τίς ἀναστήσει τὸν Ιακωβ. This question is the second clause in the prophet's direct speech. The question assumes the devastation of the land described in the vision in 7:1–2a will take place and Israel will be ruined.

τίς. Nominative subject of ἀναστήσει. The translator read מי in its normal sense, "who," rather than "how," which must be its sense in the MT (*HALOT*, 1:575.7).

ἀναστήσει. Fut act ind 3rd sg ἀνίστημι. Predictive future in a direct question. The future-tense verb has an ingressive sense (Smyth §1910). Although the transitive use of this verb can have the sense of causing "to become alive again after death," in this context it has the more general sense of restoration or raising something that is fallen (*GELS*, 53–54.I.1.4). The translator read יקום, which is *qal* in the MT ("stand, arise"), as a *hiphil* ("will raise up"). See also 7:5. He has adjusted the verb slightly, because he apparently missed the adverbial sense of מי.

τὸν Ιακωβ. Accusative direct object of ἀναστήσει. Ιακωβ is indeclinable. The article is commonly used with indeclinable proper nouns to remove any ambiguity about their case (Muraoka §5.caa). See 3:13 and 7:16 on "Jacob" in LXX Amos.

ὅτι ὀλιγοστός ἐστι. This is the third clause in the prophet's response to the vision, and the subordinating conjunction ὅτι indicates causality, i.e., "for" (BDAG, 732.4; *GELS*, 511.1).

ὀλιγοστός. Predicate nominative. Superlative form of ὀλίγος (Smyth §319), which is commonly used for the simple adjective in the LXX (*GELS*, 492). The word in its simple and superlative forms refers to being "few in quantity" (simple form) or "very small in number" (superlative form; see *GELS*, 492, s.v. ὀλίγος and s.v. ὀλιγοστός). The superlative form is always used of humans in the LXX (*GELS*, 492), and it often refers to Israel. Many times it is employed to render a simpler concept in the Hebrew like small or insignificant (see Mic 5:2; Obad 2; Isa 14:14; 60:22). In Amos 7:2 and 5 the superlative ὀλιγοστός renders קטן ("small"). Especially important for Amos 7:2 are passages in Maccabees in which Eleazer and his sons, who are small in number, depend on the Lord. Second Maccabees 2:21 states that they were successful in spite of the fact they were "few in number" (ὀλίγος), and in that context (2:22) their success is attributed to the Lord being gracious to them (ἵλεω γενομένου αὐτοῖς), as Amos requests the Lord to be in this verse. Also, in 1 Macc 3:16–17, Judas and his army are twice described as ὀλιγοστός.

ἐστιν. Pres ind 3rd sg εἰμί. Gnomic present-tense use of the equative verb, stating a timeless truth. The subject ("he") is communicated by the verb.

7:3 μετανόησον, κύριε, ἐπὶ τούτῳ. Καὶ τοῦτο οὐκ ἔσται, λέγει κύριος.

This verse continues the direct speech of Amos from verse 2, and then in the second sentence the Lord answers in the form of direct speech.

μετανόησον, κύριε, ἐπὶ τούτῳ. This is the fourth clause in the prophet's response to the vision. In the LXX the prophet's words continue in the first line of 7:3 in the form of an imperatival request to the Lord ("Repent, O Lord"), but in the Hebrew the first line of 7:3 describes what the Lord does ("The Lord relented") and introduces the Lord's words in 7:3b.

μετανόησον. Aor act impv 2nd sg μετανοέω. The aorist imperative refers to a specific command, here a request from an inferior to a superior (see also γενοῦ in 7:2). This should probably be understood as a constative aorist, summarizing the action as a whole without emphasizing any part of it. The translator apparently understood the *niphal* perfect form (נחם) as an imperative, perhaps a *piel*. Muraoka (§29.e) comments that we should not be misled by the label imperative because it "does not necessarily imply rudeness, discourtesy, some form of breach of the social etiquette"; and "in the biblical literature the use of the imperative directly addressed to God in the second person singular is a commonplace."

κύριε, See above in 7:2, where the vocative is repeated for emphasis; here the single κύριε renders the single Hebrew divine name יהוה.

ἐπὶ τούτῳ. Reference/respect. The PP modifies μετανόησον, and the preposition ἐπί has the sense "in the matter of, regarding" (*GELS*, 264.

II.4). The object of the preposition is the neuter demonstrative pronoun τούτῳ. It refers back to the judgment in the preceding vision, which is understood to be under the Lord's control and ultimately from him.

Καὶ τοῦτο οὐκ ἔσται. This direct speech is the complement of the following words, λέγει κύριος. The words καὶ τοῦτο have no equivalent in Hebrew (cf. 7:6). Since καί is part of the Lord's response to Amos, in this context it does not serve as a coordinating conjunction connecting the clauses. It is apparently adverbial ("even" NETS) or introducing a result from what precedes ("and so, and then" BDAG, 495.1.b.ζ). The logic of the conversation seems to require it to communicate the idea of result.

τοῦτο. Nominative subject. The so-called near-demonstrative is used for that which is near spatially or temporally, and it "is used to attract attention to discourse elements that are thematically important in the context" (Runge, 383), as the preceding vision of judgment is here.

οὐκ ἔσται. Fut ind 3rd sg εἰμί. The future tense here is more than a prediction. It is a command or injunction from the Lord (see Muraoka §29.ba.ii-a and the description of this use of the future in §29.gc). See 1:3 on οὐκ.

λέγει κύριος. This introductory clause occurs forty times in Amos, first in 1:3 (where it is aorist). See its use in 1:5.

Amos 7:4–6

⁴So the Lord showed me, and behold he summoned the judgment by fire, and it devoured the great deep and devoured the portion. ⁵And I said, "Lord, Lord, stop, please! Who will raise up Jacob, for he is very small in number? ⁶Repent, O Lord, concerning this!" "And this shall never come to pass," says the Lord.

Over half of the words in this vision repeat the vocabulary and language of the first vision in 7:1–3. However, the description of this vision and the discussion following it is more intense than in the first vision (Glenny 2013b, 124). This is seen by repetition of the verb "devour" (κατεσθίω; see in 7:2), the request that the judgment "stop" (κοπάζω) rather than that the Lord would repent (as in 7:3), the use of the particle δή with the prophet's request in 7:5 (*GELS*, 146.1), and the Lord's response that "this shall never come to pass," using οὐ μή with an aorist subjunctive verb (the first vision has οὐκ ἔσται).

7:4 Οὕτως ἔδειξέν μοι κύριος καὶ ἰδοὺ ἐκάλεσεν τὴν δίκην ἐν πυρὶ κύριος, καὶ κατέφαγεν τὴν ἄβυσσον τὴν πολλὴν καὶ κατέφαγε τὴν μερίδα.

Οὕτως ἔδειξέν μοι κύριος καὶ ἰδοὺ. See the discussion at 7:1.

ἐκάλεσεν. Aor act ind 3rd sg καλέω. Constative aorist, summarizing the action as a whole. Here the verb has the sense "call upon, summon" (*GELS*, 359.3).

τὴν δίκην. Accusative direct object of ἐκάλεσεν. Although *GELS* (171.2) classifies this use of δίκη as having the sense "law-suit," it is much more likely that it refers to "punishment, judgment" (*GELS*, 171.3). It is unclear how "law suit" makes sense of the following modifier ἐν πυρί. In the entry for καλέω (*GELS*, 359.3), Muraoka suggests the word has this latter sense in Amos 7:4, where the suggested rendering for the object of the verb is "the judgment by means of fire." The accusative article τήν is probably a deictic use of the article to refer to the judgment that Amos is seeing in the vision at the time he speaks (Wallace, 221); it could also be classified as the individualizing use of the article, pointing to a specific judgment (Wallace, 216–17).

ἐν πυρί. Instrumental. The PP modifies the noun δίκη, and the preposition ἐν has the sense "by means of, by using as instrument" (*GELS*, 231.6.a).

κύριος. Nominative subject of ἐκάλεσεν.

καί. This is the second of three occurrences of the coordinating conjunction in this verse, connecting independent clauses (*GELS*, 352.1.b).

κατέφαγεν. Aor act ind 3rd sg κατεσθίω. Consummative aorist, emphasizing the end point of the action (Fanning, 263–64). See the discussion of this verb in 7:2.

τὴν ἄβυσσον. Accusative direct object of κατέφαγεν. The "deep" refers to "the vast reservoirs of subterranean waters that are the source of the springs and rivers of the earth" (Glenny 2013b, 124). See its use elsewhere referring to the sources of the flood in Gen 7:11 and 8:2, the source of the rivers in Ezek 31:4, and the source of the Nile in Herodotus, *Hist.* 2.228. This is the use of the article with the "par excellence" substantive, which is in a "class by itself" (Wallace, 222–23); since the word "abyss" (ἄβυσσος) is sometimes used in the plural in the Hebrew Bible, it cannot be a monadic or one-of-a-kind noun.

τὴν πολλήν. Accusative adjective modifying ἄβυσσος. It describes the "abyss" as being "great in size" (*GELS*, 574.b). The article denotes the adjective in the second attributive position.

κατέφαγεν. See above in this verse.

τὴν μερίδα. Accusative direct object of κατέφαγεν. In view of the prophet's request in 7:5–6, this "portion is" Israel. This is the individualizing use of the article, pointing out a specific "portion." Although B and V have the possessive genitive κυρίου after μερίδα, identifying the portion as belonging to the Lord, it is not in A, Q, and W, and R-H and Ziegler do not include it in their texts. It is difficult to make sense of it in this context.

7:5 καὶ εἶπα Κύριε κύριε, κόπασον δή· τίς ἀναστήσει τὸν Ιακωβ; ὅτι ὀλιγοστός ἐστιν·

καὶ εἶπα Κύριε κύριε. See the discussion of these words in the first vision in 7:2. In B, V, and Swete κύριε is not repeated; in A, Q, W, R-H, and Ziegler it is; see 5:3 on this repetition. The words of Amos in this verse and continuing into the first part of 7:6 are direct speech.

κόπασον. Aor act impv 2nd sg κοπάζω. The aorist imperative is used here to express a specific command ("stop"), or more precisely a request, in response to the vision. Imperatives often express requests when the speaker addresses a superior (Wallace, 487–88).

δή. The particle here adds a sense of urgency to the request (*GELS*, 146.1); it is sometimes rendered "indeed" (BDAG, 222.1), and here with a request it is rendered "please," because of the power imbalance between the two individuals.

τίς ἀναστήσει τὸν Ιακωβ; ὅτι ὀλιγοστός ἐστιν. See the discussion in 7:2.

7:6 μετανόησον, κύριε, ἐπὶ τούτῳ. Καὶ τοῦτο οὐ μὴ γένηται, λέγει κύριος.

This verse is the same as 7:3, except the words οὐ μὴ γένηται, which differ from οὐκ ἔσται in 7:3. See the discussion of 7:3.

γένηται. Aor mid subj 3rd sg γίνομαι. The aorist subjunctive with οὐ μή usually expresses emphatic negation, thus adding to the intensity of the language in this vision (Smyth §2754–55; Muraoka §83.c,ca). Muraoka (§29.ba.ii-a) suggests the force of the subjunctive here is the same as, or similar to, the future in the parallel clause at the end of the first vision in 7:3. The primary difference between the two phrases is the "reduced force of negation" with the future and single negative in 7:3, and thus the increased force of the negation here, which adds to the increased intensity of the conversation in the second vision. The verb γίνομαι is always middle; see the discussion of it in 7:2 (γενοῦ).

Amos 7:7-9

⁷So the Lord showed me, and behold a man standing on a wall of hard metal, and hard metal [was] in his hand. ⁸And the Lord said to me, "What do you see, Amos?" And I said, "Hard metal." And the Lord said to me, "Behold, I am placing hard metal in the midst of my people, Israel; never again will I pass by him. ⁹And the altars of derision will be destroyed, and the mystic rites of Israel will be made desolate, and I will rise up against the house of Jeroboam with a sword."

This vision begins with the same six Greek words as the two preceding visions and the one that follows in 8:1-3, but this vision is especially parallel to the fourth vision (8:1-3). In both the Lord asks Amos what he sees and then explains the meaning of the vision. Unlike the first two visions in 7:1-3 and 7:4-6, the messages of the third and fourth visions (7:7-9 and 8:1-3) are developed in the verses following each of them (7:7-9 is developed in 7:10-17, and 8:1-3 is developed in 8:4-14).

7:7 Οὕτως ἔδειξέν μοι κύριος καὶ ἰδοὺ ἀνὴρ ἑστηκὼς ἐπὶ τείχους ἀδαμαντίνου, καὶ ἐν τῇ χειρὶ αὐτοῦ ἀδάμας.

Οὕτως ἔδειξέν μοι κύριος καὶ ἰδοὺ. See the discussion of these words above in 7:1. The translator made "the Lord" (κύριος) the subject of the verb "showed" (ἔδειξέν) rather than "standing" (ἑστηκὼς) as in the MT.

ἀνήρ. Nominative subject of the participle phrase that is in apposition to οὕτως and explains what the Lord showed the prophet (see the discussion of οὕτως in 7:1). R-H and W have ἀνήρ ἑστηκὼς (cf. Zech 1:8; 2:1[5MT]); A has κύριος ἑστηκὼς (corresponding to the MT); B and Q, followed by Ziegler, have only ἑστηκὼς, which is perhaps a desire to avoid an anthropomorphism but has a sense similar to ἀνήρ ἑστηκὼς.

ἑστηκὼς. Perf act ptc nom masc sg ἵστημι (attributive). Following R-H, the participle modifies ἀνήρ. The perfect is focusing on the present or resulting state of the action of the verb; the man is "standing."

ἐπὶ τείχους ἀδαμαντίνου. Locative. The PP modifies the preceding attributive participle, and it indicates where the ἀνήρ is standing. The preposition ἐπί with the genitive object could have the sense "on, upon" (*GELS*, 263.2) or "close by, near" (*GELS*, 263.3). Both are grammatically possible, but the first meaning ("on, upon") is more likely as it is the sense of ἐπί with a genitive every other time this construction occurs in Amos (1:11; 3:5; 5:2, 8; 6:4; 8:9; 9:6, 15, and probably 9:1 [ἐπὶ τοῦ θυσιαστηρίου]; see also Dines 1991, 222). Furthermore, BDF (§234, 1) comments that ἐπί with the genitive most frequently has the sense "'on, upon' in response to the question 'where.'"

τείχους. Genitive object of ἐπί. Although anarthrous objects of prepositions may be definite, in this context this anarthrous object is indefinite. *GELS* (673) proposes this word has the sense "protective wall" in the LXX, and that seems to be the case in the Twelve, where it occurs ten times (5x in Amos; see also 1:7, 10, 12, 14), unless it has a different sense here. In Zech 2:5 it is used metaphorically for the Lord, who will be a "wall of fire" around Jerusalem. The wall described in Amos 7:7 (and Zech 2:5) is impenetrable and formidable (see the description of its contents in the following entry; it is composed of ἀδαμάντινος). It could be a barrier, indicating the Lord's separation from his people or perhaps a barrier that the Lord will not pass. It could also represent Israel's strength or protection that the Lord (in his judgment of them) has allowed them to establish and that gives them false security, so they do not trust in him (see further Glenny 2013b, 126–28). The statements in 7:8 that the Lord is placing the "hard metal" (adamant) in the midst of his people and he will not pass by them again suggests that the τεῖχος in 7:7 is not a "protective wall," as it normally is in the LXX, and that it signifies the fact that the Lord's judgment will not pass by Israel again (see 7:8). The repetition of the words for "hard metal" (in 7:7–8) and the focus on it in the vision also suggest the wall is not a "protective wall" in 7:7, but rather a barrier of some sort, symbolizing judgment of the nation.

ἀδαμαντίνου. Genitive of content. This adjective designates what the wall is made of or consists of. This adjective only occurs twice in the LXX, here and in 4 Macc 16:13, where it refers (metaphorically) to the resolution of the mind of the mother of the martyrs (she has a "mind of adamant," NETS). The related noun ἀδάμας ("very hard metal"; *GELS*, 9) occurs three times in the LXX, all in Amos 7:7–8. LSJ (20) comments that the literal use of the substantive refers to "the hardest metal" and to a "diamond." The noun and adjective are used literally in Amos 7:7–8, where the adjective refers to a wall and the person referred to is holding "adamant, hard metal" (noun form) in his hand. In Amos 7 both words render אֲנָךְ (only these four times in the MT), which is often translated "plumbline" (KJV, ASV, NRSV, ESV), but more likely refers to a metal, such as "tin" (see the discussion in Paul, 233–35; Dines 1991, 223–25; Stuart, 372–73) or perhaps "lead" (*HALOT*, 1:71–72). Although these metals are not known for their hardness, the Greek terms used to translate this Hebrew word in Amos 7 have a connotation of incredible hardness and strength. On the meaning and use of these words, see further Glenny 2013b, 125; and Dines 1991, 225–26.

καί. Coordinating conjunction, connecting clauses and phrases (*GELS*, 352.1.a). Here the final clause in the verse, which is preceded by καί, could be considered an addition that is not technically coordinate with the preceding (see BDAG, 495–96.2).

ἐν τῇ χειρὶ αὐτοῦ. Locative. PP modifying the implied equative verb "was" and giving the location of the ἀδάμας. The preposition ἐν "indicates a place in which some object is found" (*GELS*, 231.1.a).

τῇ χειρὶ. Dative object of ἐν. The article is normally used with a head noun modified by a possessive pronoun. With the object of the preposition the article is not necessary for the object to be definite, but it clarifies that it is.

αὐτοῦ. Possessive genitive.

ἀδάμας. Nominative subject of a noun clause. It is positioned emphatically at the end of the clause. This "hard metal" is the focus of the vision. See the two occurrences of this noun in 7:8 and the discussion of the related adjective (ἀδαμαντίνου) above in this verse.

7:8 καὶ εἶπεν κύριος πρός με Τί σὺ ὁρᾷς, Αμως; καὶ εἶπα Ἀδάμαντα. καὶ εἶπεν κύριος πρός με Ἰδοὺ ἐγὼ ἐντάσσω ἀδάμαντα ἐν μέσῳ λαοῦ μου Ισραηλ, οὐκέτι μὴ προσθῶ τοῦ παρελθεῖν αὐτόν·

καί. Coordinating conjunction, connecting independent clauses (*GELS*, 352.1.b).

εἶπεν. Aor act ind 3rd sg λέγω. Probably a constative aorist, viewing the action as a whole or summary.

κύριος. Nominative subject of εἶπεν. This anarthrous, monadic noun is definite.

πρός με. Directional. This PP modifies the preceding verb, εἶπεν. The preposition πρός is often used with "verbs of speaking, addressing, etc." (*GELS*, 589.III.2), as here; it has the sense "to, toward."

Τί σὺ ὁρᾷς, Αμως;. This question is the complement of the preceding verb. The same question is found in the fourth vision (8:1). The words are reported directly (see Muraoka §79).

Τί. Accusative direct object of ὁρᾷς.

σύ. Nominative subject.

ὁρᾷς. Pres act ind 2nd sg ὁράω. The present tense is progressive in the sense that it is not instantaneous but seems to describe action over a short period of time.

Αμως. Vocative of address of this indeclinable noun.

εἶπα. Aor act ind 1st sg λέγω. Probably a constative aorist, viewing the action as a whole or summary.

Ἀδάμαντα. Accusative direct object of εἶπα. This material, which constituted the wall, is what Amos saw, rather than the wall itself. This noun occurs three times in the LXX (see 7:7).

καὶ εἶπεν κύριος πρός με. See the discussion of this same clause above at the beginning of this verse (also found in 7:15 and 8:2). Here, unlike its other three occurrences in LXX Amos, the PP πρός με is a LXX plus, perhaps added by the translator to be consistent with the preceding occurrence of the clause.

Ἰδοὺ. See the discussion of this presentative particle in 2:13. In this context it does not introduce so much the report of a vision, as in 7:1, but it introduces more the following explanation of a vision.

ἐγὼ. Nominative subject of ἐντάσσω. Emphatic pronoun.

ἐντάσσω. Pres act ind 1st sg ἐντάσσω. Progressive present, describing action over a (short?) period of time. The meaning of this verb is important for the vision, but it is also debated. In non-biblical Greek the verb has various senses: (1) to "register, insert" in a document or record; (2) to "insert" in military ranks; and (3) to "assign" a position in battle (see LSJ, 574 and Dines 1991, 229–30). The word occurs in 2 Esd 7:17; Job 15:22 (A); 4 Macc 2:8 (A); and four times in Daniel Th (5:24, 25; 6:11; 10:21). Muraoka (*GELS*, 240) lists two possible senses of the word in the LXX: (1) "to place" (in a certain location), which he suggests is the sense in Amos 7:8; and (2) "to put down in writing," which he suggests is the sense in Dan Th 5:24 and 6:10. When the verb refers to writing in the LXX, the content of the writing usually follows the verb in the accusative case, and the document or record in which the writing is done is given in the dative modified by a preposition (2 Esd 7:17 and possibly Job 15:22 [A]). Amos 7:8 does not fit either of those normal patterns *GELS* gives for ἐντάσσω referring to writing; clearly the accusative "hard metal" is not the content of the writing. It makes most sense to understand the context of Amos 7:8 to mean that the Lord is placing hard metal in the midst of his people ("I am placing"). This is also the understanding of NETS and *GELS*.

ἀδάμαντα. Accusative direct object of ἐντάσσω. See 7:7.

ἐν μέσῳ λαοῦ μου Ισραηλ. Locative. This PP modifies ἐντάσσω, and it supports the understanding of ἐντάσσω as "insert, place," for which I argued above. The preposition ἐν "indicates a place in which some object is found or placed" (*GELS*, 231.1.a), and it does not make sense to inscribe or write hard metal in the midst of Israel; the metal must be placed there (*pace* Dines 1991, 229–33, who concludes the "hard metal" is something on which or with which the Lord is writing). The dative adjective μέσῳ is functioning as a substantive, and as the object of the preposition ἐν, it has the sense "in the midst of" (*GELS*, 451.II.F.a).

λαοῦ μου Ισραηλ. This use of the genitive λαοῦ does not fit into the standard categories, because μέσος requires a genitive substantive or pronoun after it (Wallace, 135). *GELS* (450.II) explains that when the genitive following μέσος is singular, "what is inside of the expanse [e.g., in this verse what is 'in the midst of my people'] is perceived as a single whole." This anarthrous noun (λαός) must be definite, referring to a specific "people," with the proper noun Ισραηλ in apposition to it, clarifying who the people are, and with the genitive possessive personal pronoun μου modifying it.

οὐκέτι μὴ προσθῶ τοῦ παρελθεῖν αὐτόν. This clause recurs in the fourth vision in 8:2, where it clearly refers to the Lord's determination to judge his people, Israel. The asyndeton at the beginning of this clause is consistent with the change in topic from the hard metal barrier to the fact that the Lord will not pass by them again (see Runge, 21, 23).

οὐκέτι μὴ. Emphatic negation. The double negative construction with the aorist subjunctive is the most emphatic negation in Greek, and it underscores the intensity and certainty of the coming judgment (Smyth §2754–55; Muraoka §83.c,ca). The first particle, οὐκέτι, "indicates that a certain condition does not prevail or repeat itself any longer, mostly with reference to the future" (*GELS*, 513); μή is the normal negative particle with non-indicative verbals. Every time the negatives οὐκέτι μή are employed in tandem in Amos, they are followed by the verb προστίθημι and an aorist articular infinitive (5:2; 7:8, 13; 8:2), and the phrase οὐκέτι μὴ προσθῶ has the sense "no longer, no more."

προσθῶ. Aor act subj 1st sg προστίθημι. The verb προστίθημι plus an infinitive (usually with τοῦ) communicates something that the subject does still or does again as formerly. See *GELS* (599.2.a), which says this construction is most likely a Hebraism (on which, see also BDF §435; and BDAG, 885.1.c).

τοῦ παρελθεῖν. Aor act inf παρέρχομαι. Complementary infinitive. The articular infinitive τοῦ παρελθεῖν completes the complementary construction and functions as the main verb (see Muraoka §30.bg; see also Conybeare and Stock §60.d, where this usage is called the "prolative infinitive" after "extensible" verbs); Thackeray (§4) explains that προστίθημι is used in place of an adverb (here πάλιν). The aorist is a constative aorist, looking at the action as a whole or summarizing it. Dines (1991, 233–35) explains that not to "pass by" could have a positive (promise) or negative (threat) connotation. Παρέρχομαι has a good sense when it is used to describe one stopping (not passing by), as a guest or friend (Gen 18:3; Exod 23:5; Isa 33:22) or when it describes one passing by in judgment (Dan 11:10, 26); however, not passing by has a bad connotation when it means safety if one passes by (Exod 12:23b;

Isa 28:15–9). The context of judgment in this vision makes it most natural to understand "never again will I pass by him" in 7:8 negatively, referring to judgment. The identical clause in 8:2 must mean the Lord will no longer pass by Israel with his judgment; rather he will visit them with it. And the parallel in 8:2 is strong support for understanding the clause the same way in 7:8. The fact that Amos does not intercede for mercy concerning the third and fourth visions, as he did with the first two, also supports this understanding of the verb παρέρχομαι; the preceding emphatic negation means the judgment is certain. The middle voice of this verb is what Kemmer (269) calls the middle of "translational motion."

αὐτόν. Accusative object of παρελθεῖν. This masculine pronoun could refer to the "hard metal" (ἀδάμας) or to Israel. (The wall [τεῖχος] is neuter, so it does not refer to it.) The context of judgment and the fact that the pronoun clearly refers to Israel in the identical clause in the fourth vision in 8:2 support it referring to Israel here also.

7:9 καὶ ἀφανισθήσονται βωμοὶ τοῦ γέλωτος, καὶ αἱ τελεταὶ τοῦ Ισραηλ ἐξερημωθήσονται, καὶ ἀναστήσομαι ἐπὶ τὸν οἶκον Ιεροβοαμ ἐν ῥομφαίᾳ.

Verse 9 continues the direct speech of the Lord that began in verse 8; it contains specific details of the judgment that is mentioned more generally in the previous verses. "Israel's worship sites, worship, and reigning dynasty are going to be eradicated" (Glenny 2013b, 128). The prophecies in this verse also connect the vision with the following narrative in 7:10–17.

καὶ. Coordinating conjunction, connecting independent clauses (*GELS*, 352.1, b).

ἀφανισθήσονται. Fut pass ind 3rd pl ἀφανίζω. Predictive future and a simple passive without the agency expressed. The Lord is the understood ultimate agent. This verb, which occurs sixteen times in the Twelve, is often used to describe the destruction or annihilation caused by the Lord's judgment. *GELS* (105) says the passive has the sense "to suffer lack," as when something is empty.

βωμοὶ. Nominative subject of ἀφανισθήσονται. This noun, which can refer to a "raised platform" or "base," is used mostly to refer to "an altar with a base" (LSJ, 334; *GELS*, 124). In the LXX, with only a few exceptions (Num 3:10; 2 Macc 2:19; 13:8; Sir 50:12, 14; see the discussion in Glenny 2013b, 128), this word is used for pagan altars, and it is often connected to idolatry (e.g., Hos 10:8; Jer 7:31; Isa 15:2; Dines 1991, 238). First Maccabees 1:59 is a good illustration of the difference in the

LXX between βωμός and θυσιαστήριον, the word generally used for a legitimate altar. In this context the Syrians are sacrificing on an illegitimate altar that is on top of the altar of burnt offering (θυσιάζοντες ἐπὶ τὸν βωμόν, ὃς ἦν ἐπὶ τοῦ θυσιαστηρίου). Dines (1991, 238) comments that βωμός in Amos 7:9 indicates that the northern altars, which are being described, are pagan and idolatrous (see Glenny 2013b, 128).

τοῦ γέλωτος. This genitive could be classified as a descriptive genitive, giving a general description of the altars, but it is probably better to understand it as a qualitative genitive, describing the character or quality borne by the altars (Muraoka §22.xvi). The point is, the altars are a joke! LEH (117) suggests the rendering "the high places of laughter" or "the ridiculous high places"; see further Glenny 2013b, 128. Abstract nouns frequently have an article (BDF §257–58; Muraoka §5.i), but the article is seldom translated. When the article is present with an abstract noun, it often serves to focus on the quality. The corresponding Hebrew ישׂחק occurs only four times in the MT (elsewhere in Jer 33:26; Amos 7:16, and Ps 105:9); it is normally יצחק (108x in Pentateuch, Joshua, Kings, and Chronicles). The translator rendered it as "Jacob" in 7:16; here he has translated it as "laughter" (שׂחוק or שׂחק), perhaps deliberately playing on the word's etymology. If so, it appears the translator took "exegetical play one step farther" (Dines 1991, 238) and gave a sarcastic rendering to the word (so Daniel, 41 n. 23). This is entirely possible since γέλως not only means "laughter" but can also have the sense of "derision" (Wis 5:4; Mic 1:10) or "laughingstock" (Jer 20:7; 31:26; 31:39; Lam 3:14), and the "mocking at idols" motif is common in Scripture (Ps 134[135]:15–18; Isa 44; Wis 13:10–13).

αἱ τελεταί. Nominative subject of ἐρημωθήσονται. This word, which is always in the plural in the LXX (6x), refers to "pagan mystic rites" (*GELS*, 674), and in Wisdom it is connected with infanticide (Wis 14:23), idolatry (Wis 14:15), and sorcery (Wis 12:4). In non-biblical Greek the plural is used most often for "rites of initiation into the Mysteries or festivals accompanied by mystic rites" (Glenny 2013b, 128; see LSJ, 1711; Dines 1991, 239). The article with τελεταί indicates that the noun points to distinct "mystic rites." The only other time τελετή is employed in the LXX to translate Hebrew (3 Kgdms 15:12), it renders "male temple prostitutes" (קדשׁים), and it is possible that the translator understood his Hebrew text to read this in Amos 7:9.

τοῦ Ισραηλ. Possessive genitive (indeclinable noun). The article is consistent with Apollonius' canon.

ἐξερημωθήσονται. Fut pass ind 3rd pl ἐξερημόω. Predictive future ("will be made desolate"), and a simple passive without the agency expressed. The Lord is the understood ultimate agent.

ἀναστήσομαι. Fut mid ind 1st sg ἀνίστημι. Predictive future. The future middle form of ἀνίστημι is intransitive and means to "rise" or "stand" (*GELS*.54.II.1); this is sometimes called a direct middle, where the subject is acting on him- or herself (Wallace, 416).

ἐπὶ τὸν οἶκον Ιεροβοαμ. Direction or spatial. The PP modifies ἀναστήσομαι. The preposition ἐπί "indicates one to whom or that to which action, attention, thought, emotion, utterance, etc. are directed," and here it refers to "hostile action" (*GELS*, 266.III.4.a; *GE*.II.C.B) and is translated "against." The accusative object of the preposition is τὸν οἶκον, and the οἶκος here refers to a dynasty (see also 1:4). The object of a preposition is normally definite, with or without an article. Here the οἶκος is specified as "Jeroboam's" by the possessive genitive (Ιεροβοαμ.).

ἐν ῥομφαίᾳ. Instrumental. This is a second PP modifying ἀναστήσομαι. The preposition ἐν has the sense "equipped with" (*GELS*, 232.7; see Hag 2:22).

Amos 7:10–17

¹⁰And Amaziah the priest of Bethel sent a message to Jeroboam king of Israel saying, "Amos is engaged in plots against you in the midst of the house of Israel; the land will never be able to bear all his words. ¹¹For this is what Amos says, 'Jeroboam will perish by the sword, and Israel will be led away captive from its land.'" ¹²And Amaziah said to Amos, "O seer, go, depart into the land of Judah and live your life there, and you shall prophesy there. ¹³But you shall not prophecy in Bethel again, for it is the king's sanctuary, and it is the royal house." ¹⁴And Amos answered and said to Amaziah, "I was not a prophet nor a son of a prophet; I was nothing other than a goatherd and a scratcher of sycamore tree fruit. ¹⁵And the Lord took me up from among the sheep, and the Lord said to me, 'Go prophesy against my people, Israel.' ¹⁶And now hear the word of the Lord. You say, 'Stop prophesying against Israel, and never play the demagogue against the house of Jacob.' ¹⁷Therefore, thus says the Lord, 'Your wife will be a prostitute in the city, and your sons and daughters will fall by the sword, and your land will be measured out with a measuring-line, and you will meet your end in an unclean land, and Israel will be led away captive from its land.'"

The narrative of the confrontation involving Amos and Amaziah in 7:10–17 is connected to the third vision (7:7–9) by references to Jeroboam at the end of the vision and the beginning of the narrative (7:9 and 10), and by Amaziah's paraphrase in 7:11 of what Amos said in 7:9. This paragraph is divided into two main parts: the words of

Amaziah and the words of Amos. The first four verses (7:10–13) contain a brief account of Amaziah's report to Jeroboam concerning Amos (7:10–11) and his message to Amos (7:12–13). In 7:14–17 Amos attests his call and prophesies judgment against Amaziah and Israel.

7:10 Καὶ ἐξαπέστειλεν Αμασιας ὁ ἱερεὺς Βαιθηλ πρὸς Ιεροβοαμ βασιλέα Ισραηλ λέγων Συστροφὰς ποιεῖται κατὰ σοῦ Αμως ἐν μέσῳ οἴκου Ισραηλ· οὐ μὴ δύνηται ἡ γῆ ὑπενεγκεῖν ἅπαντας τοὺς λόγους αὐτοῦ·

Καὶ. Coordinating conjunction; it is not unusual for καί to be used at the beginning of a section or book (*GELS*, 353.1.h; see Amos 1:2).

ἐξαπέστειλεν. Aor act ind 3rd sg ἐξαποστέλλω. Constative aorist, describing a summary of the action ("sent").

Αμασιας. Nominative subject.

ὁ ἱερεὺς Βαιθηλ. Nominative in apposition to Αμασιας, further identifying him. The article is pointing out a specific object, here an individual, which in this case is "well-known" (or a "celebrity" type figure; Wallace, 225); the article is probably not "par excellence," because the point is not that Amaziah is the best or worst priest (Wallace, 222).

Βαιθηλ. Genitive of origin, indicating that the priest is "out of" or "sourced in" Βαιθηλ (Muraoka §22.v.iv).

πρὸς Ιεροβοαμ. Direction. PP modifying ἐξαπέστειλεν. The preposition πρός has the sense "in the direction of, towards" here with a verb of "physical movement" (*GELS*, 589.III.1). The indeclinable proper noun Ιεροβοαμ is the accusative object of πρός.

βασιλέα. Accusative in apposition to Ιεροβοαμ, further identifying him as "king."

Ισραηλ. Objective genitive, indicating the realm over which Ιεροβοαμ rules.

λέγων. Pres act ptc nom masc sg λέγω (circumstantial). Commonly in the LXX λέγων is used as "a signal marking onset of direct speech," and in such cases, as here, it "is equivalent to the double quotation marks in modern languages" (Muraoka §31.daa).

Συστροφὰς. Accusative direct object of ποιεῖται. This noun refers to an assembly or gathering, and it was used for a "tumultuous gathering" and for the "product of a clandestine gathering," a "plot," or "conspiracy" (BDAG, 979.1 and 2 [BDAG favors the second meaning, "plot, conspiracy" here]; see also *GELS*, 542; and LEH, 599). The word's position at the beginning of this speech emphasizes it.

ποιεῖται. Pres mid ind 3rd sg ποιέω. In this context the present-tense verb suggests ongoing or repeated activity. Here the middle is probably meant to present Amos as acting in his own interests, which is sometimes called the indirect use of the middle (Smyth §1719–22). Smyth (§1722) calls a combination of ποιεῖται with a verbal noun like Συστροφάς periphrasis; Muraoka (§57.b) remarks that the middle voice of ποιέω with a verbal noun in the accusative, as here, "is effectively a compound verb, a kind of syntactic hendiadys." The combination of ποιεῖται and Συστροφάς corresponds to the verb קשר ("conspire against"; *HALOT*, 2:1153.2) in the Hebrew. NETS renders the two Greek words "is conducting seditious meetings," and *LES* has "is creating conspiracies"; "is engaged in plots" works well with the following PP and allows for a wider application of the action.

κατὰ σοῦ. Disadvantage. PP modifying ποιεῖται. The preposition κατά with the genitive object σοῦ has the sense "displaying hostile attitude to and to the disadvantage of" (*GELS*, 364.I.1); I have rendered it "against."

Αμως. Nominative subject of ποιεῖται. The position of the subject near the end of the clause builds suspense and emphasizes it.

ἐν μέσῳ οἴκου Ισραηλ. Location. PP modifying ποιεῖται. The preposition ἐν has the sense "among" (*GELS*, 231.2) here with the substantive neuter of μέσος as its object (see BDF §215.3; BDAG, 635.2.b, s.v. μέσος). This use of the genitive οἴκου does not fit into the standard categories, because μέσος is one of the substantives (here the adjective functions as a substantive) that require a genitive substantive or pronoun after them (Wallace, 135). *GELS* (450.II) explains that when the genitive following μέσος is singular "what is inside of the expanse [e.g., in this verse what is 'in the midst of the house of Israel'] is perceived as a single whole." Here the indeclinable proper noun Ισραηλ functions as a genitive of apposition, i.e., the house is Israel. See the discussion of the meaning of the phrase οἴκου Ισραηλ in 3:1; 5:1; and 5:25. This PP, "in the midst of the house of Israel," refers to the royal sanctuary at Bethel (see 7:13; Glenny 2013b, 130).

οὐ μὴ δύνηται. Pres mid subj 3rd sg δύναμαι. The verb has a predictive or future sense, and it is always middle or passive voice because it describes a state or condition affecting the subject. The double negative with a subjunctive verb denotes emphatic negation. It is most commonly used with an aorist subjunctive, but it also occurs with the present subjunctive; here the construction is used in a negative prediction (Smyth §1804, 2754–55).

ἡ γῆ. Nominative subject. The γῆ refers to the kingdom. It is close to the idea of country (LSJ, 347.II; and *GELS*, 129.4.d, which mentions land "belonging to or inhabited by a particular ethnic group or nation"), but here it must refer to the kingdom, with special reference to Jeroboam's rule over it (cf. 7:12). The article points out the "land" as well known (Wallace, 225; Smyth §1120.a).

ὑπενεγκεῖν. Aor act inf ὑποφέρω. Complementary infinitive, completing the verb οὐ μὴ δύνηται. The verb has the sense "to endure, put up with" (*GELS*, 706.1)

ἅπαντας. Accusative adjective, modifying the following noun. This form (ἅπας) is the intensive of πᾶς (BDAG, 98). The substantive to which it belongs "retains the (generic) article" (BDF §275). See the discussion of ἅπας and πᾶς in Muraoka §38a–b.iβ; the construction here with ἅπας followed by the article and the plural noun has the sense "all the words" (§38.b.i).

τοὺς λόγους. Accusative object of ὑπενεγκεῖν. See the preceding entry on the use of the article with ἅπας.

αὐτοῦ. Possessive genitive.

7:11 διότι τάδε λέγει Αμως Ἐν ῥομφαίᾳ τελευτήσει Ιεροβοαμ, ὁ δὲ Ισραηλ αἰχμάλωτος ἀχθήσεται ἀπὸ τῆς γῆς αὐτοῦ.

διότι. See 3:7; here it introduces a clause which gives the reason or cause of the preceding statement: "for."

τάδε. Accusative of the demonstrative pronoun ὅδε, formed by adding the enclitic -δε to the article (old demonstrative pronoun) and declined like the article (see LSJ, 1197). Here it functions as direct object of λέγει.

λέγει. Pres act ind 3rd sg λέγω. Customary use of the present tense, referring to Amos' regular or repeated action and here introducing his speech, as reported to Jeroboam by Amaziah. These words of Amos are in the form of direct speech that is contained within Amaziah's words directly reported to Jeroboam.

Αμως. Nominative subject of λέγει.

Ἐν ῥομφαίᾳ. Instrumental. PP modifying τελευτήσει; the preposition ἐν has the sense "by means of" (*GELS*, 231.6).

τελευτήσει. Fut act ind 3rd sg τελευτάω. Predictive future, "will perish."

Ιεροβοαμ. Indeclinable proper noun, functioning as the nominative subject of τελευτήσει.

ὁ δὲ Ισραηλ αἰχμάλωτος ἀχθήσεται ἀπὸ τῆς γῆς αὐτοῦ. This exact phrase is repeated at the end of 7:17 (they are the same in Hebrew also). Prophecy of Israel's captivity is found elsewhere in LXX Amos 4:2–3; 5:5, 26–27; 6:7 and 9:4.

ὁ. Nominative. The only two occurrences of ὁ δέ in Amos are here and in the identical clause at the end of 7:17. The use of articles with place-names and other proper nouns in the LXX is not consistent (see Muraoka §5.c–h), and the use and nonuse of the article with the indeclinable noun Ισραηλ follows that pattern in Amos. The use of the article here and in 7:17 with Ισραηλ may be anaphoric, emphasizing that the Israel referred to in this clause is the Israel that has been the subject of the preceding section and is to be the recipient of the judgments described, especially in 7:8–9. It also clarifies that the indeclinable noun Ισραηλ functions as the subject of ἀχθήσεται.

δὲ. This conjunction is found only five times in Amos, and three of its occurrences are in this section (7:11, 13, 17; see also 2:9 and 4:7). Dines (1991, 240 n. 47) suggests δέ has adversative force here, and she renders it "while," which brings out some adversative force; NETS renders it "and." It is often employed in a paratactic, coordinate construction in the LXX. See Conybeare and Stock (§39–40) and Muraoka (§81) on the preponderance of paratactic constructions in Septuagint Greek. Here the sentences joined by δέ seem to be coordinate descriptions of judgment, but there is also a "new development" (Runge, 31–36) in the argument, and δέ "mark[s] a new stage in a series of events following one after another" (*GELS*, 140.1). The development marked by δέ here and elsewhere in this section (7:13, 17) is climactic and emphatic.

Ισραηλ. Indeclinable noun functioning as a nominative subject.

αἰχμάλωτος ἀχθήσεται. This construction represents an infinitive absolute construction in Hebrew, combining the infinitive absolute with an imperfect verb from the same root (גלה) for emphasis. (In 5:5 the LXX renders the same Hebrew construction with a different and more emphatic Greek construction, a participle followed by a finite verb.) The Greek construction with both words beginning with the same letter communicates the assonance of the original, but it uses words that are otherwise unrelated and does not have the intensifying force of the Hebrew containing the repetition of the verb root (see Glenny 2009, 54, 58). The nominative adjective αἰχμάλωτος functions as a substantive (*GELS*, 18.2) and is grammatically in apposition to Ισραηλ.

ἀχθήσεται. Fut pass ind 3rd sg ἄγω. Predictive future. Passive voice with no agency expressed.

ἀπὸ τῆς γῆς αὐτοῦ. Separation. PP modifying ἀχθήσεται. The preposition ἀπό has the sense "away from," signifying "removal" or "dissociation" (*GELS*, 69.1). Here the genitive object of ἀπό (γῆς) refers to the land of Israel, not the kingdom, as in 7:10 (see *GELS*, 129.4.d). The article is common with a head noun modified by a possessive genitive (αὐτοῦ), but here it is likely anaphoric, referring back to the "land" mentioned in the previous verse and preceding context (Smyth §1120, b).

7:12 καὶ εἶπεν Αμασιας πρὸς Αμως Ὁ ὁρῶν, βάδιζε ἐκχώρησον εἰς γῆν Ιουδα καὶ ἐκεῖ καταβίου καὶ ἐκεῖ προφητεύσεις·

καί. Coordinating conjunction used to introduce Amaziah's words to Amos (see *GELS*, 353.1.h on the use of καί at the "start of an utterance" and the parallel usage in 7:14).

εἶπεν. Aor act ind 3rd sg λέγω. Constative aorist, summarizing the action or describing it as a whole. The following words of Amaziah to Amos are reported directly (see Muraoka §79 on direct and indirect speech).

Αμασιας. Nominative subject.

πρὸς Αμως. Direction. PP modifying εἶπεν. The preposition πρός is commonly used with "verbs of speaking, addressing" to indicate the one spoken to (*GELS*, 589.2). The indeclinable proper noun Αμως is the accusative object of πρός.

Ὁ ὁρῶν. Pres act part nom masc sg ὁράω (substantival). This participle construction functions as a vocative (see BDF §147; and Muraoka §22.yb, who calls this "nominative substituting vocative"), introducing the direct discourse that follows. The nominative article functions as a substantiver. The present tense here refers to something that takes place customarily, regularly, or repeatedly. NETS renders the participle phrase "You that see."

βάδιζε. Pres act impv 2nd sg βαδίζω. In commands the present tense is used idiomatically with verbs of motion to emphasize the continuing or extended nature of the action (Fanning, 341, 365; see the discussion in Glenny 2013b, 131). Ironically this command is the same verb used to communicate the Lord's instructions to Amos (in 7:15), but that command told Amos to "go" to prophecy to Israel.

ἐκχώρησον. Aor act impv 2nd sg ἐκχωρέω. Aorist commands usually emphasize the specific action commanded (BDF §335), and this command is more specific (i.e., "depart" from the land) than the preceding present tense command ("go"). Here the aorist likely refers to the action as a whole. Some manuscripts have a nominative pronoun (σύ) either before (*L*) or after (B and C) this verb, making the subject more emphatic, and Ziegler, following the Hebrew, has an ethical dative (σοι) in his text, which is awkward. (Muraoka [§22.wh] defines an ethical dative as "indicating a personal and mental involvement in a situation or event on the part of the referent of the dative.") The reading without a pronoun in A and Q, and followed by R-H, is the simplest and could well be original.

εἰς γῆν Ιουδα. Direction. This PP modifies the two preceding commands, especially the immediately preceding verb (ἐκχώρησον). The preposition εἰς has the sense "towards a goal which is inside an area" (*GELS*, 196.1). Here γῆν, the accusative object of εἰς, refers to the land of Judah (see also 7:11), not to a kingdom as in 7:10 (*GELS*, 129.4.d). Nouns serving as the objects of prepositions do not need articles to be definite, as is the case here. Ιουδα is a genitive of apposition, "the land which is Judah." See BDAG, 479, and Thackeray §11.6.1, on the declension of this masculine noun.

καὶ. Coordinating conjunction, connecting independent clauses (*GELS*, 352.1.b). The following two short clauses, which are both introduced by καὶ ἐκεῖ, give more details about what Amaziah wants Amos to do when he goes back to Judah.

ἐκεῖ. Adverb with the sense "in that place already mentioned" (*GELS*, 207.1).

καταβίου. Pres act impv 2nd sg καταβιόω. With the prepositional prefix this verb has the sense of living out one's life until death (LSJ, 885.2). The present imperative is probably used here with its progressive sense emphasizing the process of living out one's life (see Fanning, 365).

καὶ ἐκεῖ. See the use of these words in the previous clause.

προφητεύσεις. Fut act ind 2nd pl προφητεύω. Imperatival future following the three preceding imperatives.

7:13 εἰς δὲ Βαιθηλ οὐκέτι μὴ προσθῇς τοῦ προφητεῦσαι, ὅτι ἁγίασμα βασιλέως ἐστὶν καὶ οἶκος βασιλείας ἐστίν.

εἰς δὲ Βαιθηλ. Direction. PP modifying the following infinitive (προφητεῦσαι); the preposition εἰς has the sense "towards an area which is inside an area" (*GELS*, 196.1). The conjunction δέ is included in the PP, because it is always postpositive. The position of the PP at the beginning of the sentence makes it emphatic; there is one place Amos is not to prophecy: Bethel. Βαιθηλ is the accusative object of εἰς.

δέ. See the discussion of δέ above in 7:11. Dines (1991, 241) and NETS both understand it to be adversative (contrastive) here (*GELS*, 140.5.b).

οὐκέτι μὴ προσθῇς. Aor act subj 2nd sg προστίθημι. Constative aorist, viewing the action of the verb as a whole. See the parallel first-person construction (οὐκέτι μὴ προσθῶ) in 7:8 and 8:2, which ironically refers to the Lord's determination to judge his people, Israel ("never again will I pass by"), and the discussion of this construction in 7:8. Here the construction expresses a prohibition, and the negative particle μή with the subjunctive is the most common way to express a prohibition with a second-person verb in the LXX and NT (Muraoka §29.e; Wallace, 469; cf. Smyth §1840–41). The verb προστίθημι is used with an infinitive (usually with τοῦ) with the sense "still to do something as formerly, do something again" (*GELS*, 599.2.a; BDAG, 885); here with the double negative it expresses emphatic prohibition: "do not do something again." Thus, Amaziah does not want Amos to ever prophesy in Bethel again. B, *L*, and C have the fut act ind 2nd pl form of προστίθημι here, but R-H and Ziegler have not followed that reading; the translator used the su junctive in the parallel constructions elsewhere in 7:8 and 8:2. The plain imperative is more polite and less solemn than the imperatival future (Muraoka §28.gc; Wallace, 569), and that difference of sense would be expected to carry over also to the subjunctive prohibition.

τοῦ προφητεῦσαι. Aor act inf προφητεύω. Constative aorist presenting the action of the verb as a whole. The infinitive is complementary, completing προστίθημι. See Muraoka (§30.bg) on the genitive article with a complementary infinitive.

ὅτι. This conjunction is introducing a causal clause ("for"), giving the reason for the preceding command (*GELS*, 511.1.a).

ἁγίασμα. Predicate nominative. This monadic noun ("sanctuary [of the king]") is definite, and it follows Colwell's rule that "definite predicate nouns which precede the verb usually lack the article" (Wallace, 256–70). The corresponding Hebrew term is מקדש, which was rendered with τελεταὶ in 7:9.

βασιλέως. Genitive of possession; it is "the king's."

ἐστὶν. Pres ind 3rd sg εἰμί. Stative verb, and the present tense is a progressive or continuous present. The subject is contained in the verb (i.e., "it is").

καὶ. Coordinating conjunction, connecting independent, coordinate clauses (*GELS*, 352.1.b).

οἶκος βασιλείας. The noun οἶκος is another predicate nominative. For its function, see the parallel noun ἁγίασμα above. Βασιλείας is an attributive genitive, identifying a quality of the head noun, i.e., it is "royal," and this is a "royal house." This house is not the palace or residence of the king, since he does not live there according to 7:10; it is the sanctuary Jeroboam established (3 Kgdms 12:26–33) that has official status (Glenny 2013b, 131).

ἐστίν. See the preceding clause.

7:14 καὶ ἀπεκρίθη Αμως καὶ εἶπεν πρὸς Αμασιαν Οὐκ ἤμην προφήτης ἐγὼ οὐδὲ υἱὸς προφήτου, ἀλλ' ἢ αἰπόλος ἤμην καὶ κνίζων συκάμινα·

καὶ. See the parallel use of καί at the beginning of 7:12.

ἀπεκρίθη. Aor pass ind 3rd sg ἀποκρίνομαι. Constative aorist, summarizing the action. See the discussion of -θη- verbs in the introduction.

This is probably a middle/passive form, which explains why it does not have the force of a passive verb.

Αμως. Nominative subject of ἀπεκρίθη.

εἶπεν. Aor act ind 3rd sg λέγω. Constative aorist, summarizing the action. Amos' words are reported in direct speech.

πρὸς Αμασιαν. Direction. PP modifying εἶπεν. The preposition πρός has the sense "in the direction of, towards," used here with a verb of "speaking, addressing" (*GELS*, 589.III.2) and an object, which is the content of the speech that follows.

Οὐκ. Negative particle (οὐ) with an indicative verb; this is the form "before a vowel with a smooth accent" (*GELS*, 511.a).

ἤμην. Impf act ind 1st sg εἰμί. The customary imperfect is used to describe a past state. The reference to the past time here casts the description of Amos that follows as what he "used to be" in contrast with what he is now, according to 7:15 (see Glenny 2013b, 131; and Dines 1991, 241)

προφήτης. Predicate nominative. This anarthrous noun is indefinite. The clause Οὐκ ἤμην προφήτης with the customary imperfect verb indicates that before the Lord's call (see 7:15) Amos was not connected with the prophetic guild.

ἐγώ. Nominative subject of ἤμην.

οὐδὲ. Negative particle (οὐ and δέ) with an indicative verb. The particle "marks negation immediately following another negation," here related to "a segment of a phrase," a second predicate nominative (*GELS*, 512, esp. h).

υἱὸς. Predicate nominative. This anarthrous noun is qualitative, stressing the traits of this class of people. Here the word refers to a "person characterized by a certain property" (*GELS*, 694.3), that of a prophet.

προφήτου. Genitive of relationship. Indefinite, anarthrous noun (see προφήτης above in this verse).

ἀλλ' ἤ. Elided form of the adversative particle ἀλλά (BDAG, 44–45; see BDF §17 on the elision) with the disjunctive particle ἤ; following a negative this combination introduces a contrast and has the sense "on the contrary, but, yet, rather" (see BDAG, 44–5.1.a; *GELS*, 26.2.b). It is possible that in this context these words are meant to have a demeaning sense ("nothing other than"; see Dines 1991, 241; BDF §448.8) and emphasize Amos' humble origins (Glenny 2013b, 132).

αἰπόλος. Predicate nominative. This anarthrous noun is qualitative, stressing the characteristic or trait of the class. This word is a LXX *hapax*; in the Targum Amos is not a "goatherd" but rather a wealthy farmer.

ἤμην. Impf mid ind 1st sg εἰμί. The customary imperfect is used to describe a past state. The subject ("I") is communicated in the verbal form.

κνίζων συκάμινα. Both these words are *hapax legomena* in the LXX. The construction could be literally rendered "one scratching sycamore fruit" (see the discussion in Glenny 2013b, 132).

κνίζων. Pres act ptc nom masc sg κνίζω (substantival). It is common for substantival participles to be anarthrous in the LXX (Muraoka §31.b). This anarthrous participle is qualitative, stressing the characteristic or trait of the class.

συκάμινα. Accusative direct object of κνίζων. It could refer to the fruit of the sycamore tree or the mulberry tree (LSJ, 1670).

7:15 καὶ ἀνέλαβέν με κύριος ἐκ τῶν προβάτων, καὶ εἶπεν κύριος πρός με Βάδιζε προφήτευσον ἐπὶ τὸν λαόν μου Ισραηλ.

ἀνέλαβέν. Aor act ind 3rd sg ἀναλαμβάνω. Constative aorist, presenting the action as a summary or whole.

με. Accusative direct object of ἀνέλαβέν.

κύριος. Nominative subject of ἀνέλαβέν. Muraoka (§5.b) comments, "In the overwhelming majority (83%) of its occurrences, κύριος as a rendering of the tetragrammaton in H[ebrew], is anarthrous," and "the articular κύριος is rather infrequent in the nominative case." He suggests that the use of a common substantive (κύριος) to render the tetragrammaton may not have triggered the factors that led to the use of the article with other divine names.

ἐκ τῶν προβάτων. Separation. This PP modifies ἀνέλαβέν. The preposition ἐκ "indicates dissociation," here with a verb of removing (*GELS*, 1.a). The genitives τῶν προβάτων comprise the object of ἐκ. The noun προβάτων is generic, referring to the class of things designated by πρόβατον rather than any other specific class of things. The point is that Amos was a shepherd, not that he was called from a specific group of sheep. Objects of prepositions are normally definite, as here, although they do not require an article to be so. The article distinguishes the class designated by the generic noun πρόβατον from other classes of things. Interestingly, B, followed by no other uncial or any modern version, has προφητῶν instead of προβάτων.

εἶπεν. Aor act ind 3rd sg λέγω. Constative aorist, presenting the action as a summary or whole. The direct speech of the Lord to Amos which follows in this verse is reported within the direct speech of Amos to Amaziah.

κύριος. See above in this verse.

πρός με. Direction. PP modifying εἶπεν. The preposition πρός has the sense "in the direction of, towards" with the verb of speaking (*GELS*, 589.III.2.b).

Βάδιζε. Pres act impv 2nd sg βαδίζω. The present tense is used idiomatically with verbs of motion to emphasize the continuing or extended nature of the action (Fanning, 341; see the discussion in Glenny 2013b, 131). Ironically, this command is the same verb used to communicate Amaziah's instructions to Amos (in 7:12), and it contrasts with that command; that command told Amos to "go" and depart from Israel to Judah.

προφήτευσον. Aor act impv 2nd sg προφητεύω. Aorist commands usually emphasize a specific action (BDF §335); here the aorist likely communicates the action "prophesy" as a whole.

ἐπὶ τὸν λαόν μου Ισραηλ. Direction. PP modifying προφήτευσον. The preposition ἐπί indicates the ones to whom the utterance is directed, and it has a sense of hostile speech, i.e., "against" (GELS, 266.4.d); see the parallel sense of ἐπί with προφητεύω in 7:16. The accusative λαόν, the object of ἐπί, is modified by the possessive genitive μου; objects of prepositions are normally definite, as here, although they do not require an article to be so.

Ισραηλ. Accusative, indeclinable noun in simple apposition with λαόν.

7:16 καὶ νῦν ἄκουε λόγον κυρίου Σὺ λέγεις Μὴ προφήτευε ἐπὶ τὸν Ισραηλ καὶ οὐ μὴ ὀχλαγωγήσῃς ἐπὶ τὸν οἶκον Ιακωβ·

The words of verses 16–17 are a continuation of Amos' direct speech to Amaziah, first repeating the words of Amaziah and then declaring the words of the Lord to Amaziah.

καὶ νῦν. The combination of these two words at the beginning of a clause "marks a new phase or turn in discourse" (GELS, 478.3, s.v. νῦν); at this point the discourse moves from Amos' defensive self-justification speech concerning his calling (7:14–15) to an offensive oracle of judgment addressed to Amaziah and Israel (7:16–17).

ἄκουε. Pres act impv 2nd sg ἀκούω. The present imperative tends to be "durative or iterative" and to be used with a "general precept (also to an individual) concerning attitudes and conduct" (BDF §335–36). Muraoka (§28.dfe) remarks that the choice of forms of the imperative in the Twelve and some other LXX books seems to be morphologically conditioned, and the translator apparently avoided the present-tense 2nd pl imperative of ἀκούω because it was easily confused with the present indicative form.

λόγον κυρίου. Accusative direct object of ἄκουε. It is definite because the genitive modifying it specifies it. On the use of genitive or accusative objects with ἀκούω, see 3:1 on ἀκούσατε. The subjective genitive (κυρίου, "of the Lord") refers to the one doing the action (speaking) implied by the head noun (a verbal noun); the monadic noun κυρίου is also definite.

Σύ. Nominative subject of λέγεις.

λέγεις. Pres act ind 2nd sg λέγω. This could be an historical present, describing a past event, but it is better to understand it as a customary present, describing what Amaziah was regularly saying. The following present prohibition (Μὴ προφήτευε) lends support to this interpretation. The following are the words of Amaziah, reported directly by Amos within his speech to Amaziah.

Μὴ προφήτευε. Pres act impv 2nd sg προφητεύω. Present prohibition with negative particle; here the context requires the sense to not continue an activity in progress (BDF §336.3).

ἐπὶ τὸν Ἰσραηλ. Direction. PP modifying μὴ προφήτευε. On the use of ἐπί, see 7:15 and below in this verse. The indeclinable noun Ἰσραηλ is the accusative object of ἐπί, and the article is often employed with indeclinable proper nouns "in the interest of less ambiguous communication" (Muraoka §5.caa); objects of prepositions are also normally definite, and thus they often have an article.

οὐ μὴ ὀχλαγωγήσῃς. Aor act subj 2nd sg ὀχλαγωγέω. See the discussion of οὐ μή with a subjunctive verb in 2:12. Here this construction is used for "stringent prohibition" (Muraoka §29.ba.ii–a). The meaning of this *hapax* is difficult, but the uses of it and its cognates in other literature are "patently uncomplimentary" (Dines 1991, 244; see Polybius 24, 7, 2; Strabo 14, 2, 5; Galen 14, 305; Vettius Valens 78, 18; Josephus, *Ag. Ap.* 2, 1). On the basis of Amaziah's words in 7:10, it seems he is "charging Amos with trying to stir up the people to win them over and threaten the king" (see Glenny 2013b, 133). *GELS* (516) suggests the rendering "to play the demagogue." The corresponding Hebrew word is נטף, which means "drip, secrete" in the *qal* stem (Joel 4:18) and "cause to drip, flow" and metaphorically "to make words flow, to drivel foam at the mouth" (Amos 7:16; 9:13; Mic 2:6 [3x], 11 [2x]) in the *hiphil* stem (*HALOT*, 1:694). Dines (1991, 244 n. 58) suggests that the LXX translation in 7:16 "may have been chosen to fit the context."

ἐπὶ τὸν οἶκον Ἰακωβ. Direction. PP modifying ὀχλαγωγήσῃς. See the similar use of ἐπί in ἐπὶ τὸν Ἰσραηλ above in this verse. The accusative object of ἐπί is οἶκον, and the indeclinable noun Ἰακωβ is a genitive of relationship, modifying οἶκον and referring to the patriarch of the "house." See the references to Jacob in 3:13; 6:8; 7:2, 5; 8:7, 9:8 ("house of Jacob" in 3:13; and 9:8). The word corresponding to "Jacob" in Hebrew is "Isaac"; see the discussion of the rendering of this Hebrew word in 7:9 (τοῦ γέλωτος).

7:17 διὰ τοῦτο τάδε λέγει κύριος Ἡ γυνή σου ἐν τῇ πόλει πορνεύσει, καὶ οἱ υἱοί σου καὶ αἱ θυγατέρες σου ἐν ῥομφαίᾳ πεσοῦνται, καὶ ἡ γῆ σου ἐν σχοινίῳ καταμετρηθήσεται, καὶ σὺ ἐν γῇ ἀκαθάρτῳ τελευτήσεις, ὁ δὲ Ισραηλ αἰχμάλωτος ἀχθήσεται ἀπὸ τῆς γῆς αὐτοῦ.

διὰ τοῦτο τάδε λέγει κύριος. Inferential. These same five words are found at the beginning of 3:11 and 5:16, where they also introduce an announcement of judgment; in each of these contexts διὰ τοῦτο is inferential. See 2:13 for a discussion of the formulaic PP διὰ τοῦτο. These words introduce the direct speech of the Lord, which is reported within the direct speech of Amos.

Ἡ γυνή σου. Nominative subject of the direct speech. An article is normally used with the head noun when it is modified by a possessive pronoun (see Smyth §1120.d; Wallace, 239; although this is not always the case, BDF §255; Muraoka §3.b). There are five examples of this pattern in this verse. Σου is a possessive genitive, "your wife."

ἐν τῇ πόλει. Locative. PP modifying πορνεύσει. The preposition ἐν "indicates a place" in which the action takes place (*GELS*, 231.1.b), and πόλει is the dative object of ἐν. Objects of prepositions are often definite, and the article may be omitted or included, as here (Muraoka §3.a; BDF §255). Here the article probably has anaphoric force pointing back to the previously mentioned city of Bethel (7:10, 13), where Amaziah lived and ministered (BDF §252.1–2).

πορνεύσει. Fut act ind 3rd sg πορνεύω. Prophetic future, "will be a prostitute."

καί. First of four coordinating conjunction, introducing the coordinate clauses which describe the judgment Amaziah will experience (*GELS*, 352.1.b).

οἱ υἱοί σου. Nominative subject (υἱοί), modified by a possessive genitive (σου). An article is normally used with the head noun when it is modified by a possessive pronoun (see Smyth §1120, d; Wallace, 239; although this is not always the case, BDF §255; Muraoka §3.b).

αἱ θυγατέρες σου. Nominative subject modified by a possessive genitive. See the discussion of the preceding article.

ἐν ῥομφαίᾳ. Instrumental. PP modifying πεσοῦνται; the preposition ἐν has the sense "by means of, by using an instrument" (*GELS*, 231.6.a; see the same phrase in 1:11; 4:10; 7:9, 11; 9:1, 10). The object of ἐν, ῥομφαίᾳ ("sword"), is best understood to be generic and definite and is apparently metonymy for armed conflict (see *GELS*, 614.b).

πεσοῦνται. Fut act ind 3rd pl πίπτω. Predictive future.

ἡ γῆ σου. Nominative subject of καταμετρηθήσεται, modified by a possessive genitive (σου). An article is often used with the head noun when it is modified by a possessive pronoun (see Smyth §1120, d; and Wallace, 239; although this is not always the case, BDF §255; Muraoka §3.b).

ἐν σχοινίῳ. Instrumental. PP modifying καταμετρηθήσεται. The preposition ἐν has the sense "by means of, by using an instrument" (*GELS*, 231.6.a), and σχοινίῳ, "measuring line," is the dative object of ἐν. Here the object of the preposition is indefinite.

καταμετρηθήσεται. Fut pass ind 3rd pl καταμετρέω. Predictive future and simple passive with no agent expressed. This verb (7x in the LXX) has the sense of "measuring" for the purpose of dividing, and here it describes an enemy or oppressor measuring conquered land (see Glenny 2013b, 134).

σὺ. Nominative subject of τελευτήσεις.

ἐν γῇ ἀκαθάρτῳ. Locative. PP modifying τελευτήσεις; the preposition ἐν "indicates a place" in which an action takes place (*GELS*, 231.1.b). The object of ἐν (i.e., γῇ) is indefinite. The dative attributive adjective ἀκαθάρτῳ modifies γῇ, "an unclean land."

τελευτήσεις. Fut act ind 2nd sg τελευτάω. Predictive future, "you will meet your end."

ὁ δὲ Ισραηλ αἰχμάλωτος ἀχθήσεται ἀπὸ τῆς γῆς αὐτοῦ. Amaziah rejected these exact words in 7:11, but the repetition of them here not only emphasizes them but also ironically reverses what Amaziah had said. See the discussion of δέ in 7:11.

Amos 8:1–3

¹So the Lord showed me and behold a fowler's cage. ²And he said, "What do you see, Amos?" And I said, "A fowler's cage." And the Lord said to me, "The end has come upon my people Israel; I will not pass by him again. ³And the coffered ceilings of the temple will wail in that day," says the Lord. "Many the fallen in every place—I will inflict silence."

This is the fourth vision in 7:1–9:7. See the introduction to the visions at the beginning of chapter 7.

8:1 Οὕτως ἔδειξέν μοι κύριος καὶ ἰδοὺ ἄγγος ἰξευτοῦ.

Οὕτως ἔδειξέν μοι κύριος καὶ ἰδοὺ. These exact words are also found at the beginning of the three previous vision accounts (7:1, 4, 7); see 7:1. In Ziegler's text the first four words are at the end of 7:17. MSS B and C follow the MT (see also 8:3 and 8:9) in having a double divine name (κύριος κύριος) in this clause; R-H and Ziegler, following MSS A and Q, have only one name in what is likely the original LXX reading.

ἄγγος. Predicate nominative of the implied verb ("there was...") or possibly subject. The rendering of this phrase is difficult. In the MT the word corresponding to ἄγγος, which occurs three times, is כלוב ("basket" [in Amos 8:1, 2], "birdcage" [in Jer 5:27]), and the word corresponding to ἰξευτοῦ is קיץ ("summer, summer fruit"). Elsewhere in the LXX ἄγγος refers to a container or vessel for various items (picked grapes, Deut 24:2[23:25 MT]; water, 3 Kgdms 17:10; grain and vegetables, Ezek 4:9) and an earthen vessel (Jer 19:11). In this context where it is modified by ἰξευτοῦ, referring to a "fowler" or "bird catcher," ἄγγος probably refers to a "a cage-like trap for birds" (see Glenny 2013b, 135; Glenny 2009, 81–82, discusses the rendering of ἄγγος ἰξευτοῦ).

ἰξευτοῦ. Possessive genitive, i.e., the trap (ἄγγος) belongs to a fowler (ἰξευτοῦ). Both words are indefinite.

8:2 καὶ εἶπεν Τί σὺ βλέπεις, Αμως; καὶ εἶπα Ἄγγος ἰξευτοῦ. καὶ εἶπεν κύριος πρός με·Ἥκει τὸ πέρας ἐπὶ τὸν λαόν μου Ισραηλ, οὐκέτι μὴ προσθῶ τοῦ παρελθεῖν αὐτόν·

Verses 2–3 contain direct discourse between the Lord and Amos designated by quotation marks in the translation.

καὶ εἶπεν Τί σὺ βλέπεις, Αμως. These words are very similar to the parallel clause in 7:8 in the second vision (καὶ εἶπεν κύριος πρός με Τί σὺ ὁρᾷς, Αμως), except the words κύριος πρός με in the parallel clause in 7:8 are not found in 8:2, following the Hebrew in both verses. The Hebrew verb (ראה), which is found in both verses, is rendered with different Greek verbs in the two verses. In this verse the translator employed βλέπεις (pres act ind 2nd sg βλέπω; progressive present), and in 7:8 he employs ὁράω (see the discussion in Dines 2013, 405). See 7:8 for the parallels.

καὶ εἶπα. See the discussion of these words in Amos' response in 7:8.
Ἄγγος ἰξευτοῦ. See the discussion of these words in 8:1.
καὶ εἶπεν κύριος πρός με. See the parallel clause in 7:8. In Ziegler's text verse 2 begins with these words.

Ἥκει. Pres act ind 3rd sg ἥκω. Perfective present, "has come"; see Muraoka (GELS, 319), who comments, "The present is used with the force of the perfect"; this is because "in contrast to ἔρχομαι, the verb emphasises the end-point of the process of physical movement, thus 'to arrive'; see esp. ἐρχόμενος ἥξει (not ἐλεύσεται) 'one who is to come will arrive' H[a]b 2:3."

τὸ πέρας. Nominative subject of ἥκει. Muraoka (GELS, 545.2) suggests this word has the sense "end of existence, extinction" in this context. The article is used here with a monadic noun, since there is only one πέρας ("end" or "furthest spot").

ἐπὶ τὸν λαόν. Direction, modifying ἥκει. The preposition ἐπί indicates the one to whom an action is directed, and here it refers to "hostile action" (*GELS*, 266.4.a) directed against the accusative object of ἐπί, "the people" (λαόν). The article is often used with the head noun when it is modified by a possessive pronoun (see Smyth §1120.d; and Wallace, 239; although this is not always the case, BDF §255; Muraoka §3.b).

μου. Possessive genitive.

Ισραηλ. The indeclinable proper noun Ισραηλ is in simple apposition to λαόν, further identifying "my people."

οὐκέτι μὴ προσθῶ τοῦ παρελθεῖν αὐτόν. See the same clause at the end of 7:8. The asyndeton at the beginning of this clause follows the Hebrew; asyndeton is often used in contexts moving from general to specific (Runge, 23). The masculine pronoun αὐτόν must refer to Israel in this context. Greek manuscripts have several variations of οὐκέτι μὴ προσθῶ (found in R-H and Ziegler, following W); οὐ προσθήσω ἔτι is in MSS B, and V and Q have οὐκέτι μὴ προσθήσω; all the readings are similar in meaning (but see the discussion of προσθῇς in 7:13). The modern editions value W, and they tend to favor the subjunctive in this construction (see 5:2; 7:8, 13).

8:3 καὶ ὀλολύξει τὰ φατνώματα τοῦ ναοῦ· ἐν ἐκείνῃ τῇ ἡμέρᾳ, λέγει κύριος, πολὺς ὁ πεπτωκὼς ἐν παντὶ τόπῳ, ἐπιρρίψω σιωπήν.

καὶ. Coordinating conjunction connecting coordinate clauses (*GELS*, 352.1.b).

ὀλολύξει. Fut act ind 3rd sg ὀλολύζω. Predictive future. This verb has the sense "howl, wail" (*GELS*, 493–94), although it can also refer to crying out in joy (see BDAG, 704; LSJ, 1217). The vast majority of the nineteen times this verb occurs in the LXX, it is employed to render the *hiphil* stem of the Hebrew verb ילל (sixteen of nineteen times; H-R, 989), perhaps trying to replicate that onomatopoetic verb form (MM, 446; BDAG, 704; *TDNT*, 5:173–74). The middle voice was employed for this verb in Attic Greek, but the active future began to supplant it, as is the case in the LXX (Thackeray §20.3).

τὰ φατνώματα. Nominative subject of ὀλολύξει. In the LXX this noun often functions as a technical term for "coffered work in a ceiling" (LSJ, 1919; and *GELS*, 711.2); this seems to be the sense here and in Zeph 2:14, where the ceiling has places (i.e., "coffers") where the "chameleons" can hide; both of these verses are in a context of the Lord's judgment. NETS renders the word "compartments." Elsewhere in the LXX it refers to the ceiling (2 Macc 1:16; Ezek 41:20; and perhaps Song 1:17). In this passage the ornamentation or decoration in the ceiling is personified and "wails." The translator apparently read the Hebrew שִׁירוֹת ("songs, singing women") as שׁוּרוֹת ("walls") or the Aramaic שָׁרִיתָא ("beam, post"); see Glenny (2009b, 93). The articles are consistent with Apollonius' canon (as a general rule in a genitive construction the head noun and its genitive modifier normally both either have the article or do not).

τοῦ ναοῦ. Partitive genitive; the "coffered ceilings" are part of the "temple."

ἐν ἐκείνῃ τῇ ἡμέρᾳ, λέγει κύριος. This construction occurs at least nine times in the LXX (Hos 2:18, 23; Amos 2:16; 8:3, 9; Mic 5:9; Obad 8; Zeph 1:10; Jer 4:9). See the discussion of these words in 2:16. There is some question whether the PP ἐν ἐκείνῃ τῇ ἡμέρᾳ, which is circumlocution for the day of the Lord (Glenny 2013b, 136), modifies the preceding verb, ὀλολύξει (NETS following MT), or the following participle, ὁ πεπτωκὼς (Dines 1991, 247; R-H; Ziegler). Because of the difficulty of connecting the PP with the awkward construction immediately following, it is best to connect it with the preceding. The order of the words in the phrase ἐν ἐκείνῃ τῇ ἡμέρᾳ differs in the manuscripts and also between Ziegler and R-H, which is followed here (see Glenny 2013b, 34); however, the difference in order makes no difference in meaning. The LXX renders two Hebrew names for the Lord (אֲדֹנָי יהוה) as one (κύριος); see also 8:1 and 8:9.

πολύς. Nominative adjective in the predicate position with relation to the following substantival participle. It could be connected to the subject by an implied linking verb, but the "verbless, asyndetic phrase is best understood as a kind of nominative absolute" (Dines 1991, 248; she refers to BDF §144, 466; Conybeare and Stock §51). Muraoka (*GELS*, 574.a) calls this use of the adjective "the singular for the plural" (see also BDAG, 848.2.a.α.א), and the adjective has the sense "great in number or quantity" (*GELS*, 574.a). See also the discussion of the unusual nature of the use of a singular in this context in Muraoka (§21.a).

ὁ πεπτωκώς. Prf act ptc nom masc sg πίπτω (substantival). The substantival construction with the article forms a generic subject, referring to a class of those who have "fallen," not an individual. One would expect a plural form here with πολύς modifying it (Muraoka §21.a).

ἐν παντὶ τόπῳ. Locative. This PP is probably best understood to be modifying the predicate adjective πολύς; the preposition ἐν is indicating a place "in which some action takes place or some state prevails" (*GELS*, 231.1.b). The dative singular τόπῳ ("place") is the object of ἐν, and the anarthrous form of πᾶς modifying a singular anarthrous noun means "every, any" (*GELS*, 459).

ἐπιρρίψω. Fut act ind 1st sg ἐπιρρίπτω. Predictive future. This verb usually means "throw, cast," but here it is more metaphorical with the sense "bring" (LEH, 233). The corresponding Hebrew verb (הִשְׁלִיךְ, "they [singular but understood to be plural] are thrown") goes with the preceding words, but in the LXX the first-person verb makes the Lord the subject; the different arrangement in the LXX is part of the reason the last part of 8:3 is somewhat awkward.

σιωπήν. Accusative direct object of ἐπιρρίψω, meaning "silence."

Amos 8:4–14

⁴Hear this now, you who destroy a poor man in the early morning and oppress the needy from the land, ⁵who say, "When will the month pass and we will do business, and the Sabbath and we will open the storehouses to make a measure small and to enlarge standard weights and to make a balance unjust ⁶to buy the poor for money and the lowly person for sandals, and we will trade in every kind of produce?" ⁷The Lord swears against Jacob's arrogant acts, "Surely none of your deeds will be forgotten forever. ⁸And for these things will not the land be shaken? And everyone who dwells in it will mourn, and destruction will rise up like a river and it will descend like the river of Egypt. ⁹And it shall be in that day," says the Lord, "and the sun will set at midday and the light will become dark upon the earth in the daytime. ¹⁰And I will turn your feasts into mourning and all your songs into lament, and I will bring sackcloth on everyone's loins and baldness on every head, and I will make him as one mourning for a beloved one and those with him as those experiencing a day of grief. ¹¹Behold, days are coming," says the Lord, "and I will send out a famine upon the land—not a famine from bread nor a thirst for water, but a famine of hearing the word of the Lord. ¹²And the waters will be shaken violently as far as the sea, and from north to east people will run about in search of the word of the Lord, but they will never find [it]. ¹³In that day the beautiful young virgins and the young men will faint with thirst, ¹⁴those who swear by the sin-offering of Samaria and those who say, 'Your god lives, Dan' and 'Your god lives, Beersheba'; and they shall fall and never rise again."

8:4 Ἀκούσατε δὴ ταῦτα, οἱ ἐκτρίβοντες εἰς τὸ πρωὶ πένητα καὶ καταδυναστεύοντες πτωχοὺς ἀπὸ τῆς γῆς,

Ἀκούσατε. Aor act impv 2nd pl ἀκούω. The aorist imperative is communicating a specific command, which is its usual use (Fanning, 327–35; BDF §335). On the use of genitive or accusative objects with ἀκούω, see 3:1 on ἀκούσατε.

δὴ. This marker is used with commands to give them a greater sense of urgency (*GELS*, 146.1; BDAG, 222.1); it is not used the other four times this command occurs in Amos (3:1, 13; 4:1; 5:1). There is nothing corresponding to this word in the Hebrew, and its only other occurrence in Amos is in 7:5.

ταῦτα. Accusative direct object ἀκούσατε. The corresponding Hebrew word is singular.

οἱ ἐκτρίβοντες. Pres act ptc nom masc pl ἐκτρίβω (substantival). This participle and the following one, both modified by the preceding article, are in apposition to the embedded second-person plural subjects of ἀκούσατε, and the participle phrases describe those subjects; the present-tense participles describe the customary, habitual, or continual actions of the addressees (Wallace, 521–22). The present-tense participle (λέγοντες) in 8:5 is a further description of these same people, but it has its own article. The basic idea of ἐκτρίβω is "to rub out" (LSJ, 523), and here it has the sense "to obliterate (as by rubbing)," thus "ruin, destroy" (BDAG, 311.2). The corresponding Hebrew verb, which also occurs in 2:7 (שׁאף), has the sense "pant, pester, press on" and perhaps here "trample upon," as it is rendered in 2:7 (*HALOT*, 2:1375).

εἰς τὸ πρωὶ. Temporal. See the discussion of this phrase in 4:4 and 5:8; there is nothing corresponding to it in the MT in this verse.

πένητα. Accusative direct object of ἐκτρίβοντες. Muraoka (§21.a) discusses the unusual nature of the use of a singular object here ("a poor person") and the plural object (πτωχούς, "the needy") with the following participle (καταδυναστεύοντες).

καὶ. Coordinating conjunction, connecting parallel substantival participle phrases (*GELS*, 352.1.a).

καταδυναστεύοντες. Pres act ptc nom masc pl καταδυναστεύω (substantival). See the syntax comments on ἐκτρίβω above. This word has the basic idea of oppressing, and "often from a position of power" (*GELS*, 371.1); see its use in parallel contexts in 4:1; Mic 2:2; and Zech 7:10.

πτωχούς. Accusative direct object of καταδυναστεύοντες. See the discussion of this word in 2:7 on πτωχῶν.

ἀπὸ τῆς γῆς. The preposition ἀπό modifies πτωχούς and could have several different senses: (1) separation from, which is the basic sense of the preposition (BDAG, 105; *GELS*, 69.1; Brenton), (2) a partitive idea ("of the land [or people]"; Dines 1991, 248 n. 1; Conybeare and Stock §92; BDF §209; *GELS*, 70.3.a), or (3) the idea of source ("from the land") (BDF §201.3; BDAG, 105–6.3; *GELS*, 70.3.a). It is simplest to understand it to have the idea of source (see Glenny 2013b, 137). Objects of prepositions are often definite, and the article with a definite object may be omitted or included (Muraoka §3.a; BDF §255). Here the article emphasizes that "the land" (γῆ) referred to is the land known above all others to the recipients, the land of Israel (on the well-known use of the article, see Wallace, 225). The noun γῆς, which is the object of ἀπό, could mean "people," but when it does it generally refers to the people of all the earth, which does not fit here; in this context it must refer to the land of Israel.

8:5 οἱ λέγοντες Πότε διελεύσεται ὁ μὴν καὶ ἐμπολήσομεν καὶ τὰ σάββατα καὶ ἀνοίξομεν θησαυροὺς τοῦ ποιῆσαι μικρὸν μέτρον καὶ τοῦ μεγαλῦναι στάθμια καὶ ποιῆσαι ζυγὸν ἄδικον

οἱ λέγοντες. Pres act ptc nom masc pl λέγω (substantival). This construction continues the Lord's words from 8:4 and introduces the speech of the subjects; it is in apposition to and thus further describes the subjects of the two parallel present participles there. See a similar construction in 8:14.

Πότε. Adverb of time, modifying διελεύσεται.

διελεύσεται. Fut mid ind 3rd sg διέρχομαι. Gnomic future, referring to a general truth (Smyth §1914); although the events described are true to life, no particular event is in view (Wallace, 571); the event is "true of any time" (Robertson, 876). This is an indirect middle in the sense that the subject is acting in relation to itself and is affected by the action of the verb. It fits more precisely in Kemmer's category of "spontaneous events associated with inanimate beings" (269–70).

ὁ μὴν. Nominative subject of διελεύσεται. This is a generic noun, not referring to a specific month but rather to the class. It is common to have an article with a generic noun, distinguishing that class from others. The noun must refer to "the religious festival of the new moon on the first day of the month" (see Glenny 2013b, 138).

καὶ. Coordinating conjunction, and here it "introduces a consequence which would ensue if what is denoted by the preceding clause is realized" (*GELS*, 354.9).

ἐμπολήσομεν. Fut act ind 1st pl ἐμπολάω. Gnomic future, referring to a generic truth, not a particular event; see the discussion of διελεύσεται above in this verse. This LXX *hapax* has the sense "to deal in" (*GELS*, 229) or "to traffic" (LEH, 197), and in this context it means "do business" (NETS); cf. the more common πωλέω (*GELS*, 609). This verb corresponds to the Hebrew verb נשביר, which is rendered with the verb ἐμπορεύομαι in verse 6; the different renderings are an example of variation or non-stereotyping. In the MT this verb has an object, "grain," that is understood but not included in the LXX.

καὶ. Coordinating conjunction connecting coordinate clauses (*GELS*, 352.1.b). The following compound clause is parallel to the preceding compound sentence, and the verb διέρχομαι from the previous parallel construction is understood in the first part of this sentence.

τὰ σάββατα. Nominative subject of διελεύσεται. The noun is parallel to μήν, and the verb is implied from the previous clause. The plural often refers to a single Sabbath day, as here (*GELS*, 616.1), and it is translated as such. This is a generic noun, not referring to a specific individual but rather to the class, and the article is common with a generic noun (see ὁ μήν above in 8:5). The MT has the singular collective form.

καὶ. Coordinating conjunction, and here it "introduces a consequence which would ensue if what is denoted by the preceding clause is realized" (*GELS*, 354.9).

ἀνοίξομεν. Fut act ind 1st pl ἀνοίγω. Gnomic future, referring to a generic event, not a particular event, "we will open."

θησαυρούς. Accusative direct object of ἀνοίξομεν. This is another generic noun. The use of the generic article is optional (Muraoka §1.d), and this noun is indefinite. The noun can refer to a place for storing something or the valuable thing that is stored (*GELS*, 330); in this context it refers to the "granaries" or "storehouses" that will be opened. This noun corresponds to the Hebrew noun בר (collective sg; the sg is followed by some Greek manuscripts; Glenny 2013b, 34), which is rendered with γένημα ("produce") in 8:6; apparently the different renderings are an example of variation or non-stereotyping.

τοῦ ποιῆσαι. Aor act inf ποιέω (purpose). On the use of this construction to express purpose, see τοῦ κατακληρονομῆσαι in 2:10.

μικρὸν. Complement in an adjectival object-complement double accusative construction. The predicate adjective tells something about the object (Wallace, 182–89); it is "small." Quantifying adjectives tend to precede the nouns they modify, perhaps influenced by cardinal numbers (Muraoka §37.baaa).

μέτρον. Accusative direct object of the infinitive ποιῆσαι in an object-complement double accusative construction. This is a generic noun, not referring to a specific "measure," but rather to the class or species.

καὶ. Coordinating conjunction connecting coordinate purpose infinitives (*GELS*, 352.1.a).

τοῦ μεγαλῦναι. Aor act inf μεγαλύνω (purpose). The verb has the sense "to enlarge." On the use of this construction to express purpose, see τοῦ κατακληρονομῆσαι in 2:10.

στάθμια. Accusative direct object of infinitive μεγαλῦναι. This is a generic noun, not referring to a specific object but rather to the class or species. The noun denotes the standard weights that were used on a balance (LSJ, 1632). The corresponding Hebrew has the generic singular "shekel" (שֶׁקֶל), and some Greek manuscripts also have a singular form (B, V, and *L*; see Glenny 2013b, 34).

καί. Coordinating conjunction connecting coordinate purpose infinitives (*GELS*, 352.1.a).

ποιῆσαι. Aor act inf ποιέω (purpose). This purpose infinite does not have a genitive article, varying from the two preceding ones and the following one in 8:6. The corresponding Hebrew is עוּת ("to falsify"; *HALOT*, 1:804.1), which the translator apparently read as עשׂה, which makes sense with the following words.

ζυγὸν. Accusative direct object of infinitive ποιῆσαι in an object-complement double accusative construction. This is a generic noun, not referring to a specific individual but rather to the class or species. Often this word denotes a yoke but in this context refers to a balance or pair of "scales" (LEH, 261; *GELS*, 315.2). The older neuter gender of this noun is replaced almost everywhere in the LXX by the masculine (Thackeray §10.24).

ἄδικον. Complement in an adjectival object-complement double accusative construction. The predicate adjective tells something about the object (Wallace, 182–89).

8:6 τοῦ κτᾶσθαι ἐν ἀργυρίῳ πτωχοὺς καὶ ταπεινὸν ἀντὶ ὑποδημάτων καὶ ἀπὸ παντὸς γενήματος ἐμπορευσόμεθα;

The previous three infinitives in 8:5 were connected by the repetition of καί, and the asyndeton before the infinitive at the beginning of 8:6 distinguishes this last infinitive; the context suggests it may be the ultimate purpose for the deceptive practices described by the preceding infinitives (Glenny 2013b, 138; Runge, 20–23).

τοῦ κτᾶσθαι. Pres mid inf κτάομαι (purpose). See two times in 8:5. In this context this verb has the sense "buy, procure for oneself" (*GELS*, 416.1; BDAG, 572.1); the middle voice could be classified as an indirect middle (Kemmer, 268). On the use of this construction to express purpose, see τοῦ κατακληρονομῆσαι in 2:10.

ἐν ἀργυρίῳ. Means, modifying κτᾶσθαι. The preposition ἐν has the sense "by means of, by using as instrument" (*GELS*, 231.6.a).

πτωχούς. Accusative direct object of κτᾶσθαι. See the discussion of this word in 2:7 on πτωχῶν and also its use in 4:1; 5:11; and 8:4. Muraoka (§21.a) discusses the unusual nature of the use of a plural object of the infinitive here (πτωχούς, "the poor") with a coordinate singular object ("lowly person," ταπεινόν).

καί. Coordinating conjunction connecting coordinate objects of the infinitive κτᾶσθαι (*GELS*, 352.1.a).

ταπεινόν. Accusative direct object of the infinitive κτᾶσθαι. See the discussion of this word for the "poor" in 2:7.

ἀντὶ ὑποδημάτων. Exchange/substitution, modifying κτᾶσθαι. The preposition ἀντί "precedes a noun of commodity or service to be obtained in return for payment or giving an equivalent amount" (*GELS*, 57.1). This preposition emphasizes the exchange or substitution that takes place in the transaction; compare the use of ἐν in the parallel above (ἐν ἀργυρίῳ), which emphasizes the means of the purchase. See the discussion of the similar phrase in 2:6; the "sandals" (ὑποδημάτων) emphasize the trivial amount the oppressors are willing to pay.

καί. Coordinating conjunction connecting coordinate clauses (*GELS*, 352.1.b); the clause introduced by this conjunction is parallel to the two main clauses in 8:5, both of which also have first-person plural future-tense verbs.

ἀπὸ παντὸς γενήματος. Partitive, modifying ἐμπορευσόμεθα. The PP with ἀπό indicates the "'source or collection' out of which selection is made" (*GELS*, 70.3.a). Preceding a singular noun, the adjective πᾶς means "every, any" (Muraoka §38.b.i), and *GELS* (127, s.v. γένημα) suggests the rendering "every kind of [produce]" in this context where it modifies γένημα. The noun γένημα, which functions as the object of ἀπό, "is a new κοινή formation from γίνομαι = 'produce of the earth,' 'fruit,' and is carefully distinguished from γέννημα, 'offspring' (from γεννάω)" (Thackeray §7.38; see also LSJ, 343, s.v. γένημα, and 344, s.v. γέννημα). This noun corresponds to the Hebrew noun בר ("wheat, grain"), which is rendered with θησαυρούς ("storehouses") in 8:5; apparently the different renderings of the noun and the following verb are an example of variation or non-stereotyping (Glenny 2009, 59). The Greek καὶ ἀπὸ παντὸς renders the Hebrew ומפל ("and the refuse"), which was apparently read as ומכל ("and from all")

ἐμπορευσόμεθα. Fut mid ind 1st pl ἐμπορεύομαι. Gnomic future, referring to a generic event, not a particular event. The indirect middle idea of "coming into possession" (Kemmer, 268) is clear in the action of commerce (i.e., "trade") communicated by this verb (*GELS*, 229.1). This verb corresponds to the Hebrew verb נשביר, which is rendered with ἐμπολάω in 8:5. See the previous entry on the translator's variation.

8:7 ὀμνύει κύριος καθ' ὑπερηφανίας Ιακωβ Εἰ ἐπιλησθήσεται εἰς νῖκος πάντα τὰ ἔργα ὑμῶν.

ὀμνύει. Pres act ind 3rd sg ὄμνυμι. Instantaneous present and the action of the verb is fulfilled at the time it is spoken. *GELS* (495.5) suggests that in this context the verb has the idea "to lash out verbally at, denounce," and the context does suggest such a rendering. However, it does not have that sense elsewhere, and it is normally rendered "to swear." See καθ' ὑπερηφανίας below.

κύριος. Nominative subject of ὀμνύει.

καθ' ὑπερηφανίας. Opposition, modifying ὀμνύει. The preposition κατά is normally employed in oath formulas with a genitive object to indicate that which the one swearing invokes to affirm the oath (*GELS*, 364.2; *GE*, 1454.1.B; see 4:4; 6:8; 8:14), but here it apparently indicates that which one swears against (so *GELS*, 698 and 495.5, s.v. ὄμνυμι). The object of the preposition κατά is usually understood to be the genitive singular ὑπερηφανίας ("arrogance"; LEH, 630; BDAG, 1030; see Glenny 2013b, 139–40), but this form could also be accusative plural and thus avoid the curious rendering of κατά with the genitive as "against," because the preposition κατά with the accusative case can possibly have the sense "against" (*GELS*, 365.II.3). The plural of the noun is unusual, occurring only about two times out of fifty-six in the LXX, but the context supports reading it as accusative plural, referring to "arrogant acts" (see the same idea in Ps 73:3), since the following parallel lines speak of "all your works"; thus, it seems best to render καθ' ὑπερηφανίας Ιακωβ as "against Jacob's arrogant acts."

Ιακωβ. The indeclinable proper noun Ιακωβ is a subjective genitive, modifying ὑπερηφανίας. The subjective genitive "functions semantically as the subject of the verbal idea implicit in the head noun" (Wallace, 113).

Εἰ ἐπιλησθήσεται εἰς νῖκος πάντα τὰ ἔργα ὑμῶν. This is a strong oath statement that the Lord will never forget the works of Jacob. The particle εἰ corresponds to the Hebrew אִם, which is used "in oath formula as conditional (self-) imprecation" (*HALOT*, 1:60.4; see also Waltke & O'Connor §40.2.2.a) with the apodosis usually left out. See the full form of the Hebrew formula in 2 Kgs 6:31 (LXX, 4 Kgdms 6:31). The expression here in the LXX indicates "strong negation after verbs of swearing" (*GELS*, 190.4), and *GE* (596.II.F) suggests the meaning "surely." This understanding of the expression assumes aposiopesis (BDAG, 278.4; BDF §372.4), and the negative force is imported into the particle because of the suppression of the apodosis (Conybeare and Stock, 90). It is probably a Hebraism (Thackeray §4 [p. 54]; *GELS*,

190.4; BDF §372.4 calls it "a strong Hebraism"). See further the excellent discussion of such expressions in Decker 2014b, 1:210–11.

ἐπιλησθήσεται. Fut pass ind 3rd sg ἐπιλανθάνομαι. Predictive future. This is a simple passive, with the plural neuter subjects receiving the action of the third-person singular verb. The verb has the idea of "forget" or "neglect," and in this context the former sense is more likely (*GELS*, 275–76.1; BDAG, 374).

εἰς νῖκος. Extent of time, modifying ἐπιλησθήσεται. See the discussion of the phrase in 1:11, where it is suggested it has the sense permanently, resolutely, or "forever" (Kraft, 155–56).

πάντα τὰ ἔργα. The neuter plural adjective πάντα modifies τὰ ἔργα, and in the construction πᾶς–article–plural noun, the adjective πᾶς refers to "all the . . ." (Muraoka §38.b.i). The main nominative and subject of the clause, τὰ ἔργα, requires the article in this construction with πᾶς (see the preceding).

ὑμῶν. Subjective genitive, modifying τὰ ἔργα (see the parallel subjective genitive Ιακωβ above in this verse). The MT reads מעשׂיהם, using the third masculine plural suffix: "their deeds."

8:8 καὶ ἐπὶ τούτοις οὐ ταραχθήσεται ἡ γῆ, καὶ πενθήσει πᾶς ὁ κατοικῶν ἐν αὐτῇ, καὶ ἀναβήσεται ὡς ποταμὸς συντέλεια καὶ καταβήσεται ὡς ποταμὸς Αἰγύπτου.

καὶ. The conjunction introduces a new or additional idea that is a consequence of the deeds described in 8:5–6, 7b (see *GELS*, 353–54.1.h and 9). The first clause of 8:8 must be a rhetorical question, since it would not make sense in this context for the Lord to promise that the land will not be shaken (see Dines 1991, 250; NETS understands the whole verse to be a question, but this is not necessary. R-H and Ziegler do not have a question mark with the verse).

ἐπὶ τούτοις. Causal, modifying ταραχθήσεται. The preposition ἐπί has the sense "on account of" (*GELS*, 265.6). The object of the preposition (τούτοις) refers to τὰ ἔργα in 8:7, which were described in 8:5–6.

οὐ. Negative particle, introducing a question expecting a positive answer (BDAG, 734.3).

ταραχθήσεται. Fut pass ind 3rd sg ταράσσω. There is no agency expressed, but it is clear that the Lord is the agent (see BDF §130.1, on what some call the "divine passive" employed to avoid using the name of God). Muraoka (§27.b) explains that "the passive brings to the fore an action or a result or effect of it," pushing the agent into the background. The passive voice of this verb is often used to describe earthquakes (Isa 24:19; Jer 4:24; Pss 17:8; 45:3, 4; 76:17).

ἡ γῆ. Nominative subject of ταραχθήσεται. Here γῆ must refer to the land of Israel. This noun is discussed in each of the clauses in this verse. The article is employed here with a well-known substantive (see the discussion of τῆς γῆς in 8:4 and τὴν γῆν in 8:11).

πενθήσει. Fut act ind 3rd sg πενθέω. Predictive future, "will mourn."

πᾶς ὁ κατοικῶν. Nominative subject of πενθήσει. One would expect a plural here in Greek, as in 9:5 (πάντες οἱ κατοικοῦντες); however, it should be noted that the translator was following closely the Hebrew in both places. In 9:5 there is a plural participle in Hebrew, and in 8:8 the participle in Hebrew is singular (see Muraoka §21.a[note 2]). Here in 8:8 the singular πᾶς modifying the substantivized participle has the meaning "every, all" (Muraoka §38.b.i).

κατοικῶν. Pres act ptc nom masc sg κατοικέω (substantival).

ἐν αὐτῇ. Locative, modifying ὁ κατοικῶν. The preposition ἐν "indicates a place in which some object is found or placed" (*GELS*, 231.1.a); αὐτῇ, the dative object of the preposition, refers to ἡ γῆ.

ἀναβήσεται. Fut mid ind 3rd sg ἀναβαίνω. Predictive future. The future of this verb is middle voice (BDAG, 58); it is clear that the subject is affected by the action, and it is probably a middle of translational motion (Kemmer, 269). In Greek there is a rhyming correspondence between ἀναβήσεται and the following καταβήσεται that matches the rhyming parallel verb endings in Hebrew (Dines 2013, 400); the rhyming is formed by the use of prepositional prefixes on the same Greek verb root.

ὡς. Introduces a comparative clause, involving ellipsis: "Destruction will rise up like a river (rises up)." The comparative particle indicates the "manner in which something proceeds" (BDAG, 1103.1.a).

ποταμὸς. Nominative subject of an implied form of ἀναβαίνω.

συντέλεια. Nominative subject of καταβήσεται. See the use of this word in 1:14 and 9:5. This word corresponds to כלה in the MT, which could be rendered "all of her [it]" as is the MT tradition or as "complete destruction," as the LXX reads (see Glenny 2009, 210–11). This word is often used in eschatological contexts referring to divine vengeance (i.e., 2 Esd 19:31; Nah 1:8; Zeph 1:18; Jer 4:27; 5:10, 18; 26:28; Ezek 11:13; 13:13; 20:17; Dan 9:27; Dan Th 9:27); see Glenny (2013b, 141).

καταβήσεται. Fut mid ind 3rd sg καταβαίνω. Predictive future. This word is middle in the future tense (BDAG, 513–14); it is clear that the subject is affected by the action, and it is probably a middle of translational motion (Kemmer, 269). The implied subject of the verb is ἡ γῆ. The Greek text has nothing corresponding to the MT's ונגרשה ("and will be tossed"), which precedes the Hebrew verb corresponding to καταβήσεται.

ὡς. See above in this verse.

ποταμὸς. Nominative subject of an implied form of καταβήσεται. The anarthrous noun "river" (ποταμός) is definite because it is specified by the following genitive modifier (Αἰγύπτου). Both times ποταμός occurs in the LXX in this verse, it corresponds to the Hebrew word for "Nile."

Αἰγύπτου. This genitive is difficult to classify, and one could use the catchall category, genitive of description; however, it seems that Αἰγύπτου functions more like an attributive genitive (like an adjective and giving a quality or attribute of the head noun), i.e., "the Egyptian river," here the well-known Egyptian river (see Robertson, 496–97; Thackeray §3[p. 23]). See Muraoka (§5.cb) on the patterns for the use of the article with the place-name Αἴγυπτος; the genitive is normally anarthrous when it is governed by a substantive (but cf. 3:9).

8:9 καὶ ἔσται ἐν ἐκείνῃ τῇ ἡμέρᾳ, λέγει κύριος ὁ θεός, καὶ δύσεται ὁ ἥλιος μεσημβρίας, καὶ συσκοτάσει ἐπὶ τῆς γῆς ἐν ἡμέρᾳ τὸ φῶς·

καὶ ἔσται. See the discussion of this phrase at the beginning of 7:2. This phrase (found in 5:14; 6:9; 7:2; and 8:9) appears to be a Hebraistic structure that "introduces an utterance indicating that which may or ought to happen, with a temporal clause or phrase or a conditional clause intervening" (*GELS*, 193.5, s.v. εἰμί, 354.12, s.v. καί); here there is a temporal PP (ἐν ἐκείνῃ τῇ ἡμέρᾳ) intervening, and the following utterance is a prophecy, as is often the case in the examples of this use of καὶ ἔσται in *GELS* (e.g., Hos 2:16; Zech 13:8).

ἐν ἐκείνῃ τῇ ἡμέρᾳ, λέγει κύριος ὁ θεός. See the discussion of these words in 2:16 and 8:3. On the word order (demonstrative–article–noun), see Muraoka (§34.c).

κύριος ὁ θεός. Nominative subject of λέγει. This title occurs eighteen times in LXX Amos; see 3:7. Here it corresponds to אדני יהוה; the other three times this Hebrew title occurs in chapter 8 (8:1, 3, and 11), it is always rendered with only one name, κύριος.

καὶ. Coordinating conjunction connecting coordinate clauses (*GELS*, 352.1.b). Here the Greek conjunction seems to be pleonastic, following the Hebrew.

δύσεται. Fut mid ind 3rd sg δύω (or δύνω; BDAG, 264; LSJ, 463). Predictive future. The active form of the future tense of δύω is causative (i.e., "cause to sink, go down"; *GELS*, 181); in the middle-voice usage the subject is affected ("sink, go into"; LEH, 165). The middle is what Kemmer (269) refers to as a "spontaneous event" associated with "inanimate beings." Mic 3:6 and Isa 60:20 also have the clause δύσεται ὁ ἥλιος.

ὁ ἥλιος. Nominative subject of δύσεται. The article is used with the monadic noun.

μεσημβρίας. Genitive of time, showing the time within which or during which something takes place, "at midday" (BDF §186.2).

συσκοτάσει. Fut act ind 3rd sg συσκοτάζω. Predictive future. This verb could be transitive (as in 5:8) or intransitive (as in Mic 3:6; see LSJ, 1733), and τὸ φῶς could be its subject (if it is intransitive) or object (if it is transitive). In this context it makes sense that φῶς is the subject, parallel to ἥλιος in the previous clause, and thus the verb is intransitive, "will become dark" (*GELS*, 663.2; Glenny 2013b, 141). See the parallel idea in 5:18 and 5:20.

ἐπὶ τῆς γῆς. Locative, modifying συσκοτάσει. The preposition ἐπί has the sense "on the surface of" (*GELS*, 263.I.2), and the genitive object of ἐπί (τῆς γῆς) refers to "land and sea" (*GELS*, 129.2), thus "the earth"; the article is used with the monadic noun.

ἐν ἡμέρᾳ. Temporal, modifying συσκοτάσει. The preposition ἐν "indicates a point in time when something takes place" (*GELS*, 231.3), and ἡμέρᾳ, the dative object of the preposition, refers to "the period of day from sunrise to sunset" (*GELS*, 320.2), thus, "daytime."

τὸ φῶς. Nominative subject of συσκοτάσει. Muraoka (*GELS*, 726.2) understands φῶς here, where it is parallel to ἥλιος, to refer to a "source of light, object which emits light," more specifically a "heavenly body." With the article the "heavenly body" would most likely be the sun, which normally shines in the "daytime" (see above in this verse).

8:10 καὶ μεταστρέψω τὰς ἑορτὰς ὑμῶν εἰς πένθος καὶ πάσας τὰς ᾠδὰς ὑμῶν εἰς θρῆνον καὶ ἀναβιβῶ ἐπὶ πᾶσαν ὀσφὺν σάκκον καὶ ἐπὶ πᾶσαν κεφαλὴν φαλάκρωμα καὶ θήσομαι αὐτὸν ὡς πένθος ἀγαπητοῦ καὶ τοὺς μετ᾽ αὐτοῦ ὡς ἡμέραν ὀδύνης.

Tobit 2:6 cites the first two clauses of 8:10, as being from Amos, in a different form than the LXX text. See Glenny (2013b, 141–42) for a discussion of this issue. First Maccabees 9:41 also contains verbal parallels to the Greek of 8:10.

μεταστρέψω. Fut act ind 1st sg μεταστρέφω. Predictive future, i.e., "will turn, change" (LEH, 397–98).

τὰς ἑορτὰς. Accusative direct object of μεταστρέψω. The article is normally used with a head noun that is modified by a possessive pronoun (see Smyth §1120.d; and Wallace, 239; although this is not always the case, BDF §255; Muraoka §3.b).

ὑμῶν. Possessive genitive.

εἰς πένθος. Spatial/transformational, modifying μεταστρέψω. The preposition εἰς "indicates transformation," i.e., "the transitive transform of the preceding" (GELS, 197.6.b). The accusative object of the preposition is πένθος ("grief, mourning, sorrow"; BDAG, 795; GELS, 544).

καί. Coordinating conjunction connecting coordinate direct objects (GELS, 352.1.a).

πάσας τὰς ᾠδὰς. The accusative ᾠδάς is a direct object of μεταστρέψω, coordinate with the preceding direct object ἑορτάς. The article is normally used in this type of construction with πᾶς (Muraoka 38.b.i), and it is normally used with a head noun that is modified by a possessive pronoun (see Smyth §1120.d; and Wallace, 239; although this is not always the case, BDF §255; Muraoka §3.b). As an adjective πᾶς is in the predicate position, and in the construction πᾶς–article–plural noun, it refers to "the entire, every, all" (Muraoka §38.b.i).

ὑμῶν. Possessive genitive.

εἰς θρῆνον. Spatial/transformational, modifying μεταστρέψω. The preposition εἰς "indicates transformation," i.e., "the transitive transform of the preceding" (GELS, 197.6.b); θρῆνον ("mourning, grief, sorrow"; see TDNT, VI, 41–42) is the accusative object of εἰς.

ἀναβιβῶ. Fut act ind 1st sg ἀναβιβάζω. Predictive future. This verb is the causative of ἀναβαίνω, and it has a wide range of meanings related to that basic sense (GE, 128; LSJ, 99), including "cause to move higher" (GELS, 36), "bring up" (BDAG, 59). Here it has the basic idea of "cause to go" (LES), "cause to come" (Dines 1991, 251), or "bring" (NETS).

ἐπὶ πᾶσαν ὀσφὺν. Spatial, modifying ἀναβιβῶ. The preposition ἐπί "indicates movement on to the surface of" (GELS, 265–66.III.1.a). Singular πᾶς followed by a singular head noun has the sense "every, any" (Muraoka §38.b.i). The object (ὀσφύν) has the sense "loin, waist," and in this context it is "where a mourner's sackcloth is worn" (GELS, 510).

σάκκον. Accusative direct object of ἀναβιβῶ.

καί. Coordinating conjunction connecting coordinate direct objects (GELS, 352.1.a).

ἐπὶ πᾶσαν κεφαλὴν. Spatial, modifying ἀναβιβῶ. On ἐπί, see just above.

φαλάκρωμα. Accusative direct object of ἀναβιβῶ and coordinate with the preceding direct object, σάκκον. This word, meaning "baldness, bald head," is a LXX neologism (LEH, 642), and this context may refer to the practice of pulling out hair or shaving the head as a sign of mourning (Isa 22:12; Ezek 7:18; and Ezek 27:31 [only in Hebrew]).

θήσομαι. Fut mid ind 1st sg τίθημι. Predictive future. In this context followed by an accusative and a ὡς phrase the verb has the sense "to cause to be, render" (GELS, 679.II.3). This use of the middle is probably best classified as a middle of self-involvement concerning intellectual activities (Miller, 427–29). See the parallel uses of τίθημι followed by an accusative object and ὡς clause in Hos 2:5 and 11:8.

αὐτὸν. Accusative direct object of θήσομαι. The intended referent of this pronoun is unclear (see Glenny 2013b, 142–43), and the change in the verse from second person ("your") to third person ("him") is awkward. The pronoun could refer to the previously described mourning and lament, but it likely refers back to Jacob (or Israel), last named in the oath formula in 8:7. This latter understanding of the pronoun yields a sense that is logical and coherent with the following context, because in the phrase τοὺς μετ' αὐτοῦ ("those with him"), the pronoun must refer to a person and not mourning or some other inanimate thing. In Hebrew the corresponding feminine pronoun apparently does refer to Israel's mourning and sorrow. This verse shares several common terms with Jer 6:26 (σάκκος and esp. πένθος ἀγαπητοῦ), a passage also referring to Israel's mourning.

ὡς. The adverb ὡς can function as a comparative particle (BDAG, 1103.1), but Muraoka notes that it can also sometimes "drift from the notion of similarity to that of identity," and he provides several examples of that use of ὡς with τίθημι and τάσσω, including this passage (*GELS*, 748.I.9; see Hos 2:5; 11:8; Mic 1:6; 2:12b; Zech 12:2; Zeph 2:13). In several of the examples Muraoka gives, some MSS have εἰς rather than ὡς, further supporting the idea that ὡς is more than a comparative particle in this construction. In this verse the ὡς phrase functions like an object-complement double accusative construction (*GELS*, 679.I.3.c, s.v. τίθημι; see also *CGCG* §30.10). Since this phrase complements the preceding accusative object (αὐτόν), it would be understood to refer to a person mourning a beloved ("one mourning") rather than the abstract quality of mourning, thus supporting the understanding favored above of αὐτόν as a reference to Israel.

πένθος. Accusative object of comparison in the comparative phrase, meaning "mourning."

ἀγαπητοῦ. Objective genitive (Muraoka §22.v.xiii). The adjective functions here as a substantive.

καί. Coordinating conjunction connecting coordinate direct objects (*GELS*, 352.1.a).

τούς. The accusative article functions as a nominalizer, changing the following PP (μετ' αὐτοῦ) into the direct object of θήσομαι and is coordinate with the preceding direct object, αὐτόν.

μετ' αὐτοῦ. Accompaniment. The preposition μετά has the sense "in the company of somebody as associate, companion, helper, etc." (*GELS*, 451.I.1), and the object of the preposition, αὐτοῦ, refers to the previous αὐτόν; it is difficult to conceive of a meaning for this phrase that does not refer to people (see the parallel phrase τοὺς μεθ' ὑμῶν in 4:2; and Glenny 2013b, 142). Dines (1991, 253) mentions the possibility that the context refers to "the ongoing tradition of mourning over Josiah (cf. 2 Chr 35:24–25; Tg. Amos 9:1)" and that the obscure pronoun αὐτόν in this verse and in Zech 12:10 refers to Josiah also. However, this is unlikely since there is nothing in this context to connect with Josiah, and in Zech 12:10 the pronoun is best explained by its correspondence to the MT (see further Glenny 2013b, 142). It is much more likely the pronoun αὐτοῦ refers to Israel; see αὐτόν above in this verse. The Hebrew corresponding to καὶ τοὺς μετ' αὐτοῦ is ואחריתה ("and the end of it").

ὡς. See the parallel ὡς phrase above in this verse. Since this phrase complements the preceding accusative object (τοὺς μετ' αὐτοῦ), it would be understood to refer to people experiencing a day of grief rather than the abstract quality of grief.

ἡμέραν. The object of comparison in the ὡς phrase is ἡμέραν, which functions like a double accusative (*GELS*, 679.3); see ὡς πένθος ἀγαπητοῦ above.

ὀδύνης. Attributive genitive.

8:11 ἰδοὺ ἡμέραι ἔρχονται, λέγει κύριος, καὶ ἐξαποστελῶ λιμὸν ἐπὶ τὴν γῆν, οὐ λιμὸν ἄρτου οὐδὲ δίψαν ὕδατος, ἀλλὰ λιμὸν τοῦ ἀκοῦσαι λόγον κυρίου·

ἰδοὺ ἡμέραι ἔρχονται, λέγει κύριος. These words are also found at the beginning of 9:13. The first three words (ἰδοὺ ἡμέραι ἔρχονται) also occur in 4:2; they announce judgment here and in 4:2, and in 9:13 they announce eschatological blessing.

ἰδού. The "presentative particle" ἰδού often introduces a new section, as here, and is "used to draw the hearer's or reader's attention to what follows," which is here an "eschatological discourse" (*GELS*, 337.b). The interjection ἰδού occurs fifteen times in Amos; see 2:13.

ἡμέραι. Nominative subject of ἔρχονται.

ἔρχονται. Pres mid ind 3rd pl ἔρχομαι. Futuristic present, emphasizing the certainty of the event, "days are coming." The action of the middle voice of translational verbs like ἔρχομαι clearly affects the subject (Kemmer, 269, calls it a middle of "translational motion").

λέγει κύριος. This clause is found forty times in Amos to introduce the Lord's words; see its first occurrences in 1:5 and 1:6. In this verse κύριος corresponds to אדני יהוה in the MT.

καί. Coordinating conjunction connecting coordinate clauses (*GELS*, 352.1.b); "with temporal designations" the use of καί is coordinate, not subordinate (BDF §442.4).

ἐξαποστελῶ. Fut act ind 1st sg ἐξαποστέλλω. Predictive future.

λιμὸν. Accusative direct object of ἐξαποστελῶ, meaning "hunger, famine" (BDAG, 596; LEH, 374).

ἐπὶ τὴν γῆν. Spatial, modifying ἐξαποστελῶ. The preposition ἐπί "indicates movement on to the surface of" (*GELS*, 265–66.III.1.a). The use of the article is probably anaphoric, referring again to the land mentioned in 8:9, but it could also be the use of the article with a well-known object. The object of the preposition (γῆν) refers to the land of Israel (see 8:8, 9).

οὐ. The negative particle is apparently negating the implied repetition of ἐξαποστελῶ, i.e., the Lord will *not* send a "famine of bread."

λιμὸν. Accusative direct object of the implied verb ἐξαποστελῶ, and it is modified by ἄρτου.

ἄρτου. Objective genitive, "famine from bread."

οὐδέ. This negative conjunction combines οὐ and δέ (see BDAG, 734.1) and introduces a negative clause following a preceding negative clause. The negative particle is apparently negating the implied repetition of ἐξαποστελῶ, i.e., the Lord will not send a famine of bread.

δίψαν ὕδατος. Acc fem sg δίψα. Direct object of the implied verb ἐξαποστελῶ. The first and third declensions of this noun are used interchangeably in this context (here and in 8:13; Thackeray §10.27).

ὕδατος. Objective genitive, where the head noun is a verbal noun with a cognate verb (Wallace, 112; cf. λιμὸν ἄρτου above in this verse).

ἀλλά. This adversative particle occurs only twice in Amos (see also 7:14). Here, preceded by a negative statement, it indicates contrast (*GELS*, 26.2.a; BDAG, 44.1.a).

λιμὸν. Accusative direct object of an implied ἐξαποστελῶ.

τοῦ ἀκοῦσαι. Aor act inf ἀκούω (epexegetical, explaining λιμόν) (BDF §394; see also Muraoka §30.bc; Wallace, 607–8; Smyth §2032, 1290). In his discussion of the substantival character of the infinitive, Muraoka (§29.aa) notes that this infinitive is parallel with the preceding genitive substantive ἄρτου and "juxtaposed with a verbal noun" (λιμόν). On the use of genitive or accusative objects with ἀκούω, see 3:1 on ἀκούσατε.

λόγον. Accusative direct object of ἀκοῦσαι. With the following genitive modifier κυρίου it is definite, and, following Apollonius' corollary, both of these anarthrous nouns have the same semantic force; they are both definite (Wallace, 250). Interestingly, the corresponding Hebrew word is plural ("*words* of the Lord").

κυρίου. Subjective genitive; the head noun has an implicit verbal idea (and a cognate verb), i.e., the word spoken by the Lord.

8:12 καὶ σαλευθήσονται ὕδατα ἕως θαλάσσης, καὶ ἀπὸ βορρᾶ ἕως ἀνατολῶν περιδραμοῦνται ζητοῦντες τὸν λόγον κυρίου καὶ οὐ μὴ εὕρωσιν.

καὶ. Coordinating conjunction connecting clauses (*GELS*, 352.1.a).

σαλευθήσονται. Fut pass ind 3rd pl σαλεύω. Predictive future. The simple passive voice has no agent expressed, but the Lord is the understood agent. The third singular form of the verb is found in MS A and *L*, apparently to be consistent with the neuter plural subject (ὕδατα), and the third plural form is found in MSS B, W, and C, followed by Ziegler and R-H.

ὕδατα. Nominative subject of σαλευθήσονται. The Hebrew corresponding to this word is מִיָּם, which can be read as "waters" (so LXX), or as "from sea" (as the MT tradition). The meaning of the preceding verb is also slightly different in the Hebrew (נוע), resulting in the clause "they shall wander from sea to sea."

ἕως θαλάσσης. Spatial extent, modifying σαλευθήσονται. ἕως is functioning as a preposition with a genitive object and has the sense "up to, as far as, giving the endpoint or limit of movement" (*GELS*, 311.A.a). The endpoint of the shaking is "the sea" (θαλάσσης); it is the object of the preposition, and it is apparently included in the action ("shaking"). It is also a monadic noun and therefore definite.

ἀπὸ βορρᾶ. Source, modifying περιδραμοῦνται. The preposition ἀπό has the sense "starting from" in an ἀπό . . . ἕως construction, "marking two extreme ends of a scale" (*GELS*, 70.2.c). Points of the compass do not take the article and are definite without it (BDF §253.5); they are monadic.

ἕως ἀνατολῶν. Spatial extent, modifying περιδραμοῦνται. ἕως is functioning as a preposition with a genitive object (ἀνατολῶν) and has the sense "up to, as far as, giving the endpoint or limit of movement" in the ἀπό . . . ἕως construction (*GELS*, 311.A.a). The plural form of ἀνατολή is used for the "quarter of sunrise," or "east" (*GELS*, 46–47.2; BDF §141.2). Points of the compass do not take the article and are definite without it (BDF §253.5).

περιδραμοῦνται. Fut mid ind 3rd pl περιτρέχω. Predictive future. Kemmer (269) calls this a middle of "translational motion," i.e., "run." In this context with the prepositional prefix the verb has the idea "run about" or "be in rapid motion here and there in an area" (BDAG, 807–8.2).

ζητοῦντες. Pres act ptc nom masc pl περιτρέχω (purpose). The adverbial participle following the main verb elaborates and explains the action of the main verb (Runge, 262).

τὸν λόγον. Accusative direct object of ζητοῦντες. The article does not follow Apollonius' canon, nor is it consistent with the parallel words at the end of 8:11 (λόγον κυρίου).

κυρίου. Subjective genitive. See λόγον κυρίου in 8:11.

καί. Coordinating conjunction indicating contrast, i.e., "but" (*GELS*, 353.4). The contrast that is developed in this verse is between the inevitability of the judgment of God on the day of the Lord and the futile efforts of the people to escape that judgment and find a word from the Lord.

οὐ μὴ εὕρωσιν. Aor act subj 3rd pl εὑρίσκω. Subjunctive used with οὐ μή to express emphatic negation. It is natural to supply an implied object after this verb; I have supplied "it" in the translation, referring back to τὸν λόγον κυρίου.

8:13 ἐν τῇ ἡμέρᾳ ἐκείνῃ ἐκλείψουσιν αἱ παρθένοι αἱ καλαὶ καὶ οἱ νεανίσκοι ἐν δίψει

ἐν τῇ ἡμέρᾳ ἐκείνῃ. Temporal, modifying ἐκλείψουσιν. This exact PP is found in 2:16; 8:3 and 9. See the discussion of the phrase in 2:16 and 8:3. It also occurs in 9:11 (ἐν ἐκείνῃ τῇ ἡμέρᾳ) with only a change in the position of the demonstrative pronoun.

ἐκλείψουσιν. Fut act ind 3rd pl ἐκλείπω. Predictive future. This word has a wide range of meanings when intransitive, but the PP ἐν δίψει ("with thirst") modifying it requires that it have the sense "to lose strength" or "fail to function properly" (*GELS*, 211.II.3.a) in this context, and thus the meaning "to faint."

αἱ παρθένοι αἱ καλαὶ καὶ οἱ νεανίσκοι. Compound nominative subject of ἐκλείψουσιν. παρθένοι is a generic noun referring to a class of people, "virgins." Although this word occurs in the masculine in the NT (Rev 14:4), in the LXX it is always feminine, referring to women and girls (BDAG, 777; *GELS*, 535). It is modified by the adjective καλαί ("beautiful" *GELS*, 360.3) in the second attributive position; νεανίσκοι is a generic noun referring to a class of people, "young men."

ἐν δίψει. Causal, modifying ἐκλείψουσιν. The preposition ἐν has the sense "on account of, due to" (*GELS*, 232.11), and δίψει ("thirst") is its dative object.

8:14 οἱ ὀμνύοντες κατὰ τοῦ ἱλασμοῦ Σαμαρείας καὶ οἱ λέγοντες Ζῇ ὁ θεός σου, Δαν, καὶ ζῇ ὁ θεός σου, Βηρσαβεε· καὶ πεσοῦνται καὶ οὐ μὴ ἀναστῶσιν ἔτι.

οἱ ὀμνύοντες. Pres act ptc nom masc pl ὄμνυμι (substantival). This participle construction is in apposition to the compound subjects of the preceding clause and further identifying them, i.e., the παρθένοι and the νεανίσκοι are "those who swear."

κατὰ τοῦ ἱλασμοῦ. Oath formula, modifying οἱ ὀμνύοντες. The preposition κατά must have the sense "by invoking," i.e., swear "by" (*GELS*, 364.I.2), indicating the object the one swearing trusts. Compare 8:7 where κατά modifying ὄμνυμι likely has the sense of swearing "against" and 4:2 and 6:8, where it has the same sense as here. The genitive noun ἱλασμοῦ, which is the object of κατά, could refer to "atonement from sin" (expiation, forgiveness, propitiation; Ps 129[130 MT]:4) or to "the means of atonement, the sin offering" (Ezek 44:27); see Dines (1991, 255–57; LEH, 287; BDAG, 474). The more concrete rendering "sin-offering" is preferred, referring to the "religious ritual in Samaria" (Glenny 2013b, 145). The MT has באשמת ("by the guilt of") rather than "by the sin-offering of"; apparently the translator read the Hebrew as באשם ("by the guilt" [or "guilt-offering"]). The article with ἱλασμοῦ indicates that the offering and ritual at Samaria are more important than all others or "in a class by themselves" ("par excellence," Wallace, 222–23); the article is not used here with a monadic noun, but the noun is more than well known.

Σαμαρείας. Genitive of place, indicating the location of the ἱλασμός. Since "Samaria" always refers to the city elsewhere in Amos (3:9, 12; 4:1; 6:1), it seems reasonable to understand it the same way here. See Glenny (2013b, 145).

καί. Coordinating conjunction connecting coordinate substantival participles (*GELS*, 352.1.a).

οἱ λέγοντες. Pres act ptc nom masc pl λέγω (substantival). This participle construction is in apposition to the subjects of the preceding clause and further describes them.

Ζῇ. Pres act subj 3rd sg ζάω. This form could be an indicative or subjunctive. The indicative would signify a statement of faith or acclamation (see NETS; 2 Kgdms 22:47), and the subjunctive is the mood used in this common oath formula, "Your god lives" (Dines 1991, 255; Ruth 3:13). Since there are no other acclamations in the Twelve and there is a reference to making an oath earlier in this verse, it is more likely the two uses of this verb in 8:14 are part of oath formulas, invoking the gods in

Dan and Beersheba to guarantee their promises (see the fuller discussion in Glenny 2013b, 145–46).

ὁ θεός. Nominative subject of ζῇ.

σου. Genitive of subordination.

Δαν. Vocative of address of this indeclinable noun (BDAG, 212).

καὶ. Coordinating conjunction connecting parallel oath formulas (*GELS*, 352.1.a).

ζῇ ὁ θεός σου. See the discussion of the first occurrence of this clause above. The MT has "the way (דרך) of Beersheba," rather than "your God lives, Beersheba."

Βηρσαβεε. Vocative of address. In 5:5 the LXX translates this placename ("well of the oath"); see also Gen 26:33 and 21:31.

καὶ. Coordinating conjunction connecting coordinate clauses, ἐκλείψουσιν αἱ παρθένοι αἱ καλαὶ καὶ οἱ νεανίσκοι ἐν δίψει and πεσοῦνται (*GELS*, 352.1.a).

πεσοῦνται. Fut act ind 3rd pl πίπτω. Predictive future. The plural subjects of this verb are the subjects of the preceding articular participles, who swear and express their loyalty to the gods of Dan and Beersheba.

καὶ. Coordinating conjunction connecting coordinate clauses, πεσοῦνται and οὐ μὴ ἀναστῶσιν ἔτι (*GELS*, 352.1.a).

ἀναστῶσιν. Aor act subj 3rd pl ἀνίστημι. Subjunctive used with οὐ μή to express emphatic negation. Muraoka (§83.ca) mentions this as an example of emphatic negation with the aorist subjunctive, which is "immediately followed or preceded by a future" (πεσοῦνται); with this arrangement the aorist subjunctive takes on a predictive aspect, much like the future.

ἔτι. Used with emphatic negation, this adverb has the sense "never again" (*GELS*, 295.1.c).

Amos 9:1–7

¹I saw the Lord standing upon the altar, and he said, "Strike the place of propitiation, and the gateways will be shaken; and cut through the heads of all. And I will slay the survivors of them with a sword; any one of them who attempts to flee will never escape, and any one of them who attempts to rescue himself will never succeed. ²If they hide in Hades, from there my hand will drag them up; and if they ascend to heaven, I will bring them down. ³Even if they hide in the summit of Carmel, from there I will search them out, and I will seize them. And if they should sink from my sight into the depths of the sea, there I will command the dragon, and it will bite them. ⁴And if they go into captivity ahead of their enemies, there I will command the sword, and it will slay them; and I

will firmly set my eyes against them for the purpose of calamities and not good things." ⁵And the Lord, the Lord God, the Almighty One, he who takes hold of the land and shakes it so that all those inhabiting it mourn and the destruction of it will rise up like a river, and it will descend like the river of Egypt; ⁶he who builds his ascent into the heavens and establishes his promise on the earth; he who summons the water of the sea and pours it out on the surface of the earth, the Lord, the God, the Almighty One, is his name. ⁷"Are you not like the sons of the Ethiopians to me, sons of Israel?" says the Lord. "Did I not bring up Israel out of the land of Egypt and the foreigners out of Cappadocia and the Syrians out of the pit?"

See the introduction to the structure of this vision at the beginning of Amos 7.

9:1 Εἶδον τὸν κύριον ἐφεστῶτα ἐπὶ τοῦ θυσιαστηρίου, καὶ εἶπεν Πάταξον ἐπὶ τὸ ἱλαστήριον καὶ σεισθήσεται τὰ πρόπυλα καὶ διάκοψον εἰς κεφαλὰς πάντων· καὶ τοὺς καταλοίπους αὐτῶν ἐν ῥομφαίᾳ ἀποκτενῶ, οὐ μὴ διαφύγῃ ἐξ αὐτῶν φεύγων, καὶ οὐ μὴ διασωθῇ ἐξ αὐτῶν ἀνασῳζόμενος.

The beginning of the fifth vision is marked by asyndeton, which is normal with the introduction of a new topic (Runge, 21).

Εἶδον. Aor act ind 1st sg ὁράω. Constative aorist, presenting the action as a whole (BDF §332).

τὸν κύριον. Accusative direct object of εἶδον. This is the use of the article with a "par excellence" substantive, one that is in a class by itself and the only one deserving the appellation (see the discussion in Wallace, 222–23).

ἐφεστῶτα. Prf act ptc acc masc sg ἐφίστημι (attributive, modifying κύριος). Thackeray (§23.7 [p. 253 n. 1]) notes that this form reflects a revision to the classical form of the participle of ἵστημι "a little before the beginning of the Christian era." The intransitive verb has the sense "be present, located, in position," and in this context refers to the Lord "standing" (GELS, 343.I; see also GE, 881.2). The basic aspect of the perfect tense is past completed action with results that exist in the time of the speaker or writer (Wallace, 573–74); here the emphasis is on the present state produced by the action of the verb. Fanning (291–97) calls it the "perfect of resulting state."

ἐπὶ τοῦ θυσιαστηρίου. Location, modifying ἐφεστῶτα. The preposition ἐπί with the genitive following ἐφίστημι has several different senses in the LXX: (1) "on" or "upon" in Num 14:14; (2) "at" or "by" in Gen

24:43; Num 23:17; Obad 14; or (3) "over" in Num 23:6; Sir 23:2. "On" is the more likely rendering; it is the more common understanding of the preposition with the genitive (BDF §234.1; Dines 1991, 261–62, has "upon," and NETS has "on"). See also the discussion at 7:7 and Glenny (2013b, 148).

θυσιαστήριον could refer to an illegitimate altar (2:8; 3:14 [2x]), but "it usually refers to an altar of the true God" (Glenny 2013b, 148; see also LEH, 281 and the discussion of βωμοί at 7:9). The article is used with a well-known substantive.

εἶπεν. Aor act ind 3rd sg λέγω. Constative aorist summarizing the action.

Πάταξον. Aor act impv 2nd sg πατάσσω; a specific command (BDF §335).

ἐπὶ τὸ ἱλαστήριον. Direction, modifying πάταξον. The preposition ἐπί indicates that to which the action of the preceding imperative is directed and here refers to "hostile action" (*GELS*, 266.4.a). More specifically ἐπί indicates a "place to be hit" (*GELS*, 539.i, s.v. πατάσσω). See the discussion of this phrase in Glenny (2013b, 148) and Dines (1991, 261–62). "Normally in the LXX ἱλαστήριον (here the accusative object of ἐπί) refers to the golden cover on top of the ark ('mercy seat') in the Holy of Holies" (Glenny 2013b, 148; see the discussion on pp. 148–49); thus, it is a monadic noun, and the situation in view in the LXX is apparently in the Temple in Jerusalem. Apparently, the translator read כפרת ("the gold cover on top of the ark") and not כפתור ("capital of a pillar"), the reading in the MT (see the discussion in Glenny 2009, 250; LXX.E, 2359).

καί. Coordinating conjunction connecting clauses (*GELS*, 352.1.b), and here the conjunction introduces "a result that follows from what precedes" (BDAG, 495.1.b.ζ), which is common after a command (Sir 2:6; 3:17; Matt 4:19).

σεισθήσεται. Fut pass ind 3rd sg σείω. Predictive future. The corresponding verb is plural in the MT, but the Greek requires a collective singular with the neuter plural subject.

τὰ πρόπυλα. Nominative subject of σεισθήσεται. This architectural term ("gateways"), which has the same meaning as προπύλαια (LSJ, 1496), occurs only in the LXX here and in Zeph 1:9. It "commonly refers to gateways or entrances to both Egyptian and Greek temples" (Glenny 2013b, 149; see Herodotus, *Hist.* 2.63, 101, 121; 5.77). The article is used to identify specific πρόπυλα, perhaps in the Temple in Jerusalem; they are well known, and thus the article points them out as such.

καί. Coordinating conjunction connecting clauses (*GELS*, 352.1.b), and here the conjunction introduces "a result that follows from what precedes" (BDAG, 495.1.b.ζ); this is apparently a second result of the preceding command.

διάκοψον. Aor act impv 2nd sg διακόπτω. Specific aorist command (BDF §335). This verb is used in a similar context in Hab 3:14, and Muraoka suggests it has the sense "gash" in these two contexts (*GELS*, 152.1).

εἰς κεφαλὰς. Direction, modifying διάκοψον. The unusual use of the preposition εἰς here is debated (Dines 1991, 261; LXX.E, 2359, suggests the MT, which the Greek follows fairly closely here, is corrupt), and Brenton suggests the sense "into" ("cut through into [onto] the heads"); Muraoka (*GELS*, 152.1) and NETS render it "cut through the heads of all," apparently understanding the preposition to denote the object of the verb (see Glenny 2013b, 149). This last understanding is simplest; the Lord is apparently commanding his agent to cut through the heads of people (and the remainder of the verse supports this interpretation).

πάντων. Possessive genitive.

τοὺς καταλοίπους. Accusative direct object of ἀποκτενῶ. The article with the noun indicates it refers to a specific group, "the survivors of them" (apparently the survivors out of the "all" mentioned in the previous phrase).

αὐτῶν. Partitive genitive.

ἐν ῥομφαίᾳ. Instrumental, modifying ἀποκτενῶ. The preposition ἐν has the sense "by means of, by using as an instrument" (*GELS*, 231.6.a).

ἀποκτενῶ. Fut act ind 1st sg ἀποκτείνω. Predictive future.

οὐ μὴ διαφύγῃ. Aor act subj 3rd sg διαφεύγω. Subjunctive used with οὐ μή to express emphatic negation (see 2:12). The sense of this word is "to manage to escape" (*GELS*, 162), and here it is parallel with διασῴζω. The simple form of the verb, which occurs later in the verse, has more the sense of attempting to flee or escape (see φεύγων below). This verb and the following cognate participle follow the pattern of finite verb and participle from the same verb that is found in the Hebrew: לֹא יָנוּס לָהֶם נָס (Dines 2013, 401).

ἐξ αὐτῶν. Partitive, modifying φεύγων; the preposition ἐκ "indicates and entity out of which a component is singled out ('partitive')" (*GELS*, 201.2).

φεύγων. Pres act ptc nom masc pl φεύγω (substantival). This is a generic use of the substantival participle, referring to a class (similar to a gnomic present participle). There is a "high frequency" of anarthrous participles functioning substantivally in the LXX (Muraoka §31.b). See the similar substantival use of this participle in Obad 14. These two substantival uses of a participle form of φεύγω both have the sense "attempting to flee" (so NETS; see *GELS*, 712.a), and in Amos 9:1 it is clear the attempt does not succeed.

οὐ μὴ διασωθῇ. Aor pass subj 3rd sg διασῴζω. Subjunctive used with οὐ μή to express emphatic negation (see 2:12).

ἐξ αὐτῶν. Partitive, modifying the following substantival participle; the preposition ἐκ "indicates an entity out of which a component is singled out ('partitive')" (*GELS*, 201.2).

ἀνασῳζόμενος. Pres mid ptc nom masc sg ἀνασῴζω (substantival); the middle form of this verb often has the sense of attempting to save oneself (*GELS*, 46.2 gives the sense of the middle as "to escape in an attempt to rescue oneself"; see Obad 14). This is a generic use of the substantival participle, referring to a class (similar to a gnomic present participle). There is a "high frequency" of anarthrous participles functioning substantivally in the LXX (Muraoka §31.b).

9:2 ἐὰν κατορυγῶσιν εἰς ᾅδου, ἐκεῖθεν ἡ χείρ μου ἀνασπάσει αὐτούς· καὶ ἐὰν ἀναβῶσιν εἰς τὸν οὐρανόν, ἐκεῖθεν κατάξω αὐτούς·

ἐάν. Conditional particle, introducing the protasis of a future more vivid condition (Smyth §2321–25; BDF §373). There are five of these conditional constructions in 9:2–4; the two conditions in 9:2 are merely hypothetical (see Wallace, 696–99, for the discussion of what he calls "third class conditions"), and they are coordinate, joined by καί. Beginning the verse with asyndeton is consistent with the introduction of a new thought (Runge, 20–23).

κατορυγῶσιν. Aor act subj 3rd pl κατορύσσω. This is an aorist subjunctive in a future more vivid condition (see ἐάν above). On the second aorist passive form of this verb, see *GELS* (392; LSJ, 930; and Thackeray §21.4 [p. 237]). This verb (10x in the LXX) can have the sense "dig down" (Dines 1991, 269), but its more common sense is to "bury" (LSJ, 930; LEH, 251; *GELS*, 392; Gen 48:7; Ezek 39:11–13; NETS). Normally when the verb has the sense "bury," it has an object, but twice elsewhere in the LXX it does not (Josh 24:32; Jer 32:33), as also seems to be the case here. Some LXX renderings that have the sense "bury" make the verb reflexive (LXX.D), and some make the verb passive "be buried" (NETS); NETS adds an implied object in the translation of Josh 24:32. The sense of the verb here seems to be to dig down to hide themselves, which I have rendered "hide." The Hebrew gives the impression of a living person breaking through to Sheol (יחתרו; "dig"), but the Greek has the more common idea of one going to the realm of the dead after death. This Greek reading is found in R-H and Ziegler, but MS B and

Swete have κατακρυβῶσιν; perhaps the copyist of B was influenced by the first verb in 9:3 (see there).

εἰς ᾄδου. Locative, modifying κατορυγῶσιν. In this context the preposition εἰς is "synonymous with ἐν" (*GELS*, 197.8; BDAG, 289.1.a.δ). Because εἰς takes the accusative case, a word like οἶκον must be supplied, i.e., in the house of Hades (BDF §162, 8; LSJ, 36.I.1, s.v. ᾄδης; BDAG, 19.1). In this construction, ᾄδου functions as a genitive of possession (in the idiom εἰς ᾄδου).

ἐκεῖθεν. Adverb of place (BDAG, 301). Here it indicates "a point from which a physical movement starts" (*GELS*, 207.a). This word begins the apodosis of the condition, and as with all conditions, if the protasis is true the apodosis follows (Smyth §2280).

ἡ χείρ. Nominative subject of ἀνασπάσει. The Lord's χείρ ("hand") is an anthropomorphism, representing his power and authority.

μου. Possessive genitive. Head nouns modified by possessive pronouns are normally articular.

ἀνασπάσει. Fut act ind 3rd sg ἀνασπάω. The future tense in the apodosis of a future more vivid condition expresses a future consequence of the condition, which will happen if the condition is met (BDF §2326.a). And here with the Lord speaking, if the condition is met, the future tense has the force of a predictive future.

αὐτούς. Accusative direct object ἀνασπάσει.

καί. Coordinating conjunction connecting coordinate conditional sentences (*GELS*, 352.1.b). It is possible that καί is functioning adverbially with ἐάν, and the two words have the sense "even if" (so NETS; see also BDAG, 267.1.c.α; *GELS*, 354.8.b); however, if that were the case, then these words would describe an extreme case or invite comparison with something less plausible in the preceding (*GELS*, 354.8.a), and in this verse the two conditional sentences are coordinate, giving opposite hyperbolic extremes.

ἐάν. Conditional particle, introducing the protasis of a future more vivid condition (Smyth §2321–25; BDF §373).

ἀναβῶσιν. Aor act subj 3rd pl ἀναβαίνω. This is an aorist subjunctive in a future more vivid condition (see ἐάν above).

εἰς τὸν οὐρανόν. Direction, modifying the preceding verb. The preposition εἰς has the sense "toward a goal which is inside an area or in the direction of it," used here with a verb of movement (*GELS*, 196.1). No corresponding preposition is required in Hebrew. The singular of this noun refers to "space far above the earth" and together with the γῆ constitutes "the whole material universe" (*GELS*, 513.1; see LXX Gen 1:1); thus, it is a monadic noun, like γῆ.

ἐκεῖθεν. Adverb of place (BDAG, 301). See earlier comments on this adverb in 9:2.

κατάξω. Fut act ind 1st sg κατάγω. The future tense in the apodosis of a future more vivid condition expresses a future consequence of the condition, which will happen if the condition is met (BDF §2326.a). And here with the Lord speaking, if the condition is met, the future tense has the force of a predictive future.

αὐτούς. Accusative direct object of κατάξω.

9:3 ἐὰν ἐγκρυβῶσιν εἰς τὴν κορυφὴν τοῦ Καρμήλου, ἐκεῖθεν ἐξερευνήσω καὶ λήμψομαι αὐτούς· καὶ ἐὰν καταδύσωσιν ἐξ ὀφθαλμῶν μου εἰς τὰ βάθη τῆς θαλάσσης, ἐκεῖ ἐντελοῦμαι τῷ δράκοντι καὶ δήξεται αὐτούς·

ἐάν. Conditional particle, introducing the protasis of a future more vivid condition (Smyth §2321–25; BDF §373). The two conditional sentences in this verse are parallel, contrasting two extreme places of height and depth on this earth, and thus joined by καί. These two related conditional sentences introduce a new thought in this verse, and asyndeton is often found when a new thought is introduced (Runge, 20–23).

ἐγκρυβῶσιν. Aor pass subj 3rd pl ἐγκρύπτω. This is an aorist subjunctive in a future more vivid condition (see ἐάν above). The verb has the sense "to conceal; put out of view" (GELS, 188). MS B, followed by Swete, has ἐγκατακρυβῶσιν; cf. 9:2. MSS A, W, R-H, and Ziegler have ἐγκρυβῶσιν. The reading in B appears to be a conflation of its reading in 9:2 (κατακρυβῶσιν) and this verb.

εἰς τὴν κορυφὴν. Location, modifying ἐγκρυβῶσιν. The preposition εἰς is "synonymous with ἐν" (GELS, 197.8; BDAG, 289.1.a.δ). The four words that comprise the object of the preposition (τὴν κορυφὴν τοῦ Καρμήλου) are also found in 1:2, functioning as a subject.

τοῦ Καρμήλου. Partitive (sometimes called wholative) genitive (BDF §164), denoting the whole mountain of which the "summit" is a part. The "summit of Carmel" is a geographical extremity contrasting the "depths of the sea" later in the verse. The use of an article with the head noun and genitive modifier follows Apollonius' canon, but both nouns are monadic and thus normally articular. Καρμήλος occurs five times in the LXX (see also 1:2; Mic 7:14; Isa 32:16; Jer 27:19), and it always has an article.

ἐκεῖθεν. Adverb of place (BDAG, 301). Here it indicates "a point from which a physical movement starts" (GELS, 207.a). See also the two occurrences in 9:2. This word begins the apodosis of the condition, and, as with all conditions, if the protasis is true, the apodosis follows (Smyth §2280).

ἐξερευνήσω. Fut act ind 1st sg ἐξερευνάω. The verb has the sense "search, search out" (*GELS*, 249.1). The future tense in the apodosis of a future more vivid condition expresses a future consequence of the condition, which will happen if the condition is met (BDF §2326.a). And here with the Lord speaking, if the condition is met, the future tense has the force of a predictive future.

καὶ. Coordinating conjunction, connecting coordinate verbs (*GELS*, 352.1.a).

λήμψομαι. Fut act ind 1st sg λαμβάνω. The sense of λαμβάνω in this context is "seize" (see *GELS*, 423.5). See the coordinate verb ἐξερευνήσω above.

αὐτούς. Accusative direct object of the two preceding verbs.

καὶ ἐάν. See the discussion of these two words at the beginning of the second conditional sentence in 9:2.

καταδύσωσιν. Aor act subj 3rd pl καταδύω [καταδύνω]. An aorist subjunctive in a future more vivid condition (see ἐάν in 9:2 [2x] and 9:3). The basic sense of this verb is "to sink, go down" or "to cause to sink" (LSJ, 890), but here it has the idea "to slink away and lie hidden" (*GELS*, 371.2). Thackeray (§21.1) uses this verb as an example of the infringement of the first aorist endings into the sphere of the old second aorist endings.

ἐξ ὀφθαλμῶν. Separation, modifying καταδύσωσιν. The preposition ἐξ (form of ἐκ before a vowel) "indicates dissociation" by removal (*GELS*, 201.1.a). ὀφθαλμῶν, the genitive object of ἐξ, is an anthropomorphism, referring to the Lord's sight or awareness. See 9:4.

μου. Possessive genitive, referring to the Lord.

εἰς τὰ βάθη. Direction, modifying καταδύσωσιν. The preposition εἰς has the sense "toward a goal that is inside an area" (*GELS*, 196.1).

τῆς θαλάσσης. Partitive (sometimes called wholative) genitive, modifying the head noun (BDF §164), i.e., the deep parts of the whole sea. The employment of articles follows Apollonius' canon, and θαλάσσης is also a monadic noun.

ἐκεῖ. Adverb with the sense "in that place already mentioned" (*GELS*, 207.1), i.e., "the depths of the sea."

ἐντελοῦμαι. Fut mid ind 1st sg ἐντέλλω. This verb is always in the middle voice in biblical literature (*GELS*, 240; BDAG, 339). The future tense in the apodosis of a future more vivid condition expresses a future consequence of the condition, which will happen if the condition is met (BDF §2326.a). And here with the Lord speaking, if the condition is met, the future tense has the force of a predictive future. The middle seems to be an indirect middle in that the will of the commander is expressed in the command "I will command."

τῷ δράκοντι. Dative of person commanded. "Verbs of commanding prefer the dative of the person addressed with the infinitive [containing the contents of the command]" (BDF §409.1). Here the content of the command is contained in the following clause (see below). See Glenny (2013b, 150–51) on the wide-ranging use of this noun in the LXX (34x). It is often rendered "dragon" (e.g., all four times it occurs in Bel and the Dragon [23, 25, 27, 28 in LXX and Th]); it is sometimes the sea personified as a dragon of chaos (Job 7:12) or a many-headed dragon that God destroys (Ps 73:13–14). It is possible early Christians could have understood it to refer to Satan in this context (*TDNT*, 2:283; see also Ps 103:26; Job 26:13; Isa 27:1; Ezek 29:3; 32:2). The article is employed here with the monadic noun.

καί. Coordinating conjunction, connecting clauses (*GELS*, 351.1.b). The clause following this conjunction reveals the content of the Lord's command, i.e., "bite them" (see ἐντέλλεται; there is a similar construction in 9:4 and 9:9; Muraoka §81.a; *GELS*, 241.1, s.v. ἐντέλλομαι).

δήξεται. Fut mid ind 3rd sg δάκνω. Predictive future. This verb has the sense "bite, harm, sting" (LSJ, 367), and the middle voice is used (esp. in the future tense), apparently because the subject's will or intention is involved or it is a two-participant event (Kemmer, 149, 269).

αὐτούς. Accusative direct object of δήξεται.

9:4 καὶ ἐὰν πορευθῶσιν ἐν αἰχμαλωσίᾳ πρὸ προσώπου τῶν ἐχθρῶν αὐτῶν, ἐκεῖ ἐντελοῦμαι τῇ ῥομφαίᾳ καὶ ἀποκτενεῖ αὐτούς· καὶ στηριῶ τοὺς ὀφθαλμούς μου ἐπ᾽ αὐτοὺς εἰς κακὰ καὶ οὐκ εἰς ἀγαθά.

καί. Coordinating conjunction, connecting coordinate clauses (*GELS*, 352.1.b). The clause that follows is the last of five consecutive conditional sentences, and after the four preceding hyperbolic examples, this condition is not an "extreme case" (*GELS*, 354.8), as one might expect with an adverbial use of καί with ἐάν, i.e., "even if" (so NETS); this is rather a coordinate use of the conjunction.

ἐάν. Conditional particle, introducing the protasis of a future more vivid condition (Smyth §2321–25; BDF §373). The condition presented is entirely possible.

πορευθῶσιν. Aor mid subj 3rd pl πορεύομαι. This is an aorist subjunctive in a future more vivid condition (see ἐάν in 9:2 [2x] and 9:3). This intransitive verb occurs only in the so-called passive-voice forms in the aorist (θη-) in biblical literature (BDAG, 853); it is a verb of "translational motion" (Kemmer, 269), and these types of verbs are typically expressed with middle-voice forms. The -θη- passives often have middle meanings (Aubrey, 563–625; Caragounis, 153; and see the comments in the Introduction).

ἐν αἰχμαλωσίᾳ. Location, modifying πορευθῶσιν. The preposition ἐν has the sense "into (of movement or transformation)," and it is equal to εἰς (*GELS*, 233.17); αἰχμαλωσίᾳ ("captivity") is the dative object of ἐν.

πρὸ προσώπου τῶν ἐχθρῶν αὐτῶν. Location, also modifying πορευθῶσιν. The preposition πρό has the sense "in front of, ahead of," indicating place (*GELS*, 583.II; NETS); Dines (1991, 270) renders it "in the sight of," and Brenton has "before the face of"; however, the idea of "face" or "sight" is not required here and is awkward (see Glenny 2013b, 151).

τῶν ἐχθρῶν. Possessive genitive. This adjective, which has the sense of "hostile, inimical," is mostly used as a substantive in the LXX (*GELS*, 310), and it is sometimes modified by "the genitive of the person who is the object of the enmity" (BDAG, 419.2.b.β).

αὐτῶν. Objective genitive.

ἐκεῖ. Adverb; see 7:12 and 9:3.

ἐντελοῦμαι. Fut mid ind 1st sg ἐντέλλω; see the same form and usage in 9:3.

τῇ ῥομφαίᾳ. Dative of person or thing commanded. The personified "sword" is the Lord's agent and represents judgment by "warfare, bloodshed, and violence" (see Glenny 2013b, 151). "Verbs of commanding prefer the dative of the person [or thing] addressed with the infinitive [containing the contents of the command]" (BDF §409.1). The content of the command is contained in the following clause (see below). The article functions like a possessive pronoun ("my").

καὶ. Coordinating conjunction, connecting clauses (*GELS*, 352.1.b). The clause following the conjunction is the content of the Lord's command (see ἐντέλλεται; there is a similar construction in 9:3 and 9; Muraoka §80.a; *GELS*, 241.1, s.v. ἐντέλλομαι).

ἀποκτενεῖ. Fut act ind 3rd sg ἀποκτείνω. Predictive future, i.e., "will kill, slay."

αὐτούς. Accusative direct object of ἀποκτενεῖ.

καὶ. Coordinating conjunction, connecting coordinate clauses (*GELS*, 352.1.b). In this clause, which is parallel with the apodosis in the first clause in 9:4, the Lord strongly affirms by the use of anthropomorphic language that he will fix his attention on Israel for judgment.

στηριῶ. Fut act ind 1st sg στηρίζω. Predictive future. See the similar use of the verb in Prov 16:30 and Jer 24:6; *GELS* (636.1) suggests the sense of the verb in these three contexts is "to place firmly and determinedly."

τοὺς ὀφθαλμούς. Accusative direct object of στηριῶ. The anthropomorphism refers to the Lord's awareness and attention (see also 9:3). It is normal for a head noun modified by a possessive pronoun to be articular. The MT has the singular "eye" (עֵינִי) here, but the translator rendered it with a plural, as he did the dual Hebrew form in 9:3; the spelling of the two forms is identical (עֵינַי), and perhaps he did not distinguish the difference.

μου. Possessive genitive.

ἐπ᾽ αὐτούς. Direction, modifying στηριῶ. The preposition ἐπί "indicates one to whom or that to which action, attention, thought, emotion, utterance, etc. are directed" (*GELS*, 266.III.4); here it has the meaning "against them."

εἰς κακὰ καὶ οὐκ εἰς ἀγαθά. Purpose. Coordinate PPs modifying στηριῶ. The preposition εἰς in the parallel phrases "indicates a target, aim, or focus" (*GELS*, 196.3). The two coordinate accusative objects of εἰς (κακά and ἀγαθά), which are neuter plural, probably indicate acts or experiences of calamity and good, i.e., "calamities not good things." Since objects of prepositions are often definite without an article, the anarthrous adjective need not be indefinite and qualitative; the word could refer to concrete experiences. Furthermore, anarthrous Greek abstract nouns are often definite, and there is much freedom concerning the use or nonuse of the article with them (see Robertson, 758; on 794 he writes, "No vital difference was felt between articular and anarthrous abstract nouns"; and Wallace, 249–50, comments that abstract nouns "are commonly anarthrous though they are not indefinite"). The negative particle (οὐκ) is the form of οὐ before a vowel with smooth breathing.

9:5 καὶ κύριος κύριος ὁ θεὸς ὁ παντοκράτωρ, ὁ ἐφαπτόμενος τῆς γῆς καὶ σαλεύων αὐτήν, καὶ πενθήσουσιν πάντες οἱ κατοικοῦντες αὐτήν, καὶ ἀναβήσεται ὡς ποταμὸς συντέλεια αὐτῆς καὶ καταβήσεται ὡς ποταμὸς Αἰγύπτου·

Verses 5–6 comprise the third doxology in Amos (see also 4:13; 5:7–9). The doxology or hymn is clearly marked by the change from the Lord speaking (first person) to a description of the Lord (third person) and by the use of participles to describe the works of the Lord. The last half of 9:6 is exactly the same as the last half of 5:8. The end of the doxology is also marked by the shift to the Lord's direct speech in 9:7.

κύριος. Nominative and part of the divine appellation, describing the Lord, who is the subject of this doxology; this word corresponds to the Hebrew word אֲדֹנָי, and this is the only time this name for God (κύριος κύριος ὁ θεὸς ὁ παντοκράτωρ) is found in the Septuagint. The whole appellation at the beginning of the verse could be considered a nominative absolute, which is not part of the main clause of the verse. See 5:3 on the repetition of κύριος; it is not found in Ziegler's text, but it is in MSS B, W, V, A, Q, Swete, and R-H.

κύριος ὁ θεὸς ὁ παντοκράτωρ. This phrase recurs ten times in Amos (3:13; 4:13; 5:8, 14, 15, 16, 27; 9:5, 6, 15) and three other times in the Twelve (Hos 12:6; Nah 3:5; Zech 10:3); see the discussion of it in 3:13. Here it corresponds to הצבאות יהוה.

ὁ ἐφαπτόμενος τῆς γῆς καὶ σαλεύων αὐτήν. This phrase is in apposition to the divine appellation at the beginning of the verse. The two substantival participles form a Granville Sharp construction, with both referring to the Lord. This rule applies when two substantives are linked by καί and governed by a single article, providing the substantives are not plural, impersonal, or proper nouns (see Wallace, 270–77).

ὁ ἐφαπτόμενος. Pres mid ptc nom masc sg ἐφάπτω (substantival). Nominative in apposition to the divine appellation at the beginning of the verse. This verb is always middle voice in the LXX (Amos 6:3; 2 Macc 7:1), and in this verse it has the sense "to hold fast to" (*GELS*, 308.1) and thus is a reflexive, indirect middle (Kemmer, 268). The present tense could have a future sense, but more likely it should be understood as describing something the Lord customarily or repeatedly does (possibly iterative); the sense is not gnomic (proverbial, timeless). The article with the substantive participle is individualizing. This verb normally takes its object in the genitive case.

τῆς γῆς. Genitive complement of ἐφαπτόμενος. The article is normal with a monadic noun. This noun can have several different referents; here, in light of the following description of its inhabitants (πάντες οἱ κατοικοῦντες αὐτήν), it probably refers to the "sphere of human inhabitation" (*GELS*, 129.4.b).

καί. Coordinating conjunction, connecting coordinate substantival participles in a Granville Sharp construction (*GELS*, 352.1.a).

σαλεύων. Pres act ptc nom masc sg σαλεύω (substantival). The participle appears in a Granville Sharp construction and in apposition to the divine appellation at the beginning of the verse. The present tense could have a future sense, but more likely it should be understood as describing something the Lord customarily or repeatedly does (possibly iterative); the sense is not gnomic (proverbial, timeless).

αὐτήν. Accusative direct object of σαλεύων and referring to the preceding γῆς.

καί. Coordinating conjunction, connecting coordinate clauses (*GELS*, 352.1.b). The following clauses describe the consequences of the Lord's actions described by the preceding participles (*GELS*, 354.9).

πενθήσουσιν. Fut act ind 3rd pl πενθέω. Predictive future ("will mourn").

πάντες. Nominative adjective modifying the following substantival participle. For this use of πᾶς (followed by an article and plural nominative, meaning "all the . . ."), see Muraoka (§38.b.i).

οἱ κατοικοῦντες. Pres act ptc nom masc pl κατοικέω. Substantival participle with the article, functioning as subject. The plural present participle of κατοικέω is often used substantivally to refer to the "inhabitants" (permanent residents) of a place.

αὐτήν. Accusative direct object of κατοικοῦντες, referring to the preceding γῆς.

καὶ ἀναβήσεται ὡς ποταμὸς συντέλεια αὐτῆς καὶ καταβήσεται ὡς ποταμὸς Αἰγύπτου. This clause is exactly the same as the end of 8:8, with the exception that the pronoun αὐτῆς (here, an objective genitive) is not found in 8:8.

9:6 ὁ οἰκοδομῶν εἰς τὸν οὐρανὸν ἀνάβασιν αὐτοῦ καὶ τὴν ἐπαγγελίαν αὐτοῦ ἐπὶ τῆς γῆς θεμελιῶν, ὁ προσκαλούμενος τὸ ὕδωρ τῆς θαλάσσης καὶ ἐκχέων αὐτὸ ἐπὶ πρόσωπον τῆς γῆς· κύριος ὁ θεὸς ὁ παντοκράτωρ ὄνομα αὐτῷ.

ὁ οἰκοδομῶν. Pres act ptc nom masc sg οἰκοδομέω (substantival). Another participle in apposition to the divine appellation at the beginning of 9:5, continuing the string of these in the doxology. The present tense ("he who builds") should probably be understood as timeless (gnomic). The LXX has four participles in this verse, describing the work of the Lord and rendering two finite verbs and two participles in the Hebrew.

εἰς τὸν οὐρανὸν. Direction, modifying ὁ οἰκοδομῶν. The preposition εἰς has the sense "towards a goal which is inside an area or in the direction of it" (*GELS*, 196.1). The object of the preposition (οὐρανόν; "heaven") is much more often singular than plural (only 8 percent) in the LXX; it refers to "the space far above the earth" (*GELS*, 513.a); NETS renders it "sky."

ἀνάβασιν. Accusative direct object of οἰκοδομῶν. In the doxology in 4:13 the Lord is described as treading on the earth; in 9:6 he is involved in both heaven and earth. The ἀνάβασις is apparently his means of ascending from earth to heaven (LXX.E, II, 2360), not "his upper chambers" (מעלותו) in heaven, as in the MT. The monadic, anarthrous Greek noun is definite; the pronoun modifying it also contributes to its definiteness.

αὐτοῦ. Possessive genitive.

καί. Coordinating conjunction, connecting coordinate phrases (*GELS*, 352.1.b).

τὴν ἐπαγγελίαν. Accusative direct object of θεμελιῶν. The position of the object at the beginning of the clause emphasizes it. The Hebrew word corresponding to ἐπαγγελίαν in the MT is אגדה ("vault" in NRSV), which was apparently understood to be a *hiphil* form of the verb נגד, resulting in the LXX rendering, meaning "promise" (see the discussion in Glenny 2009b, 83–84); see also the use of the related word ἀπαγγέλλω ("proclaim, announce") in the doxology in 4:13. The article appears with a monadic noun; it is also common to have an article with a head noun modified by a possessive pronoun.

αὐτοῦ. Subjective genitive; the Lord is the one promising.

ἐπὶ τῆς γῆς. Locative, modifying θεμελιῶν. The preposition ἐπί has the sense "situated, moving, happening or performed on the surface of" (*GELS*, 263.I.2). In parallel with "heaven" in the preceding clause, the γῆ apparently refers to the "earth" and not the land of Israel (see Glenny 2013b, 153, and 2009, 84). The article is frequently used with monadic nouns, like γῆ.

θεμελιῶν. Pres act ptc nom masc sg θεμελιόω (substantival). Another substantival participle in apposition to the divine appellation at the beginning of the verse. The article at the beginning of the previous clause modifies the parallel participles in both clauses. The present tense should probably be understood as timeless (gnomic). The sense of this word is "to set up on a firm basis," thus "establish" (*GELS*, 326).

ὁ προσκαλούμενος τὸ ὕδωρ τῆς θαλάσσης καὶ ἐκχέων αὐτὸ ἐπὶ πρόσωπον τῆς γῆς· κύριος ὁ θεὸς ὁ παντοκράτωρ ὄνομα αὐτῷ. See the discussion of these words in 5:8b. In the R-H edition of the LXX, these words are exactly the same as 5:8b, with only one exception; the object of the preposition ἐπί in 5:8 is genitive (προσώπου), and in 9:6 the object is accusative (πρόσωπον). There is probably little difference in meaning. With the accusative in 9:6, ἐπί could indicate a "movement from a higher position on to something, descending on to something" (*GELS*, 266.1.b), while with the genitive in 5:8 is probably a more general idea, indicating the surface on which the action takes place (*GELS*, 263.I.2). In both contexts there are MSS that have the other reading; in 9:6 the genitive is found in MSS A, Q, and L. The exact Greek name for the Lord at the end of 6:6 (κύριος ὁ θεὸς ὁ παντοκράτωρ) occurs ten times in Amos and only three times elsewhere in the LXX (Hos 12:6; Nah 3:5; Zech 10:3). See the discussion of it at 3:13; here it corresponds to the single word יהוה. MSS B, W, V, and Swete have the title κύριος παντοκράτωρ.

9:7 οὐχ ὡς υἱοὶ Αἰθιόπων ὑμεῖς ἐστε ἐμοί, υἱοὶ Ισραηλ; λέγει κύριος. οὐ τὸν Ισραηλ ἀνήγαγον ἐκ γῆς Αἰγύπτου καὶ τοὺς ἀλλοφύλους ἐκ Καππαδοκίας καὶ τοὺς Σύρους ἐκ βόθρου;

οὐχ. The negative at the beginning of the sentence anticipates a positive answer to the rhetorical question. Asyndeton is often found where there is the introduction of a new thought or a change in topic, as seems to be the case here (Runge, 20–23).

ὡς. The comparative particle introduces the predicate in the equative sentence (*GELS*, 748.7.a), and it introduces the perspective from which the subject is "to be viewed or understood as to character, function, or role" (BDAG, 1104–5.3).

υἱοὶ. Nominative in comparative phrase with ὡς. Muraoka (*GELS*, 748.6, s.v. ὡς) comments that in the LXX "in similes the noun following ὡς is usually anarthrous," although here with the genitive modifier, υἱοί is definite.

Αἰθιόπων. Genitive of relationship (BDF §162).

ὑμεῖς. Nominative subject of ἐστε.

ἐστε. Pres act ind 2nd pl εἰμί. The state described by the verb is gnomic, a timeless, general state. The original reading of B is future tense (ἔσται), but all modern editions and B[ab] have the present tense.

ἐμοί. Ethical dative. Here it is "denoting the interest of the speaker" (Smyth §1486; see also Wallace, 146–47). The genitive ἐμοῦ is the reading in MS B and Swete.

υἱοὶ. Nominative for a vocative of direct address (BDF §147; Conybeare and Stock §50).

Ισραηλ. Genitive of relationship (BDF §162). Although an indeclinable proper noun, Ισραηλ functions as a genitive here.

λέγει. Pres act ind 3rd sg λέγω. Introductory formula use of the present tense, emphasizing the continuing results of the Lord speaking in the past (his words still have relevance, like an OT quotation in the NT; see Eph 4:8; 5:14; Wallace, 532–33).

κύριος. Nominative subject of λέγει.

οὐ. The negative at the beginning of this sentence anticipates a positive answer to the rhetorical question.

τὸν Ισραηλ. Accusative direct object of ἀνήγαγον, and article with this monadic noun; Ισραηλ normally has an article.

ἀνήγαγον. Aor act ind 1st sg ἀνάγω. Consummative aorist, stressing the cessation of the action.

ἐκ γῆς. Separation, modifying ἀνήγαγον. The preposition ἐκ indicates dissociation from (*GELS*, 201.1) or separation from (BDAG,

295–96.1) the object of the preposition (γῆς); this differs from the simple idea of origin or source.

Αἰγύπτου. Genitive of apposition, clarifying which land is in view (Wallace, 95). This same phrase is found in 2:10 and 3:1; see the discussion at 2:10.

καὶ. Coordinating conjunction, connecting coordinate clauses (*GELS*, 352.1.b); the verb in the previous clause (ἀνήγαγον) is understood in the following two clauses.

τοὺς ἀλλοφύλους. Accusative direct object of the implied ἀνήγαγον. Hebrew has פלשתיים ("Philistines"), and this is the normal rendering of that word in the LXX; this common Greek word has the sense "of another tribe, race" (*GELS*, 29; LEH, 29); see 1:8. This is the use of the article with an ethnic group (Muraoka §5.cae).

ἐκ Καππαδοκίας. Source (*GELS*, 201–2.5.a), modifying an implied ἀνήγαγον. Hebrew has "Caphtor" (כפתור) instead of "Cappadocia" (Καππαδοκίας) for the object of the preposition. Cappadocia is apparently the plateau area in central Asia Minor. See Glenny (2009, 174–76).

τοὺς Σύρους. Accusative direct object of the implied ἀνήγαγον; ethnic groups are usually articular (Muraoka §5.cae).

ἐκ βόθρου. Source (*GELS*, 201–2.5.a), modifying an implied ἀνήγαγον. The genitive object of the preposition (βόθρου) has the sense "a hollowed out area in the ground" (BDAG, 180) and is often rendered "pit" in this context (*GELS*, 120); Hebrew has "Kir" (קיר), which the translator may not have known and renders in 1:5 with ἐπίκλητος ("called" or perhaps "foreign" in that context); see 1:5; Glenny (2009, 64–67); and Dines (1991, 274–82).

Amos 9:8–15

⁸"Behold, the eyes of the Lord God are upon the kingdom of sinners, and I will destroy it from the face of the earth; except that I will not destroy completely the house of Jacob," says the Lord. ⁹"For behold I will give an order and I will winnow the house of Israel among all the nations, just as [grain] is winnowed with a winnowing fan, and destruction shall never fall upon the land. ¹⁰All the sinners of my people will perish by the sword who say, 'Calamities will never approach nor ever be upon us.' ¹¹In that day I will raise up the tent of David, which has fallen, and I will build up the collapsed part of it, and I will raise up the ruined parts of it, and I will build it up as in the remote past ¹²so that the remnant of people and all the nations upon whom my name is called upon them may seek [me]," says the Lord, the God who accomplishes these things. ¹³"Behold, days are coming," says the Lord, "when the reaping shall last

up to the vintage, and the grapes shall ripen at seedtime, and the mountains shall drip sweetness, and all the hills shall be thickly planted. ¹⁴And I will bring back the captivity of my people Israel, and they will build the demolished cities, and they will inhabit [them], and they will plant vineyards, and they will drink their wine, and they will plant gardens, and they will eat their fruit. ¹⁵And I will plant them upon their land, and they will never again be dragged out of their land, which I gave to them," says the Lord, the God, the Almighty One.

LXX Amos 9:8–15, which is made up of two parts (9:8–10 and 11–15), comprises the final unit of the book. In these verses the judgment theme that dominated the preceding (esp. 7:1–9:7) is replaced by hope.

9:8 Ἰδοὺ οἱ ὀφθαλμοὶ κυρίου τοῦ θεοῦ ἐπὶ τὴν βασιλείαν τῶν ἁμαρτωλῶν καὶ ἐξαρῶ αὐτὴν ἀπὸ προσώπου τῆς γῆς· πλὴν ὅτι οὐκ εἰς τέλος ἐξαρῶ τὸν οἶκον Ιακωβ, λέγει κύριος.

Ἰδοὺ. A presentative particle that draws attention to what follows (*GELS*, 337.b; BDAG, 468); here it is introducing a prophetic pronouncement. The form is aor mid impv 2nd sg of εἶδον, accented on the ultima when used as a particle.

οἱ ὀφθαλμοὶ. Nominative subject of an implied copula. See 9:4 also on the eyes of the Lord. The use of the article is individualizing or particularizing, making the noun definite.

κυρίου. Possessive genitive, modifying ὀφθαλμοί.

τοῦ θεοῦ. Genitive in simple apposition to κυρίου. The construction without the article modifying κυρίου does not follow Apollonius' canon, but this is one of the exceptions to the canon Robertson (780) mentions: "[T]he genitive may be anarthrous if it is a proper noun." Muraoka (§5.b) discusses the use or absence of the article with κύριος and demonstrates it is normally anarthrous in the LXX (although proper nouns are always definite); he states that "the articular κύριος is rather infrequent in the nominative case" (18). The phrase κύριος ὁ θεός (in various cases) occurs eighteen times in Amos in the R-H text, and κύριος is always anarthrous; here it corresponds to אדני יהוה. See the discussion of the first occurrence of this phrase in Amos in 3:7.

ἐπὶ τὴν βασιλείαν. Spatial, modifying the understood equative verb in the clause. The preposition ἐπί indicates one to whom or that to which attention is directed (*GELS*, 266.III.4). It could have the sense "against" here as in 9:4, but that sense is less likely here. The noun βασιλεία could refer to a particular kingdom and then the article would be individualizing, or it could be generic, referring to the class of sinful kingdoms. The latter is more likely here, in contrast with τὸν οἶκον Ιακωβ in the next clause, which will be treated differently.

τῶν ἁμαρτωλῶν. Genitive of possession or, more likely, subjective genitive. With a verbal noun serving as the head noun (here related to the verb βασιλεύω), the category of subjective genitive takes precedence (i.e., "the kingdom ruled by sinners" or "the kingdom where sinners are in authority"); see the helpful discussion in Wallace (81–82). This plural adjective is functioning as a substantive ("sinners"), as it does most of the time in the LXX (*GELS*, 31.b), and the use of articles in this phrase is consistent with Apollonius' canon. The MT has "upon the sinful kingdom" (בממלכה החטאה), which could be taken to be an abstract idea, but the Greek is more concrete with its "upon the kingdom of the sinners."

ἐξαρῶ. Fut act ind 1st sg ἐξαίρω. Predictive future. In this verse (2x) this verb has the sense "to remove, get rid of, efface, obliterate" (*GELS*, 244.4; see also Muraoka 1990, 31–32), and I have rendered it "destroy" (see this verb also later in the verse).

αὐτήν. Accusative direct object of ἐξαρῶ, referring back to βασιλείαν and "the kingdom of sinners."

ἀπὸ προσώπου. Separation, modifying ἐξαίρω. The preposition ἀπό has the sense "away from ('removal or dissociation')" (*GELS*, 69.1.a). πρόσωπον refers to the "outer surface" of the earth (BDAG, 888.3).

τῆς γῆς. Partitive genitive, modifying προσώπου. The monadic noun γῆς refers to the "land and sea" opposite the sky (*GELS*, 129.1). See the same use of the word in 8:9.

πλὴν ὅτι. These two words often function as a unit meaning "except that, save that" (LSJ, 1419.II.4, s.v. πλήν; see also BDAG, 826.1.δ, s.v. πλήν). This phrase occurs nine times in the LXX; see also the other occurrence in the Prophets in Amos 4:12, where it seems the two words function independently. Here the two words introduce "a parenthetical after-thought" and have the sense "however"; see also 1 Kgdms 8:9 (*GELS*, 564.a.4).

οὐκ. Negative with an indicative statement.

εἰς τέλος. Spatial, modifying ἐξαίρω. The preposition εἰς is probably best understood to be a "marker of degree" with the sense "up to, until" (BDAG, 289–90.3). The phrase can have the idea "in the end, utterly, completely" (*GELS*, 675–76.3.b.iii, s.v. τέλος), and with the negative particle and a future verb, it can even have the sense "never" (Jdt 7:30; Hab 1:4). Thackeray uses this rendering of the Hebrew infinitive absolute with a finite verb (in השמיד אשמיד) as an example of the translators "employing an adverb, particle or other form of paraphrase" to translate the infinitive (Thackeray §4; see also LXX.E, 2360).

ἐξαρῶ. See the discussion of this verb above in 9:8.
τὸν οἶκον Ιακωβ. See the discussion of this phrase in 3:13. Here it functions as the accusative direct object of ἐξαίρω. The context (9:9–15) suggests it refers to all the nation of Israel, Northern and Southern Kingdoms.
λέγει κύριος. This introductory formula occurs forty times in Amos; see the first occurrence in 1:5.

9:9 διότι ἰδοὺ ἐγὼ ἐντέλλομαι καὶ λικμιῶ ἐν πᾶσι τοῖς ἔθνεσιν τὸν οἶκον τοῦ Ισραηλ, ὃν τρόπον λικμᾶται ἐν τῷ λικμῷ καὶ οὐ μὴ πέσῃ σύντριμμα ἐπὶ τὴν γῆν.

διότι. This conjunction, which occurs thirteen times in Amos (3:7, 14; 4:2, 13; 5:3, 4, 17, 22; 6:8, 11, 14; 7:11; 9:9), could be causal ("for, because") or inferential ("therefore") (*GELS*, 172; BDAG, 251; LEH, 156). Here it explains the discriminating destruction in 9:8, apparently giving the reason or cause for it.
ἰδοὺ. See 9:8. This Greek word is not in MSS B and V.
ἐγώ. Nominative subject of ἐντέλλομαι. This grammatically unnecessary pronoun adds emphasis to the role of the subject of ἐντέλλομαι, who is the Lord. It is unlikely that it is meant to be understood with the second verb (λικμιῶ), which describes the result of the action of ἐντέλλομαι.
ἐντέλλομαι. Pres mid ind 1st sg ἐντέλλω. Futuristic present tense, "I will command, give an order" (see *GELS*, 241.1). The middle seems to be an indirect middle in that the will of the one commanding is expressed in the command. See the discussion of this verb in 9:3 and 9:4, where the future tense is employed.
καί. Coordinating conjunction, connecting coordinate clauses (*GELS*, 352.1.b). The following clause gives the result of the previous one (see BDAG, 495.1.b.ζ).
λικμιῶ. Fut act ind 1st sg λικμίζω = λικμάω (*GELS*, 431). Predictive future. The "normalized" reading λικμήσω (from λικμάω) is in MS B, L, and Swete; λικμιῶ is also found in Q, W, Aᵃ, and Ziegler (the original of A omits the κ); see the discussion of Attic future forms in Conybeare and Stock §21. The imagery of "winnowing" was used metaphorically in the LXX to describe destruction or punishment by scattering more than it was used literally (see Glenny 2013b, 155–56). In this context (see esp. 8:8b, 10) the winnowing imagery must be understood to be positive (as in Jer 38[31 MT]:10; see Glenny 2009, 212–13), describing the salvaging of the remaining valuable grain in the dispersed "house of Israel."

ἐν πᾶσι τοῖς ἔθνεσιν. Locative, modifying λικμίζω. The preposition ἐν could indicate "a place" in which an action takes place (*GELS*, 231.1.b), or it could have the sense "among," which fits the LXX's historical context better (also in NETS; see *GELS*, 231.2), i.e., Israel is "among all the nations." The dative adjective πᾶσι is in the predicate position modifying τοῖς ἔθνεσιν, the dative object of ἐν, and the syntagm with πᾶς requires an article modifying the head noun (see Muraoka §38.b.i).

τὸν οἶκον. Accusative direct object of λικμιῶ.

τοῦ Ισραηλ. Genitive of apposition (i.e., the members of the house, or nation, are specifically Israel; see Wallace, 95–100) or, possibly, genitive of source, if the emphasis is on the fact that the nation is made up of the descendants of Israel. This phrase is also found in 6:1 and 6:14 without the first article and in 5:25 without any article. The articles here with the head noun and its modifier are consistent with Apollonius' canon. The genitive article before the indeclinable noun Ισραηλ is absent in MSS B, Q, L, Swete, and Ziegler.

ὃν τρόπον. This phrase occurs five times in Amos; see also 2:13; 3:12; 5:14 and 19. The phrase emphasizes "comparability and analogy" (*GELS*, 688.2.a).

λικμᾶται. Pres pass ind 3rd sg λικμίζω = λικμάω. Gnomic present tense. The implied subject of this verb ("grain") must be supplied. See the discussion of this verb above in the verse.

ἐν τῷ λικμῷ. Instrumental, modifying λικμάω; the preposition ἐν has the sense "by means of, by using as instrument" (*GELS*, 231.6.a). The noun λικμῷ, which is the dative object of ἐν, is cognate to the verb λικμάω, which occurs twice above in this verse, rendering נוע. This cognate noun, meaning "winnowing fan," is an "additional cognate" in the Greek, which is not found in the Hebrew reading I כברה meaning "sieve" (see Dines 2013, 404). MSS B and W have λικνῷ (from λίκνον = λικμός); modern editions have λικμῷ.

καὶ. Coordinating conjunction, connecting independent clauses (*GELS*, 352.1.b). The following clause gives the final result of the previous two clauses (see BDAG, 495.1.b.ζ).

οὐ μὴ πέσῃ. Aor act subj 3rd sg πίπτω. Aorist subjunctive with a double negative to express emphatic negation (see 2:12).

σύντριμμα. Nominative subject of πέσῃ. The meaning of this word is difficult (see Dines 1991, 286–89). According to LSJ (1729) this noun has the same meaning as συντριμμός, but Muraoka (*GELS*, 662) understands the two words to differ in meaning in the LXX. The MT has צרור ("pebble"), and the context in the MT ("no pebble will fall to the ground") suggests that no one will escape the Lord's judgment. The Hebrew word occurs only elsewhere in the MT in 2 Sam 17:13, and it is very likely the translator did not know the word (Glenny 2013b, 156–57; see Glenny 2009, 213–14, for a discussion of the origin of the Greek rendering). The word σύντριμμα (cf. συντρίβω) has the sense "fracture, ruin" (LSJ, 1729; *GELS*, 662); when it refers to a "fracture," the fracture is often severe and ruinous, as in the destruction of Jerusalem (Lam 2:11; 3:48; 4:10). Dines summarizes that in its thirty-two occurrences in the LXX, it does not have a connection with harvesting or corn, nor does it refer to a small object like a pebble (with the possible exception of "the smashed jar" in Isa 30:41); it refers to a concept or category of disaster, which can be described in specific examples (Dines 1991, 289). Thus the suggestion that it should be rendered "crushed grain" here (*GELS*, 662.2; NETS has "nothing crushed" and in the notes gives the suggestion "no crushed grain") does not seem to do justice to the use of the word elsewhere in the LXX. The context of deliverance (9:8, 11–15) and the use of the word elsewhere in the LXX suggest it means "destruction, ruin" here (Glenny 2013b, 156); thus, "destruction shall never fall upon the land."

ἐπὶ τὴν γῆν. Locative, modifying πίπτω. This exact PP also occurs in 3:5, 14; and 8:11. In 3:5 and 3:14 it also modifies πίπτω, describing items falling "to the ground" (NETS), and the context in 8:11 describes a famine sent "on the land" (NETS). The preposition ἐπί indicates that to which hostile action is directed (*GELS*, 266.III.4.a). The concept in 8:11 is similar to this passage; in both places "fall to [upon] the land [earth]" is a negative idea (see also 2 Kgdms 17:12; Ps 139[140 MT]:11; Job 1:16 [A]; Amos 3:14; Ezek 38:20; it is a positive idea in 1 Kgdms 3:19; 14:45; cf. 1 Kgdms 26:20; 2 Kgdms 14:11; 3 Kgdms 1:52). Here describing "destruction" (σύντριμμα) falling on the land, the concept must be negative. The emphatic negation supports this understanding of the phrase; to say God's judgment would never be averted contradicts 9:8, 11–15. Thus, the clause is "a confident oracle of salvation" (Dines 1991, 289; see also Glenny 2013b, 156–57). The noun γῆν, which is the object of ἐπί, is monadic, referring to the land of Israel and its inhabitants (BDAG, 196.3); thus, it is natural for it to be articular.

9:10 ἐν ῥομφαίᾳ τελευτήσουσι πάντες ἁμαρτωλοὶ λαοῦ μου οἱ λέγοντες Οὐ μὴ ἐγγίσῃ οὐδ᾽ οὐ μὴ γένηται ἐφ᾽ ἡμᾶς τὰ κακά.

The asyndeton at the beginning of 9:10 follows the Hebrew; in the LXX verse 10 contrasts with verse 9, perhaps correcting the notion that verse 9 promises God will not judge his people if they sin (see the same contrast in 9:8).

ἐν ῥομφαίᾳ. Instrumental, modifying τελευτάω. The preposition ἐν has the sense "by means of, by using as instrument," here a "sword" (*GELS*, 231.6.a). In 9:1 and 9:4 the sword (ῥομφαίᾳ) is the Lord's agent of destruction.

τελευτήσουσι. Fut act ind 3rd pl τελευτάω. Predictive future, "will perish."

πάντες ἁμαρτωλοί. Nominative subject of τελευτάω, modified by the adjective πάντες. The genitives modifying the noun ἁμαρτωλοί specify which sinners are in view.

λαοῦ. Partitive genitive, so the sinners are a part of God's people. There will be a remnant that will survive (9:8–9).

μου. Possessive genitive.

οἱ λέγοντες. Pres act ptc nom masc sg λέγω (attributive, modifying ἁμαρτωλοί). Introduces direct speech.

Οὐ μὴ ἐγγίσῃ. Aor act subj 3rd sg ἐγγίζω. Aorist subjunctive with a double negative to express emphatic negation (see 2:12).

οὐδ'. The negative with οὐ μή is a triple negation (Muraoka §83.cf); the non-contracted form is οὐδέ. This negative conjunction "marks negation immediately following another negative" and often can be translated "nor" (*GELS*, 512). See Zeph 1:12, where it is also preceded and followed by a clause with οὐ μή (*GELS*, 512.d).

Οὐ μὴ γένηται. Aor mid subj 3rd sg γίνομαι. Aorist subjunctive with a double negative to express emphatic negation (see 2:12). The sense of the verb is "happen, take place" (*GELS*, 130.1; cf. "be" in NETS), and "come" (Dines 1991, 293) fits the context with the prepositional phrase modifying it. The copular verb γίνομαι is naturally reciprocal and does not have an active voice. The emphatic double negative with both verbs in this sentence, combined with οὐδ', intensifies the rhetoric (Satterthwaite, 6; De Waard, 347; see also 4:6–11; and 7:1–6). The negative οὐ is not found in this construction in MS B, *L*, and Swete.

ἐφ' ἡμᾶς. Locative, modifying γίνομαι. The preposition ἐπί indicates that against which a hostile action is directed (*GELS*, 266.III.4.a).

τὰ κακά. Nominative subject of both ἐγγίσῃ and γένηται. The neuter plural adjective refers to concrete deeds or phenomena bearing the character of the adjective, i.e., "calamities" (Muraoka §20.eb, §23.fb; see 5:14), and with the article it functions like a generic noun, describing a class of events (Wallace, 233). The article appears with an abstract adjective. The location of the subject at the end of the sentence emphasizes it.

9:11 ἐν τῇ ἡμέρᾳ ἐκείνῃ ἀναστήσω τὴν σκηνὴν Δαυιδ τὴν πεπτωκυῖαν καὶ ἀνοικοδομήσω τὰ πεπτωκότα αὐτῆς καὶ τὰ κατεσκαμμένα αὐτῆς ἀναστήσω καὶ ἀνοικοδομήσω αὐτὴν καθὼς αἱ ἡμέραι τοῦ αἰῶνος,

The LXX version of Amos 9:11–12 is quoted in the account of the Jerusalem Council in Acts 15:16–17. The LXX rendering of 9:11 is more stylish than the MT, harmonizing the Hebrew pronominal suffixes, so they all refer to the σκηνή. Also, in the LXX the first and third verbs are identical (ἀναστήσω), as are the second and fourth (ἀνοικοδομήσω). The fourfold repetition of the prepositional prefix (ana-) and the two perfect passive participles from πίπτω add to the assonance. The stylistic refinements just mentioned suggest they are more likely "logical and stylistic improvements" of the translator than refinements found in the LXX's *Vorlage* (Dines 1991, 294; see further Glenny 2012).

ἐν τῇ ἡμέρᾳ ἐκείνῃ. Temporal, modifying the four finite verbs in this verse. The preposition ἐν "indicates a point in time when something takes place" (*GELS*, 231.3). In the prophets this phrase often refers to "a future time of divine intervention in the affairs of the world" (Glenny 2013b, 158; see also 8:13), the day of the Lord. The noun ἡμέρᾳ refers to "the eschatological day" (*GELS*, 320.1.a), which is "an extended period," and it has the sense "time" (BDAG, 438.4). The demonstrative pronoun (ἐκείνῃ) is in the predicate position, modifying ἡμέρᾳ.

ἀναστήσω. Fut act ind 1st sg ἀνίστημι. Predictive future. The repetition of the prepositional prefix (ἀνα-) with all four verbs in this verse adds assonance to the LXX rendering and emphasizes rebuilding and restoration (Glenny 2013b, 158).

τὴν σκηνήν. Accusative direct object of ἀνίστημι. This term (σκηνή) occurs 421 times in the LXX, and it can refer to a tent, hut, booth, or the tabernacle (*GELS*, 624; LEH, 555–56; BDAG, 928). In Amos 5:26 it refers to the portable tabernacle or sanctuary of Moloch, and here it is likely used metaphorically for the dynasty and kingdom of David (see Glenny 2013b, 158–59; Glenny 2009, 218–24; the parallel in Isa 16:5; and the similar understanding in 4Q174 1–3 I, 12). It cannot refer to the Temple, since David did not build the Temple, and it cannot refer to Jerusalem (so Van der Kooij), because the building of Jerusalem would not accomplish the purpose clause in the next verse ("so that the remnant of people and all the nations . . . may seek me"). CD VII 16 takes σκηνὴν Δαυιδ to refer to the books of the Law, which will be reestablished and interpreted by an interpreter of the Law raised up to lead the nation. The article is standard with the head noun modified by a possessive genitive or an articular participle, and this head noun has both.

Δαυιδ. Possessive genitive.

τὴν πεπτωκυῖαν. Prf act ptc acc fem sg πίπτω (attributive, with the article, modifying σκηνήν). The perfect tense emphasizes the state resulting from past action.

ἀνοικοδομήσω. Fut act ind 1st sg ἀνοικοδομέω. Predictive future.

τὰ πεπτωκότα. Prf act ptc acc neut pl πίπτω (attributive, modifying σκηνήν). The participle functions similarly to the previous perfect participle from πίπτω, emphasizing the state resulting from past action. It is the direct object of the preceding verb, ἀνοικοδομήσω.

αὐτῆς. Possessive genitive, referring to the σκηνή. The corresponding pronominal suffix is feminine plural in the MT, perhaps referring to the walls (see Garrett, 283). Paul (291 n. 20) notes that the Hebrew suffixes in this verse "seem to be in total disarray."

τὰ κατεσκαμμένα. Prf pass ptc acc neut pl κατασκάπτω (substantival). Direct object of ἀναστήσω. It functions similarly to the previous two perfect participles, emphasizing the state resulting from past action. It is normal to have an article with a head noun when it is modified by a possessive pronoun.

αὐτῆς. Possessive genitive, again referring to the σκηνή. The corresponding pronominal suffix is masculine singular in the MT. See the previous occurrence of αὐτῆς.

ἀναστήσω. See the same form and function above in this verse.

καὶ. The third coordinating conjunction, connecting independent clauses, in this verse (*GELS*, 352.1.b).

ἀνοικοδομήσω. See the same form and function above in this verse.

αὐτήν. Accusative direct object of ἀνοικοδομήσω; its antecedent is σκηνή.

καθώς. This conjunction shows similarity or comparison (see BDAG, 493.1); it functions adverbially here, modifying the preceding verb (ἀνοικοδομήσω) and comparing the past state of the σκηνή with its condition in the future (ἐν τῇ ἡμέρᾳ ἐκείνῃ). See also 2:9 and 4:11. A substantive indicating a point in time is employed here following καθώς instead of the expected prepositional phrase (ἐν . . .); see Muraoka (§26.n).

αἱ ἡμέραι. Nominative in a comparative phrase with καθώς.

τοῦ αἰῶνος. Attributive genitive, giving an innate quality of the head noun. This word can refer to future time or the "remote past" (*GELS*, 19.1 and 2; Glenny 2013b, 158). Every time the phrase καθὼς αἱ ἡμέραι τοῦ αἰῶνος occurs in the LXX with the comparative (Mic 7:14; Mal 3:4) and without it (Sir 50:23; Isa 63:9), it refers to the past, and the comparison here also requires that sense. Apollonius' canon applies here.

9:12 ὅπως ἐκζητήσωσιν οἱ κατάλοιποι τῶν ἀνθρώπων καὶ πάντα τὰ ἔθνη, ἐφ' οὓς ἐπικέκληται τὸ ὄνομά μου ἐπ' αὐτούς, λέγει κύριος ὁ θεὸς ὁ ποιῶν ταῦτα.

ὅπως. Conjunction indicating purpose (final) with a subjunctive verb (*GELS*, 502.4; BDAG, 718.2.a.α; BDF §369).

ἐκζητήσωσιν. Aor act subj 3rd pl ἐκζητέω. Used in a purpose clause with ὅπως (BDF §369.1). The verb does not have an object, but the context and the previous reference to seeking the Lord (5:4, 6) suggest με should be understood after the verb "they may seek [me]," as found in several Lucianic MSS and versions; A, which is apparently influenced by Acts 15:17, has τὸν κύριον. Instead of the corresponding Hebrew יירשו ("they may possess"), the translator read ידרשו ("they may seek"). There is some debate whether the LXX of the Hebrew represents the original text here (see LXX.E, 2361), but most believe a text similar to the MT was original (see Glenny 2012).

οἱ κατάλοιποι τῶν ἀνθρώπων καὶ πάντα τὰ ἔθνη. Compound nominative subject of ἐκζητήσωσιν.

οἱ κατάλοιποι. First element of the compound nominative subject of ἐκζητήσωσιν. The use of articles is consistent with Apollonius' canon. The corresponding Hebrew word (שארית) serves as the direct object in the MT, marked by the particle את; it is very possible this refinement marking the direct object was not present in the LXX's *Vorlage*.

τῶν ἀνθρώπων. Partitive genitive, referring to human beings or people, not particularly to maleness (*GELS*, 52.1; BDAG, 81.1.c). The following words (πάντα τὰ ἔθνη) suggest it refers specifically to gentiles, as it also does in 4:13. The Greek ἀνθρώπων corresponds to אדום ("Edom") in the MT, and the translator apparently read אדם ("man"); it is possible the Hebrew word did not have a vocalic *waw*. For my fuller discussion of the issues involved in the translation of Amos 9:11–12 and its use in Acts 15, see Glenny 2012 and 2013b, 158–60.

καὶ. Coordinating conjunction, connecting compound subjects, which are coterminous, i.e., "the remnant of people" and "all the nations upon whom my name is called" are the same (*GELS*, 352.1.e).

πάντα τὰ ἔθνη. Second element of the compound nominative subject of ἐκζητήσωσιν. For the construction with the adjective πάντα and article, see Muraoka (§38.b.i).

ἐφ' οὓς. Spatial, modifying ἐπικέκληται. The preposition ἐπί indicates those to whom speech is directed (*GELS*, 266.III.4.d). The prepositional phrase renders the Hebrew relative particle אשר (see ἐπ' αὐτούς below).

ἐπικέκληται. Prf pass ind 3rd sg ἐπικαλέω. The perfect tense emphasizes the state of the gentiles described in this verse. The construction ἐπικαλεῖται τὸ ὄνομά τινος ἐπί τινα indicates ownership, control, or protection (BDAG, 373.2; GELS, 273.A.3) consistent with a covenant relationship. This is the only place in the LXX this phrase is applied to gentiles (Dines 1991, 303; see the use of this passage in Acts 15:17). The phrase has covenant connotations when applied to Israel, as God's people (Deut 28:10; 2 Chr 7:14). The repetition of ἐπί in the compound noun (2x elsewhere in the verse) emphasizes movement toward gentiles. See the discussion of this verb in Glenny (2013b, 160).

τὸ ὄνομά. Nominative subject of ἐπικαλέω. The article is normal with a head noun modified by a possessive pronoun.

μου. Possessive genitive.

ἐπ᾽ αὐτούς. Spatial, modifying ἐπικέκληται. The preposition ἐπί indicates those to whom speech is directed (GELS, 266.III.4.d). The pleonastic PP repeats or resumes the previous ἐφ᾽ οὕς. The pronoun αὐτούς could be called a resumptive pronoun, referring back to the previous relative (οὕς); Robertson (723) calls the repetition a "pleonastic antecedent." See Garrett (282) on the corresponding Hebrew construction.

λέγει κύριος ὁ θεὸς. This oath-like confirmation formula occurs also in Amos 3:11, 13; 4:3, 5; 5:16, 27; 8:9, and 15; see 3:11 and 13. The divine speech formula λέγει κύριος occurs forty times in Amos. This form of the divine name is found in MSS A, W, and Rahlfs; L, B, Q, Ziegler, and Swete have κύριος.

ὁ ποιῶν. Pres act ptc nom masc pl ποιέω (substantival). Nominative in apposition to κύριος ὁ θεός.

ταῦτα. Accusative direct object of ποιῶν.

9:13 ἰδοὺ ἡμέραι ἔρχονται, λέγει κύριος, καὶ καταλήμψεται ὁ ἀλοητὸς τὸν τρύγητον, καὶ περκάσει ἡ σταφυλὴ ἐν τῷ σπόρῳ, καὶ ἀποσταλάξει τὰ ὄρη γλυκασμόν, καὶ πάντες οἱ βουνοὶ σύμφυτοι ἔσονται·

ἰδοὺ ἡμέραι ἔρχονται, λέγει κύριος. See the same formula in 8:11. The divine speech formula λέγει κύριος occurs forty times in Amos (see 9:12). In Amos ἰδού occurs fourteen times, and it normally introduces a statement of judgment; the only exceptions are 4:13; 9:9, and here; in the last two occurrences it introduces statements of deliverance (9:9) and salvation (9:13). The shorter formula, ἰδοὺ ἡμέραι ἔρχονται, occurs also in in 4:2 and in Amos always announces judgment.

καὶ. This coordinating conjunction is used instead of subordination "when καί connects an expression of time with that which occurs in the time"; thus it is rendered "when" (BDAG, 494.1.b.γ; see also BDF §442.4).

καταλήμψεται. Fut mid ind 3rd sg καταλαμβάνω. Predictive future. The verb could have the sense "overtake" or "reach up to" in this context, referring to the ingathering of crops.

ὁ ἀλοητός. Nominative subject of καταλήμψεται. Generic noun referring to a class, "harvest, reaping" in general. MSS B, Q, and W, followed by Swete, have the synonym ἄμητος (*GELS*, 32). The only other occurrence of ἀλοητός in the LXX is in the covenant promise in Lev 26:5, which is echoed in this passage. The noun refers to the "act of threshing" grain in the spring of the year (*GELS*, 29; see also the discussion in Glenny 2013b, 160–61).

τὸν τρύγητον. Accusative direct object of καταλήμψεται. Generic noun referring to a specific class. This noun could refer to the harvest of grain (4:7; Joel 1:11; LSJ, 1829) or grapes (e.g., Lev 26:5; Judg 8:2; 2 Kgdms 8:12; Isa 24:13); since the word normally has the latter sense in the LXX, since this is the sense of the passage in LXX Lev 26:5, which is probably the source of the phrase here (see Wevers 1997, 439), and since the fall harvest of grapes makes most sense here (the harvest of grain in the spring and summer overtakes the harvest of grapes in the fall), it is better to understand the reference here to the harvest of grapes, "the vintage." This Greek word renders the Hebrew participle from קצר (i.e., "reaper"); the meaning of the Hebrew verb is "gather in, harvest" (*HALOT*, 2:1126).

καί. Coordinating conjunction, connecting coordinate clauses (*GELS*, 352.1.b). The following clause differs slightly from the Hebrew of Lev 26:5 and Amos 9:13, but it could be a free translation of either (see Glenny 2013b, 161).

περκάσει. Fut act ind 3rd sg περκάζω. Predictive future. The verb has the sense "to turn dark," and here and in Sir 51:15 it refers to grapes when they begin to ripen (*GELS*, 555).

ἡ σταφυλή. Nominative subject of περκάσει. Generic noun referring to a specific class of objects, "grapes, a cluster of grapes" (*GELS*, 633).

ἐν τῷ σπόρῳ. Temporal, modifying περκάζω. The preposition ἐν "indicates a point in time when something takes place" (*GELS*, 231.3.a; LSJ, 1630), "at seedtime." In Israel this would be in November–December before the early rains (see Glenny 2013b, 161).

καί. Coordinating conjunction, connecting coordinate clauses (*GELS*, 352.1.b). The following clause is exactly the same as the Joel 3:18, and both render the same exact Hebrew clause (see Joel 4:18 MT).

ἀποσταλάξει. Fut act ind 3rd sg ἀποσταλάζω (= ἀποστάζω; LSJ, 218). Predictive future. Third-person singular verb with a neuter plural subject; this phenomenon "especially preponderates with words having non-personal meaning" (BDF §133.2). This neologism has the sense "drip, drop" (LEH, 75), and it is found elsewhere in the LXX only one time, in Joel 3:18.

τὰ ὄρη. Nominative subject of ἀποσταλάξει. Generic noun referring to a class, "the mountains."

γλυκασμόν. Since the verb ἀποσταλάζω is intransitive (LSJ, 218, s.v. ἀποστάζω), Muraoka (§22.xj) suggests this accusative is a variation of an accusative of respect. The only other occurrence of this rare word in the LXX is in the same phrase in Joel 3:18.

πάντες οἱ βουνοί. Nominative subject of ἔσονται (βουνοί = "hills"). See Muraoka (§38.b.i) for a discussion of this construction with the adjective πᾶς in the predicate position.

σύμφυτοι. Predicate adjective. Although it has been suggested that this adjective means "grow together" in this context (*TDNT*, 7:786), Greek usage suggests the idea of thickly wooded or planted (LSJ, 1689), and the context emphasizes the idea of things being planted, here "thickly planted" (so *GELS*, 650.1; see the repetition of verbs related to "planting" [φυτεύω] in 9:14–15 [3x]).

ἔσονται. Fut mid ind 3rd pl εἰμί. Predictive future. This is one of many verbs that does not have an active future form. It is easy to see why εἰμί would have a middle form, since its subject is involved in, or affected by, the state communicated by the verb.

9:14 καὶ ἐπιστρέψω τὴν αἰχμαλωσίαν λαοῦ μου Ισραηλ, καὶ οἰκοδομήσουσιν πόλεις τὰς ἠφανισμένας καὶ κατοικήσουσιν καὶ καταφυτεύσουσιν ἀμπελῶνας καὶ πίονται τὸν οἶνον αὐτῶν καὶ φυτεύσουσιν κήπους καὶ φάγονται τὸν καρπὸν αὐτῶν·

ἐπιστρέψω. Fut act ind 1st sg ἐπιστρέφω. Predictive future. The verb has the sense "to bring back to the point of origin or home" (*GELS*, 282.1).

τὴν αἰχμαλωσίαν λαοῦ μου. Accusative direct object of ἐπιστρέφω. The corresponding word in the MT is "restoration, turning" (שבות; *HALOT*, 2:1385–86), and the Hebrew expression has the idea of "restoring the fortunes" (see Paul, 294, on the Hebrew expression). The article is expected with the monadic noun; λαοῦ is an objective genitive, since the "people" are the ones being taken into captivity, and μου is a genitive of possession. The rendering of the Hebrew שבות ("fortune") by αἰχμαλωσίαν ("captivity") results in a more specific meaning.

Ισραηλ. Genitive of this indeclinable noun, in simple apposition with λαοῦ. This word indicates this passage has implications that go beyond the southern Kingdom of Judah.

καί. Coordinating conjunction, connecting coordinate clauses (*GELS*, 352.1.b), and continuing the string of future blessings for Israel.

οἰκοδομήσουσιν. Fut act ind 3rd pl οἰκοδομέω. Predictive future, "will build." Cf. ἀνοικοδομέω (2x) in 9:11.

πόλεις. Accusative direct object of οἰκοδομέω. It should probably be understood to be definite with the attributive participle modifying and specifying it.

τὰς ἠφανισμένας. Prf pass ptc acc fem pl ἀφανίζω (attributive, modifying πόλεις). The perfect tense emphasizes the state the cities are in. See Muraoka (§31.ce) on the construction here (anarthrous noun[πόλεις]–article[τάς]–participle[ἠφανισμένας]). Although such participle construction often functions as a relative clause, Muraoka suggests in this case it be understood as modifying the head noun (i.e., "demolished cities").

καί. Coordinating conjunction, connecting clauses (*GELS*, 352.1.b), and "introducing a result that comes from what precedes" (BDAG, 495.1.b.ζ).

κατοικήσουσιν. Fut act ind 3rd pl κατοικέω. Predictive future. The implied object of the verb is the cities mentioned before, thus the supplied word "them."

καί. Coordinating conjunction, connecting coordinate clauses (*GELS*, 352.1.b), and continuing the string of future blessings for Israel.

καταφυτεύσουσιν. Fut act ind 3rd pl καταφυτεύω. Predictive future. See the simple form of the verb later in this verse and the same compound in verse 15. The meaning of the compound form of the verb is difficult to distinguish from the simple form (i.e., "to plant"; *GELS*, 387).

ἀμπελῶνας. Accusative direct object of καταφυτεύω. The noun is generic, referring to the class "vineyard."

καί. Coordinating conjunction, connecting clauses (*GELS*, 352.1.b), and "introducing a result that comes from what precedes" (BDAG, 495.1.b.ζ).

πίονται. Fut mid ind 3rd pl πίνω. Predictive future, "will drink." On the future form of this word, see BDF (§74.2; 77). This is an indirect middle, which category is used for verbs of coming into possession or ingestion (Kemmer, 268).

τὸν οἶνον. Accusative direct object of πίονται. The noun is generic, referring to a class.

αὐτῶν. Genitive of source; i.e., they will drink the wine derived from the vineyards they plant.

καί. Coordinating conjunction, connecting coordinate clauses (*GELS*, 352.1.b), and continuing the string of future blessings for Israel.

φυτεύσουσιν. Fut act ind 3rd pl φυτεύω. Predictive future, "will plant." Note the compound form of this verb above in this verse. Two other compounds of this verb occur in verses 14 and 15, and both translate the Hebrew verb נטע ("plant"); here the simple form of the verb renders the Hebrew verb "make" (עשׂה).

κήπους. Accusative direct object of φυτεύσουσιν. The noun is generic, "gardens."

καὶ. Coordinating conjunction, connecting clauses (*GELS*, 352.1.b), and "introducing a result that comes from what precedes" (BDAG, 495.1.b.ζ).

φάγονται. Fut mid ind 3rd pl ἐσθίω. Predictive future, "will eat." On the future form of this word, see BDF (§74.2). This is an indirect middle, which category is used for verbs of coming into possession or ingestion (Kemmer, 268).

τὸν καρπὸν. Accusative direct object of φάγονται. Generic noun. The plural (τοὺς καρπούς) is found in MSS B, W, and Swete; Rahlfs and Ziegler have the singular, which agrees with the Hebrew and is preferred.

αὐτῶν. Genitive of source, i.e., they will eat the fruit derived from the gardens they plant.

9:15 καὶ καταφυτεύσω αὐτοὺς ἐπὶ τῆς γῆς αὐτῶν, καὶ οὐ μὴ ἐκσπασθῶσιν οὐκέτι ἀπὸ τῆς γῆς αὐτῶν, ἧς ἔδωκα αὐτοῖς, λέγει κύριος ὁ θεὸς ὁ παντοκράτωρ.

καὶ. Coordinating conjunction, connecting coordinate clauses (*GELS*, 352.1.b), and continuing the string of future blessings for Israel.

καταφυτεύσω. Fut act ind 1st sg καταφυτεύω. Predictive future. See the simple form of the verb and the same compound form in verse 14, where the people are promised that they will "plant" vineyards and gardens; here the Lord "plants" the people.

αὐτοὺς. Accusative direct object of καταφυτεύσω.

ἐπὶ τῆς γῆς. Locative, modifying καταφυτεύω. The preposition ἐπί marks a position "on the surface of" (*GELS*, 263.I.2; BDAG, 363.1.a). This exact prepositional phrase occurs only seven times in the LXX (with this form of the possessive personal pronoun). In Josh 24:15 it refers to the land of the Amorites, and in its other five occurrences it refers to the land of Israel, which the Lord promised to Jacob and gave to them (Isa 14:1; Ezek 28:25; 34:27; 36:17; 37:25). It also refers to the land of Israel here; thus, the object of ἐπί (the monadic noun γῆς) refers to a specific region of the earth "belonging to or inhabited by a particular ethnic group or nation," as is clear from the following possessive pronoun (see *GELS*, 129.4.d).

αὐτῶν. Possessive genitive.

καί. Coordinating conjunction, connecting coordinate clauses (*GELS*, 352.1.b), and continuing the string of future blessings for Israel. This is the final and essential blessing.

οὐ μὴ ἐκσπασθῶσιν. Aor pass subj 3rd pl ἐκσπάω. Aorist subjunctive with a double negative to express emphatic negation (see 2:12). It is a simple passive with no agency expressed.

οὐκέτι. The negative with οὐ μή is a triple negation (Muraoka §83.cf). Used with another negative this adverb means "never again" (BDAG, 736.1).

ἀπὸ τῆς γῆς. Separation, modifying ἐκσπάω. The preposition ἀπό has the sense "away from" in a context of "removal or dissociation" (*GELS*, 69.1). See the discussion above in this verse on the words τῆς γῆς αὐτῶν. Swete, following MS B, does not have the personal pronoun αὐτῶν here; Rahlfs and Ziegler have it, matching the previous occurrence of this phrase in 9:15.

αὐτῶν. Possessive genitive.

ἧς. Genitive relative pronoun functioning as the direct object of ἔδωκα; the relative is genitive by attraction to the case of its antecedent (τῆς γῆς αὐτῶν). The case of a relative pronoun is normally determined by its function in its clause or phrase, but an accusative or nominative relative pronoun is often attracted to the case of its genitive or dative antecedent, and in such cases the relative clause is restrictive, further defining the antecedent of the pronoun (Muraoka §86.a; see also BDF §294).

ἔδωκα. Aor act ind 1st sg δίδωμι. Constative or complexive aorist, "surveying at a glance the course of a past action from beginning to end" (Smyth §1927).

αὐτοῖς. Dative indirect object.

λέγει κύριος ὁ θεὸς ὁ παντοκράτωρ. This divine speech formula is found five times in the LXX, and four of those occurrences are in Amos (3:13; 5:16, 27; 9:15; see also Nah 3:5); see the discussion of the individual words in the previous occurrences of this title. In the MT the corresponding Hebrew text for the name for God is different in each of the four occurrences of this phrase in LXX Amos, so this was apparently a divine name that was favored by the translator; see the discussion of this title in 3:13. The Hebrew corresponding to the phrase in this verse is אמר יהוה אלהיך ("says the Lord your God"); interestingly, the verb λέγει is used in the LXX to render the verb in the divine speech formulas נאם יהוה and אמר יהוה in this chapter (see 9:7, 8, 12, 13, and 9:15, respectively). See Glenny (2009, 186–89) for a discussion of the meaning of παντοκράτωρ in LXX Amos; that title emphasizes that the Lord is God of all nations and peoples, and the difference between the Hebrew and the corresponding Greek in this verse suggests that the translator wanted to emphasize the theme of the Lord's universal sovereignty, which is also emphasized elsewhere in LXX Amos (see esp. 9:11–12).

GLOSSARY

Adjectivizer—An article used to change a nonadjective into an adjectival modifier.
Alliteration—The conspicuous repetition of the same sound or letter at the beginning of successive or adjacent words.
Anacoluthon—A grammatical interruption or lack of implied sequence within a sentence.
Anaphoric—Referring back to a preceding word or groups of words. Thus, pronouns are anaphoric references to participants that have already been introduced into the discourse.
Anarthrous—Lacking an article.
Antecedent—An element that is referred to by another expression that follows it. Thus, the antecedent of a relative pronoun is that element in the preceding context with reference to which the relative clause provides additional information.
Apodosis—The second part ("then" clause) in a conditional construction.
Apollonius' canon—The second-century AD grammarian Apollonius Dyscolus set out the general rule that when one noun (usually in genitive case) modifies another noun, both will be articular or both will be anarthrous.
Apollonius' corollary—The corollary to Apollonius' canon: when one noun (usually in genitive case) modifies another noun and both are anarthrous, usually the semantic force of both is the same (i.e., definite, indefinite, or qualitative).
Apposition—When two nouns occur together in the same case and they explain each other, they are said to be in apposition.
Aramaism—See *Semitism*.
Arthrous/articular—Including an article.

Ascensive—Being intensive or expressing a final addition or point of focus. In Greek, this term is most often used in relation to conjunctions, especially καί. In such instances, the conjunction is typically translated "even."

Aspect—The writer's/speaker's viewpoint of an action, event, or state. Specifically, how the writer or speaker presents the action unfolding in time.

Assonance—The repetition of a vowel or consonant sound in a literary work.

Asyndeton—The omission of conjunctions between clauses, often resulting in a hurried rhythm or vehement effect.

Attendant circumstance—A verbal participle expressing an action or circumstance that prepares for or accompanies the action of the main verb. Although the participle is semantically dependent on the main verb, it is often translated as a finite verb conjoined to the main verb by "and." Structural clues include the following: tense of both the participle and main verb is aorist, mood of main verb is imperative or indicative, participle precedes the main verb in word order and time, typically found in narrative and infrequently elsewhere.

Attraction—Some relative pronouns at times take on or are "attracted" to the case of their antecedent.

Background—Information that is off the event line, or storyline—that is, those events or materials that do not move the narrative forward. Instead, background information comments on, amplifies, or otherwise supports the narration.

Cataphoric—Referring forward to a following word or group of words.

Chiasm—"The crosswise arrangement of contrasted pairs to give alternate stress" (Smyth §3020).

Clausal complement—A direct object expressed in the form of a clause rather than a noun phrase. For example, ὅτι is often used to introduce complement clauses after verbs of speech.

Clitic—A word that is written as a separate word in the syntax but that is pronounced and accented as if it were part of another word. There are two types. Enclitics shift their accents to the preceding word; proclitics shift their accents to the following word.

Collocation—The conventional association of two or more words so as to produce a particular nuance.

Complement—In addition to its use in the phrase "clausal complement," this term is also used in two additional ways. It may refer to (1) a constituent, other than an accusative direct object, that is required to complete a verb phrase. Verbs that include a prepositional prefix often take a complement whose case is determined by the prefix. For example, verbs with the prefix συν characteristically take a dative complement; or (2) the second element in a double accusative construction, which completes the verbal idea.

Construction *ad sensum* — Literally "construction according to sense." A construction that follows the sense of the expression rather than strict grammatical rules, as when a plural verb is used with a collective singular subject.

Copula/copular clause — A linking verb that joins a subject and predicate into an equative or copular clause.

Crasis — The merging of two words through the use of contraction.

Deponency — This label is often used to refer to verbs whose morphology is middle, passive, or middle/passive and are considered to be "active" in meaning. As discussed in the Introduction, middle and passive forms are treated as such in this Handbook.

Development — The use of δέ does not mark either semantic continuity or discontinuity (since either can be present) but instead signals a new development in the narrative or argument.

Direct discourse — A direct object clause often introduced by ὅτι that records direct speech.

Double accusative construction — Constructions in which a verb takes two accusatives. There are two types. In a double accusative of person and thing, the verb is often thought to have two accusative direct objects, a thing and a person. But many of these constructions are better understood as instances of the cross-linguistic phenomenon of advancement. In a double accusative of object-complement construction, a verb will have an object and the complement of that object in the accusative case, the latter predicating something about the former.

Elative — An adjectival form denoting intensity or superiority.

Elision — This term may be used morphologically to describe the omission of a letter in a word (e.g., the final vowel) in some prepositions or conjunctions or syntactically with reference to a word being omitted, which must be supplied from the context.

Ellipsis — The omission of an element of language that technically renders the sentence ungrammatical but that is usually understood in context.

Enclitic—A clitic is a word that is written as a separate word in the syntax but that is pronounced and accented as if it were part of another word. Enclitics donate their accent to the preceding word.

Epexegetical—In reference to an infinitive, denotes its function in clarifying, explaining, or qualifying. Regarding a clause beginning with the conjunction ἵνα or ὅτι, refers to a clause that completes the idea of a noun, verb, or adjective. Epexegetical genitives specify a particular example of the category introduced in the head noun.

Equative verb/clause—An equative verb joins a subject and predicate to form an equative clause.

External evidence—In textual criticism the evidence available from manuscripts and versions is described as external evidence. See also *internal evidence*.

First-class conditional—Used to introduce neutral conditions where the realization of the action in the protasis is assumed for the sake of argument.

Genitive absolute—A participial construction consisting of a genitive substantive and anarthrous genitive participle, typically at the beginning of a sentence, and (usually) grammatically independent of the main clause verb. It can express any adverbial idea attested for participles but is most often temporal.

Gloss—A brief explanation or short definition of a word that may not reflect the wider range of meaning of the word.

Hapax legomenon—A word that occurs only one time in the designated corpus (e.g., LXX) or, in the case of absolute *hapax legomenon*, occurs only once in a language as a whole.

Haplography—The accidental omission of text.

Hebraism—See *Semitism*.

Hendiadys—Two words joined by καί and used to express a single idea.

Homoiarchton—In textual criticism, an unintentional error of eyesight committed when copying a text, due to words or lines that begin similarly.

Homoiteleuton—Used in rhetoric to refer to the use of similar sound endings to words, phrases, or sentences.

Hyperbaton—Refers to the "separation of two or more syntactically closely connected words or groups of words, for signaling or reinforcing the end of syntactical and semantic units in the Greek (and, by analogy, Latin) literary sentence" (Markovic, 127).

Hypotaxis—The subordinate relationship of clauses, indicated by conjunctions or other grammatical relationships (e.g., genitive absolute construction).

Imperfective (verbal aspect)—A semantic value, associated with verbs in the present and imperfect tenses, with which the writer/speaker means to portray the action as a process or as continuous. See also perfective (verbal aspect) and stative (verbal aspect).

Indirect discourse—Reported speech or thought.

Intermediate agent—The agent (introduced with διά + the agent in the genitive case) is not the ultimate cause of the action; the action took place through him/her/it.

Internal evidence—In textual criticism the evidence for a variant reading that is based on consideration of what the author is most likely to have written (intrinsic probability) or what a scribe may have changed (transcriptional probability) is described as internal evidence. See also *external evidence*.

Intransitive—A type of verb that does not require a direct object. Some verbs may function either transitively or intransitively depending on the statement in which they are used.

Litotes—A figure of speech in which a statement is made by negating the opposite idea.

Marked—Departing from the normal or neutral pattern or having additive features. See also *unmarked*.

Matrix clause—A linguistic term describing a clause (sometimes described as superordinate), which is modified by a subordinate clause or modifier (*CGCG* §39.1–2; 47.9).

Merism—A figure of speech in which two or more contrasting or complementary parts are invoked to represent the whole.

Metonymy—A figure of speech in which one term is used in place of another with which it is closely associated.

Neologism—A word not attested prior to the work in question.

Nominalizer—An article that is used to change a word, phrase, or clause into a substantive. Most commonly, nominalizers are used to make an adjective or participle substantival.

Oblique case—The cases that can appear in roles other than that of subject, i.e., genitive, dative, and accusative; sometimes they are called the objective cases.

Parataxis—The linking of clauses or phrases together without utilizing conjunctions that mark subordinate relationships.

Parenthesis—Describes a distinct thought not completely unrelated to the ideas in the discourse but somewhat disruptive.

Paronomasia—Refers to the repetition of the same word root in order to make a connection or wordplay.

Perfective (verbal aspect)—A semantic value associated with verbs in the aorist tense with which the writer/speaker means to portray the action in summary or as a complete whole, without reference to any process that might be involved. See also imperfective (verbal aspect) and stative (verbal aspect).

Periphrasis—An indirect way of saying something. For example, ποιέω + abstract noun (e.g., λιτανείαν) when the verb alone (e.g., λιτανεύω) would have sufficed.

Periphrastic construction—An anarthrous participle used with a verb of being to constitute a finite verbal idea, yielding a roundabout way of saying something that could have been expressed with a single verb.

Pleonasm—The use of more words than necessary.

Point/counterpoint set—A construction typically involving a negated statement (with οὐ or μή) followed by a corresponding phrase or clause initiated by ἀλλά. Such sets are one particular type of correlative emphasis.

Predicate nominative/accusative/adjective—An anarthrous noun or adjective sharing the same case as the subject and connected to the subject with an equative verb (expressed or implied).

Prolepsis—The use of a descriptive word or phrase in anticipation of its becoming applicable.

Prominence—The "semantic and grammatical elements of discourse that serve to set aside certain subjects, ideas, or motifs of the author as more or less semantically or pragmatically significant than others" (Reed, 75–76).

Protasis—The first part ("if" clause) in a conditional construction.

Semitism—The influence of a Semitic language (Hebrew or Aramaic) on a Greek writer. This phenomenon sometimes produces a form of expression that is atypical of a native Greek speaker.

Solecism—A violation of standard grammatical usage.

Stative (verbal aspect)—A semantic value associated with verbs in the perfect and pluperfect tenses with which the writer/speaker means to portray the action as a state or condition, without reference to any process or expenditure of energy. See also perfective (verbal aspect) and imperfective (verbal aspect).

Third-class conditional—Used to introduce prospective conditions, where the fulfillment of the condition is likely. Sometimes called a future more vivid condition.

Transitive—A type of verb that requires a direct object (see Intransitive).

Ultimate agent—The person ultimately responsible for the action without necessarily being directly involved. The agent may be introduced in the genitive case with ὑπο, ἀπό, or παρά.

Unmarked—The default option among two or more grammatical choices. See also *marked*.

Vorlage—A prototype or source document behind a manuscript copy or recension; or an underlying tradition.

WORKS CITED

Aejmelaeus, Anneli. "OTI *Causale* in Septuagintal Greek." Pages 11–29 in *On The Trail of the Septuagint Translators*. Edited by Anneli Aejmelaeus. Contributions to Biblical Exegesis and Theology 50. Leuven: Peeters, 2007.

Aitken, J. K. *No Stone Unturned: Greek Inscriptions and Septuagint Vocabulary*. Corpus Scriptorum Historiae Byzantinae 5. Winona Lake, Ind.: Eisenbrauns, 2014.

Arieti, James A. "A Study in the Septuagint of Amos." PhD diss., Stanford University, 1972.

Aubrey, Rachel. "Motivated Categories, Middle Voice, and Passive Morphology." Pages 563–625 in *The Greek Verb Revisited: A Fresh Approach for Biblical Exegesis*. Edited by Steven E. Runge and Christopher J. Fresch. Bellingham, Wash.: Lexham Press, 2016.

Baillet, M., J. T. Milik, and R. de Vaux. *Les "petites grottes" de Qumran*. Discoveries in the Judaean Desert 3. Oxford: Clarendon Press, 1962.

Bakker, Egbert. "Voice, Aspect and Aktionsart: Middle and Passive in Ancient Greek." Pages 23–47 in *Voice: Form and Functions*. Edited by B. Fox and P. Hopper. Amsterdam: John Benjamins: 1994.

Bauer, Walter, Frederick W. Danker, William F. Arndt, and F. Wilbur Gingrich. *A Greek-English Lexicon of the New Testament and Other Early Christian Literature*. 3rd ed. Chicago: University of Chicago, 2000.

Blass, F., and A. Debrunner. *A Greek Grammar of the New Testament and Other Early Christian Literature*. Translated and revised by R. W. Funk. Chicago: University of Chicago, 1961.

Blomqvist, Jerker. "Gender Assignment of Boiotian Settlement Names." *Classica et Mediaevalia: Danish Journal of Philology and History* 65 (2014): 5–21.

Bons, Eberhard. "Amos." Pages 437–45 in *Introduction to the LXX*. Edited by Siegfried Kreuzer. Waco, Tex.: Baylor University Press, 2019.

Boyd-Taylor, Cameron. *Reading between the Lines: The Interlinear Paradigm for Septuagint Studies*. Leuven: Peeters, 2011.

Brenton, Lancelot C. L. *The Septuagint Version, with Apocrypha, Greek, and English*. London: Samuel Bagster & Sons, 1844. Repr., Grand Rapids: Zondervan, 1976.

Bruce, F. F. "Prophetic Interpretation in the Septuagint." *Bulletin of the International Organization for Septuagint and Cognate Studies* 12 (1979): 17–26.

Burk, Denny. *Articular Infinitives in the Greek of the New Testament: On the Exegetical Benefit of Grammatical Precision*. New Testament Monographs 14. Sheffield: Sheffield Phoenix Press, 2006.

Caird, G. B. "Towards a Lexicon of the Septuagint, II." Pages 133–52 in *Septuagintal Lexicography*. Edited by Robert A. Kraft. Septuagint and Cognate Studies 1. Missoula: University of Montana, 1972.

Caragounis, C. C. *The Development of Greek and the New Testament: Morphology, Syntax, Phonology, and Textual Transmission*. Wissenschaftliche Untersuchungen zum Neuen Testament 1/167. Tübingen: Mohr Siebeck, 2004.

Cathcart, K. J., and R. P. Gordon. *The Targum of the Minor Prophets. The Aramaic Bible 14*. Edinburgh: T&T Clark, 1989.

Conrad, Carl W. "New Observations on Voice in the Ancient Greek Verb." Washington University in St. Louis website, 2002.

———. "Ancient Greek Voice." Washington University in St. Louis website, 2015. https://pages.wustl.edu/cwconrad/ancient-greek-voice.

Conybeare, F. C., and St. George Stock. *Grammar of the Septuagint: With Selected Readings, Vocabularies, and Updated Indexes*. Boston: Ginn, 1905. Repr., Peabody, Mass.: Hendrickson, 1995.

Cripps, Richard S. *A Critical and Exegetical Commentary on the Book of Amos*. London: SPCK, 1969.

Dafni, Evangelia G., and Aaron Schart. "Amos." Pages 2:2339–61 in *Septuaginta Deutsch: Erläuterungen und Kommentare zum griechischen Alten Testament*. Edited by M. Karrer and W. Kraus. 2 vols. Stuttgart: Deutsche Bibelgesellschaft, 2011.

Daniel, S. *Recherches sur le vocabulaire du culte dans la Septante*. Etudes et Commentaires 61. Paris: C. Klincksieck, 1966.

Decker, R. J. *Reading Koine Greek*. Grand Rapids: Baker, 2014a.

———. *Mark 1–8: A Handbook on the Greek Text*. Baylor Handbook on the Greek New Testament. Waco, Tex.: Baylor University Press, 2014b.

Dines, J. M. "The Septuagint of Amos: A Study in Interpretation." PhD diss., London, 1991.
———. *The Septuagint*. New York: T&T Clark, 2004.
———. "Stylistic Invention and Rhetorical Purpose in the Book of the Twelve." Pages 23–48 in *Et Sapienter et Eloquenter: Studies on Rhetorical and Stylistic Features of the Septuagint*. Edited by Eberhard Bons and Thomas J. Kraus. Göttingen: Vandenhoeck & Ruprecht: 2011.
———. "Was LXX Pentateuch a Style-Setter for LXX Minor Prophets?" Pages 397–411 in *XIV Congress of the International Organization for Septuagint and Cognate Studies: Helsinki 2010*. Atlanta: Society of Biblical Literature, 2013.
———. "The Minor Prophets." Pages 438–55 in *T&T Clark Companion to the Septuagint*. Edited by James K. Aitken. London: Bloomsbury T&T Clark, 2015.
———. "Design or Accident? Rhetorical Touches in the XII with Special Reference to the Book of Amos." Pages 29–42 in *Les Douze Prophètes dans la Septante*. Edited by Cécile Dogniez and Philippe Le Moigne. Supplements to Vetus Testamentum 180. Leiden: Brill, 2019.
Dogniez, Cécile. "Dodekapropheton / The Twelve Prophets: An Overview." Pages 419–30 in *Introduction to the LXX*. Edited by Siegfried Kreuzer. Waco, Tex.: Baylor University Press, 2019.
Ehorn, Seth M. *2 Maccabees 1–7: A Handbook on the Greek Text*. Baylor Handbook on the Septuagint. Waco, Tex.: Baylor University Press, 2020.
Emde Boas, Evert van, Albert Rijksbaron, Luuk Huitink, and Mathieu de Bakker. *The Cambridge Grammar of Classical Greek*. Cambridge: Cambridge University Press, 2019.
Fanning, Buist M. *Verbal Aspect in New Testament Greek*. Oxford Theological Monographs. Oxford: Clarendon Press, 1990.
Freedman, David Noel. *Anchor Bible Dictionary*. 6 vols. New York: Doubleday, 1992.
———. *Eerdmans Dictionary of the Bible*. Grand Rapids: Eerdmans, 2000.
Fuller, Russell. "The Form and Function of the Book of the Twelve: The Evidence from the Judean Desert." Pages 86–101 in *Forming Prophetic Literature: Essays on Isaiah and the Twelve in Honor of John D. W. Watts*. Edited by J. W. Watts and P. R. House. JSOTSup 235. Sheffield: JSOT Press, 1996.
Garrett, D. A. *Amos: A Handbook on the Hebrew Text*. Baylor Handbook on the Hebrew Bible. Waco, Tex.: Baylor University Press, 2008.

Gelston, A. "Some Hebrew Misreadings in the Septuagint of Amos." *Vetus Testamentum* 52, no. 4 (2002): 493–500.

———. *The Twelve Minor Prophets*. Biblia Hebraica Quinta 13. Stuttgart: Deutsche Bibelgesellschaft, 2010.

Gignac, Francis T. *A Grammar of the Greek Papyri of the Roman and Byzantine Periods*. 2 vols. Rome: Istituto editoriale cisalpino–La goliardica, 1976, 1981.

Glenny, W. Edward. "Hebrew Misreadings or Free Translation in the Septuagint of Amos?" *Vetus Testamentum* 57, no. 4 (2007): 524–47.

———. *Finding Meaning in the Text: Translation Technique and Theology in the Septuagint of Amos*. Supplements to Vetus Testamentum 126. Leiden: Brill, 2009.

———. "The Septuagint and Apostolic Hermeneutics: Amos 9 in Acts 15." *Bulletin for Biblical Research* 22, no. 1 (2012) 1–26.

———. *Hosea: A Commentary Based on Hosea in Codex Vaticanus*. Leiden: Brill, 2013a.

———. *Amos: A Commentary Based on Amos in Codex Vaticanus*. Leiden Brill, 2013b.

———. "The Septuagint and Biblical Theology." *Themelios* 41, no. 2 (2016): 263–78.

———. "9.3 Minor Prophets: Septuagint." Pages 614–23 in *Textual History of the Bible*, vol. 1: *The Hebrew Bible, Part 1b: Pentateuch, Former and Latter Prophets*. Edited by A. Lange and E. Tov. Leiden: Brill, 2017.

———. "Textual History of the Minor Prophets: Hebrew Manuscripts and Versions." Pages 41–56 in *The Oxford Handbook of the Minor Prophets*. Edited by Julia M. O'Brien. Oxford: Oxford University Press, 2021.

Harl, M., C. Dogniez, L. Brottier, M. Caseviz, and P. Sandevoir, eds. *La Bible d'Alexandrie*. Vol. XXIII.4–9: *Les Douze Prophètes—Joël, Abdiou, Jonas, Naoum, Ambakoum, Sophonie*. Paris: Cerf, 1999.

Hatch, E., and H. A. Redpath. *A Concordance to the Septuagint and Other Greek Versions of the Old Testament*. 2nd ed. Repr., Grand Rapids: Baker, 1983.

Hermann, Johannes, and Friedrich Baumgärtel. *Beiträge zur Entstehungsgeschichte der Septuaginta*. Berlin: W. Kohlhammer, 1923.

Howard, George E. "Some Notes on the Septuagint of Amos." *Vetus Testamentum* 12 (1970): 108–12.

———. "The Twelve Prophets: To the Reader." Pages 777–81 in *A New English Translation of the Septuagint*. Edited by Albert Pietersma and Benjamin G. Wright. Oxford: Oxford University Press, 2007.

Jastrow, Marcus. *Dictionary of the Targumim, the Talmud Babli and Yerushalmi, and the Midrashic Literature*. Repr., Peabody, Mass.: Hendrickson, 2005.

Jobes, Karen H., and Moisés Silva. *Invitation to the Septuagint*. 2nd ed. Grand Rapids: Baker, 2015.

Johnson, Sherman Eldridge. "The Septuagint of Amos." PhD diss., University of Chicago, 1936.

Jones, Barry A. *The Formation of the Book of the Twelve: A Study in Text and Canon*. SBLDS 149. Atlanta: Scholars Press, 1995.

Joosten, Jan. "Rhetorical Ornamentation in the Septuagint: The Case of Grammatical Variation." Pages 11–22 in *Et Sapienter et Eloquenter: Studies on Rhetorical and Stylistic Features of the Septuagint*. Edited by Eberhard Bons and Thomas J. Kraus. Göttingen: Vandenhoeck & Ruprecht, 2011.

Karrer, Martin, and Wofgang Kraus, eds. *Septuaginta Deutsch: Erläuterungen und Kommentare zum griechischen Alten Testament*. 2 vols. Stuttgart: Deutsche Bibelgesellschaft, 2011.

Kelly, J. N. D. *Early Christian Doctrines*. Rev. ed. San Francisco: Harper & Row, 1978.

Kemmer, Suzanne. *The Middle Voice*. Typological Studies in Language 23. Amsterdam: John Benjamins, 1993.

Kittel, G., and G. Friedrich, eds. *Theological Dictionary of the New Testament*. Translated by Geoffrey W. Bromiley. 10 vols. Grand Rapids: Eerdmans, 1964–1976.

Koehler, Ludwig, and Walter Baumgartner. *The Hebrew and Aramaic Lexicon of the Old Testament*. 2 vols. Leiden: Brill, 2001.

Kooij, A. van der. "The Septuagint of Zechariah as Witness to an Early Interpretation of the Book." Pages 53–64 in *The Book of Zechariah and Its Influence*. Edited by Christopher Tuckett. Burlington, Vt.: Ashgate, 2003.

Kraft, Robert A., ed. *Septuagintal Lexicography*. Society of Biblical Literature Septuagint and Cognate Studies 1. Missoula: University of Montana, 1972.

Kraus, Wolfgang, and Martin Karrer, eds. *Septuaginta Deutsch: Das griechische Alte Testament in deutscher Übersetzung*. Stuttgart: Deutsche Bibelgesellschaft, 2009.

Lee, John A. L. "The Present State of Lexicography of Ancient Greek." Pages 66–74 in *Biblical Greek Language and Lexicography: Essays in Honor of Frederick W. Danker*. Edited by Bernard A. Taylor. Grand Rapids: Eerdmans, 2004.

———. *The Greek of the Pentateuch: Grinfield Lectures on the Septuagint, 2011–2012*. Oxford: Oxford University Press, 2018.

Liddell, Henry George, and Robert Scott. *A Greek-English Lexicon with a Revised Supplement*. 9th ed. Revised by Henry Stuart Jones. Oxford: Clarendon Press, 1996.

Lust, Johan, Erik Eynikel, and Katrin Hauspie. *A Greek-English Lexicon of the Septuagint*. 3rd ed. Stuttgart: Deutsche Bibelgesellschaft, 2015.

Markovic, Daniel. "Hyperbaton in the Greek Literary Sentence." *Greek, Roman, and Byzantine Studies* 46 (2006): 127–45.

Mathewson, David L., and Elodie Ballantine Emig. *Intermediate Greek Grammar: Syntax for Students of the New Testament*. Baker: Grand Rapids, 2016.

Mayser, Edwin. *Grammatik der griechischen Papyri aus der Ptolemäerzeit mit Einschluss der gleichzeitigen Ostraka und der in Ägypten verfassten Inschriften*. Vol. 2. Berlin: Satzlehre, 1926–1934.

Miller, Neva. "Appendix 2: A Theory of Deponent Verbs." Pages 423–30 in *Analytical Lexicon of the Greek New Testament*. Edited by T. Friberg, B. Friberg, and N. Miller. Grand Rapids: Baker, 2000.

Montanari, Franco. *The Brill Dictionary of Ancient Greek*. Leiden: Brill, 2015.

Moule, C. F. D. *An Idiom Book of New Testament Greek*. 2nd ed. Cambridge: Cambridge University Press, 1959.

Moulton, J. H. *A Grammar of New Testament Greek*. Vol. 1: *Prolegomena*. Edinburgh: T&T Clark, 1908.

Moulton, J. H., and W. F. Howard. *A Grammar of New Testament Greek*. Vol. 2: *Accidence and Word-Formation*. Edinburgh: T&T Clark, 1929.

Moulton, J. H., and Nigel Turner. *A Grammar of New Testament Greek*. Vol. 3: *Syntax*. Edinburgh: T&T Clark, 1963.

Mounce, William D. *The Morphology of Biblical Greek*. Grand Rapids: Zondervan, 1994.

Muraoka, T. "Is the Septuagint Amos VIII 12–IX 10 a Separate Unit?" *Vetus Testamentum* 20 (1970): 496–500.

———. "Hebrew Hapax Legomena and Septuagint Lexicography." Pages 205–22 in *VII Congress of the International Organization for Septuagint and Cognate Studies Leuven 1989*. Edited by Clause E. Cox. Atlanta: Scholars Press, 1989.

———. "Septuagintal Lexicography: Some General Issues." Pages 17–47 in *Melbourne Symposium on Septuagint Lexicography*. Septuagint and Cognate Studies 28. Edited by T. Muraoka. Atlanta: Scholars Press, 1990.

———. *A Greek-English Lexicon of the Septuagint: Chiefly of the Pentateuch and the Twelve Prophets*. Louvain: Peeters, 2002.

———. *A Greek-English Lexicon of the Septuagint*. Paris: Peeters, 2009.

———. *A Syntax of Septuagint Greek*. Paris: Peeters, 2016.

Nogalski, J. D. *The Book of the Twelve: Hosea–Jonah*. Smyth & Helwys Bible Commentary. Macon, Ga.: Smyth & Helwys, 2011.

Olmstead, Wesley G. *Matthew 1–14: A Handbook on the Greek Text*. Baylor Handbook on the Greek New Testament. Waco, Tex.: Baylor University Press, 2019.

Palmer, James Karol. "Not Made with Tracing Paper: Studies in the Septuagint of Zechariah." PhD diss., Cambridge University, 2004.

Palmer, Leonard R. *A Grammar of the Post-Ptolemaic Papyri*. Vol. 1: *Accidence and Word-Formation*. London: Oxford University Press, 1946.

Park, A. W. *The Book of Amos as Composed and Read in Antiquity*. Studies in Biblical Literature 37. New York: Peter Lang, 2001.

Paul, Shalom M. *A Commentary on the Book of Amos*. Hermeneia. Minneapolis: Fortress, 1991.

Penner, Ken W., ed. *Lexham English Septuagint*. Bellingham, Wash.: Lexham Press, 2019.

Pennington, J. T. "Deponency in Koine Greek: The Grammatical Question and the Lexicographical Dilemma." *Trinity Journal* 24 (2003): 55–76.

Pietersma, A., and B. G. Wright III, eds. *A New English Translation of the Septuagint*. Oxford: Oxford University Press, 2007.

Porter, Stanley E. *Verbal Aspect in the Greek of the New Testament with Reference to Tense and Mood*. 2nd ed. Studies in Biblical Greek 1. New York: Lang, 1993.

———. *Idioms of the Greek New Testament*. 2nd ed. Biblical Languages: Greek 2. Sheffield: Sheffield Academic, 1994.

Pouchelle, Patrick. "The Septuagint *Paideia* and the Construction of a Jewish Identity during the Late Hellenistic and Early Roman Period." *Catholic Biblical Quarterly* 81 (2019): 33–45.

Rahlfs, Alfred, and Robert Hanhart, *Septuaginta: Editio Altera*. 2nd rev. ed. Stuttgart: Deutsche Bibelgesellschaft, 2006.

Rajak, Tessa. *Translation as Survival: The Greek Bible of the Ancient Jewish Diaspora*. Oxford: Oxford University Press, 2009.

Reed, Jeffrey T. *A Discourse Analyses of Philippians: Method and Rhetoric in Debate over Literary Integrity*. Journal for the Study of the New Testament Supplement Series 136. Sheffield: Sheffield Academic, 1997.

Robertson, A. T. *A Grammar of the Greek New Testament in Light of Historical Research*. 4th ed. Nashville: Broadman & Holman, 1934.

Runge, Steven E. *Discourse Grammar of the Greek New Testament: A Practical Introduction for Teaching and Exegesis*. Peabody, Mass.: Hendrickson, 2010.

Runge, Steven E., and Christopher J. Fresch, eds. *The Greek Verb Revisited: A Fresh Approach for Biblical Exegesis*. Bellingham, Wash.: Lexham Press, 2016.

Satterthwaite, Philip E. "The Translators as Imperialists: And Other Aspects of the Septuagint Translation of the Book of the Twelve." An expanded version of a paper given to the Cambridge University OT Seminar, October 1997.

Sawyer, J. F. A. "'Those Priests in Damascus': A Possible Example of Anti-sectarian Polemic in the Septuagint Version of Amos 3,12." *Annual of the Swedish Theological Institute* 8 (1970–1971): 123–30.

Seeligmann, Isac L. *The Septuagint Version of Isaiah: A Discussion of Its Problems*. Mededelingen en Verhandelingen 9. Leiden: Brill, 1948.

Seitz, Christopher R. *Prophecy and Hermeneutics: Toward a New Introduction to the Prophets*. Grand Rapids: Baker, 2007.

Siebenthal, Heinrich von. *Ancient Greek Grammar for the Study of the New Testament*. Oxford: Peter Lang, 2019.

Silva, Moisés, ed. *New International Dictionary of New Testament Theology and Exegesis*. 2nd ed. Grand Rapids: Zondervan, 2014.

Smyth, Herbert Weir. *Greek Grammar*. Cambridge, Mass.: Harvard University Press, 1956.

Sollamo, Raija. *Renderings of Hebrew Semiprepositions in the Septuagint*. Helsinki: Suomalainen Tiedeakatemia, 1979.

Spicq, Celsas. *Theological Lexicon of the New Testament*. 3 vols. Translated and edited by James D. Ernest. Peabody, Mass.: Hendrickson, 1994.

Stuart, Douglas. *Hosea–Jonah*. Word Biblical Commentary 31. Waco, Tex.: Word Books, 1987.

Sweeney, Marvin A. "Sequence and Interpretation in the Book of the Twelve." Pages 49–64 in *Reading and Hearing the Book of the Twelve*. Edited by James D. Nogalski and Marvin A. Sweeney. SBL Symposium Series 15. Atlanta: SBL Press, 2000.

Swete, Henry Barclay. *The Old Testament in Greek According to the Septuagint*. 3 vols. Cambridge: Cambridge University Press, 1925–1930.

———. *An Introduction to the Old Testament in Greek*. Reprint of the 1914 Cambridge University Press edition. Peabody, Mass.: Hendrickson, 1989.

Thackeray, Henry St. J. *A Grammar of the Old Testament in Greek According to the Septuagint*. Vol. 1: *Introduction, Orthography, and Accidence*. Cambridge: Cambridge University Press, 1909.

———. *The Septuagint and Jewish Worship*. London: British Academy, 1921.
Theocharous, Myrto. *Lexical Dependence and Intertextual Allusion in the Septuagint of the Twelve Prophets*. The Library of Hebrew Bible / Old Testament Studies 570. London: T&T Clark, 2012.
Tov, Emanuel. *The Septuagint Translation of Jeremiah and Baruch*. Harvard Semitic Monographs 8. Missoula, Mont.: Scholars Press, 1976.
———. *Textual Criticism of the Hebrew Bible*. 3rd ed. Minneapolis: Fortress Press, 2012.
Tov, Emanuel, and Frank Polak. "The Revised CATSS Hebrew/Greek Parallel Text." Electronic text hypertexted and prepared by OakTree Software, Inc. Version 1.2, 2009.
Turner, Nigel. *Grammatical Insights into the Greek New Testament*. Edinburgh: T&T Clark, 1965.
VanGemeren, Willem A., ed. *New International Dictionary of Old Testament Theology and Exegesis*. 5 vols. Grand Rapids: Zondervan, 1997.
Waard, Jan de. "Translation Techniques Used by the Greek Translators of Amos." *Biblica* 59 (1978): 339–50.
Wallace, Daniel B. *Greek Grammar beyond the Basics: An Exegetical Syntax of the New Testament*. Grand Rapids: Zondervan, 1996.
Waltke, Bruce K., and M. O'Connor. *An Introduction to Biblical Hebrew Syntax*. Winona Lake, Ind.: Eisenbrauns, 1990.
Wevers, John William. *Notes on the Greek Text of Exodus*. Society of Biblical Literature Septuagint and Cognate Studies 30. Atlanta: Scholars Press, 1990.
———. *Notes on the Greek Text of Leviticus*. Society of Biblical Literature Septuagint and Cognate Studies 44. Atlanta: Scholars Press, 1997.
Wolff, Hans Walter. *Joel and Amos*. Hermeneia. Philadelphia: Fortress Press, 1977.
Wright, Benjamin G. "Sirach (Ecclesiasticus)." Pages 410–24 in *T&T Clark Companion to the Septuagint*. Edited by James K. Aitken. London: Bloomsbury T&T Clark, 2015.
Young, Richard A. *Intermediate New Testament Greek: A Linguistic and Exegetical Approach*. Nashville, Tenn.: Broadman & Holman, 1994.
Zerwick, Maximilian. *Biblical Greek: Illustrated by Examples*. Rome: Pontificii Instituti Biblici, 1963.
Ziegler, J. *Die Einheit der Septuaginta zum Zwölfprophetenbuch*. Beilage zum Vorlesungsverzeichnis der Staatlichen Akademie zu Braunsberg im ws 1934/35; Braunsberg, 1934.
———. *Duodecim Prophetae: Septuaginta*. Vol. 13. 2nd ed. Göttingen: Vandenhoeck & Ruprecht, 1984.

GRAMMAR INDEX

accusative (adverbial), 2:10, 5:14, 5:19
accusative (extent of time), 5:25
accusative (object of ὡς), 8:10^2
accusative (of respect), 9:13
accusative direct object, 1:1, 1:2, 1:4^2, 1:5^2, 1:6^2, 1:7^2, 1:8, 1:9^2, 1:10^2, 1:11^5, 1:12^2, 1:13^2, 1:14^2, 2:1^2, 2:2^2, 2:3^2, 2:4^5, 2:5^2, 2:6^3, 2:7^2, 2:8^2, 2:9^3, 2:10^3, 2:14, 2:15, 2:16, 3:1^2, 3:2^2, 3:3, 3:4^3, 3:5, 3:6, 3:7^2, 3:9^2, 3:10^2, 3:11^2, 3:12^3, 3:14, 3:15, 4:1^3, 4:2, 4:4^2, 4:5^3, 4:6^2, 4:7, 4:8, 4:9^5, 4:10^3, 4:11^3, 4:12, 4:13^5, 5:1^2, 5:2, 5:3, 5:4^2, 5:5, 5:6^2, 5:7^2, 5:8^5, 5:9^2, 5:10, 5:11^5, 5:12^4, 5:14^2, 5:15^4, 5:16^2, 5:18, 5:19^2, 5:20, 5:21, 5:22^4, 5:23^2, 5:25^2, 5:26^3, 5:27, 6:1^2, 6:4^2, 6:6^2, 6:8^4, 6:10^2, 6:11^2, 6:12^2, 6:13, 6:14^2, 7:2^2, 7:4^3, 7:5, 7:8^4, 7:10^2, 7:11, 7:14, 7:15, 7:16, 7:17, 8:2^2, 8:3, 8:4^3, 8:5^2, 8:6^2, 8:10^5, 8:11^5, 8:12, 9:1^2, 9:2^2, 9:3^2, 9:4^2, 9:5^2, 9:6^4, 9:7^3, 9:8^2, 9:9, 9:11^2, 9:12, 9:13, 9:14^6, 9:15
accusative direct object (person) in a person-thing double accusative construction, 2:12
accusative direct object (thing) in a person-thing double accusative construction, 2:12
accusative direct object in an object-complement double accusative construction, 8:5^2
complement in an object-complement double accusative construction, 8:5^2
accusative in apposition, 5:1, 5:26, 6:2, 7:10, 7:15, 8:2
accusative of person, 1:3, 1:6, 1:9, 1:11, 1:13, 2:1, 2:4, 2:6
accusative subject (of infinitive), 1:6, 1:11, 2:4
adjectivizer, 3:9
adverb of comparison, 3:12
adverb of manner, 2:13, 3:12, 9:9
adverb of place, 2:9^2, 3:11, 4:5, 6:2^2, 7:12^2, 9:2^2, 9:3^2, 9:4
adverb of time, 5:8, 6:7, 8:5

dative (ethical), 9:7
dative (indirect object), 2:12, 3:9, 3:13, 4:1², 4:6, 4:12², 5:22, 5:25, 7:1, 7:4, 7:7, 8:1, 9:15
dative (of advantage or interest), 5:3, 5:6, 5:18, 5:26
dative (of material), 2:8
dative (of means or instrument), 1:3, 6:11²
dative (of person commanded), 9:3, 9:4
dative (of place or sphere), 5:20
dative (of possession), 4:13, 5:8, 5:27, 9:6
dative (of respect/reference), 2:15
dative complement (object), 2:4, 5:19

future (deliberative), 3:3, 3:4², 3:5², 3:6³

genitive (attributive), 1:14², 3:2, 7:13, 8:8, 8:10, 9:5, 9:11
genitive (interpositional), 1:1
genitive (objective), 1:6, 1:9, 4:6, 4:10, 6:1, 6:6, 6:10, 7:10, 8:10, 8:11², 9:4², 9:5, 9:14
genitive (of apposition), 2:10, 3:1², 3:9, 4:1, 5:1, 5:2, 5:3, 5:4, 5:6², 5:22, 5:25, 6:1, 6:12, 6:14, 7:10, 7:12, 9:7, 9:9
genitive (of comparison), 6:2
genitive (of content), 2:13, 7:7
genitive (of description), 1:1², 5:5, 5:8, 6:1, 6:14
genitive (of destination), 4:10
genitive (of material), 7:1
genitive (of place), 1:5⁴, 2:5, 2:7, 3:9, 3:14², 4:1, 7:2, 8:14
genitive (possessive), 1:1, 1:2², 1:4², 1:7², 1:8, 1:10², 1:11², 1:12, 1:13, 1:14³, 1:15³, 2:1, 2:2, 2:4³, 2:7³, 2:8³, 2:9⁴, 2:10, 2:11, 2:14², 2:15², 2:16, 3:4³, 3:7, 3:9, 3:10,
3:11³, 3:12, 4:2, 4:4², 4:6², 4:9⁴, 4:10⁴, 4:12, 4:13, 5:2, 5:12², 5:17, 5:18², 5:19², 5:20, 5:21², 5:22, 5:23², 5:26², 6:2², 6:10³, 7:7, 7:8, 7:9², 7:10, 7:11, 7:13, 7:15, 7:17⁵, 8:1, 8:2², 8:10², 9:1, 9:2, 9:3, 9:4, 9:6, 9:8, 9:11², 9:12, 9:14, 9:15²
genitive (of price or value), 2:6
genitive (of relationship), 1:1, 1:4, 1:11, 1:13, 2:4², 2:7, 2:11², 3:12, 3:13, 4:1, 4:5, 7:14, 7:16, 9:7², 9:8
genitive (of source), 2:2, 5:1, 5:8, 5:23², 6:5, 7:10, 9:6, 9:14²
genitive (of subordination), 1:1², 2:1, 2:3, 5:26, 8:14²
genitive (of time), 8:9
genitive (partitive), 1:2, 1:8, 1:12, 1:13, 2:2, 3:12, 4:13, 5:8, 5:15, 6:7, 8:3, 9:1, 9:3², 9:6, 9:8, 9:10, 9:12
genitive (qualitative), 7:9
genitive (representative), 5:26
genitive (subjective), 1:3, 1:6, 1:9², 1:11, 1:13, 2:1, 2:4, 2:6, 2:7, 2:9², 3:2, 3:7, 3:14, 4:6, 5:22, 6:7, 6:8, 7:16, 8:7², 8:11, 8:12, 9:6, 9:8
genitive complement (object), 1:9, 2:8, 2:14, 3:1, 6:3, 9:5, 9:15
genitive in apposition, 1:1², 3:7, 5:26, 7:8, 9:8, 9:14

hyperbaton, 1:1, 4:7, 6:4

infinitive (cause with ἕνεκα), 1:11, 2:4
infinitive (cause with ἕνεκεν), 1:6
infinitive (complementary), 4:4, 5:2, 6:10, 7:2, 7:8, 7:10, 7:13, 8:2
infinitive (epexegetical), 8:11

Grammar Index 293

infinitive (purpose with τοῦ), 1:6, 2:10, 4:8, 4:12, 6:10, 8:5³, 8:6
infinitive (result), 6:14
infinitive (substantival), 3:5

merism, 1:2

neuter plural subject with a singular verb, 2:11, 6:2, 8:7, 9:10², 9:13
nominalizer, 1:3, 4:1, 4:2, 4:4, 5:8, 8:10
nominative (in comparative phrase), 2:9², 9:7, 9:11
nominative (pendant), 5:3
nominative (predicate), 2:9, 3:6, 4:11, 4:13, 5:8, 5:13, 5:16, 5:17, 5:18², 5:20³, 5:27, 7:1², 7:2, 7:5, 7:13², 7:14³, 8:1, 8:2, 9:6
nominative absolute, 1:1, 9:5
nominative for vocative, 3:1, 3:11, 5:1, 5:25, 6:1, 6:14, 9:7
nominative in apposition, 3:7, 3:8, 3:11, 3:13², 4:3, 4:5, 4:13², 5:2, 5:8², 5:14², 5:15², 5:16², 5:27², 7:1, 7:10, 7:11, 7:17, 8:9, 9:5³, 9:6², 9:12, 9:15²
nominative subject, 1:2³, 1:3, 1:5², 1:6, 1:8³, 1:9, 1:11, 1:13, 1:15³, 2:1, 2:2, 2:3, 2:4³, 2:6, 2:9², 2:10, 2:11², 2:13², 2:14³, 2:15³, 2:16², 3:1, 3:3, 3:4², 3:5², 3:6³, 3:7, 3:8⁴, 3:10², 3:11³, 3:12³, 3:13, 3:14, 3:15³, 4:2³, 4:3, 4:5², 4:6², 4:7³, 4:8², 4:9², 4:10, 4:11², 4:13², 5:1, 5:3³, 5:4, 5:5², 5:6², 5:7, 5:8, 5:12, 5:14, 5:15, 5:16², 5:17, 5:18², 5:19³, 5:20, 5:24², 5:27, 6:1, 6:2², 6:7, 6:8², 6:9², 6:10, 6:11, 6:12², 6:14, 7:1², 7:2, 7:3², 7:4², 7:5, 7:6², 7:7, 7:8⁴, 7:9², 7:10³, 7:11³, 7:12, 7:14², 7:15², 7:16, 7:17⁷, 8:1, 8:2³, 8:3², 8:5², 8:6, 8:7, 8:8⁵, 8:9³, 8:11², 8:12, 8:14², 9:1, 9:2, 9:5³, 9:6, 9:7², 9:8², 9:9², 9:10², 9:12², 9:13⁶, 9:15
compound nominative subject, 2:7, 5:24, 8:13, 9:12
nominative subject (of noun clause), 7:7
nominative subject (of participle phrase), 7:7

participle (attributive), 2:13, 3:12, 4:1³, 4:2, 4:11, 6:5², 7:1, 7:7, 9:1, 9:10, 9:11², 9:14
participle (causal), 5:12³
participle (circumstantial), 2:8, 5:5, 7:10
participle (conditional), 3:4
participle (customary present), 2:8
participle (means), 2:12, 3:1
participle (predicate), 5:5
participle (purpose), 8:12
participle (result), 5:20
participle (substantival), 1:3, 1:5, 1:8, 1:13, 1:15, 2:7, 2:12, 3:10, 4:13⁵, 5:2, 5:6, 5:7, 5:8⁶, 5:9², 5:10, 5:13, 5:16, 5:18, 6:1², 6:3³, 6:4³, 6:5, 6:6³, 6:8, 6:10, 6:13², 7:12, 7:14, 8:3, 8:4², 8:5, 8:8, 8:14², 9:1², 9:5³, 9:6⁴, 9:11, 9:12
predicate adjective, 5:12, 6:2, 6:7, 9:13
predicate adjective of an implied verb, 5:12

relative clause, 1:1²
relative pronoun, 1:1²

subjunctive with oath formula, 8:14²
subjunctive with ἐάν, 3:3, 3:4, 3:7, 5:22, 6:9, 7:2, 9:2², 9:3², 9:4

Grammar Index

subjunctive with ὅπως, 1:13, 2:7, 4:1, 5:6, 5:14, 5:15, 9:12
subjunctive with ὅταν, 3:12, 3:14, 5:19[5]
subjunctive with οὐ μή, 2:12, 2:14[2], 2:15[3], 3:7, 4:8, 5:11[2], 5:21, 7:6, 7:10, 7:16, 8:12, 8:14, 9:1[2], 9:9, 9:10, 9:15
subjunctive with οὐκέτι μή, 5:2, 7:8, 7:13, 8:2
synecdoche, 1:4, 1:5

vocative of address, 2:11, 3:12, 4:1, 4:12, 7:2[2], 7:3, 7:5[2], 7:6, 7:8, 8:2, 8:14[2]

ἄνευ (separation), 3:5[2]
ἀνθ' ὧν (causal), 1:3, 1:9, 1:13, 2:1, 2:6, 5:11
ἀντί (exchange/substitution), 8:6
ἀπό (partitive), 6:7, 8:6
ἀπό (separation), 5:23, 7:11, 7:17, 9:8, 9:15
ἀπό (source), 8:4, 8:12
αὐτός (identical), 2:7

διά (causal), 2:13, 3:2, 4:12
διά (inferential), 5:11, 5:13, 5:16, 6:7, 7:17
διά (locative), 5:17
διά (result), 3:11
διότι (cause), 5:3, 6:11, 7:11, 9:9
διότι (inferential), 5:22, 6:14

ἐάν (introducing vivid future [or third class] conditional), 3:3, 3:4, 3:7, 5:22, 6:9, 7:2, 9:2[2], 9:3[2], 9:4
εἰ (introducing direct question), 6:10, 6:12[2]
εἰ (introducing indirect question), 3:3, 3:4[2], 3:5[2], 3:6[2], 6:2
εἰ (in oath formula), 8:7

εἰς (direction), 1:4, 1:12, 2:7, 4:10, 4:13, 5:8[2], 5:16, 6:2[2], 6:3, 7:12, 7:13, 9:1, 9:2, 9:3, 9:6
εἰς (extent of time), 1:11, 8:7
εἰς (location), 1:6, 1:9, 4:3, 4:4[2], 4:8, 5:5, 5:7[2], 5:19, 9:2, 9:3
εἰς (purpose), 2:11[2], 5:16, 9:4[2]
εἰς (result/resulting state), 1:11, 2:1
εἰς (spatial), 4:2, 6:12[2], 6:14, 9:8
εἰς (temporal), 4:4[2], 8:4
εἰς (transformational), 8:10[2]
ἐκ (derivation), 1:8
ἐκ (dissociation), 1:5, 2:9, 6:7
ἐκ (origin), 1:2[2], 3:4[2], 5:3[2]
ἐκ (partitive), 1:1, 2:11[2], 3:2, 6:2, 6:4, 9:1[2]
ἐκ (separation), 1:8, 2:10, 2:14, 3:1, 3:11, 3:12, 4:7, 4:11, 5:19, 7:15, 9:3, 9:7
ἐκ (source), 1:5, 2:3, 2:8, 5:11, 6:4, 6:10, 9:7[2]
ἐν (causal), 8:13
ἐν (direction), 1:15
ἐν (instrumental), 4:2, 4:10, 6:13, 7:4, 7:9, 7:11, 7:17[2], 9:1
ἐν (locative), 1:1, 1:3[2], 1:13, 2:8, 2:10, 3:6[2], 3:9[3], 3:10, 3:12[2], 4:1, 4:6[2], 4:10, 5:10, 5:11, 5:12, 5:15, 5:16[2], 5:17, 5:21, 5:25, 6:9, 6:12[2], 7:7, 7:8, 7:10, 7:17[2], 8:3, 8:8, 9:4, 9:9
ἐν (manner), 1:11, 2:2
ἐν (means), 4:9[2], 4:10, 8:6, 9:9, 9:10
ἐν (source), 2:16
ἐν (stative), 4:10
ἐν (temporal), 1:1[2], 1:14[2], 2:16, 3:14, 5:13, 8:3, 8:9[2], 8:13, 9:11, 9:13
ἕνεκα (causal), 1:11, 2:4
ἕνεκα (purpose), 6:10
ἕνεκεν (causal), 1:6, 2:6
ἕνεκεν (exchange), 2:6

ἐπέκεινα (locative), 5:27
ἐπί (addition), 3:15
ἐπί (causal), 1:3², 1:6², 1:9², 1:11²,
   1:13², 2:1², 2:4², 2:6², 6:6, 6:13,
   8:8
ἐπί (direction), 1:7, 1:8, 1:10, 1:14,
   1:15, 2:2, 2:4, 3:3, 3:9, 3:14²,
   4:2, 5:1, 5:5, 5:9², 6:1, 7:9, 7:15,
   7:16², 8:2, 9:1, 9:4
ἐπί (locative), 1:11, 2:7, 3:5², 3:9,
   3:14, 4:7⁴, 4:13, 5:2, 5:8, 5:19,
   6:4, 7:7, 8:9, 9:1, 9:6², 9:9, 9:10,
   9:15
ἐπί (opposition), 3:1, 3:2
ἐπί (reference or respect), 7:3, 7:6
ἐπί (spatial), 6:14, 8:10², 8:11, 9:8,
   9:12²
ἕως (spatial), 6:14, 8:12²

ἵνα τί, 5:18

καθώς (similarity and
   comparison), 2:9, 4:11, 9:11
κατά (disadvantage), 7:10
κατά (oath formula), 4:2, 6:8, 8:14
κατά (opposition), 3:1, 8:7
κατέναντι (locative), 3:12, 4:3

μετά (accompaniment), 1:14, 2:2²,
   2:3, 4:10, 8:10
μετά (association), 4:2, 5:14
μή, 2:11, 2:12, 2:14², 2:15³, 3:3, 3:4,
   3:7², 4:8, 5:2, 5:5³, 5:6, 5:11²,
   5:14, 5:21, 5:25, 6:10, 6:14, 7:6,
   7:8, 7:10, 7:13, 7:16², 8:2, 8:12,
   8:14, 9:1², 9:9, 9:10², 9:15

ὅπως (introducing purpose
   clause), 1:13, 4:1, 5:6, 5:14,
   5:15, 9:12

ὅπως (introducing result clause),
   2:7
ὅτι (causal), 4:12, 5:5, 5:12, 5:13,
   6:8, 7:2, 7:5, 7:13
ὅτι (indirect causality), 6:12
ὅτι (indirect discourse), 4:5
οὐ μή, 2:12, 2:14², 2:15³, 3:7, 4:8,
   5:11², 5:21, 7:6, 7:10, 7:16, 8:12,
   8:14, 9:1², 9:9, 9:10², 9:15
οὐκ, 1:3, 1:6, 1:9, 1:11, 1:13, 2:1,
   2:4², 2:6, 2:11, 2:12, 2:14²,
   2:15⁴, 3:4, 3:6², 3:7, 3:8, 3:10,
   4:6, 4:7², 4:8², 5:2, 5:5, 5:6,
   5:11², 5:18, 5:20², 5:21, 5:22²,
   5:23, 6:5, 6:6, 6:13, 7:3, 7:6,
   7:10, 7:14², 7:16, 8:8, 8:11, 8:12,
   8:14, 9:1², 9:4, 9:7², 9:8, 9:9,
   9:10², 9:15
οὐκέτι μή, 5:2, 7:8, 7:13, 8:2
οὐχί, 5:20

παρά (source), 5:11
παρά (spatial), 6:10
πρό (location), 9:4
πρό (temporal), 1:1, 4:7
πρός (direction), 2:7, 3:7, 4:6, 4:8,
   4:9, 4:10, 4:11, 5:4, 7:8², 7:10,
   7:12, 7:14, 7:15, 8:2
πρός (reference), 6:5

σύν (accompaniment), 6:8

ὑπέρ (reference), 1:1
ὑποκάτω (locative), 2:13

ὡς (adverb), 4:9, 4:10, 4:11
ὡς (comparative), 2:9, 5:5, 5:6,
   5:24², 8:8², 9:5², 9:7
ὡς (functioning like an object
   complement), 8:10²
ὡς (relative adverb), 4:11, 6:5²

AUTHOR INDEX

Aejmelaeus, A., 182
Aitken, J. K., viii, x
Arieti, J. A., 62, 66, 112, 160
Aubrey, R., xxxv, 20, 249

Baillet, M., Milik, J. T.,
  de Vaux, R., 12
Bakker, E., 19
Blomqvist, J., 105
Bons, E., xxii, xxix, xxx, xxxi,
  xxxii, xxxvii
Bruce, F. F., 188
Burk, D., 46, 99, 100

Caird, G. B., 23
Caragounis, C. C., 20, 249
Cathcart, K. J., Gordon, R. P., 29,
  58, 165
Conrad, C. W., 147, 151
Conybeare, F. C., Stock, St. G., xii,
  19, 57, 59, 113, 152, 178, 181,
  185, 202, 209, 221, 224, 228,
  254, 258
Cripps, R. S., 158

Daniel, S., 149, 204
Decker, R. J., xxxvi, 11, 12, 39, 60,
  129, 170, 229

Dines, J. M., xxi, xxiv, xxix, xxx,
  xxxi, xxxii, xxxvii, 2, 3, 11,
  16, 19, 22, 23, 28, 37, 39, 45,
  47, 52, 53, 54, 57, 65, 66, 75,
  78, 79, 81, 85, 87, 89, 94, 95,
  101, 102, 108, 109, 112, 118,
  119, 122, 134, 136, 142, 149,
  150, 152, 153, 154, 155, 158,
  159, 160, 164, 166, 168, 170,
  171, 174, 176, 177, 180, 181,
  188, 189, 190, 198, 199, 201,
  202, 203, 204, 209, 211, 213,
  216, 219, 221, 224, 229, 230,
  233, 235, 239, 242, 243, 244,
  249, 255, 259, 260, 261, 262,
  265
Dogniez, C., xxix

Ehorn, S. M., xxxv, 46, 60, 99
Emde Boas, E. van,
  Rijksbaron, A., Huitink, L.,
  Bakker, M. de, xii

Fanning, B. M., xxxv, 22, 42, 44,
  46, 56, 70, 71, 79, 92, 93, 94,
  96, 100, 137, 140, 196, 210,
  211, 215, 223, 241
Fuller, R., xxiv

Garrett, D. A., 5, 26, 29, 80, 263, 265
Gelston, A., xxxi, 27, 168, 188, 190
Gignac, F. T., xii
Glenny, W. E., xxii, xxiii, xxv, xxvi, xxvii, xxix, xxx, xxxi, xxxii, xxxiii, 2, 5, 13, 14, 15, 17, 18, 23, 24, 26, 27, 28, 32, 33, 34, 37, 38, 39, 40, 41, 51, 54, 55, 65, 66, 68, 69, 70, 72, 73, 75, 78, 79, 80, 81, 82, 85, 87, 88, 89, 90, 91, 92, 94, 97, 100, 101, 104, 106, 107, 108, 109, 112, 113, 114, 115, 116, 117, 118, 120, 122, 123, 124, 127, 128, 129, 130, 131, 133, 136, 141, 146, 147, 148, 149, 150, 151, 152, 153, 154, 155, 158, 159, 160, 161, 163, 164, 165, 167, 168, 170, 171, 172, 175, 176, 177, 178, 180, 184, 185, 186, 188, 190, 191, 192, 193, 195, 196, 199, 203, 204, 207, 209, 210, 212, 213, 214, 215, 216, 218, 219, 221, 224, 225, 226, 227, 228, 230, 232, 234, 235, 239, 240, 242, 243, 248, 249, 253, 255, 258, 260, 262, 263, 264, 265, 266, 270

Hermann, J., Baumgärtel, F., xxvii
Howard, G. E., xxviii, xxxi

Jastrow, M., 165
Jobes, K., Silva, M., viii, x
Johnson, S. E., xxviii, 112
Jones, B. A., xxv
Joosten, J., xxxii

Kelly, J. N. D., 108
Kemmer, S., xxxvi, 5, 27, 30, 39, 48, 61, 87, 115, 117, 118, 121, 128, 130, 139, 145, 147, 148, 150, 151, 163, 164, 167, 172, 175, 176, 180, 181, 189, 193, 203, 224, 226, 227, 230, 231, 235, 237, 248, 251, 268, 269
Kooij, A. van der, 103, 171, 262
Kraft, R. A., 24, 229

Lee, J. A. L., viii

Markovic, D., 277
Mathewson, D. L., Emig, E. B., xxxvi
Mayser, E., xii
Miller, N., 234
Moule, C. F. D., 57
Mounce, W. D., 12, 63
Muraoka, T., ix, x, xii, xxviii, xxix, 4, 5, 9, 14, 17, 18, 21, 22, 29, 30, 31, 33, 34, 36, 37, 38, 39, 41, 43, 44, 45, 47, 49, 51, 52, 53, 54, 55, 56, 57, 58, 59, 60, 61, 62, 63, 64, 67, 70, 71, 73, 80, 81, 82, 83, 84, 85, 87, 90, 93, 96, 97, 98, 101, 102, 103, 104, 105, 106, 107, 112, 113, 114, 115, 117, 119, 120, 121, 125, 128, 130, 132, 133, 135, 136, 138, 139, 141, 142, 144, 145, 146, 149, 150, 152, 154, 155, 156, 161, 162, 163, 166, 167, 173, 174, 176, 177, 178, 179, 180, 181, 183, 185, 189, 190, 191, 192, 193, 194, 195, 197, 200, 202, 204, 206, 207, 208, 209, 210, 211, 212, 214, 215, 216, 217, 218, 220, 221, 223, 224, 225, 227, 229, 230, 231, 232, 233, 234, 236, 240, 243, 244, 248, 249, 252, 255, 256, 257, 259, 261, 263, 264, 267, 268, 270

Nogalski, J. D., 9, 36, 56, 187

Author Index

Palmer, J. K., 90
Palmer, L. R., xii
Park, A. W., xxiii, 3, 7, 57, 62, 160, 183, 188
Paul, S. M., 4, 12, 13, 14, 23, 113, 186, 199, 263, 267
Penner, K. W., xi
Pietersma, A., Wright, B. G., xi
Porter, S. E., xxxv, 17, 22, 33, 37, 38, 116, 136, 140, 192
Pouchelle, P., 67

Rajak, T., viii
Reed, J. T., 278
Robertson, A. T., 4, 11, 29, 33, 36, 39, 40, 61, 62, 63, 67, 97, 123, 127, 156, 224, 231, 250, 256, 265
Runge, S. E., xxxvi, 42, 55, 68, 82, 83, 86, 92, 93, 98, 100, 123, 131, 134, 138, 140, 142, 160, 195, 202, 209, 220, 226, 238, 241, 244, 246, 254
Runge, S. E., Fresch, C. J., xxxvi

Satterthwaite, P. E., 261
Sawyer, J. F. A., 78
Seeligmann, I. L., 171
Seitz, C. R., xxv
Siebenthal, H. von, xii
Smyth, H., ix, xii, 1, 4, 8, 9, 21, 33, 36, 41, 46, 47, 49, 50, 56, 57, 60, 63, 67, 68, 75, 76, 99, 120, 136, 147, 148, 150, 152, 154, 174, 175, 176, 177, 184, 193, 197, 202, 207, 208, 209, 211, 217, 218, 220, 224, 232, 233, 236, 244, 245, 246, 247, 248, 254, 270, 274
Sollamo, R., 43, 73, 140, 144
Spicq, C., 40, 133, 147, 148
Stuart, D., 34, 199
Sweeney, M. A., xxiv

Swete, H. B., xxiv

Thackeray, H. St. J., xii, xxvii, 8, 10, 17, 28, 32, 66, 76, 79, 105, 113, 117, 121, 158, 178, 202, 211, 220, 226, 227, 228, 231, 236, 241, 244, 247, 257
Theocharous, M., 34, 168
Tov, E., xxviii, xxxi
Tov, E., Polak, F., 62
Turner, N., 25

Waard, J. de, 261
Wallace, D. B., 1, 3, 4, 6, 8, 9, 10, 13, 15, 16, 18, 20, 21, 22, 23, 25, 26, 27, 29, 30, 31, 33, 36, 37, 38, 39, 40, 41, 42, 43, 44, 45, 46, 47, 48, 49, 51, 52, 54, 55, 56, 57, 58, 60, 61, 62, 63, 64, 65, 67, 68, 69, 71, 72, 73, 75, 76, 77, 78, 79, 80, 81, 82, 83, 84, 86, 87, 92, 93, 94, 95, 103, 105, 113, 114, 115, 116, 119, 120, 123, 125, 126, 130, 131, 133, 136, 138, 141, 142, 145, 146, 149, 151, 154, 161, 162, 168, 172, 173, 174, 178, 179, 191, 192, 193, 196, 197, 202, 205, 206, 207, 208, 211, 212, 217, 218, 220, 223, 224, 225, 226, 228, 232, 233, 236, 239, 241, 244, 250, 251, 254, 255, 257, 259, 261
Waltke, B. K., O'Connor, M., 228
Wevers, J. W., 85, 148, 149, 266
Wolff, H. W., xxx, 7, 8, 96
Wright, B. G., xxix

Young, R. A., 22, 111

Zerwick, M., 49, 75